TAGORE LAW LECTURES - 1950

TAGORE LAW LECTURES - 1950

EVOLUTION OF ANCIENT INDIAN LAW

NARES CHANDRA SEN GUPTA

GYAN

Published by

GYAN

Gyan Publishing House
5, Ansari Road
Daryaganj, New Delhi-110002
Phone: 011-47034999, 9811692060
E-mail: books@gyanbooks.com

Distribution Network
gyanbooks.com
India, USA, Canada, UK, Australia

ISBN: 978-93-7316-123-5 (HB)

First Published, 1950

2nd Impression 2025

Printed at: Gyan Press, Delhi.

TAGORE LAW LECTURES - 1950
Author: NARES CHANDRA SEN GUPTA

UNIVERSITY OF CALCUTTA

TAGORE LAW LECTURES, 1950

EVOLUTION OF ANCIENT INDIAN LAW

NARES CHANDRA SEN-GUPTA, M.A., LL.D.,

Senior Advocate, Supreme Court of India, Advocate, Calcutta High Court, Tagore Law Professor 1950, Late Dean of the Faculty of Law, University of Dacca, Author of "Sources of Law and Society in Ancient India", "Evolution of Law", "Pratnavidhana", etc., etc.

LONDON
ARTHUR PROBSTHAIN
41, GREAT RUSSEL STREET,
LONDON, W.C.1.

CALCUTTA
EASTERN LAW HOUSE
LTD.
54, GANESH CHANDRA AVENUE.

Dedicated with gratitude
to the memory of
THE LATE SIR ASHUTOSH MOOKERJEE
The maker of the Calcutta University of to-day,
to whose interest and encouragement
I owe so much.

THE AUTHOR

PREFATORY

This book embodies the matter of twelve lectures delivered by me as Tagore Law Professor of the Calcutta University in April 1952.

The work, such as it is, is an imperfect fulfilment of a dream and an ambition which I contracted in my youth more than forty years ago. Since then I have devoted all the time I could spare to follow up the indistinct trails that I could discover in the gloaming, in the hope of presenting, one day, a really complete picture of the Evolution of Ancient Indian Law.

With every step forward however I realised more and more the vast area and incredible complexity of the problem before me. I soon shed the easy confidence with which I started on the enterprise. For I found that the task involved a study of a vast mass of material beyond the powers of a single investigator. For, a proper sociological study of the evolution would embrace not only a deep knowledge of the legal literature but also of the entire cultural history of ancient India, assisted by a thorough critique of anthropological material which, by the way, has been only imperfectly exploited as yet. The literary material alone is vast, as one could find from Mahamahopadhyay P. V. Kane's monumental work on the *History of Dharmasastras*. The rest of the material has to be gathered from a great mass of studies scattered over numerous books and periodicals.

After being engaged in this study off and on for over forty years, I cannot yet claim to have covered more than a small fraction of the entire field for research. I thus feel like an indifferently equipped woodsman in a vast uncharted forest of which he has dependable knowledge of only small patches.

I could have wished the work to be not only more comprehensive but also more acute and convincing. But I felt that time was against me. A septuagenerian in Bengal has no right to expect much longer time for active work. And I did not care to see such glimmerings of light that I have got to die out altogether. I have, therefore, decided to give to the world the result of my studies so far as they went.

As I have said at the conclusion, the last thing that I could wish is to be dogmatic about any opinion I have expressed in it. I should naturally welcome any criticism which may help to throw further light on any of the points made by me. I venture to think however that the outstanding features of my thesis, *e.g.* that the evolution of Ancient Indian law has not been a simple development from within of a single culture, *viz.* the Aryan, but has at all stages been influenced by various cultures, and that positive law emerges in time with the assumption of judicial authority by the King and grows with the expansion of King's justice, will stand the test of closer examination. The other cultures which have contributed to the development of law I have often described as non-Arya, but not for that reason necessarily inferior to the Arya culture.

There is a none too uncommon feeling in India that Arya culture was in every respect a superior one and every contribution of a non-Arya race or culture must have been inferior, morally and materially. Every student of history knows that this was not a fact, and I need hardly warn my readers that the term non-Aryan, for me, does not bear the derogatory implication of the word Anārya as used in ancient Indian literature.

It is needless to say that I am indebted to a vast number of previous workers in the field. But I must single out Mahamohopadhyay Kane's *History of Dharmasastras,* a magnificent storehouse of information on which I have drawn copiously with the confidence that the care and industry of the learned author richly deserves. And the recently published work, *Vedic India* edited by Dr. R. C. Majumdar and Stuart Piggot's *Prehistoric India* have also been of great assistance to me.

I have followed the scheme of transliteration in use to-day, but for facility of understanding I have ventured to make one change by using *Ṛi* for ঋ, instead of Ṛ. I have not been too punctilious however with diacritical marks where the pronunciation seemed to be obvious.

My thanks are due to Dr. D. C. Sarkar who was good enough to look over the manuscript and make valuable suggestions. I am also indebted to Sri Harideb Chatterjee, M.A., LL.B., for looking over the proofs and to him and Sri Satyabrata Datta, M.A., LL.B. for helping with the index. I have also had material assistance from my grand-daughter Miss Neelakshi Sen Gupta, M.A., B.Mus. in preparing the manuscript for the Press and looking over proofs.

N. C. Sen-Gupta.

CONTENTS

CHAPTER I

INTRODUCTORY

SECTION I

Hindu Law proper as it has come down to us is a product of the middle ages, applied and developed by British Indian Courts. Its source books are the great commentaries and text books, compiled mostly at a time when the Muslim conquerors were already establishing themselves.

The basic assumption of the law of these text books is that the law is eternal and is entirely derived from one source—the Veda.

The law proper in their view is only a part of the comprehensive code which governed all sides of men's conduct and which is wholly attributable to the eternal Veda.

This theoretic exposition of the law hides much of its real source and history. The mediaeval text writers purport to expound the law almost exclusively with reference to texts of the Smṛitis which are supposed to be only *'interpreted'* by them. But even this exposition betrays the existence of other factors which determine the law as laid down by them, if we examine closely the controversy between different jurists with regard to many a topic of law. In these discussions each protagonist professes to be out to justify his own view by reference to the Śāstric texts. It appears however that in point of fact they are only seeking justification in the Śāstra for the law as they found practised in their own community. Thus the development of the law by commentaries was not, as might be easily supposed, but a logical evolution from within, but was determined by historical facts without.

A poignant instance of this fact is to be found in the discussion on the validity of marriage with a maternal uncle's daughter.

The history of marriage with the maternal uncle's daughter is interesting if somewhat obscure. There are one or two passages not only in the Smṛitis but also in the Ṛigveda which seem to suggest the validity of marriage with the maternal uncle's daughter.[1]

RV आयाहीन्द्र पथिभिरीलितेभि यज्ञभागमिमं न भागधेयं जुषस्व ।
तृप्तां जुहुर्मातुलस्य व योषाभागस्ते पितृष्वसेयीव पामिव ॥ Khila.

They show that there was a time, at any rate during the early Aryan settlement in the northern India when maternal uncle's daughter was not regarded as a sapiṇḍa,—sapiṇḍa relationship being purely agnatic.[1] On this basis the texts of law prohibiting marriage with a Sapiṇḍa girl which can be traced to earliest times would not affect the maternal uncle's daughter or the father's sister's daughter. But already, long before these commentaries, the Dharmaśāstras had unanimously accepted the position that the maternal uncle's daughter would be a sapiṇḍa and the law texts are unanimous that a sapiṇḍa girl cannot be married.

The text books of northern India and among others the Tantravārtika of Kumārilaswāmi, who was himself a South Indian though settled in Benares, are unanimous that the maternal uncle's daughter cannot be married and that such a marriage would be sinful in the extreme. Yet great works of South Indian expositors in law, Parāśaramādhava, Smṛitichandrikā, etc., are equally strong in seeking to establish, again by reference to Vedic and Smṛiti texts, that such marriages are not only permissible, but even praiseworthy.

The true inwardness of the controversy lies below the surface of the legal exigesis, in the social background of the law. In Northern India generally such marriages are not permitted even now, while in the South India and the Deccan they are very much in vogue. Nor is the vogue one of recent origin but has existed from very early times. It is noticed by Baudhāyana in his Dharmasūtra (c. 500 B.C.) as an established custom in the south like fish eating in the east.[2] This custom has in fact existed in the south from very ancient times and therefore, when these great southern writers were struggling to establish its validity by their own interpretation of śāstras they were really out to seek śāstric support for a usage to which they were born.

The fact is that the laws of the Hindus like every other human institution have grown out of rudiments in the remote past. That basic law has gathered volume and content like a snowball as it rolled on in time. The law of the Mitākṣara of Vijñāneśvara or of the Dharmaratna of Jimūtavāhana is not the law as it was about three to four thousand years ago when the Ṛigveda was probably compiled.

This fact would be readily recognised by any one who takes the trouble to read the mediæval and modern text books by the side of

1 See *post*. Baudhyana Dh. S. I. 5, 113—115.

2 Baudhāyana Dharmasūtra I. 1, 19.

the hymns of the Ṛigveda or even the much later Dharmasūtras which were the more proximate sources of the law. But what is not equally recognised is that the whole of the development of this law is not entirely from within, by a more or less logical development of the basic principles to be found in those remote sources. It will be one of the purposes of these lectures to show that this is not a fact, but that the law has grown into its fully developed form by a liberal absorption not only of the growing usages of a single homogeneous community who were the *fons et origo* of the laws, but, at least equally, of the customs and usages of communities and races alien to the Aryans whose laws were the ultimate source.

The original kernel of this law was undoubtedly the laws of the races known as Aryans who came and established themselves in India between three and four thousand years ago. Law proper emerges in that society for the first time in the works known as the Dharmasūtras. A part of these works deals with the duties of the king—one of whose duties is to administer justice (vyavahāra). Law proper so far as envisaged in these works is laid down as parts of this duty (dharma) of kings. With the expansion of the administration of king's justice positive law grows and ultimately develops into an elaborate code.

But behind and beyond this stage of law embodied in the Dharmasūtras there was a long history of the development of society down to this stage. Law existed then not as rules administered by kings but as rules developed in fact by custom and usage but obeyed from a sense of inner constraint promoted by magic and the religious compulsion associated with it.

In the Ṛigveda there is no trace of the king administering justice or enforcing the law. But there runs through the whole of it a concept of binding law—*Rita*, sometimes also called *dharma*—which is generally associated with magic rituals which give it strength and obligatoriness. Transgression of these rules (anṛita) is not a mere violation of human laws to be enforced by human sanctions but was supposed to be punished in this life and hereafter by supernatural forces.

The human element in the enforcement of this law was furnished by the seers or wise men of the community who knew the rituals of penance (prāyaśchitta) by which these wrongs could be righted. These wise men were resorted to for remedy when a transgression was committed and in all cases of doubt they were the persons who could lay down what was the law.

The laws of the Āryas never completely got clear of this association with magic and religion and even in its latest stages of growth the law was always dharma and when the king came to administer the law, it was because it was his duty (Dharma) to maintain the dharma.

Nevertheless with the development of society even the traditional law of Dharma, corresponding to the *Fas* of Rome, followed a more or less independent development. The king's duties and statecraft itself became an independent subject of study and developed along lines, not out of alliance with dharma but yet peculiarly its own.

The history of the development of this law is only partially to be found in written records. Down to the stage when law proper took a definite shape, the picture has to be reconstructed by piecing together fragments of social life to be gathered from religious and ritual literature that preceded the age of the Dharmasūtras. In this task we are fortunately able now to find some valuable links though not plentiful in archæological and anthropological researches into the pre-history of India and of races and kingdoms of neighbouring lands. With all that aid, one has still to roam in a wilderness lighted only by a dim and uncertain light. For though archæology has now thrown considerable light on the history of India of the middle ages, with regard to remoter times, we still have to grope in a dense mist where only shadowy outlines are visible.

SOURCES

It will be worth while at this stage to take stock of the sources from which we have to draw our materials for this pre-history as also of the later history of ancient Indian law.

The ultimate traditional source of all law, and necessarily the oldest historical material are the Vedas. Of these the texts of the Rigveda are the oldest. None of these works purport to lay down the law. The Vedas are mainly collections of hymns addressed to different gods the compilation of which is ascribed by tradition to Kriṣṇadvaipāyana Vedavyāsa. The texts *e.g.* of the Ṛigveda themselves, apart from the tradition that they were revealed to different seers, clearly indicate their origin, long before their compilation, in the inspired composition of different Ṛiṣi authors which had already acquired, at the date of their compilation, magic virtue and were on that account in use in rituals connected with diverse activities of the life of the ancient Āryas. The texts of the other Vedas, notably the Yajurveda, are more frankly associated with rituals and endowed with magic properties.

Of the Vedas, the Ṛigveda is in a sense the root, the Sāman and Yajus having arisen, in a way, as efflorescences for purposes of uses in ritual sacrifices. These three together are referred to in the literature down to a much later date as the Trayī—or the three revealed texts.

The Atharva Veda which is substantially a book of magic and charms was, till a comparatively late date, called Atharvāngirasa, associated with dark and frightening deeds of its votaries.

It consists substantially of magic charms and seems to have had an origin and history independent of the Vedas as the special science of men of dark deeds. But in its present form it has absorbed and sometimes enlarged a large body of Mantras of the Ṛigveda. It is probable that as the number of believers in these magic rites increased among Vedic worshippers it became mixed up with these mantras from Ṛigveda and on the strength of this it was admitted to the rank of a fourth Veda.

The ritual tradition is carried through and developed in the Brāhmaṇas, a great deal of which is concerned with the elaboration of the rituals, often with mystic and quasilogical and esoteric explanations of the reasons for each element of the ritual, and in the Āraṇyakas some of which develop a more philosophic outlook on the ultimate realities. These are found crystallised later in the Upaniṣads.[1]

None of these works are works on law. But a study of the mantras of the Saṃhitās, and perhaps even more, of the Brāhmaṇas and the Upaniṣads with their stories and traditions, throw a great deal of light on the life and mind of the society in which they had vogue and give us a valuable, if scanty, collection of the germs from which Ārya law grew, which were revered in all later ages as Śruti or absolutely binding revealed rules of conduct of Āryas.

The nearest approximation to the character of law is made by the works which historically followed the Veda or Śruti, the Śrauta and Gṛihya Sūtras. These are compilations in the form of brief rules which *ordain* the forms of ritual in all their detail, including, in the course of exposition, the verses of the Veda which have to be recited at each stage of the ritual to attain the magic effect sought by the ritual. These works do not directly concern the lawyer's law, but are of invaluable assistance in giving a fuller picture of the life of the Ārya.

The broad outline of the picture that we get of the life of the

[1] For a clear uptodate account of the general character and contexts of the Vedic literature see the *Vedic India* Book III Chap. 12 by Dr. B. K. Ghosh p. 225 seq.

Ārya in these works is that from conception in the mother's womb to death and cremation every minute act of his life is accompanied by a ritual. In that way it gives us a very complete picture of that life. And their very character as manuals of magico-religious ritual gives us some assurance that the picture they give is a more or less faithful one of the life of the people from the most ancient times, though inevitably affected no doubt by later variations. For rituals which are believed to have magic effects are not lightly varied in ancient societies, though they may grow by accretion as well as by quasi-logical extensions of ancient rules. In this way these works are not only a valuable guide to the life of the time when they were compiled, but also of the life of far more ancient times.

The works which followed these and were in a manner consolidated with the Śrauta and Gṛihya sūtras bring us as near the concept of the lawyer's law as ancient Indian law ever came to. These are the Dharmasūtras. These too like the Gṛihyas ordain rules of conduct of Āryas divided by classes with reference to each stage of life. While the Gṛihyas give the rules for the rituals of every day life of the Ārya, these Dharmasūtras lay down detailed rules of conduct of Āryas, for the most part apart from rituals, in every stage of life or āśrama. The earliest of these Āśramas is Brahmacharyya, (studentship), followed, after completion of studies, by marriage and the status of Gṛihastha (householder). Then follow the stages of Vānaprastha and Sannyāsa. All the rules of conduct are laid down with meticulous detail and varied with reference to the varṇa or the caste of each man.

In this comprehensive code of duties for all, the Dharmasūtras deal also with the duties of the king—and along with his other duties, that of administering the law in disputes (Vyavahāra). In dealing with this Vyavahāra these works also lay down the laws which the king must observe and enforce and great prominence is given to the king's duty to award punishment (Daṇḍa) to offenders. Thus the Dharmasūtras are the first works to lay down the lawyer's law, the law to be administered by the king in his administration of justice.

The next stage in the evolution of ancient law is marked by more elaborate and comprehensive codes in which the aphoristic style of the sūtras is replaced by a metrical form. The whole series of the texts from the sūtra works down to the metrical works are comprehensively known by the name of Smṛiti (Recollections). These works mark the last stage of ancient Indian law with which I shall be directly concerned in these lectures.

The development of law in Ancient India has taken place not by mere logical process or natural development out of the sacred works of ancient India but has, at every stage, received considerable development from the customs and usages of many races who surrounded the community which professed the Vedic culture. So too various new religious systems, some of whom claimed millions of votaries in India, including Kings and Emperors have grown up from time to time and assisted in the development of the law.

Furthermore, the basic law itself has again been diversified by reason of the mere vastness of territory over which it ultimately came to prevail.

SECTION II

Social Background of Ancient Indian Law

In order to appreciate the development of the law, it is necessary to bear in mind the basic social organisation of ancient India and the changes which came over it in course of time to which the law naturally reacted. Here it will be necessary to remember that much of what existed in the earliest times may have to be found not in the records of those times alone, but in many cases in those of succeeding ages.

I shall give here a brief outline of the society as I imagine it to have been. Several aspects of it will require a further treatment later.

The materials for a complete picture of society in the Vedic times are not very abundant but there are materials which show certain outstanding features. In the first place, the society was a society of villages. The whole community was organised in villages. These villages were in the Vedic times apparently purely agnatic, that is to say, the principal inhabitants of villages consisted of persons who were descended in the male line from a common male ancestor. We do not find any trace of cognatic relations living in the same villages.

It seems that families of the Vedic times consisted of the father, mother and his immature sons. Grown-up sons upon their marriage set up houses of their own. But the houses of brothers were contiguous to one another. This is indicated by one little detail in the ceremony of Baliharaṇa in Baudhāyana's Gṛihyasūtra (II, 8, 1—40). Baliharaṇa is a ceremony connected with the offer of oblations to the *Viśvedevāh* i.e. to all the gods of the universe. These offerings had to be made at different places in the house. And from this ceremony we get an idea of the constitution of the house in those times. There was a place for the gods (devatāvakāśa), a bed-room, the room where the fire was placed, the cattle shed, the sabhā room which was probably also a place for gambling, a husking shed (Ulukhala-muṣalāvakāśa). The offerings had to be made at each of these places, and, after every part of the house was exhausted, the last offering being made at the door or gate of the house. Thereafter the offering had to be made in the house of the elder brother *after going out of the house.* (*Upaniṣkramya Jyeṣṭhāvakāśe*—II. 8, 30). This indicates, to my mind, that descendants of a common ancestor normally lived grouped together in adjacent but different houses, each of which had its full compliment of the various parts indicated in the Baliharaṇa ceremony.

By the expansion of the family in several generations, accordingly, the wider group was formed of persons descended from a common ancestor who would constitute what later law books call the *Kula* corresponding to the gens of Roman Law. This *Kula* which is probably the same as *Janma* of the Vedas is frequently referred to in later legal literature as a group by themselves.

The village however, strictly speaking, did not consist of the *Kula* alone. The *kulas* like the Roman gentes included only the men who mattered, the owners and masters of the village. But by the side of them there lived other people who performed various social services for the members of the *Kula*. In the ancient Indian villages from the Vedic times we can notice the existence of a two-fold division in the community, corresponding to similar divisions in the city states of Greece and Rome, of an upper and superior class and a lower class of commoners corresponding to some extent to the Plebians of Rome. There were persons who would perhaps be attached to the families of the upper classes as inferior members who did necessary services to the principal families like the clients in ancient Roman society.[1] These included cultivators, barbers, traders, artisans, herdsmen and so forth. This population is referred to in the Vedas as the Viś.

The evidence of later literature shows that these lower classes also had their own group organisations or guilds for regulating their

[1] This is probably indicated by Gautama Dh. S. Chap. X, 61-62 which suggests a relation between a Sūdra and his Ārya patron similar to that of patr[on] and client in Rome. यञ्चायमाश्रितो भतव्यस्तेन । क्षीणोऽपि तेन चोत्तरस्तदर्थोऽस्य निचयः । They were free and not slaves but were *āśrita* of the twice born with mutual obligations like those of patron and client in Rome.

own affairs. The sacred laws of the Āryas governed the life of the upper classes but these inferior classes of people had their own guild usages which were binding on them irrespective of any reference to the sacred law. This is indicated in the earliest of the law books, Gautama's Dharmasūtra, in which, while the sources of law are first stated to be (1) the Vedas, (2) the recollections of sages who knew the Vedas and (3) their usages and practices, it is further stated that cultivators, traders, herdsmen who live by tending cattle, usurers and artisans have authority in their particular groups (*Krisivaṇik-pāśupālyah Kuśīda Kāravah sve sve varge*).

The village so organised was a more or less autonomous unit in which each of the groups, the Kulas and guild groups had a certain measure of autonomy in determining the law and also of deciding disputes amongst their members, though the upper classes were however chiefly governed, by sacred traditions, where there were any, of which the custodians were men specially learned in the sacred law.

Bodies of such learned men seem to have existed from very ancient times and colleges of these men called Pariṣads were resorted to for determination of any doubtful or disputed question of theology. We have got evidence of the existence of the Pariṣads of communities which were evidently in the nature of universities or perhaps of the College of Pontiffs of ancient Rome. In the Brihadāraṇyaka Upaniṣad (VI, 2, 1) reference is made to the Pariṣad of the Pānchālas to whom Śvetaketu went for learning after finishing his education. It would thus seem that these Pariṣads of learned men had authority from the earliest times in matters involving the sacred law.

Though thus each of the groups in the village was in some measure autonomous, the village as a whole constituted a special group or unit which had authority in matters concerning the whole village. At its head was the Grāmaṇi who is mentioned in the Rigveda and elsewhere. In later literature, the Grāmaṇi is an official of the king. But evidently in the Vedic times he was merely the leader of the village, not necessarily elected, but going to the top by some sort of common acquiescence. As the leader of the community, these village and group chiefs (grāmaṇis and gaṇapatis) led their own contingents in war under the king and attended at sacrifices as the king's entourage, but they were in no sense officers appointed by the king.

In course of time the villages grew. Groups of villages formed a larger settlement and consistuted a tribe like the many who are referred to in the Rigveda, Anu, Druhyu, Turvasu, Kuru etc. and also others like Pānchālas who are referred to in the Upaniṣads. These tribes had their kings who were primarily the leaders of hosts, military captains and had undefined powers of coercion in aid of Dharma.

Of administration of justice in Vedic times, the Vedic literature itself says little. The king had apparently not yet become a judge. It was his duty no doubt to keep order and to compel people to perform their duties, but a regular system of administration of king's justice had not yet come into existence. Disputes between people were apparently decided by the community, the Kula or the guild to which they belonged. Cases must have been very rare in which the king was called upon to meddle in such disputes and in fact it is doubtful whether the king had at all the authority to interfere when it did not involve any question of public importance such as, a great violation of the Dharma to maintain which was the duty of the king.

Tribunals

The sort of tribunals which must have existed in these times is not to be found in any Vedic texts but is probably indicated in much later literature. As we have seen, Gautama in giving the source of law gives authority to the cultivators, artisans etc. in their own communities. In his time as well as in the time of the other Dharmasūtras already the king was administering justice. Decision of litigations (Vyavahāra) formed an important head of the duties of the king. And these manuals of law in their treatment of Vyavahāra or litigation give details as to the sort of disputes which came before the king for decision and show how the topics of litigation increased and developed in course of time.

Gradually we find that the king is assisted in his work by other judges appointed by the king until the whole cadre of *Partiṣṭhita* courts, *i.e.*, courts established by the king seems to have grown up. But even in these latest developments, for instance, in the works of Yājñavalkya, Nārada, Bṛihaspati etc. we find that, besides the king's court, there were other courts which had authority to decide disputes. They are variously enumerated and they include the Kulas, Śreṇis, Pūgas, Vrātas and Gaṇas. Roughly, these include the gens, the various guild organisations and the village as a whole, which had, by the time of these works, been organised on a different basis. Thus later authorities lay down that these Kula and guild organisations were primary courts, but their decisions were liable to appeal or review by higher courts and there was a heirarchy of tribunals from the Kula, Śreṇi, Pūgas etc. upto the king's judge and the king himself. That was the result of the ultimate concentration of judicial administration in the hands of the king which necessitated the organisation of all tribunals under his authority. But the existence or survival of these Kula, Śreṇi etc. organisations indicates that they were mere modified survivals of an ancient order of things when they were tribunals with final authority in the Vedic society.

The law, *i.e.*, the lawyer's law, was gradually isolated from the great body of customs and sacred laws which were binding on society, in the course of the development of the king's judicial administration or Vyavahāra. Our primary concern would be with the development of this law. But in the earliest times, apparently long before the king had taken up the administration of justice, it was administered in the various gentile, communal or local organisations.

Laws

What was the law which these bodies administered? With regard to the upper classes, in matters which were within its scope, it was obviously the sacred law consisting of traditions and customs of great sages of the past and the authoritative Vedic texts where they existed. There had already grown up a body of persons who were specially learned in that subject. They were not Ṛiṣis or seers themselves but persons who had special knowledge and had risen to a rank approximate in authority to that of the Vedic Ṛiṣis. Āpastamba in his Dharmasūtras says that Ṛiṣis who were seers of the Vedic texts did not exist amongst the *Avaras* or modern men, but there are some persons who were *Śrutarsis* who had risen almost to te rank of Seers or Ṛiṣis by having heard or learnt about the law, like Śvetaketu. That indicates that Vedic learning and knowledge of law had, for ages before Āpastamba, been a special study of a class of learned men who apparently came together in the Pariṣads and had authority in all doubtful matters which were not primarily governed by any definite Vedic texts or which involved special knowledge of the interpretation of these texts or reconciling of apparent oppositions between them. It is these men who, like the Pontiffs of ancient Rome or the Druides of Gaul, developed the law, such as it was, before it was formulated in definite codes so far as the upper classes were concerned. They formed schools, and gradually defferentiation arose between different schools leading to the development of the various *śākhās* and *charaṇas* of the Vedas.

The Dharmasūtras were the manuals of the various charaṇas which had their complete codes of law in the three sets of Sūtra works, Śrauta, Gṛihya and Dharmasūtras. They are attributed, each of them, to a particular person such as Gautama, Vasiṣṭha, Baudhāyana, Āpastamba, Hiraṇyakeśi etc.

These were not codes of law for the general body of people but apparently *memoria technica* or manuals for the use of the learned men of the schools for help in teaching pupils or laying down the law when appeals were made to them by the people. They constituted, each of them, a complete body of authoritative and authentic rules in force in that particular charaṇa. As has been indicated before, they were not strictly speaking, original works of certain individuals but embodied the traditional learning of the school to which the traditional author belonged. That is why Āpastamba calls the rules in his Dharmasūtra, *sāmayāchārika* rules or rules settled by concensus of the learned (*Dharmajñasamaya*).

While the sacred law was laid down by these Pariṣads, there was also a body of laws, purely secular, which governed the relations of tradesmen, artisans, cultivators etc. which did not form a subject of appeal to the Pariṣads but were regulated entirely by guilds or communities themselves. The result was that, in the earliest law books, we find two different sets of sources of law. One set which was primarily the law of the upper class, divided now into Brāhmanas and Kṣatriyas and to some extent of the Vaiśyas, but not of the lower class. The source of law for this upper class was, as mentioned before, the Vedas and these manuals or Dharmaśāstras and sacred custom, that is to say, the customs of people who were presumed to be acting according to lost Vedic texts. On the other hand, the law of the lower class and also laws on purely secular matters were founded on mere custom as such, which was not required to answer to the character of custom which can be presumed to be based on lost Śruti. This custom was administered even in the days of the Dharmasūtras by the respective guilds.

Then again while the clean men of villages consisted of these people, there were besides, beyond the villages proper but on their outskirts, settlements of communities which were regarded as unclean, the Antyajas of whom the names of Chandāla, Svapāk, Niṣāda, obviously of non-Arya origin and also of washermen appear to be referred to from old times with whom social intercourse was altogether forbidden. So too there were persons who were deemed to be outcastes *Abhiśastas* and *Apapātras*, who had to live outside the village and with whom, as with the dediticii of ancient Rome, no clean men could have any intercourse. In later law we find it definitely mentioned that even these were governed by their own customs.

India was then, as it is more emphatically now, a land of a multitude of races and cultures.—Its grades of culture extend from men who can hold their own against, and, in some respects, even give points to the foremost races and peoples of the world, to almost the lowest rungs of civilisation. Hindu law givers of early days concerned themselves primarily with the cultured classes and left to the rest their own laws, usages and institutions.

SECTION III

Stages of Law

At the stage when justice was administered by the kula or the guilds or the villages, the law which they would administer would naturally be founded upon usage and custom, except in matters which definitely fall within the sphere of sacred law as laid down by religious authority. Custom then was necessarily the pre-eminent factor in developing and determining the law to be administered. In course of time then, customs which were studied by the scholars of the community assembled in pariṣads tended to crystalise into definite rules which were embodied in the manuals of law in these schools. These manuals became the Dharmasūtras of the particular schools.

Dharmasūtras

As I have indicated above, the Dharmasūtras themselves are far from being regular codes of laws. Law proper *i.e.*, laws enforced by state authority forms only a part of the Dharmasūtras and goes under Rājadharma. There are indeed even elsewhere some texts of a legal character spread out in the different chapters dealing with other topics. Thus, for instance, under studentship or *Brahmacharya* in Gautama we find a rule that the teacher should discipline the pupil without corporal punishment and, failing that, with no more than flogging with a rope or a light cane. To this rule is added a rider—if the teacher gives other corporal punishment, the king will punish him.[1] As will be seen later, a great deal of what became the lawyers' law in later times *e.g.* marriage inheritance etc. were also treated in other parts of these early works and not under Vyavahāra.

As we proceed further in the development of Dharmasūtras we find the contents of Rājadharma being expanded and more elaborate rules of positive law formulated which tend to be sêparated from Rājadharma proper under the different heads or topics of Vyavahāra or determination of disputes by the king. The contents of this chapter of Vyavahāra are found growing from the time of Gautama and Āpastamba till it becomes a fairly elaborate code in what is believed to be the latest of Dharmasūtras, *viz.*, the Viṣṇu-smṛiti, which, as willl be seen later, was, in its present form a much later work than the other Sutras.

In the Dharmasūtras we find that the rules of conduct which are of legal obligation are becoming less and less dependent upon custom and are stated more and more in definite propositions of law and laid down in these several manuals. In other words, the law becomes increasingly *lex scripta.* The authority of customs is still recognised as a subsidiary source of law but under a theory of a presumption of their being founded on the revealed law.[2]

In all this development however these sutras are only manuals of certain schools or *charaṇas* and are practical authorities only among the followers of the respective schools. Each of them no doubt appears to claim universal authority but, in point of fact, their authority was practically confined to Āryas who belong to that particlar Vedic school. At the next stage however, we come upon a class of Dharmaśāstras which are not only of an encyclopædic character but which are no longer manuals of schools. These are the metrical dharmaśāstras of Manu, Yājnavalkya, Nārada and others.

Metrical Smritis

The growth of these Dharmasāstras of universal authority marks an important stage in the development of Hindu society. There has apparently been, before this, a great inter-mixture and consolidation

1 Gautama II, 42; शिष्यशिष्टिरवधेन। तदशक्तौ रज्जुवेणुविदलाभ्याम्। अन्यथा अन् राज्ञा शास्यः।

2 Apastamba II, 29, 13-14, I, 4, 8.

of the different communities belonging to the different schools and also a development of a synthetic common culture among persons professing the laws in the various schools. The Vedic society with its divisions of *śākhās* and *charaṇas* was maintained in tradition in so far as purely sacred law is concerned, but has apparently broken down outside that sphere and a common society with a common culture has grown up which required for its manual of law a book of universal authority. The answer to this need for such works were these metrical dharmaśāstras.

Gautama, Āpastamba, Vaśiṣṭha and Baudhāyana do not contemplate the application of their law to any but Āryas, any more than the Jus Quiritium in early Rome contemplated its application to Plebs or Peregrines. It was only by stages that Latins and, later, plebs were admitted to some of the laws of the Quirites, until by Praetorian law all Roman citizens were governed by a universal law Characteristically, while the Dharmasūtras expressly or implicitly confine their application to Āryas, Yājñavalkya and Manu contemplate their code to apply to all classes including paṣandis, gaṇas, mixed castes etc. No one was outside the law of these codes.

I am inclined to think that the development of this literature was the result of a rebuilding of the Indian culture after a great break down of the basic Ārya culture as a result of the inroads of heretic cults and also of the intermixture of the original Āryas with other races. Possibly also the development of great kingdoms and empires may have contributed to this call for a common code governing the entire community. In any case we find a definite stage in the evolution of the law indicated by these encyclopædic books of law,—a stage in which distinctions of Śākhā and charaṇas are eliminated and a common code is compiled for all.

Manusaṃhita

These codes however were not really all new. To take the leading work amongst them—the Manusaṃhita as it has now come down to us—we find in it many texts which are cited either verbatim or in substance in the sūtra manuals that preceded it and some are reproductions of Vedic texts. I am inclined to think that the Manusaṃhita was a compilation of all known texts which, from the most ancient times, had been attributed to Manu, whom tradition from Vedic times credited as the first law-giver of the human race.

(a) But it was also an attempt to lay down a complete code of laws on the basis of known and existing texts of Manu by additions from Vedas, customs and other sources which were incorporated into it.

Illustrations can be found in history of similar attempts elsewhere, made under auspices of great kings at a time when there was a great confusion about the law, to prepare authoritative compilations of the texts of law. The most outstanding of such attempts of course is the great Corpus Juris of Justinian which purports to bring together all the law that was in force at that date— whether in the works of authoritative jurists or in the statutes of the Empire. A similar and more ancient illustration is furnished by the mode of compilation of the Zend Avesta which was compiled under the authority of king Ardeshir by the high priest Tansar. The original Avesta in the only two copies that existed of it was lost after Alexander's invasion. Fragments however were retained either in memory or in writing. These were collected by Valkhas and the extant original Zend Avesta was compiled by Ardeshir's high priest, Tansar. In making this compilation, Tansar not merely collected and sorted his materials but freely brought in his own contribution when he thought fit as appears from a letter[1] of Tansar which says in almost so many words that, invoking the authority of Shahinshah, he freely altered the old laws which were unsuitable to his age. And, later, Shahpuhr I developed the Avesta by ordering the wisdom of the Avesta relating to profane sciences scattered amongst the Hindus and Greeks to be collected and embodied in Tansar's text of the Avesta,—a veiled confession, as Darmesteter takes it, of the fact that the Zend Avesta was enriched by Shahpuhr by scientific materials gathered and collected from other sources.

We know as a fact that many ancient works to which reference is found scattered in extant works are lost and may well have been lost even at the time when the present text of Manu was compiled. If there was an original Manusaṃhitā other than the texts which were retained in memory or in fragments only, it may have been similarly lost; and some great king may have ordered, like Ardeshir or Shahpuhr that the text of Manusaṃhitā should be reconstructed and entrusted some learned scholars with the task. In making the reconstruction and producing a work which would be complete in itself, that scholar may have taken recourse to the methods which

(a) यत्तु मनुरब्रवीत्तद्भेषजम्, Taittīriya Saṃhita quoted in Tantravāttika.

1 Tansar's letter quoted in Darmesteter's Zend Avesta (Sacred Books of the East) Pages xliv to xlvi.

were followed by Tansar and Shahpuhr of re-adjusting the old law to new condition as also of enriching the surviving texts by borrowing from other sources.

It is more difficult to say anything about the other metrical Smṛtis. But it appears that during a rather long period such metrical Smṛtis sprang up in some abundance. Although we have got only a few in full, a large number of metrical Smṛtis made for the students of law such as, those of Kātyāyana, Yama, Bṛihaṣpati and others are scattered about in quotations in the Nibandhas. Sixteen authors are named by Yājñavalkya. Paithinasi cited in Smṛiti Chandrikā gives as many as twenty six names. Other authorities, like Śankha and Angirā quoted there give an even larger number. Although it is not possible to say anything about their origins, it seems possible to infer that they were the results of reconstruction of ancient law by adaptation to existing conditions, and the matrical form was preferred in the period when they were compiled on account probably of its mnemonic value. Of the metrical Smṛitis now current under the names of old authors like *e.g.* Āpastamba, however, many are rank forgeries.

Of the metrical Smṛitis comparatively few are available now in full. But both with regard to the metrical Smṛitis as well as to many Dharmasūtras which have likewise disappeared, there is abundance of quotations of their texts in the literature of the commentaries and Nibandhas which marked the next most important step in the development of Hindu Law. And in the case of some of these Smṛitis, it is possible to reconstruct a fair part of the contents of the lost Smṛitis as has been done by Jolly and by Kane with regard to Bṛihaṣpati and Kātyāyana.

It is impossible to say how long the compilation of the metrical Smṛitis in the name of reputed saints, and even of gods continued. But apparently the output had ceased some long time before the commencement of the commentaries on the Smṛitis, the earliest of which did not go beyond the eighth century A.D. From that time on, the entire development of law has taken place from the numerous commentaries and text books. The works of this character which have up till now been unearthed either in full or in part are set out in Kane's History of Dharmaśāstras (Vol. I, pages 135-246).

NIBANDHAS

Although they are outside the scope of these lectures certain characteristics which mark out the literature of the commentaries as a whole may be stated,—though there has been considerable development among them in the course of the ages. In the first place, it appears that when the commentaries were written all the reputed Smṛitis had acquired equal authority and common acceptance, as a result of the consolidation of all India into a single social complex; and the task of commentator was like that of the Roman Jurisconsults to reconcile the numerous texts and to adapt them to the existing conditions of society. In the second place, we notice that although the commentaries were often the work of scholars and were full of scholastic disquisitions, the principal works bear unmistakable trace of being the works of practical lawyers, persons who had made the administration of law,—both law as administered by the Courts as well as the law of *āchāra*—their vocation in life. Even before this, as we shall see, the development that we find in the Smṛitis and notably in the works of Nārada, Bṛihaspati, Kātyāyana, Yama and others clearly indicates that, by the time when these works were written, the matter had come into the hands of the practical lawyers. They developed the law not only with reference to the sacred traditions but also with equal regard to the practical needs of the society of the times. This becomes very prominent in the commentaries from Viśvarūpa and Vijñāneśvara down to authors like Chaṇḍésvar of Mithila and Nīlakaṇṭha, who were practical lawyers and who tried to expound the law as much with reference to śāstras as to the practical needs of the society. It will appear from a study of these commentaries that it is by reference to the social usages and the needs of the society that each of the commentaries has been developed.

Scope of the Present Work

As has been indicated already, the development of the law has not, in India any more than anywhere else, been a completely logical process. It was conditioned by historical events and by the pressure of environments and circumstances, amongst which were the changing needs of society as well as the pressure of communities who were previously outside the pale of Ārya law.

Even the works on law, so far as they are available, though they give a deceptive appearance of a continuous and systematic growth are full of enormous gaps which we have yet no means to fill up. Between the Vedas and the Dharmasūtras we can feel that customs were developing over a wide area before they are finally embodied in the various Dharmasūtras. But we have no tangible evidence to construct a systematic story of the growth.

Then again the Dharmasūtras themselves cite several authors who are either followed or controverted. Of their works we have no trace. What we have is just a handful out of the many works which must have been compiled probably through centuries in different parts of India.

Between these again and the metrical Smṛitis, only a few of which are intact, there is a yawning gap of apparently troubled history about which this literature gives us no trace. During this period Vedic culture and society must have suffered great shocks from heterodox societies or opinions of which traces have been obliterated, though not altogether. The reference to Pakhaṇḍis and Vrātas in the Smṛitis who are said to be governed by their own laws indicates the prior existence of such elements. Manusaṃhitā however purports to say that its laws applies even to Pakhandis. Even the Buddhists apparently purported to follow the law of Manu, though much altered, as would appear from the fact that the Dhammatat of Burma professes to lay down the law in Manu's name. That probably indicates an ultimate consolidation of the entire society, but we can only guess.

A great deal too much of the facts of history which thus contributed to the growth of the law has been lost. Necessarily our principal recourse in the study of the evolution of the law would be these legal works. It is only occasionally that we can hope to get a glimpse into the factors other than traditional law which have actually influenced the development. Our main source books and the principal evidence in respect of our study must, therefore, be these law books.

As already indicated however the task of giving the entire evolution of ancient Indian law even from law books alone is formidable and utterly impossible in the course of the present series of lectures. What I propose to do is to give you the course of evolution of law with reference to a few selected features and indicate what, to my mind, is the history of the development of those particular topics of law from their origins. The topics selected will not necessarily be the most important for the practical application of the law but important for the purpose of giving an insight into the course of evolution of law in ancient time.

I shall confine my investigation only to the Smṛitis and not later works, to works, that is to say, before the age of commentaries and nibandhas. The history of the development of the law in the commentaries is interesting and its ramifications many. But that is a develoment which must await future treatment, probably by other hands and cannot be attempted in these lectures.

SECTION IV

SEQUENCE OF SOURCE BOOKS

In trying to construct a history from written records, the first thing would apparently be to fix the ages of the various source books. Attempts have pretty often been made by various scholars down to Prof. Kane in history of Dharmaśāstras. I do not propose to go over that ground or attempt to reason out a chronological sequence of the works.

For, to my mind the mere arrangement of these works in a chronological order, even if anything like the approximate chronology can possibly be ascertained would be very different from the study of the evolution of the law. In the first place, the chronology of the texts relied upon for constructing the history is as yet little more than a mass of guesses. In most cases the texts which we have to rely upon have been quoted from books, the whole of which is not available, and has not in fact been available for long ages, and there is unmistakable proof of numerous other lost works of other authors which were in existence from the remote past down to the comparatively recent times.[2] Further most of the books, such as the Dharmasūtras, were compilations clearly made at different times and probably, in widely different places of the subcontinent, of the law and customs prevailing in the schools where the law and customs themselves may have been in actual use long before they were reduced to their present form in their manuals, so that the mere

[2] That many of these original works had ceased to be available even in the days of text-writers like Devaṇṇa Bhatta and Jimūtavāhana is indicated by the fact that they often purport to quote Smṛiti texts not from original works but from Saṁgrahas. "*Iti Samgrahakāra*" is often stated in the Smṛitichandrikā. Jiūtavāhana too in his Vyavahāramātrika quotes texts from such works and, in one instance, he says that a particular text, though not found in Dhāreśvara has been quoted in many nibandhas and therefore must be genuine (वृद्धधातातप-वचनन्तु बहुज्ञजीर्णोक्त निबन्धेऽस्माभिर्दृष्टं न पुनर्भोजदेवे । Vyavahāra Mātrika p. 305). Dhāreśvara *i.e.*, King Bhoja of Dhāra was the author of samgraha which all commentators considered to be an authentic work par excellence.

reference by one book to another in these manuals of schools which have been handed down from generation to generation is no evidence of the relative antiquity of the author quoted in relation to the author who makes a quotation. It would thus be clear that in attempting to arrange the texts in a chronological order by mere reference to the succession in time of the several books of these authors must be more or less futile.

Moreover, the Sūtra texts that have come down to us either in their originals or from the quotation in the Nibandhas and commentaries by no means exhaust the sources of the laws or the influences which have assisted in their development. Behind these laws as formulated in the texts there must have been a more or less long history of the development of the customs which are embodied in them. Unless we can make some reasonable guess about that history, we cannot be sure of having made any valuable contribution to the evolution of the law.

Our main purpose would be not so much the external history of the laws but, what Ihering calls, their inner chronology, that is the inner history of the evolution of legal institutions embodied in the books. Time sequence of the works themselves is not necessarily an infallible indication of the sequence of the laws and institutions embodied in them. It will often be found that early statements of law are not really complete expressions of the whole actual law and leave unexpressed limitations or amplifications which are only expressly formulated in a later work. In particular, late compilations like Manu often contain strange survivals of laws which had already become archaic at the time. Thus Manu speaks at one place that sons and wives are incapable of owning property, and that what they acquire belongs to the house-father :[3]—this is in clear conflict with other parts of the law in which the separate ownership of property by sons and wives is acknowledged. The text nevertheless survives. The law about secondary sons like Putrikāputra is given in elaborate details when they have clearly gone out of use. Instances like these will be found in many parts of these works as we shall have occasion to note as we go on.

Our task would therefore be to go behind these apparent sequences in the expressed laws (called by Ihering Rechtssätze) and to find out the real sequence of the institutions by a critique of the expressed laws, (geschichtsphilosophisce Kritik) or in other words to reconstruct the inner evolution thereof.[4]

3 Manu VIII. 416.

4 See Ihering Geist der Rômischen Rechts (Aufl VI) p. 38 seq.

Nevertheless we have for this purpose to start with a working idea of the sequence of legal works though not their actual dates. For this purpose we have to look at their general make up and contents and find out the stage of development that the law has reached in them. In this manner we can place our source books in some sort of order of sequence. We may be sure that of the Vedic literature, the Rigveda came first and the other Saṃhitās were later The Brāhmaṇas, Āraṇyakas, Upaniṣads as a class generally speaking, followed one another in this order, though there is little doubt that the oldest Upaniṣads were some of them older than some works known as Āraṇyakas. The Śrauta and Gṛihya Sūtras came next and then the Dharmasūtras of each school, though of the extant sūtra works the oldest Dharmasūtras were probably older than the Gṛihya sūtras e.g. of Āpastamba and Hiranyakeśī.

Among the extant Dharmasūtras I am inclined to think that the Gautama Dharmasūtra is the oldest. Baudhāyana and Vasiṣṭha followed, but the question of priority between them may be doubtful. Āpastamba and Hiranyakeśī were later, though it will be seen that these works retain in many respects survivals of old laws which have been displaced in the earlier works.

While this sequence seems to be indicated, it is also clear that all these works did not fall in the same line of development. Each may have been, and some of them clearly seem to have been the last of a line developed independently of others and probably widely separated in space and time. Some may have been developed in the Punjab, others in far away South and yet others in the east and may have been separated from one another by centuries. Thus, we should not be surprised to find an institution highly developed in an early work of the North while in a much later work of the peripheral areas of distant South the more archaic law is reproduced. This probably accounts for the occasional finding of more archaic law in Baudhāyana and notably in Āpastamba than the law in Gautama and Vaśiṣṭha.

Of the Sūtra works Viṣṇu gives us the law in its most developed form. It would seem to be separated by a whole history of growth from the older sūtra works and is much nearer to the later metrical Smritis like Manu and Yājñavalkya, and, in its present form, probably incorporates some features and expressions of even later dates though retaining a core of a more ancient text.

Of the metrical Smritis one may confidently say that Manu-samhitā was the oldest, though later manipulations of its texts are far from ruled out. Yājñavalkya's work is of independent growth in a line perhaps, following Viṣṇu and probably later in age. The works and fragments of Nārada, Brihaṣpati, Kātyāyana and some others follow one another.

While this sequence of the works in time may be taken as a working hypothesis, we must concentrate more on the inner evolution of the laws and institutions than on that of their literature. It will be seen that in making this search we shall often find ourselves on surer ground than in the more slippery region of the chronology of works.

By the side of these Smṛitis there is a whole literature which has an important bearing on legal history in what is called Arthaśāstra. The oldest work among these is the Arthaśāstra of Kauṭilya. Kāmandaka's Nītisāra, so far as it goes, is in essence a metrical rendering of the teachings of the school of Kauṭilya. Another work of the same character is Śukranīti. And a substantial chapter in the Sāntiparva of the Mahabhārāta also deals with the same topic of Politics.

There is a great deal of law in these works and a chapter of Kauṭilya, Dharmasthīyam, expressly deals with law and its administration. But the ages of these works are not free from controversy. Kauṭilya's work has been placed very differently by different scholars. But it is undoubtedly very old, how old, it would be rash for me to guess.

Whatever its age it is difficult to place the work as a whole in the order of evolution of laws as evidenced by the Dharmaśāstras. Kauṭilya recognises the authority of Dharmaśāstra, but of what precise works, it is difficult to surmise. In many parts, the laws laid down by him are almost identical with those of the Dharmaśāstras. But there are important differences. And in his treatment of the political organisation of society and administration he makes remarkable departures from the law of the Dharmasūtras generally, where the administrative authority is not nearly so fully organised on the basis of centralisation under the king. On some topics of law Kauṭilya gives us laws much more developed than in any of the Dharmasūtras.

On the whole, I am inclined to place the work of Kauṭilya later in the order of evolution than the Dharmasūtras. His law is much more developed and the society he depicts is much more highly organised under a central authority than in any of the Dharmasūtras. This does not necessarily mean that every Dharmasūtra was older in age than Kauṭilya. Some may have been later in date, though they followed an independent line of development. It seems to me that the school of politics founded by Kauṭilya flourished in some powerful and extensive centralised monarchy established in some part of India where developments had taken place very much ahead of the traditional law of dharmaśāstras. The school fourished and may have spread to other kingdoms, but the indications are that it decayed in later times leaving the field clear to dharmaśāstras. This seems to be indicated by the fact, among others, that the great commentaries and nibandhas of the middle ages which laid down the practical law for the people based on dharmaśāstras do not, so far as I have been able to trace, refer at all to the Arthaśāstra of Kauṭilya. Kauṭilya's school must have influenced political organisation in later ages but did not definitely influence legal works.

SECTION V

Evolution of Ancient Indian Society.

The main purpose of these lectures is to place before you what I conceive to be the story of the development of the law in the Dharmaśāstras starting from the Dharmasūtras down to the latest metrical Smṛitis. But the story of this evolution can only be properly appreciated against the background of the history beyond the stage of the Dharmasūtras and beyond the stage when positive law, that is, law administered by the king as judge came into existence.

Aryan Theory

Scholars of the last century assumed that the entire civilisation and culture of ancient India was one of which the primary, and probably the single root was the Vedas. Early Indologists traced the culture back to what they call the Aryan Race who were the common ancestors of the Indian Aryans, the Iranians as well as the Romans, the Greeks and practically all the European races. The result, in the words of a distinguished linguist, was "When the hypothesis of an Aryan invasion and occupation of India was first proposed some four generations ago, it was believed that the white-skinned, blue-eyed, and golden-haired Aryans, like their kinsmen of Northern Europe, entered India from the plateau of Central Asia, which was then a land of romantic mystery, came to this land of the black-skinned non-Aryans, made an easy and matter-of-course conquest of them, and imposed upon an inferior race or races their superior religion, culture and language. It was believed that all the better elements in Hindu religion and culture—its deeper philosophy, its finer literature, its more reasonable organization, everything in fact which was great and good and noble in it—came from the Aryans as a superior white race, and whatever was dark and lowly and superstitious in Hindu religion and civilization represented only an expression of the suppressed non-Aryan mentality."[5] A great deal of this attitude has now to be abandoned in the light of modern research.

First of all, the theory of a common Aryan race, founded as it was on the basis of vital linguistic affinities has to be considerably modified. Linguistic affinities, as well as the existence of practically common religious notions and social institution among the several peoples in Europe and Asia no doubt go long to establish a common root culture from which the different cultures of these peoples have been largely derived, but it does not necessarily imply that they are all descended from a common race. The movement of cultures even in the remote past often overstepped the limits of races and tribes. Thus we know now that a very substantial part of the culture of Greece, more in fact than the elements which can be definitely traced to common Indo-Germanic roots, was derived from the Minoan culture of Crete as also Babylonian and Egyptian cultures.[6] So too, much of the ancient Roman culture was derived from Etrusean and other neighbouring races whom they conquered and some of whom, in later times swarmed into the city of Rome, becoming Plebians and Peregrins. The culture of Iran, including the chief aspects of its political structure was largely based on what she derived from Sumer and Accad through Babylonians and Assyrians. In India itself in historical times, aliens like the Śakas and Yuehchis who were not of the same race as the Vedic Aryas are seen to have adopted the language and culture of the country. The same is true of the great South Indian races of Dravidian stock from whom came the Andhras, Cholas, Cheras and Pāṇḍyas who almost completely absorbed the religion and culture of the Aryans.

In fact the nature of the movement of cultures even in the remotest past cannot yet be said to have been sufficiently understood, in absence principally of a sufficient body of materials to

[5] S. K. Chatterjee in "The Vedic Age", p. 157.

[6] Nilsson: The Minoan and Mycenaean Religion etc. p. 157 Bertrand Russell: History of Western Philosophy p. 25 seq.

4

construct a picture of such movement. It cannot therefore be said that the mere existence of common language roots and even of common social and religious conceptions and institutions such as can be traced between ancient India, Greece, Rome and Germanic races for instance, necessarily implies their descent from a common race.

On the contrary the evidence of anthropology is quite otherwise. For among the races speaking Indo-Germanic languages there are totally different racial types, as different, for instance, as the Nordics of Northern Europe and the Mediterranean races of Southern Europe. It seems probable therefore that though the language and institutions of these races may disclose a common root culture, they were very likely acquired in some manner in the dark remote past by intercourse between these races. This common cultural root developed among these different races, each on its own lines, everywhere enriched by fresh accessions from the indigenous culture of these races and of neighbours among whom they came to live. (a)

In the next place, archaeological researches and a more intensive study of linguistics have demolished the foundation of the theory that the Aryans of India who composed the Vedas came into a country inhabited only by savages whom they conquered and civilised.

With regard to the Vedic civilisation the evidence of the Vedas themselves and post-Vedic literature as well as anthropological and archaeological researches seem to establish clearly firstly, that the people who composed the Vedas were not themselves quite as homogeneous a race as is generally supposed. In the second place, these people were associated with other peoples in a larger society with contacts not only within the land of the Five Rivers but also beyond the hills as far at least as Central Asia,—a large territory which was peopled by races with which the Vedic Indians were in intimate social contact. Thirdly, the Aryans, that is to say, the race who composed the Vedas did not come into a country inhabited solely by savages whom they conquered and civilised but also by civilised races whose culture contributed to the further development of ancient Indian institutions.

Let us take first of all the evidence of the Ṛigveda. There is a reference in it to a number of tribes and races not only in the land of the Five Rivers, the home of the Vedas, but also beyond them which were probably, many of them, not of the same culture as the Vedic Aryans.

(a) The entry of different races speaking the Ārya language into India from the earliest times has been shown by R. P. Chanda in his *Indo-Aryan Races*.

The races whom the Vedas describe as Dāsas and Dasyus were apparently indigenous peoples who are treated with contempt in the same manner as the Greeks looked down upon the non-Greeks whom they called Barbarians. They are the enemies of the Āryas. But though enemies they were not, according to the description of the Ṛigveda itself, savages. They lived in fortified towns built of stone (ayasipurah) (Ṛigveda II, 2, 4) and were organised in clans (viśah). Physically they were described as black-skinned, (krisṇatvachah) and flat nosed (anāsah) (Ṛigveda II, 12, 4) and they were said to be foul in speech (Mṛidhṛavāch—Ṛigveda V, 29, 10). They were very wealthy. Kirātas, Kikātas, Chandālas etc. were some of them. Their religious life was very different from that of the Āryas. They are described as akarman, because they performed no Vedic rites, adevayu, because they did not recognise Vedic gods or rites, abrahmana, because they did not conform to Vedic modes of devotion, and avrata and anyavrata as they did not follow Vedic laws of life.[7]

Notwithstanding the wealth of vituperative epithets applied to them, these Dāsas were obviously civilised peoples of a different race and culture and on that account looked down upon, for they were wealthy and lived in stone built cities. Piggott,[8] is of opinion that the description of their physique suggests that they were the same people as built the Harappa Empire. This may or may not be correct, and it seems that there were at the time other civilised races than the Harappans also to which this description might have applied.

Besides these enemies of a totally different culture and mode of life, the Ṛigveda refers to a number of peoples with whom they had contacts, friendly as well as hostile, who could not all have been Aryans. The peoples frequently referred to as Panchajanah, viz. Puru, Yadu, Anu, Druhyu and Turvasu were clearly Aryans and possibly also the five others referred to as allies of four of these peoples against Turvasu in the Battle of the Ten Kings, viz. Alina, Paktha, Bhatanas, Siva and Visanin. But the Ṛigveda refers to others, Yakṣu, Vaikarna, Kabaṣa, Nahusa, Chedi, Gandhāri, Mujabant, Mahabriṣa, Bāhlika, Pani, Aja, Sigma, Matsya and others all of whom could not have been Aryans.[9]

7 The Vedic India Book III Chap. XIII by Dr. Pusalkar at page 249. *Vedic Index* sub. nom. Dasyu & Dāsa.

8 Pre-historic India (Pelican).

9 Zimmer: Altindischen Leben (page 120 seq.) He holds, contrary to the oponion of Roth, that these were all names of Aryan races.

Of some of these races it can be said with some amount of confidence that they were of a different culture. The Panis are definitely described as not worshipping the gods. Kikātas were also, according to Zimmer, non-Aryans living in Magadha. Gandhāra, Mujabant and Bāhlika were races living in trans-montane regions and were most likely non-Aryan. Mujabants are people who are reviled in the Atharva Veda and therefore not presumably of the Ārya culture.

Of Bāhlikas we have further material for saying that they were of an alien stock though in social contact with the Bharatas. According to the Mahābhārata tradition in Udyoga Parva, Pratīpa, the king of the Bharatas had three sons. Devāpi the eldest was disqualified from succeeding to him on account of his disease. The second brother Bāhlika renounced the throne of Hastinā in favour of Śāntanu, and became attached to his maternal uncle's family (mātulakulaṃ samāsritah) where he succeeded to his maternal uncle in the kingdom of Bahlika.[10] This story is partially confirmed by the Vedas. For the Ṛigveda refers to Śāntanu, king of Hastinā and his elder brother Devāpi whom he appointed his Purohit (RV. X, 98, 5-8). In the Satapatha Brāhmana (XI, 8, 4-6) the Kuru prince Bāhlika is mentioned.[11] There is therefore no need to doubt the authenticity of the Mahābhārata tradition as has been done by the learned authors of the Vedic Index. If that is accepted, we find that among the Bāhlikas, sister's sons lived in the family of their maternal uncle on whose death inheritance passed to the sister's son, a rule which prevails in matriarchal societies but which was unknown in the laws of the Āryas, where a sister's son only became a remote heir at a much later date and only as a Bandhu.

The Bāhlikas would thus appear to have been a matriarchal or semi-matriarchal race among whom marital relations were apparently, according to Vedic ideas, irregular. Even in later days,

10 Mahabharata V, 149, 27-8.

वाह्लीको मातुलकुलं त्यक्त्वा राज्यं समाश्रितः ।
पितृण भ्रातृण परित्यज्य प्राप्तवान् परमर्धिमत् ॥
वाह्लीकेन त्वनुज्ञातः शान्तनुर्लोक विश्रुतः ।
पितर्यूपरते राजन् राजा राज्यमकारयत् ॥

11 तदूह वाह्लीकः प्रातिपेयः कौरव्यो राजा । Sat. Brah. XII, 3, 3.

The name Bāhlika Prātipiya given to a Kuru prince of Hastinā may have only indicated that he was the son of the Bāhlika princess married by Pratipa to distinguish him from the others born of other mothers.

Vātsyāyana in his Kāmasūtra refers to Bāhlikas, Strīrājya and other trans-Himalayan races as people whise sexual relations were known to be irregular.[12]

It would further seem from the character of the Ṛigvedic hymns themselves that the people who composed them were not quite as homogeneous as is generally supposed. Attempts have been made by learned scholars to frame a picture of Rigvedic society from several hymns as one whole. To my mind, these attempts have never succeeded in harmonising the several conflicting views expressed at different texts.

Deeply conscious of the narrow limits of my knowledge of the Vedas, I hesitate to tread on the shifting soil of controversies on Vedic literature where even seasoned scholars have failed to find a footing yet, far less to dogmatise on any part of it; but, if I may venture to throw out just a hint for further investigation, I would suggest that the hymns of the Ṛigveda were composed by peoples separated from one another, who may have started with a common theology, but developed it each in his own way, until a time when these various peoples were consolidated into one people and all their separate hymns of magico-religious import were compiled into one great work for ritual purposes of the composite people. This hypothesis seems to be supported by the character of the various hymns.

Max Müller characterised the Vedic theology as Henotheism, because in different hymns different gods are regarded as the highest. That is undoubtedly the character of the Ṛigveda taken as a whole. But let us take each hymn or perhaps a group of several hymns as individual creations or inspired poems of people apart from one another. One of them, belonging to a family or clan of Varuṇa worshippers may then be supposed to have composed the hymns in which Varuṇa is the sole deity invoked and praised. So too there were others who according to their respective convictions composed hymns in praise of Agni, Indra, Aśvins, Marut etc. At a later stage when these worshippers of the several gods came

[12] Kāmaśātra p. 140 quoted by Chakladar, Social Life in Ancient India p. 50,

ग्रामनारीविषये स्त्रीराज्ये च वाह्लीके बहवो युवानोऽन्तःपुरधर्मान् एककस्याः परिग्रहभूताः ।

This, like many other statements of Vatsyāyana about distant people, was probably based on tradition and hearsay which probably somewhat distorted facts. The fact probably was that Bāhḷikas were a polyandrous race where women consorted with many visiting husbands.

into closer contact, the Varuṇa worshipper in his hymn would take cognisance of some other deities but place Varuṇa above all. Similarly the Indra worshipper would place Indra above other gods and perhaps one would make a joint prayer to several gods. As the contacts between the several groups of worshippers increased the number of gods mentioned would grow.

As is well known, there are several hymns which belong to the first category in which one god alone is invoked and is often endowed, particularly in Varuṇa hymns, with the attributes of one sole ruler of the universe. Then there are others in which Mitra, Indra, Agni etc. are also named, giving primacy to Varuṇa. The attributes assigned to the gods in different hymns would then naturally be very different and often conflicting with one another. In the composite society made up of the worshippers of different deities these would all be lumped together into a common liturgy and their mantras with all their magic virtues would be equally honoured by all.

If this hypothesis is proved to be correct, it would follow that no particular passage of any mantra, whether descriptive of a god or embodying a story or rule indicating a social rule or habit can be taken necessarily to be a characteristic of Ṛigvedic society as a whole. It would follow also that in the course of the growth of this literature the original common stock of beliefs and institutions with which the different composers started would be developed by accretion either from the worshippers' own thoughts or by borrowings from diverse sources. On this view it would seem that the Ṛigveda is itself to some extent syncretic and it is a fabric made up of warp and weft from different sources including alien sources. The traces discovered by scholars of alien influences in some of the Ṛigvedic texts would in this view be fully explicable.

Vedic literature also shows the existence of other civilised races of considerable importance in the country apparently to the east of the land of the Five Rivers.

In the Atharva Veda (Book XV) reference is made to a great empire of a powerful sovereign the Eka Vrātya. The term "Vrātya" is used in later literature for the twice-born who have fallen from the purity of the Āchāra of the Āryas and from the performance of the obligatory duties of the twice-born by reason of which they have been reduced to the status of the Śūdras. But evidently, the Vrātya of the Atharva Veda does not imply such a person. It was the designation of a powerful king who, though not performing the Vedic rituals and following the Vedic laws, was a cultured person and was also spiritually eminent. In the Panchaviṃsa Brāhmaṇa we find a ritual of Vrātyastoma by which a whole race of Vrātyas were purified and raised to the status of Āryas. This tradition of conversion of Vrātya race was carried on in several Śrautasūtras which give details of Vrātyastoma.

The evidence of these works has been referred to and analysed by the late Prof. Nagendra Nath Ghosh in his book "Indo-Aryan Literature and Culture". His conclusions, so far as they have been worked out with dramatic details, may not be acceptable in their entirety, but the authorities cited by him undoubtedly establish his broad conclusion that there were, in the days of Atharva Veda, one or more great empires and kingdoms in the East who did not have the essentials of the Vedic culture but adopted it under the influence of Vedic Brāhmaṇas and that these people were definitely not Aryans. The continuity of this variety of the ritual of Vrātyastoma from the Panchaviṃsa Saṃhita down to the Śrautasūtras indicates that such conversion continued in post-Vedic times of other non-Vedic or non-Aryan communities than the Eka-Vrātya referred to in the Atharva Veda.

Furthermore, all these evidences make it probable that at even a remoter age peoples and races not belonging originally to the Ārya culture but with a civilisation and culture of an approximately equal standard were absorbed into the Aryan community even without any formal conversion. The ritual of Vrātyastoma must have been invented for these mass conversions at a later stage. But when the ritual was invented, it must have been utilised for the conversion of other similar races with whom the Aryans came into contact in other places of India.[13]

Coming down to historical times we know that the Aryan

[13] See Vedic India page 255.

The learned author of this chapter in Vedic India, Dr. Pusalkar, at page 256 thinks that the Vrātyas were not non-Āryas, as Roth, Whitney, Bloomfield and Chanda hold, on the following grounds:

(1) Their speech was Prākrit.
(2) They had priestly and military classes called Arhants and Yaudhas and
(3) They were allowed to become members of the Brāhmana class by performing the Vrātyastoma.

And he holds that there were early Aryans outside the sphere of Brahmana culture. None of these grounds seem to be satisfactory reasons to prove their Aryan origin.

With regard to their speech the evidence is inadequate. Even assuming that degenerated parts of the Aryan speech characterised their language, that might have been the result of intercourse between these people and the neighbouring Aryans during the long period between the early Rigvedas and the days of the Atharvaveda and Tāndya Brāhmaṇa, particularly if we suppose, as I have suggested,

culture spread over India in time and it absorbed the races and peoples who belonged to a different culture. The Śaka or the Yuehchi invaders of a definitely alien stock founded great empires. But their kings were absorbed into the Aryan culture and professed the gods of India, as well, probably as their own gods. In the South the Andhras, who later established a great empire of their own, were apparently originally a non-Ārya race probably of a matriarchal stock. This conclusion seems to be indicated by the names of their kings who were called Gautamiputra, Vāsiṣṭhi-putra etc. The metronymic attached to their names seems to indicate a matriachal origin. Similarly other great South Indian kingdoms of the Cholas, Cheras anl the Pāndyas were all completely Aryanised. Even the Greeks who established themselves in Bactria and at one time carried their kingdoms to parts of India were not uninfluenced by Ārya civilisation and the Milindapanha indicates that Menander became a good Buddhist. Other instances in more recent times can be found in the Ahoms and other immigrants in the territories which is now covered by Manipur, parts of Assam and Cooch Behar who were all similarly Aryanised. But, as has been recognised in judicial decisions in British India, they did not adopt

that such intercourse of Āryas with non-Ārya neighbours had already started in the days of the Rigveda.

As regards Arhants and Yaudhas, we cannot be sure of the exact words in Vrātya language for these words. They might have been Sanskritised in these Śruti passages in the same manner as Indian names have been transformed by Greek writers, sometimes unrecognisably and later by the early English who for instance called Humayun Badshah Emmaupaxda. As for the existence of priently and military classes, that was a natural division which one finds almost in every primitive society and also in philosophical theories like that of Plato in his Republic.

As for their eligibility for the Vrātyastoma, in the first place it clearly presupposes that these people were not normally eligible for Vedic rituals. Secondly, somewhat later Smṛiti works indicate that the fiction by which the Ārya law brought the whole human race in the scheme of the classification of varṇas was by a theory of miscegenation and, where that could not be applied, by a theory that they were Vrātyas or Vriṣalas i.e. Āryas who had fallen from the correct conduct of Ārya. We have plenty of evidence to show that foreign races like Śakas and Dravidians had at some time or another been admitted to Ārya society and their kings and priests often became afterwards pillars of Vedic faith and learning. Where this happened, what was evidently done was that therr priestly classes, kings and soldiers were recognised as Brahmanas and Kastriyas and common people as Vaiśyas. This may have often happened in fact in the remote past without any regular ceremonial, and when it became common, ritualism, kept its pace with the progress later by devising a special ceremony and called it Vrātyastoma on the fictitious assumption that the Vrātyas were Āryas who had fallen from their status by foregoing the āchāra of their supposed castes.

the whole of Hindu Law but retained many of their old customs and usages.

Apart from the evidence of the Vedic and post-Vedic literature which has shown the existence of great civilised kingdoms outside the pale of the Aryan kingdoms, archaeological researches have disclosed the existence of a great civilisation in the North-West of India in the very land in which the Ṛigvedic Āryas later flourished. The discovery of the great Harappan culture in a large empire extending from Sind and Baluchistan to the Punjab if not to the further east has proved that long before the Vedic Ārya could be supposed to have come into North-West India the bulk of that territory was occupied by a race, probably of Dravidian stock, whose material civilisation was very superior to that of the Āryas and who were culturally definitely not inferior to them. It seems probable that this empire was conquered and their great cities destroyed by the Vedic peoples. But the destruction of the empire did not destroy the people, nor necessarily involved the driving of the entire apparently teeming population out of the country. They certainly survived and, in all probability they were gradually absorbed in the Ārya societies, by their adopting the chief elements of Ārya culture, though they must have continued to retain original elements of their own prior culture, some of which they communicated to the Vedic society itself.

The full measure of the implications of Harappa civilisation and its influence on the society and institutions of its conquerors has not and cannot yet be correctly gauged, though since the publication of Sir John Marshall's great volumes on Indus Valley Civilisation some considerable further excavation and research has been made. On the basis of such knowledge as we now have, it is nevertheless possible to say that it must have considerably influenced Aryan culture after the age of the Ṛigveda. The worship of Siva and the mother goddess can be definitely traced to the Harappa culture. The mode of worship in later Hindu society of images by offerings of flowers etc. which has all but displaced the Vedic worship by *homa* and offerings to the fire is probably traceable to the same source, or at any rate to Dravidian influence. The imperial polity inaugurated by Chandragupta Mauryya has also been traced by some scholars to the Harappan model.[14]

[14] See *The Vedic India* Ed. Dr. R. C. Majumdar Book II Chap. IX for results of the latest researches. Also Stuart Piggout Pre-historic India (Pelican) Chap. VII. In Book II Chapter VIII of The Vedic India Dr. S. K. Chatterjee has made a valuable contribution showing among other things the contribution of Dravidians generally to the culture, as a result of linguistic researches.

Even the Ṛigveda itself cannot be said to be a product of pure Ārya culture uninfluenced by foreign elements. Piggott has shown how the material culture indicated in the Ṛigveda was partly based on foreign sources, notably the war chariot of the Āryas, particularly described in the Ṛigveda, as well as other mechanical implements must have been borrowed from other races of greater antiquity and might have been ultimately derived from Sumer (Piggott, op. cit. p. 273 seq).

An intensive study of linguistics in recent times has also disclosed the existence of Dravidian influence not only in the later history of India but also in the Vedas themselves. (See S. K. Chatterji in XVI JRASB p. 146 seq.)

The evidence of the Vedic literature as well as of history and archaeology thus establish that India has not only been a great complex of numerous races who have all made their contributions to this culture and civilisation in comparatively later times but that such mixture of races and cultures has taken place from the remotest times.

This continued admixture of the peoples in the soil of India could not but have influenced the customs and laws of the Āryas themselves, and the laws and rituals of later days may be accepted to be the result of great synthesis carried out through thousands of years.

We have, therefore, to consider the history of the law not as an independent evolution from the single Vedic stock, but as a growth influenced not merely by the natural growth of customs among the single Aryan race, but also to a large extent by the customs and usages brought into the Hindu culture by the numerous races adopted. It is not possible as I have already stated, to trace all the various influences which operated upon the history of ancient Indian law with any great assurance but, as I shall endeavour to show, there are indications in some places of the introduction of institutions as a result of non-Ārya influence either by the gradual adoption by the Ārya community of the customs of their non-Ārya neighbours or immigrants or by the survivals amongst the non-Āryas, converted to the Aryan cult, of their native customs and usages.

No doubt the books of law from the Dharmasūtras downwards must be our main source for the knowledge of the history but, in studying the evolution, it would be worth our while to bear in mind the possible foreign influences which might have moulded the development.

How precisely the infusion of non-Ārya laws in the sacred law of the Āryas could have taken place is a matter largely of guess work. But a few pointers exist from which we may imagine some of the ways in which this may have happened.

The Panchaviṃśa Saṃhitā with its institution of Vrātyastoma probably indicates one of the ways. A band of Āryas led by a Brahman sage may have settled in a country under a non-Ārya King. The sage may have won the respect and admiration of the local people by his sanctity and higher spiritual life or possibly by performing miracles through Vedic rites and may have attracted the ruler himself who may have adopted his teaching and his discipline, as Constantine adopted Christianity in Rome. Such ruler may have brought his people under the banner of Ārya law by example, precept or by royal decrees in the manner that Asoka propagated Buddhism or Constantine spread Christianity in Rome.

For conversion of rulers ahd peoples to the Ārya cult the sages may have devised a new ritual of Vrātyastoma. The stoma itself was a part of the Ārya liturgy from much older times for purification of Āryas who had fallen from the strict discipline of the law of their varṇas. In this new environment the sages may have used them with modification suited for the purpose and thus devised a new form of Vrātyastoma for the admission of non-Ārya peoples into Ārya law.[15]

A second way in which Ārya law may have been affected by non-Ārya laws is probably indicated by the texts of Manu, Yājñavalkya and others that when a country was conquered by a king, he should maintain the laws and customs of the country as they were.

> Yasmin deśe ya āchāra vyavahāra kulasthiti
> Stathaiva pratipālyosau yadā vaśamupāgatah.

That it was a part of the pious duty of Ārya kings to expand their sway over other kingdoms is indicated by the ancient rituals of Rājasūya and Aśvamedha. There can be no doubt that Ārya kings of old, in this manner conquered many territories. But their idea of conquest, as laid down in the śāstras was to restore the throne to the old king or some scion of his family after an acknowledgment of suzerainty. In such kingdoms Brāhmanas from the conqueror's territory would be settled and they would spread Ārya law and ritual, keeping intact however the ancient laws and customs of the vanquished people. In such territories the law which would finally be rebuilt would thus naturally consist primarily of the customs of

[15] For a description of the different varieties of Vrātyastoma see N. N. Ghosh: Indo-Aryan Literature and Culture p. 6 seq.

the vanquished non-Āryas with a veneer, light or heavy according to circumstances, of the essentials of Ārya ritual and law.

A third way was apparently one indicated by historical facts. Even powerful conquerors of Ārya territory as well as neighbouring non-Ārya rulers who were impressed with the higher spiritual value of Ārya culture or influenced by the prestige which it acquired in their eyes sometimes voluntarily invited sages of repute from Ārya land to give instructions or to initiate people into the Ārya mysteries. This was what happened to the Yuehchi conquerors and probably also to the Andhras, the Cholas, Cheras and Pāndyas. The peoples of the Eastern territories were also similarly Aryanised. Naturally Aryan law with its claim of spiritual values would prevail in these territories, but they would necessarily be greatly affected by the old laws of the native races which were retained by the people in greater or less quantity. The strength and tenacity of native laws which continued would depend upon a number of circumstances. We shall find some very prominent instances in which such laws were very substantially continued inspite of Aryanisation in the races on the Malabar coast. As will be seen later that Marumakattayam and Alya Santana law which prevail in those territories were the old laws of the natives of those territories with only a more or less light veneer of Ārya laws.[16]

[16] See infra.

CHAPTER II

King's Justice

Definite history of the evolution of law proper starts with the emergency and growth of the King as judge. As we have seen, in the earliest stages of the society in ancient India administering justice between persons was the function of the social groups of Kulas and guilds. But already, in the earliest Dharma Sūtras we find the King's administration of justice firmly established as an important function of the King.

The evolution of Kingship in ancient India would be an interesting study for the student of the history of its polity. With that study, at any rate, in its earlier stages we are not directly concerned. But we may note at once that the King in Vedic times had not the overwhelming might and personality that he acquired in later literature. From Manu in its present form, onward, the King is deemed to be a god himself, Viṣṇu himself in human form; he is made up of parts of eight great gods and therefore a person who must be implicitly obeyed. Yet in early law the concept of the divine personality of the King seems to be entirely absent. Gautama for instance, while he insists that everybody must respect the King, the Brāhmanas only in a lesser degree, nowhere says that the King is in any sense a divine personality. The Puranic story of King Vena (possibly representing a non-Ārya Conqueror) who presumed to be God and was destroyed for it, reflects, to my mind the attitude of the early Indian Aryan who would not tolerate the idea of divinity of Kingship. From such historical evidence as exists it is possible to suggest that the concept was imported into India if not by the Kushān Kings at any rate from foreign sources.[17] This concept was a familiar one among the races which surrounded the Ārya in his Vedic home, including the Sumerians and the Semitic races.

Manu in VII, 3-13 elaborates an idea of the divinity of kings on which he founds the absolute obligation of subjects to obey whatever commands or laws the king lays down. His opinion has no doubt greatly influenced and pervaded subsequent literature. But looking at the prior works like the Vedic literature and the

[17] See *Advanced History of India* by Majumdar, Roy Chaudhuri and Datta Macmillan Part I p. 124.

Dharmasūtras it seems clear that the doctrine propounded in these texts was a later innovation based on a growing theory probably under alien influences.[18]

The judicial authority of the King, as we find it in the earliest laws, is not founded on any fiction of his divine personality but upon positive law and had its ultimate historical basis in his function as the military chief. As such, he would naturally concentrate in himself in a growing measure the power to coerce people to obedience. The law accordingly looks on him as a person whose duty it was to compel each person to adhere to the law of the varṇa to which he belongs.[19] He is looked upon as the upholder of social and moral order, though, characteristically for India, in conjunction with the learned Brāhmaṇa.[20] For the purpose of maintaining Dharma he is endowed with the power of Daṇḍa or awarding punishment.

The association of Daṇḍa (Punishment) with the king meets us at the very threshold of early law and is to be found also in the Brāhmaṇas. Daṇḍa is looked upon as the weapon to enforce obedience to Dharma, and, in a somewhat later conceit, is described as Dharma himself created in that shape by Brāhmaṇ.[21] Daṇḍanīti or the laws about punishment is, from very early times conceived

18 As against the view here put forward and as evidence of the prior existence of a theory of the divinity of kings, Kane (Vol. III page 32 q.v.) refers to Ṛigveda IV, 42, 3—4 where, in the opening mantras Trasadasyu says "I am Indra and Varuṇa, I am the wide and deep Heaven and Earth etc." and other passages from Atharvaveda VI, 87, 1—2 and Śatapatha Brāhmṇa V, 4, 3, 4. With due deference to the author's wide scholarship I do not think that these mantras indicate a theory of the divine personality of the king. The mantras of the Ṛigveda appear in a Sukta by which Trasadasyu invokes the gods Indra and Varuṇa apparently on the eve of a battle. The identification of himself with Indra and Varuṇa are apparently parts of the ritual sacrifice. Kane himself points out (loc cit) that in Agnisṭoma and Vājapeya sacrifices the sacrificer is often spoken of as identical with Indra and other gods. But this is so not only in these two sacrifices but in several others too. The identification of the god worshipped with the worshipper himself by magic mantra is a familiar technique not only in ancient India but elsewhere also. It is possible that by repeating "I am He" at the ritual the worshipper while engaged in the sacrifice is believed by the magic of the mantras to attract to himself the power and attributes of the divinity he invokes. At the most it means that while initiated for the sacrifice he becomes imbued with divine attributes not that he is always so.

19 Vas. Dh. S. IX, 5; देशधर्म जातिधर्म कुलधर्मान् सर्वान् त्वै तानानुप्रविश्य राजा चतुरोवर्णान् स्वधर्मे स्थापयेत् ।

20 Gau. Dh. S. VIII, 14; द्वौ लोके धृतव्रतौ राजा ब्राह्मणश्च बहुश्रुतः ।

21 Manu VII, 14, Yajn I, 354 "धर्मो हि दण्डरूपेण ब्रह्मणा निर्मितं पुरा ।

as a most essential part of the education of a King. But Daṇḍa is to be applied according to established canons of dharma.

The ancient Aryan did not look upon the king as either the source or even the repository of law. The law was what had come down from past ages which was in the special knowledge of the sages who had specialised in its study. The duty of the king to maintain and uphold that law was itself imposed upon him by that law. The power and prestige of the king no doubt appear to have grown with time but the essence of Ārya law from the earliest Vedic times was that he should place himself under the guidance of the sages. The Ṛigveda shows that it was his duty to choose his Purohita and be guided by him. The choice of the Purohita made all the difference to the fortunes of Triṣṭu in the battle of the Ten Kings. The early text of Viṣṇu places the king's duty to choose a Purohita and be guided by him in the forefront of his obligations.

When the king's authority and duty to administer justice was firmly established as we find already in the Dharmasūtras, we find it laid down immediately that he has to ascertain the law from learned men and from the Kulas and guilds.

No doubt his power over the law is found to increase in later times. Later law-givers give him authority to give directions to local and guild organisations which they are bound to carry out. And Manu goes so far as to give him power to legislate and makes it obligatory on his subjects to follow this Rājakṛita laws or royal decrees provided, however, that they are not opposed to dharma or sacred law. This directive power of the king however never proceeded very far, as we shall see in a later chapter. It was mainly confined to mere secular matters and only within the law.

In the earliest law books we thus find that where authority to administer justice is given to kings they are also given strict injunctions as to where they should find the law. This led in time to constitutional limitations on his powers to do justice with resulting important developments, as we shall presently find.

Gautama lays down that, in administering justice the King has to get his law from three sources:

(1) The scriptures, including the Veda, Dharmasūtras, Vedāngas and Purāṇa;

(2) Customs and usages of countries, communities and Kulas unopposed to sacred texts;

(3) Customs and laws prevailing among cultivators, traders, herdsmen, moneylenders and artisans determined by each community in matters relating to themselves.[22]

[22] Gautama Dh. S. XI. 19-21.

He goes on to mention that in respect of each of these different heads the King must ascertain the law from those who have authority to decide about the law.[23] And lastly, that in the case of Vipratipati, i.e. doubt or difficulty, the king is to ascertain the law from aged persons who are learned in sacred lore.[24]

These texts no doubt make the King a judge of disputes and require him to ascertain the law from the several competent sources. It does not yet indicate that the King is always to be assisted by any constituted advisers. Nor do the texts speak of any other person except the King as administering justice, though in another text an officer called Prāḍvivāka is mentioned.[25] In later law, as we shall presently see, the Prāḍvivāka is a permanent judge who rises to even greater importance in the end, but in this text he seems to have been mentioned only as a person who performs the subsidiary function of examining witnesses. It is not without significance that none of the extant Sūtra works except Visṇu mentions the King's sabhā which fills an important place in later literature of law in connection with the administration of justice. Viṣṇu too only mentions qualifications to be possessed by persons appointed sabhāsadas or members of the sabha, and only the context indicates that the sabhā functions in the administration of justice.[26]

As will be seen later, in the days of the Dharmasūtras, although the sphere of King's justice was growing the matters which came before the King's Court were nevertheless comparatively few. Civil justice must have been rarely required to be done by the King whose important functions were concerned with protection of people, punishment of crimes, and the maintenance of Dharma or social order.[27]

As the judicial functions of the King grew, we find a twofold development. In the first place, the obligation of the King to know

23 Gau. Dh. S XI, 22.

24 Gau. Dh. S XI, 25.

25 Gau. Dh. S XIII, 26. राजा प्राड्विवाको वा धर्मवित्। प्राड्विवाको मध्यो भवेत्।

26 Viṣṇu III, 72. स्वयमेव व्यवहारान् पश्येद्विद्वद्भिः ब्राह्मणै सह। जन्मकर्म-व्रतोपेताश्च राज्ञा सभासदः कार्या रिपौ मित्रे च ये समाः कामक्रोधलोभादिभिः कार्यार्थिभिरनाहार्याः।

27 See Gautama X & XI, Apastamba II, 5, 11, 11. It is interesting to note
22 See Gautama X & XI, Apastamba II, 5, 11, 11. It is interesting to note
that Megasthenes whose knowledge was confined to the King's Court says kings were much occupied with criminal cases and but little with civil suits (Schwanbeck frag. XXVII, Trans. Mc. Crindle). See post on topics of Law for a fuller treatment.

the law from competent authorities was crystallised into a definite constitutional authority to advise the king in the shape of the king's sabhā and secondly, the judicial authority of the king came to be delegated to permanent judges.

The King's Sabhā

The existence of a sabhā of the King in the text of Viṣṇu has been referred to before, but the first definite rule of the position of the sabhā in the decision of disputes we find in Manu and Yajñavalka.[28] In both we find that the King administers justice with Sabhāsadas. Later texts of Nārada and other authorities like Kātyāyana and Bṛihaspati quoted in nibandhas go into more elaborate details.

The texts of Viṣṇu and Yājñavalkya indicate that the members of these sabhās were appointed by the King as permanent adjuncts to the Court and we get it that it was their duty to give their opinions on the cases heard before them.

But besides these "appointed" or *niyukta* members of the sabhā any learned Brāhmaṇa who came in would be invited to take his place in the sabhā and it would be his moral duty and right to give his opinion likewise.[29] The function of the sabhā in respect of litigations was of course advisory like that of assessors but, naturally the king would follow their advice as a rule.

As administration of King's justice grew in volume we find later texts going into greater details about this sabhā. One

व्यवहारान् दिदृक्षुस्तु ब्राह्मणैः सह पार्थिवः ।
मन्त्रज्ञैर्मन्त्रिभिश्चैव विनीतः प्रविशेत् सभाम् ॥
तत्रासीनः स्थितो वापि पाणिमुद्यम्य दक्षिणाम् ।
विनीतवेशाभरणः पश्येत् कार्याणि कार्यिनाम् ॥

Manu VIII. 1. 2. See also Yajnavalkya II 1-2.

व्यवहारान्नृपः पश्येद्विद्वद्भिः ब्राह्मणैः सह ।
धर्मशास्त्रानुसारेण क्रोधलोभ विवर्जितः ॥
श्रुताध्ययनसम्पन्नाः धर्मज्ञाः सत्यवादिनः ।
राज्ञा सभासदः कार्या रिपौ मित्रे च ये समाः ॥

[29] See anonymous text quoted by Mitākṣarā under Yaju I. 1-2. नियुक्तो वाऽनियुक्तो वा धर्मज्ञो वक्तुमर्हति ।

important development was the inclusion of merchants in the sabhā. The older texts like Manu and Yājñavalkya provide for only Brāhmaṇa advisers. Though the still older text of Gautama already indicated that cultivators, merchants, herdsmen, usurers and artisans had authority in matters pertaining to them, neither they, not Viṣṇu, Manu and Yājñavalkya contemplated that they should find a place in the sabhā. A text of Kātyāyana, however, quoted in various commentaries says that the sabhā should include a few merchants of good birth and conduct, aged, wealthy and free from greed.[30] This development must have occurred at a social stage when merchants had risen to a place of great importance in society. When Gautama classed *vaniks* with cultivators and herdsmen they were apparently a community of little importance and held in low esteem. But in later times Śreṣṭhis became wealthy and important citizens as we find in numerous Jātaka stories as well as in literary works like the Mṛichchhakaṭika. Besides, as will appear later on, trade disputes which are not to be found in earlier law books came, in course of time, to fill an increasingly important place in the King's vyavahāra and necessitated the advice of reliable and respectable merchants for their decision.

The King's sabhā which thus grew in importance is dignified in the text of Manu by the epithets "Brahmasabhā" (VIII 11) and by Bṛihaṣpati as Yājñasadrisī or "adhvarasammita"—like a sacrificial assembly. That indicates that the opinion of this sabhā had attached to it sanctity like what attached to Pariṣads of early law. In fact this sabhā, which satisfied the definition of a Pariṣad, and had authority to lay down the law, had thus risen to the position of an authoritative body whose opinion the King would be expected to follow. The growth of this sabhā thus placed an important constitutional limitation on possible whims and caprices of Kings in doing justice, though of course it was not always effective in practice.

From another side also we find the exercise of judicial functions by the King personally gradually declining as, apparently the

30 कुलशीलवयोवृद्धैः वित्तवद्भिरमत्सरैः ।
वणिग्भिः स्यात् कतिपयैः कुलभूतैरधिष्ठितम् ॥

Kane's Collection verse 58.

An earlier stage is probably marked by the text of Vyāsa cited by Mayukha (also cited elsewhere as Nārada's text but not found in extant Nārada Smṛiti).

वणिक्शिल्प प्रभृतिषु कृषिरङ्गोपजीविषु ।
अशक्यो निर्णयो ह्यन्यैस्तज्ज्ञैरेवकारयेत् ॥

number of cases coming before the King grew. Viṣṇu already provided that the King might at his option employ a Brāhmaṇa to decide litigations.[31] Yājñavalkya in one passage says that the King might engage a Brāhmaṇa to deputise for him in deciding disputes if he does not decide himself on account of other work and provides that such deputy shall also act with the advice of sabhyas appointed by the King.[32]

Permanent Judges

The deputies contemplated by these texts are casual and not permanent appointees. In the later texts of Nārada and Bṛihaṣpati the judicial functions are found to be exercised by the Prāḍvivāka. Prāḍvivāka is mentioned in much earlier texts and also in Gautama Dharma Sūtras. His function then seems to have been that of a chief or chairman or foreman of the sabhā. His duty was originally performed, while the King himself presided over the Court, in asking questions to witnesses and giving his opinion. This seems also to have been his position in the text of Kātyāyana quoted in commentaries.

> saprāḍvivāk sāmātyah sabrāhmaṇapurohitah
> sasabhyo prekṣako rājā svarge tiṣṭhati dharmatah

which contemplates the Prāḍvivaka as assisting the King together with other members of the sabhā.

But in later texts apparently the Prāḍvivāka is an independent judge who permanently deputises for the king and his position reaches its zenith when the King is directed to decide "according to the opinion of the Prāḍvivāka." (Prāḍvivāka matesthitah)[33] as much as the King of England decides according to the opinion of the Judicial Committee of the Privy Council.

Bṛihaṣpati in a text cited in the Vyavahāra Mayūkha gives ten

---

31 स्वयमेवव्यवहारान् पश्येत् । ब्राह्मणं वा नियुञ्ज्यात् ।

32 अपश्यता कार्यवशात् व्यवहारान्नृपेण तु ।
सभ्यैः सह नियोक्तव्यः ब्राह्मणः सर्वधर्मवित् ॥
Yajn II, 3 so too Manu VIII, 9-10.
यदा स्वयं न कुर्यात्तु नृपतिः कार्यदर्शनम् ।
तदा नियुञ्ज्याद्विद्वांसं ब्राह्मणं कार्यदर्शने ॥
सोऽस्य कार्याणि संपश्येत् सभ्यैरेव त्रिभिर्वृतः ।

33 Narada Introd I, 85 see SBE Vol. XXXIII p. 14.

limbs of the King's Court (Karaṇa) and gives the division of functions as follows "vaktādhyakṣo nṛipah śāstā sabhyāh kāryaparikṣakāh," which seems to give the power to give decisions to the sabhā while the adhyakṣa, by which is probably meant the Prāḍvivāka, is the speaker and the King is the one who pronounces the sentence.

Already in the days of Yājñavalkya, however, we find that there have grown up permanent Judges appointed by the King to decide disputes. Instead of the King deciding disputes or appointing *ad hoc* judges occasionally, he appoints permanent judges who decide all disputes. These Courts, as distinguished from the ancient people's courts are called by Yājñavalkya adhikṛita or adhiṣṭhita courts.[34] But from these courts an appeal lies to the King's own Court. In Kauṭilya's Arthaśāstra we find many such courts spread all over the Kingdom.

By the time of Bṛihaṣpati[35] a multitude of regular courts have been established, which are classified under four heads (1) pratiṣṭhitā (2) aparatiṣṭhita (3) mudrita (4) Śāsita. By *pratiṣṭhita* Courts he means Courts in cities and villages, evidently appointed by the King; *mudrita* probably means the court of the Prādvivāka, if he is the official called by Bṛihaṣpati adhyakṣa; *śāsita* means the Court over which the King presides. *Apratiṣṭhita* is significant. It means a travelling Court not sitting at a fixed place.[36] Apparently therefore there were travelling Courts for doing justice on the spot. Another text of Bṛihaṣpati cited by the Mayūkha says "For forest dwellers the Court (Karaṇa) shall be in the forest, for soldiers in the army, and in the market for merchants."[37] This probably

34 नृपेनाधिकृताः पूगाः श्रेणयोऽथ कुलानि च। पूर्वं पूर्वं गुरु ज्ञेयं व्यवहारविधौ नृणाम्। Yajn II, 30.

35 Bṛihaṣpati cited in Smṛiti Chandrikā:

प्रतिष्ठिताऽप्रतिष्ठिता मुद्रिता शासिता तथा।
चतुर्विधा सभा प्रोक्ता सभ्याश्चैव तथाविधाः॥
प्रतिष्ठिता पुरे ग्रामे चला नामाऽप्रतिष्ठिता।
मुद्रिताऽध्यक्ष संयुक्ता राजयुक्ताश्च शासिता॥

See SBE Vol. XXXIII p. 277 verse 2-3. Gaekwad ed. p. 9-10.

36 Bṛihaṣpati cited by Smṛiti Chandrikā See note (35) above.

37 ये चारण्यचरास्तेषामरण्ये करणं भवेत्।
सेनायां सैनिकानान्तु सार्थे तु वणिजस्तथा॥

Gaekwad ed. p. 2 text 75.
also cited in Jimūṭavāhana's Vyavahāra mātrikā (Memoirs of ASB Vol. III No. 5 p. 281).

indicates that these circuit courts went round these special places to decide these disputes. These Karaṇas were King's courts and not the ancient popular tribunals.

The ancient popular tribunals of Kula Śreṇi etc. do not figure prominently in the Smṛitis which are concerned only with the King's Courts. They did not disappear however and are mentioned in the latest of the Smṛiti works. Yājñavalkya (II, 30) and Nārada refer to them. But in these texts these ancient tribunals have been subordinated to the King's Courts to which an appeal lies against their decisions[38] and it would seem that they themselves have begun to be appointed by the King.

Growth of King's Justice

The gradual enlargement of the sphere of King's justice is evidenced by the contents of the various Smṛiti works. In the late works like Manu, Nārada and Bṛihaṣpati there are enumerations of eighteen topics of Vyavahāra which were subjects of litigation enumerated by Manu and they were squeezed into the eighteen topics by Nārada only by manipulations and by the introduction of a head called miscellaneous (Prakīrṇaka).

These topics of litigation do not seem to have been as rigid forms as the forms of action in ancient Roman law or the writs of English Common Law. They would appear to have been merely attempted classifications of the various kinds of litigation which came into vogue from time to time and place to place.

Now, looking at the more ancient Dharmasūtras we find most of these topics of litigation missing in their chapters on Vyavāhara. Thus Gautama in his chapter XII, where he deals with the various topics which came before the King's Court but which he did not

[38] Yājñavalkya, II, 30

नृपेणाधिकृता पूगाः श्रेणयोऽथ कुलानि च ।
पूर्वं पूर्वं गुरुज्ञेयं व्यवहारविधौ नृणाम् ॥

Nārada (sometimes quoted as Katyayana and Bṛihaṣpati)

कुलानि श्रेणयश्चैव गणाश्चाधिकृतो नृपः ।
प्रतिष्ठा व्यवहाराणां पूर्वेभ्यस्तूत्तरोत्तरः ॥

Gatha quoted by Asahaya

ग्रामे दृष्टः पुरे याति पुरे दृष्टस्तु राजनि ।
राज्ञा दृष्टः कुदृष्टो वा नास्ति पौनर्भवो विधिः ॥

classify, does not deal with questions of partition, inheritance, marital rights and duties or secondary sonship, all of which entered into the lists of Vyavahāra topics in Manu, Nārada and Bṛihaspati. It is not as if there were no laws on these topics in Gautama's time; for he deals with these several topics in other chapters. Only these disputes did not come to the King's Courts as litigation. The reason is that in those early days these were disputes exclusively within the jurisdiction of the popular or gentile tribunals. This view is further strengthened by the text that there can be no *vyavahāra* between father and son, husband and wife, preceptor and pupil.[39] The reason is that Vyavahāra means litigation before the King's Court[40] while these disputes were matters entirely for domestic tribunals.

As we go on to the works of later dates, we find the number of topics dealt with under Vyavahāra going up almost by leaps and bounds until we come to the enumerations of Manu, Nārada and others. In fact as I have mentioned before, these enumerations in fact exceeded eighteen in time and the law ultimately reached a stage at which all form was ignored and any complaint made to the King by a person on being harassed by another's act against smṛiti and āchāra became a possible topic of Vyavahāra.

This indicates a course of development of King's justice not dissimilar to developments elsewhere. As we shall find more fully later, originally people's tribunals were the authorities for deciding all disputes. The King's justice was first confined to punishment of crimes and more serious social offences. Gradually the King began to deal with a few matters of a civil nature not involving punishment. For some reason or other, administration of justice by the King became popular and people began to flock to King's Courts for redress of their grievances which were previously

39 Bṛihaspati quoted in Jimūtavāhana op. cit p. 285.

गुरुशिष्यौ पितापुत्रौ दम्पती स्वामीभृत्यकौ ।
विरोधेऽपि मिथस्तेषां व्यवहारो न सिध्यति ॥

also cited as

"गुरोः शिष्ये पितु पुत्रे दम्पत्योः स्वामीभृत्ययोः । etc.

Jimūtavāhana in his Vyahahāra mātrika would confine these text to small wrongs and cites texts indicating a possibility of such Vyavahāra loc cit. See post under Toprcs of Law.

40 Yājñavalkya II. 5.

स्मृत्याचार व्यपेतेन मार्गेनाधर्षितः परैः ।
आवेदयति चेद्राज्ञे व्यवहार पदं हि तत् ॥

adjudicated by popular tribunals, with the result that topics of law which, being matters for domestic tribunals, were kept by early law outside the King's justice were absorbed under Vyavahāra step by step.

We knaw that King's or the Praetor's justice in Rome and the King's Courts in England similarly absorbed the functions of the Pontiffs, the Curiae, the Hundred and the Baronial Courts until the latter were totally supplanted. A similar process, which is natural with the growth in the prestige and power of the King apparently accounted for the gravitation of all judicial authority in ancient India to the King.

There are points in the history of King's justice in England and of the Praetor's justice in Rome which may give us some light on the growth of the King's justice in India. In the Legis Actio Sacramento of Rome which is probably a symbolic survival of the first interference of the king in the administration of justice, there is a little drama in which each of the contestants claims the property in dispute by laying his *festuca*—which is the survival of a spear according to Gaius—upon the thing. It is then that the Praetor intervenes and calls upon the parties to refer the matter to the decision of a judex. The show of fight with spears was an indispensable pre-requisite for the Praetor's, and before him of the King's, interposition in a dispute, it being his duty to maintain peace.[41] So too in England the fictitious averments in the writ of trespass of an attack *vi et armis* and *contra pacem* hark back to an earlier stage when the King could only take up decision of a dispute if a breach of peace was threatened. This survived as a fiction which was made use of for assuming jurisdiction over civil disputes which would otherwise fall to be exercised either by the Hundred moot or, in feudal times, by the Baronial Courts.

Such traces of early law as we have, also indicate that the king's jurisdiction in India was first invoked only in cases of what were regarded as serious crimes by reason of the king's duty to maintain peace and social order. How it developed in course of time we shall consider when we come to discuss the topics of Litigation.

Administration of Justice in King's Court

One result of the enlargement of the jurisdiction of King's Courts was that law became more and more systematic and its study

[41] Maine Ancient Law pp. 375-376. Ihering points out the origin of adjudication in Rome with a process before the Pontiffs with religious sanctions before the L. A. Sacramento came into existence. Geist der Römischen Rechto I, 245 ft.

and practice went into the hands of practical lawyers who specialised in it. In their hands the Corpus Juris of ancient India received enormous development to keep pace with the progress of times and went more and more into minute details. While ancient Indian jurists could not compare with the classical jurists of ancient Rome in respect of scientific classification or systematic exposition, their laws were, in their most developed stage, far from inferior in the wealth of detail, founded on practical knowledge of law and its administration.

The subject which I shall now deal with, legal procedure in ancient India, is a fine illustration of the kind of development that the law had in the hands of practical jurists.

Judicial procedure of the King's Court fills but little space in the early works, the Dharmasūtras.

Indeed the law of Procedure, which rose to great importance in later law under the name Vyavahāra Mātrikā, is only meagrely dealt with as a part of the substantive law in the earliest works. The law of Evidence, which is slightly more elaborate, is also lightly touched in these works. I must not be taken to suggest however that because rules of procedure are not found formulated here or in other early Dharmasūtras, there were necessarily no rules of procedure at all. There can be no question that in these as in all early texts of law everywhere, much is taken for granted and not stated because they were facts of common knowledge among contemporaries. It may also be that, at any rate, some of the rules which we find stated in later works were already in vogue and assumed in the early works. In any event there must already have been some usages and practices which were habitually resorted to in the King's Court without their being recorded in the laws. But the absence of such rules in the law books certainly shows that such practices had not yet hardened into concrete rules or, at any rate, assumed sufficient importance to be recorded in texts of law.

Gautama on Procedure

All that Gautama has to say about Procedure is this (Gaut. Dh. S. XI. 23-25):

"Reasoning is the means for determining the truth and by that he (the King) shall decide properly. In case of difficulty decision shall be given by learning from Brāhmaṇas grown old in the learning of the three Vedas. In difficulties, truth and falsehood is determined (by examination of) witnesses by the King, the Prādvivāka or a

Bhāhmaṇa who knows the law. Prāḍvivāka will be the intermediary." (Madhyah).

Meagre as this statement is, it is interesting in one respect. It shows that in that early stage of King's justice questions of fact requiring evidence seem not to have been always involved; oftentimes the facts were known or admitted and only the legal consequences or rather, liability to and the measure of punishment to be awarded were in question. That is why witnesses are necessary only in cases of Vipratipatti but not always. This is a feature which one notices in other primitive laws.[42]

Apastamba, Vasistha and Visnu

Āpastamba and Vaśiṣtha are almost equally laconic on the law of procedure. Āpastamba's law on this subject is interesting only in the recourse to ordeal as a primary means of determining the truth. After providing that learned Brāhmaṇas should determine disputes he adds "In case of doubt by means of indications and by daiva (ordeal)". He then goes on to say "Sarvānumato mukhyah satyaṃ praśnam vrūyāt." The meaning of this passage is somewhat obscure. Does it imply that instead of examining witnesses of the parties the judges should call upon the leading man, by general consent, of the community or place to come and tell the truth? (Āpast. Dh. S. II, 11, 29, 5-7).

The procedure indicated in this passage is of a summary nature. It shows the law of procedure in a rudimentary stage not very different from that in Gautama, where questions of fact were of secondary importance, and when they arose they were ascertained by ordeal or by the testimony of a man of eminence.

In other Dharmasūtras we find a fuller treatment of evidence, as we shall see later, but of procedure proper we find very little indeed. Even Viṣṇu, whose work contains substantive law in a form more elaborate than in any other Sūtra work and whose treatment of the law of evidence is much more elaborate, dismisses the law of procedure proper with nothing more than a statement that the King should decide disputes with learned Brāhmaṇas or should employ a Brāhmaṇa to decide disputes.

Manu

Manu too, in spite of all the elaboration with which he deals with substantive law and also the law of evidence, has precious

42 See the author's Evolution of Law (2nd Ed.) p. 74.

little to say about procedure proper. Practically all that we get from him on the law of procedure is that (1) the King is to hear cases in the sabhā ; (2) that he should take up cases in the order of the varṇa or caste of the complainant (VIII, 24); (3) that neither the King nor his officers should initiate any legal proceedings nor should they smother any case brought by another (VIII, 43) and some provisions about how a litigant loses his suit for various kinds of default.

Yajnavalkya on Procedure

In Yājñavalkya the law of procedure takes a great step forward.

Vyavahārapada or litigation is defined by him as arising when a person complains to the King having been oppressed by illegal acts (II, 1, 5).[43]

After the complaint is made it has to be written down by officers of the Court in the presence of the defendant with full particulars of the precise date and identity of the defendant (II, 1, 6). This is followed by the reply of the defendant which also has to be written down, in the presence of the complainant. Then the complainant is to make a statement of the evidence on which he relies (II, 1, 7). Decision follows proof. These four stages, *Plaint, Answer, Proof* and *Decision* are called by him the four feet of a litigation.

This is followed by more detailed and specific rules, some of which are as follows :—

(1) No recrimination or counter-claim is allowed until the complaint is discharged ;

(2) No departure from pleading is permissible. II 9

(3) Counter claim or recrimination is permitted in certain criminal charges. II 9

(4) Each party is required to find a surety for satisfaction of judgment. II 10

(5) Where a contesting defendant loses, he pays an amount equal to the claim to the King ; while, where the complaint is found to be false the complainant pays double the amount to the King.

(6) Distinction between cases which have to be tried immediately and those where decision is to be adjourned.

(7) Order of examination of witnesses, Plaintiff's witnesses first examined.

43 स्मृत्याचारव्यपेतेन मार्गेणाधर्षितः परैः ।
आवेदयति चेद्राज्ञे व्यवहारपदं हि तत् ॥

These and the other rules show that already in Yājñavalkya's time a detailed law of procedure has been evolved as a result of the administration of justice having passed into the hands of specialists in laws.

Some of the outstanding provisions of the law of Yājñavalkya on the topic of Vyavahāra are given below.

Wager

An interesting point is the reference to sapaṇa vyavahāra or a litigation with a wager.[44] It is strange that we hardly find any mention of this wager in litigation in any earlier text of Indian law, or any further particulars about it, though analogous practices can be found very far away. In Rome, for instance, in the Legis Actio Sacramento after the parties have made their claims with their *festuca* and the Praetor intervenees, each party is to lay a wager on the truth of his claim. Possibly also the offer of a talent by a litigant in the Homeric legend, referred to by Sir H. Maine, was similarly a wager laid. It seems that in India as elsewhere the wager was a means of strengthening the pledge of the truth of the claim upon which alone the court would take up the case, a function which is now performed only by oath, affidavit or verification insisted upon by modern laws as necessary to start a legal proceeding. In Yājñavalkya's time apparently the paṇa or wager was not always required but could be laid at the option of the litigant or probably had to be laid only in certain classes of cases. When a wager was laid, if the party lost the suit he forfeited the wager to the king in addition to whatever other penalty might be imposed on him.

Surety or Security

Apart from wager where it was laid, each of the parties had to offer sureties (pratibhū) according to Yājñavalkya, who is sufficient to satisfy whatever decree might be made (Samarthah Kāryanirṇaye). Nārada (Introd. II Jolly page 24) however requires the Plantiff to offer a pledge of sufficient value before the Plaint is written.

Rule of Justice

Another striking point in Yājñavalkya is the text (II 19)[45] which requires the King to determine cases according to the substance of the thing (bhūta) by eliminating all false pleas

44 Yājña II, 18 Nārada I-46.

45 छलं निरस्य भूतेन व्यवहारान्नयेन्नृपः ।

(chhala). This probably implies that decision should be according to the justice of the case irrespective of technical flaws.

Plus Petitio

There is a rule of *plus petitio* in II, 9 which says that the case in the Plaint shall not be departed from or a new case made at the trial. A corresponding rule against the defendant is that if the defendant denies the whole claim, then, if a part of it is proved, there would be a judgment for the whole. (II, 10).

Void Litigations

Sensible rules are laid down for nullifying litigations, like other transactions, for force or fraud. The same rule is applied to transactions done by women, or at night, or in the inner rooms of a house or outside villages or by enemies (II, 31). The latter restrictions, artificial as they seem, might have been due to the social conditions of the times. So too, litigations by inebriates, lunatics, persons in distress, by children, as well as those which are incoherent are to be rejected (II, 32). Yājñavalkya likewise has a somewhat elaborate code of rules of evidence which will be dealt with in its proper place. His code is the first in which a definite law of procedure worked out in some detail is found in ancient law. It indicates that when this work was compiled, administration of justice by trained practical lawyers had been fully established.

Later Laws

This development is carried forward by other Smṛitis of which the work of Nārada alone is available in full.

More important even are numerous texts of Bṛihaṣpati, Kātyāyana and Yama which are however only to be found in quotations scattered all over the text books and commentaries. From these it is possible to construct a complete picture of the law of procedure in its most developed form some outlines of which I shall of procedure in its most developed form some outlines of which I give below.

One observation I should like to make here on the basis of the history so far outlined. It is sometimes said that extreme formality is the characteristic of early law of procedure, and that it is only gradually that the law shakes off its forms and becomes rationalised. The histories of the law of Procedure in Rome and in England bear out this proposition. But the examination of the history of procedure in ancient India outlined above clearly proves the contrary to have been the case here. Here administration of justice evidently began with hardly any rule of procedure. The latter grew up in time with practice gradually hardened into more rigid rules such as we find in the later law of procedure.

It will be seen however that procedure never hardened in India into inflexible rules such as those of ancient Rome or English Common Law whose hard crust could only be broken by the independent agency of Equity. In the Indian law there appears always to have been an undercurrent of sound common sense and justice wearing down the rigidity of rules without any outside interference. It is hard however to be too dogmatic about it, having regard to the fragmentary character of our knowledge of the history. In the available books we have to deal with a finished product with only occasional glimpses of past history and it is just possible that the various steps by which the finished rules were achieved have been too far obliterated to enable us to know what they were. It is possible that our judgment in this respect may be as fallacious as if a student were to take a modern text book of the English law of Contract or of Real Property and say, on looking at it, that there had never been behind it a long history of laborious work of forces breaking down senseless forms and bringing out the essential rules of justice.

Final Stage of Procedure

I shall now give an account of the law of procedure in its fullest development in the *Smṛitis*.

Summons and Injunction (Āhvāna and āsedha)

As in the ancient law of Rome and elsewhere, there does not appear to be any provision in the earliest Indian law for bringing the defendant before the Court by a process of the Court. Litigation starts with the complaint and apparently, it was the business of the complainant to bring the defendant before the Court. In later law, however, provisions appear for the Court summoning parties and witnesses.[46]

The first definite law for summoning the defendant is to be found in a text of Kātyāyana cited in the commentaries. After the King has ascertained the facts alleged from the plaintiff by questions, Kātyāyana says, if he is satisfied that the complaint is lawful, he should summon the defendant, by sending him a message (Mudrā)

[46] For epigraphic evidence of such summons in the 6th Century A.D. See JRASB (Letters) Vol. XVI p. 111.

or by sending an officer to bring him.[47] There are detailed exceptions provided for both in Kātyāyana and Nārada e.g. of persons who may not be summoned.[48]

Apart from the duty of the King to summon, there is a provision made by Nārada, to prevent the defendant escaping justice, by a process which is called "Āsedha." It is clear, that the prohibition of Āsedha was not an act of the Court but merely a private act of the plaintiff. The text of Nārada on Āsedha is as follows :

Vaktavyārthe natiṣṭhantam utkrāmantaṃcha tadvacham
Āsedhayed vivādārthī yāvadāhvāna darśanam
Sthānāsedhah kālakṛitah pravāsāt karmanastathā
Chaturvidhāh syādāsedho nāsiddhastam vilanghayet
Āsedhakāla āsiddhah āsedham yo'tivartate
Sa vineyo'nyathā kurvan-nāsedha daṇḍabhāgbhavet

Jolly translates āsedha as arrest. But as the Mitākṣarā and Asahāya explain it, it seems to be rather an injunction placed on the defendant by the plaintiff (and not by the Court) pending the issue of summons (Yāvadhāhvānadarśanam) violation of which involves penalties. Nārada's text above says āsedhayed vivādārthī—"the plaintiff should forbid", if the defendant seeks to act against the claim of the plaintiff in the suit or disregards his words.

Plaint

Yājñavalkya provides for the writing down of the plaint apparently first when he complains and again in the presence of the defendant when he appears, with particulars about the time and the description of the defendant.[49]

"That which the plaintiff relates should be recorded in the presence of the defendant specified by the year, the month, the fortnight, the day, the name, caste etcetera."

47 एवं पृष्टः स यद्ब्रूयात् ससभ्यैर्ब्राह्मणैः सह ।
विमृश्य कार्यं न्याय्यश्चेत् आह्वानार्थमतः परम् ॥
मुद्रां वा निक्षिपेत्तस्मिन् पुरुषं वा समादिशेत् ।
Quoted in Mitākṣarā under Yājñ. II, 5. Kane's collection of texts of Kātyāyana, Versee 88.

48 See text of Kātyāyana quoted in Mitāksarā loc. sit. and Kane Kātyāyanasmṛiti pages 15-16.

49 प्रत्यर्थिनोऽग्रतो लेख्यं यथावेदितमर्थिना ।
समामासतदर्धाह नामजात्यादि चिह्नितम् ॥
श्रुतार्थस्योत्तरं लेख्यं पूर्वावेदक सन्निधौ ।

"The answer of the defendant who has heard the plaint should be taken down in writing in the presence of the complainant."

Brihaspati and other text writers who have been quoted in the commentaries give detailed rules about the characteristics of a good and valid plaint (bhāsa).[50] Defective plaints are to be rejected by the King without summoning the defendant. Defect (called Pakṣābhāṣa) is variously described. If the plaint speaks of something which is opposed to human experience (aprasiddha), or if it does not disclose any cause of action (Nirāvādha) or, if it is a jumble of meaningless words (Nirartha) or, if it is something which does not call for any action (Nisprayojana), or incapable of proof (asambhava) or, if it is contradictory in terms, and also if it is against the interest of the city and the kingdom (Purarāṣṭra viruddha), the plaint must be rejected.[51] Multifarious suits where several causes of action and several independent parties are joined together, is a fatal defect in a plaint.

There is a prohibition against the making of recrimination or cross claim until the case against the defendant is disposed of, but subject to the exception that where the dispute relates to a quarrel or to "Sāhasa" (i.e. violent injuries) recrimination is allowable,

50 अर्थबद्धमसंयुक्तं परिपूर्णमनाकुलम् ।
साध्यवद्वाचकपदं प्रकृतार्थानुबन्धी च ॥
प्रसिद्धमविरुद्धं च निश्चितं साधने क्षमम् ।
संक्षिप्तं निखिलार्थं च देशकालाविरोधी च ॥
वर्षर्तुमासपक्षाहा वेला देशप्रदेशवत् ।
स्थानावसथसाध्याख्या जात्याकार वयोयुतम् ॥
साध्यप्रमाणसंख्यावदात्मप्रत्यर्थी नामवत् ।
परात्मपूर्वजानेक राजनामाभिरङ्कितम् ॥
क्षमालिङ्गात्मपीडावत् कथिताहर्तृ दायकम् ।
यदावेदयति राज्ञे तद्भाषेत्यभिधीयते ॥

Quoted in Mitākṣara under Yājñ. II. 6.

51 अप्रसिद्धं निराबाधं निरर्थं निष्प्रयोजनम् ।
असाध्यं वा विरुद्धं वा पक्षाभासं विवर्जयेत् ॥
पुरराष्ट्रविरुद्धश्च यश्च राज्ञा विसर्जितः
अनेक पदसङ्कीर्णः पूर्वपक्षो नसिध्यति

Kātyāyana cited in Jimūtavāhana Vyāvahara Mātrikā. Kane's collection V. 136 & 140 which reads यश्च राष्ट्रविरुद्धं etc. Translation at Kane p. 142.

apparently for the obvious reason that in such cases much would turn upon who started the quarrel.[52]

Who can start Litigation ?

Reference has already been made to the text of Manu, who lays down that the King or his officers should not start any litigation or, in other words, that there could be no litigation unless the person injured complained before the King. That this was a rule more or less rigidly followed is illustrated by the trial scene in "Mṛichchhakaṭika" where, although the King's brother-in-law Śakāra had laid a complaint before the Court that Chārudatta had killed Vasantasenā the court thought that it could not be a litigation as Śakāra had no right in the matter ; and the judge sent for Vasantasenā's mother to ascertain whether she had any complaint. But in course of time, exceptions had to be recognised and in a few cases it was provided that prosecution may be started by the King and his officers.[53]

The ordinary rule was that the person injured must himself come and complain and there is provision for punishment prescribed for the making of a vicarious or champartous complaint by a person who himself is not interested in the dispute. But Manu and Nārada provide for a complaint made by a brother or father, acting as Agent.[54] To this again Kātyāyana adds certain exceptions and lays down that in some very serious offences, attorneys (Prativādi) are not allowed.

52 अभियोगमनिस्तीय नैनं प्रत्यभियोजयेत् , but कुर्यात् प्रत्यभियोगं च कलहे साहसेषु वा । Yājñ. II, 9-10

Nārada (Introd. II, SBE XXXIII p. 24 seq) gives elaborate rules of pleading which are almost modern in character.

53 See translation under caption "Trial of Chārudatta" in 15 CWN notes.

Manu says—नोत्पादयेत् स्वयं कार्य्यं राजा नाप्यस्य पुरुषः
न च प्रापितमन्येन ग्रसेदर्थं कथञ्चन ॥

54 योऽदत्तव्यवहारत्वादनियुक्तः प्रवर्तते ।
वचनं तस्य न ग्राह्यं लिखित प्रेषिताद्दते ॥
यो न भ्राता पिता वापि न पुत्रो न नियोगकृत् ।
परार्थवादी दण्डयः स्यात् व्यवहारेषु विब्रुवन ॥

Quoted as Bṛihaspati in Vyāvahara Mātrikā p. 288.

लिखित means written authority, प्रेषित means appointed in the presence of a third party according to Jīmūtavāhana loc. cit.

Classes of Complaints

Nārada distinguishes between two classes of plaints, "Śankābhiyoga" and Tattvābhiyoga". "Tattvābhiyoga" arises where the complaint is about a wrong or injury already committed, while Sankābhiyoga arises where no mischief has been actually done but is only apprehended (like bills *quia timet* of English Equity). Where, although mischief has not been actually done but there are signs (Hoḍa), suggesting attempt or preparation visible of the contemplated offence, the complaint would be Tattvābhiyoga".[55]

Defence (Uttara)

After the complaint has been recorded and heard by the defendant, he has to get his defence (uttara) recorded, provided, according to Bṛihaspati, that the King has decided that the complaint is maintainable. It is only if the complaint is free from the faults of Pakṣābhāsa that the defendant can be called upon to have his defence recorded.

With regard to the time for making the defence Yājñavalkya provides that in the case of 'Sāhasa' 'Steya' 'Pāruṣya', offence regarding cattle, and violation of women, the answer should be given immediately; in other cases time may be given as desired. The text of Nārada, Bṛihaspati and Kātyāyana, however, introduced limits of time which may be allowed to a defendant to enter on his defence, the time limited may be one day, two days, three days, five days or a week. According to Bṛihaspati four months or even three years may be given to the defendant on a consideration of his capacity for making his defence.[56]

In another text Kātyāyana lays down that the time to be given should be regulated by considering the time, the power and the strength or weakness of the case, without sticking to any hard and fast rule.[57]

55 अभियोगन्तु विज्ञेयं शङ्का तत्त्वाभियोगतः ।
शङ्काऽसत्यं तु संसर्गात्तत्त्वं होढाभिदर्शनात् ॥
Quoted in Jīmūtavāhana's Vyāvahara-mātrikā.

56 एकाहं त्र्यहं पञ्चाहं सप्ताहं पक्षमेव वा ।
मासं चतुस्त्रयं वर्षं लभते शक्त्यपेक्षया ॥

57 कालं शक्तिं विदित्वा तु कार्यानाञ्च बलाबलं ।
अल्पं वा बहु वा कालं दद्यात् प्रत्यर्थिने प्रभू ॥

Defects and classes of defence

The characteristics of a good defence as well as defects justifying the rejection of the defence have been laid down in several texts. Nārada says that a defence should not be irrelevant, (Anyārtha), meaningless (Arthahīna) or without any evidence and must not cover more or less than the grounds of the plaint.[58]

Defences may be of four kinds. (1) True (Satya), (2) False (Mithyā), (3) Confession and avoidance (Pratyavaskandana) and (4) the bar of previous decision, or Res judicata (Prangnyāya).[59]

An answer which is mixed up of any two or more of these varieties of defence is bad for what is called Uttarasankara or mixing up of defences. There is a text of Vriddhaśātātapa quoted in Jimūtavāhana's Vyavahāramātrika, (p. 305) however, which admits the possibility of a defence which is partly of one and partly of another kind and accordingly adds to the four defences mentioned before, a fifth and a sixth called Saṃśliṣṭa or mixed and Vipratīti, or contradiction of facts.

The hearing: (Kriyā)

I have referred to the text of Yājñavalkya to the effect that after the ansmer is written both parties have to provide sureties (Pratibhū) for the implementation of the ultimate decision of the suit. Kātyāyana goes into details as to who can be a Pratibhū.

After the 'sureties' are provided, the hearing begins. There are somewhat elaborate rules with regard to what may be called the right to begin or the burden of proof. The faults of proof are also dealt with in detail. Proofs are of two kinds, human and divine or the testimony of witnesses or documents or ordeals. These matters will be dealt with more fully later.

One matter which may be noted here is that the law recognised the loss of title by prescription. Possession of a property was one of the kinds of evidence which could be given about title. Starting

सद्यः कृते सद्य एव समातीते दिनं भवेत् ।
षड्ब्दिके त्रिरात्रं स्यात् सप्ताहं द्वादशाब्दिके ॥
विंशत्यब्दे दशाहं तु मासार्धं वा लभेत सः ।
मासं त्रिंशत्समातीते त्रिपक्षं परतो भवेत् ॥
Verses 147 and 154-155 in Kanes' Kātyāyana Smriti.

58 अन्यार्थमर्थहीनञ्च प्रमाणागमवर्जितम् ।
लेख्यं हीनाधिकं भ्रष्टं भाषादोषास्तूदाहृताः ॥

59 Nārada II, 5-6.

from this, the lawgivers from pretty early times went to the length of holding that where possession has been held by even a trespasser in the presence of the owner for twelve years the latter's title is lost.[60] In cases where possession was without knowledge of the owner a longer period of prescription is provided and it is further laid down that in the case of certain classes of transactions title cannot be destroyed by any length of time.

The Judgment (Siddhi)

Judgment can be given when the evidence of both parties has been fully heard. Two texts of Nārada Kātyāyana and Bṛihaṣpati lay down that the party who wins should be given a decree (jayapatra) in writing. The contents of such decrees are meticulously laid down. It should contain a statement of the cases of the plaintiff and defendant respectively, the points at issue, the particulars of the evidence, the decision of the Court and the names of the sabhāsadas who were present.[61]

We find no reference to jayapatra in any text in any earlier smṛitis but epigraphic evidence has established that the practice of giving such Jayapatras did prevail in later times.

Res Judicata

Praṇgnyāya has been referred to above as one of the possible defences to an action. Once a decision has been given, it becomes final and cannot be reopened by leading fresh evidence. As Nārada picturesquely puts it (Introd. I, 62).

> Yathā pakveṣu dhānyeṣu niṣphalāh pravṛiṣo gunāh
> Nirṇītevyavahāranam pramānam aphalaṃ tathā.

[60] See infra p. 74 ff.

[61] यद्वृत्तं व्यवहारेषु पूर्वपक्षोत्तरादिकम् ।
क्रियावधारणोपेतं जयपत्रेऽथ संलिखेत् ॥
पूर्वोत्तर क्रियायुक्तं निर्णयान्तं यदा नृपः ।
प्रदाद्यात् प्रार्थिने लेख्यं जयपत्रं तदुच्यते ॥

Kātyāyana says,

अर्थिप्रत्यर्थिवाक्यानि प्रतिज्ञा साक्षीवाक् तथा ।
निश्चयश्च तथा तस्य यदाचार वृतः स्वयम् ॥
एतद्यथाक्षरं लेख्यं यथापूर्वं निवेशयेत् ।
सभासद्श्च ये तत्र स्मृतिशास्त्रविदः स्मृताः ॥

This description corresponds very nearly to the Rubakaris of Indian Courts during early British rule.

There are texts however which indicate some limitations upon this finality of the decision. In the first place, this is a rule which applied only to the King's Court which had now become the final court of appeal. Decision of inferior courts could always be re-opened by appeals to the next higher tribunal and finally to the King. Even in the case of a decision by the King, Yājñavalkya provides that the King may review and set aside a decision which has been wrongly given and in that case the party who had won before as well as the sabhyas who decided the case are punishable with a fine equal to double the value of the suit.[62] Nārada too in (I, 50) lays down the same rule, but is not so clear about the persons who are to pay the fine.

This rule is limited by the commentators as applying only to cases where the previous wrong decision was due to the fault of witnesses or sabhyas, but not where the parties have been defeated by his own words or acts.

[62] Yājñ. II 305.

CHAPTER III

KING'S JUSTICE—EVIDENCE

In Yājñavalkya's work four kinds of proof are recognised (1) documents (Lekhya), (2) possession (Bhukti), (3) witnesses (sākṣī) and (4) Divya. We shall attempt here to trace the evolution of these different kinds of proof in the early legal literature.

In Gautama's Dharmasūtra the emphasis is all on the evidence of witnesses and rules are laid down with some elaboration as to how witnesses are to be examined after being solemnly adjured to speak the truth. An opinion of "some" (eke) is mentioned that witnesses must give evidence on oath. Ordeals are also referred to, but Gautama is altogether silent about documentary evidence, which, as we shall presently see, acquired increasing importance in later law.

Āpastamba too, like Gautama, speaks of the examination of witnesses, probably only one, and Ordeal (Divya) and is equally silent about documents. From Vaśiṣṭha onwards however documents are mentioned and the law regarding documents and documentary evidence grows increasingly more detailed and minute.

Divya as a means of defence always existed from the earliest times and oath was also a mode of divine testimony, though the details about divya are elaborately worked out only in later works. In the Tāṇḍya Brāhmaṇa we find a reference to Vatsa clearing himself from a foul charge by entering fire. And Manu (VIII, 1 10) refers to Vaśiṣṭha clearing himself from a charge of having swallowed his sons by a solemn oath calling on the gods to punish him if he was guilty.[63]

The law of evidence, like the law of procedure grew with time. The earliest laws contain little about evidence. But as litigation in the King's Court increases, the need for rules for determining truth is felt and the law of proof tends to grow out of growing usages.

The story of this evolution has to be studied against the background of social conditions leading up to litigation in primitive and ancient society. When the King starts deciding disputes, his function at the start is only to determine the penalty. Facts are either

[63] The oath is in Ṛigveda VII, 105, 15 which does not itself indicate that it was taken by Vaśiṣṭha to clear himself. In the Ṛigveda, of course, this oath and ordeal is not taken before a king or a court.

known or admitted or found by other competent authority. Failing that, divine testimony in some form or other is sought. It is only gradually that human testimony comes to be resorted to and with it the need for weighing evidence.[64]

In the text of Ṛigveda (VII, 14-15) where Vaśiṣṭha apparently appeals to the fire ordeal and oath, we have an instance of a person clearing himself by divine testimony. Probably the evidence of the first form of human testimony is the text of Āpastamba (II, 11, 29, 6-7) where the King is enjoined, in case of doubt, to ascertain the truth by linga (signs or circumstances) or by daiva and then is instructed to question a person described as *sarvānumato mukhyah ;* which seems to imply that the King does not examine any witnesses cited by either party but calls a person of eminence holding a leading position by common consent and asks him about facts.

As indicated above, in an early stage of society where communities were small and matters of litigation comparatively simple, facts of such disputes would be generally known, so that, when the community itself is the judge no question of fact would normally arise. When, after this stage, the King becomes judge he might ascertain facts by simply calling one of the leading members of the community as in this rule of Āpastamba.

In this respect, this particular rule of Āpastamba probably represents an earlier state of affairs than is found in Gautama. Gautama (XIII, 1-6) contemplates the determination of the truth by examining witnesses. The qualifications of a witness as prescribed by Gautama (XIII, 2)[65] do not indicate however that any person who knows the facts can be a witness but only such as are worthy to be trusted by the King. This apparently is reminiscent of the earlier requirement in Āpastamba of a Sarvānumato mukhyah, but it is no longer one, but many witnesses who are examined.

As a natural evolution, after this, witnesses come to be cited by the parties and, gradually, as will presently appear, elaborate rules for the testimony of witnesses appear.

Documents as evidence are not contemplated either in Gautama or Āpastamba. It appears however in Vaśiṣṭha who not only refers to documentary evidence but goes further to distinguish different kinds of documents laukika and Rājakṛita (May. ed. Mandlik, p. 9). But it would seem that as yet, according to Vaśiṣṭha, documents are

[64] See the author's "Evolution of Law", Chap. IX.

[65] विप्रतिपत्तौ साक्षिणि मिथ्यासत्यव्यवस्था । नहव स्युरनिन्दिताः स्वकर्मसु प्रात्ययिकं राज्ञश्च निष्प्रीत्यानभितापाश्च ॥

used as evidence only in specified cases which are not many. And in one passage of Vaśiṣṭha documentary evidence holds a secondary position, next to evidence of witnesses.[66]

In later smṛiti texts, as will be presently seen, documents rise to primary importance and the law of documentary evidence is treated in great detail in provisions of law which were obviously founded on practical experience of courts.

Divya

As documentary and oral evidence rise in importance and practical rules for testing such evidence are evolved, the use of divine testimony recedes to the background. From being an ordinary method of proof at option, it becomes more and more exceptional and is on the one hand gradually made both humane and feasible, on the other, the scope of appeal to divya tends to be limited to more or less exceptional cases of a serious nature.

I have mentioned before that appeal to divine testimony was very ancient and is indicated by the testimony of the Ṛigveda and the Tāṇḍya Brāhmana. The later specification of the several kinds of divyas may possibly only be an enunciation of ancient traditions. In these works, śapatha or oath, apparently of the defendant himself, is also mentioned by one authority as a species of divya. But the ordeals which are more commonly meant by Divya fall under five classes. Tulā, Agni, Āpah, Viṣa and Kośa.

Tula

Tulā is the name given to the ordeal by balance. It is also called 'ghata' by Viṣṇu. A full description of this particular mode of proof is given in Viṣṇu and also in a text of Kātyāyana. In substance it consists of weighing the accused in the balance. A large balance is set up on which the accused is weighed against weights placed in the other pan. The height to which the pan in which the defendant is set rises is marked on a post set up beside it. After he is weighed, he gets down and mantras are uttered. Then he is placed on the balance once again. If, on this occasion, his pan goes up beyond the original mark, he is found innocent. If it goes below the mark, he is guilty. It is not clear what happens when the pan stands even with the first mark. The basis of the faith in this result lies in the magic of the mantra uttered between the two weighments.

66 In Chapter XVI Vaśiṣṭha refers to लिखितं as evidence, but gives into details only of witnesses.

From this description one is reminded at once of the famous writing on the wall in Belshazzar's dream, "You have been weighed in the balance and found wanting." That expression probably indicates a custom in Babylon of weighing accused persons not dissimilar to the ordeal by the balance as described by Kātyāyana. It may be that this practice was borrowed by one community from another, or it may be that it was an institution common to all races inhabiting the area from India to Palestine. No one knows.

Agni

If, as Manu and Nārada say, the reference to the Ṛigvedic text about Vaśiṣṭha's oath relates to his clearing himself of an accusation by oaths it would seem that something like an ordeal of fire is also indicated by the passage immediately preceding it. The reference in Tāṇḍya Brāhmaṇa to an ordeal by fire has already been mentioned and the story of Sītā, in the Rāmāyana, clearing herself by entering the fire, is well known. It is possible that in the earliest stage of society, in extreme cases, this method of divine proof was actually resorted to. Nor need this cause any surprise in a community which prescribed penances at least equally drastic to be voluntarily gone through by persons to expiate their deadly sins and which believed in miracles worked by magic mantras.

But none of the Smṛiti texts prescribe anything so fatal. The descriptions of ordeal by fire in Yājñavalkya, Viṣṇu and Kātyāyana are far less drastic and more feasible. In this the person to be tested has seven *Aśvattha* leaves placed on his hands and then upon these a red hot iron ball of a specified weight is placed. With the ball in hand the accused had to walk seven steps across seven circles placed round the fire and then throw it out. If his hands are not burnt or badly seared he is found innocent (Yājñavalka II. 104. Viṣṇu XI 12. Manu in VIII 114 says "Agniṃ hārayet", possibly implying ordeal by entering fire; and in VIII 116 Vatsa's ordeal is referred to).

The Water Test

The test of water appears to have gone out of use quite early. At any rate in the days of the Smṛiti Chandrīka it is mentioned as obsolete. It is difficult to say what form the water test took in its primary stages. But the form in which it survives in the Smṛitis consists in the ability of the accused persons to be under water for a length of time which is not unreasonably long. He is to dive under water taking hold of the knees of a person standing in the water beside him while another person, shoots three arrows at a target a hundred and fifty cubits away. A third man who stands near the target goes and picks up the arrows one after another. If the accused can keep himself completely immersed under water during all this time he is innocent.

Poison

The ordeal of poison in the form in which we find it in the smṛitis provides that, after certain rituals, the poison is eaten by the accused and then the accused is kept in the shade and watched for the rest of the day. If by that time he discloses no sign of the effect of poison, he is innocent. The poison prescribed is śārṇga (probably derived from some kind of horn, śringa) which does not appear to have been very lethal in its effect and the dosage is very small.

This form of ordeal also seems to have gone out of use quite early.

Kosa

The ordeal of koṣa is even lighter. In it, the images of Rudra, Durgā and Āditya are worshipped by the accused and they are bathed by him with water. Then the accused is required to drink three handfuls of that water and if, within fourteen days of the taking of the ordeal, no serious calamity comes upon the accused in the shape of an act of the King or of God or serious illness or death of his near relations or loss of his wealth, then he is innocent.[67]

These are the principal forms of ordeals which are vouched for by the smṛiti texts.[68]

Later developments

It will be noted that the more drastic ordeals by fire or lethal poison or even by drowning which seem to have been the original forms of ordeals, yielded place to milder forms of tests which could possibly be successfully undergone without a miracle.

We find also that in course of time ordeals tended to be restricted in their application. Thus Yājn. II 22 mentions documents, possession and witnesses as modes of proof and "*in the absence of any of these* Divya is a mode of proof." Kātyāyana (cited in Mayukha p. 8) says "that if one party relies on human testimony and another on daiva, then the human proof and not the daiva is to be adopted

67 Manu VIII 11b, Nārada IV 251 Yājñ. II 95 Viṣṇu XXIV.

68 Brihaspati and Pitāmaha quoted in Aparārka give four more forms of ordeal.

by the King. If there is human proof even in respect of only a part of the cause of action that is to be accepted and not divine testimony even if it apertains to the whole. Divya proof is not admissible when there are witnesses." Then he goes on to specify certain particular topics of litigation in which Divya is absolutely excluded. Other texts restrictive of Divya testimonies are cited in the commentaries (see Mayukha Ed. Mandlik p. 9). Thus Bṛihaṣpati says that in complaints of Mahāpāpa and abhiśāpa, divya is the only evidence, as also where a doubt arises upon the oral and documentary evidence. A text of Hārita cited in Mitākṣarā under II 92 allows divya where a document is alleged to be forged as well as in the cases where the transactions in question took place in a lonely forest or at night or in the inner compartments as also in cases of Sāhasa, or of breach of trust. Bṛihaṣpati says on the other hand, that divya may be resorted to optionally with witnesses in Vākpāruṣya, Daṇḍapāruṣya and sāhasa and certain cases of debts, while Kātyāyana absolutely forbids divya in Vākpāruṣya and disputes about land, and Pitāmaha in a text cited in Mayukha similarly forbids divya in disputes about immovable property. These texts indicate that, with the growth of the law of oral and documentary evidence ordeal tended to be pushed back and probably practically went out of vogue except in exceptional cases.

In comparatively modern times however it appears that in some places ordeals were revived and frequently resorted to down to the nineteenth century where they seem to have been employed as ordinary modes of proof. New forms of divya not to be found in these texts also appear to have been evolved. (See Kane History of Dharmaśāstras Vol. III p. 337). The evidence of the extensive use of divya in modern Hindu states of the 18th and 19th centuries which also indicate notable departure, from the sastric forms of the tests indicates only a local feature. In these localities divya may have survived as local customs after its general discouragement in later smritis or may have been revived by orthodox pandit ministers of the reborn Hindu States.

Witnesses

As already mentioned, the decision of disputes by testimony of witnesses properly so called, as distinguished from the testimony of a person of eminence consulted by the king about the facts, gradually came into vogue. The works of Dharmaśāstra go into great details as to time at which and the ways in which witnesses are to be examined and how they are to be tested. As early as in the text of Gautama we find that witnesses are to be sworn according to some (SBE II p. 247). We have seen before that in Vaśiṣṭha's time the testimony of witnesses gets a primacy over documents.

Gautama on witnesses

Gautama's law in Chapter XIII (SBE Vol. II p. 246) with regard to witnesses is as follows:

"1. In disputed cases the truth shall be established by means of witnesses.

2. The (latter) shall be many, faultless as regards the performance of their duties, worthy to be trusted by the king, and free from affection for, or hatred against either (party).

3. (They may be) Śūdras even.

4. But a Brāhmaṇa must not be forced (to give evidence) at the word of a non-Brāhmaṇa except if he is mentioned (in the plaint).

5. (Witnesses) shall not speak singly or without being asked.

6. And if, (being asked) they do not answer, they are guilty of a crime.

7. Heaven is their reward, if they speak the truth ; in the contrary case hell (will be their portion).

8. (Persons) not mentioned (in the plaint), must also give evidence.

9. No objection (can be raised against witnesses) in a case of (criminal) hurt.

10. Nor if they have spoken inadvertently.

11. If the sacred law or the rules (referring to worldly matters) are violated, the guilt (falls) on the witnesses, the assessors, the king, and on the offender.

12. Some (declare, that the witnesses) shall be charged on oath to speak the truth.

13. In the case of others than Brāhmaṇas that (oath shall be sworn) in the presence of the gods, of the king, and of Brāhmaṇas.

14. By false evidence concerning small cattle a witness kills ten.

15. (By false evidence) regarding cows, horses, men, or land, in each succeeding case ten times as many (as in the one mentioned before).

16. Or (by false evidence) regarding land the whole (human race).

17. Hell (is the punishment) for a theft of land.

18. (By false evidence) concerning water (he incurs) the same (guilt) as (for an untruth) about land.

19. Likewise (by false evidence) regarding (criminal) intercourse.

20. (By false evidence) regarding honey or clarified butter (he incurs) the same (guilt) as (by an untruth) about small cattle.

21. (By false evidence) about clothes, gold, grain, and the Veda, the same as (by an untruth) about kine.

22. (And by false evidence) regarding a carriage (or a beast of burden) the same as (by an untruth) about horses.

23. A witness must be reprimanded and punished for speaking an untruth.

24. No guilt is incurred by giving false evidence, in case the life (of a man) depends thereon.

25. But (this rule does) not (hold good) if the life of a very wicked (man depends on the evidence of a witness)..

26. The king, or the judge, or a Brāhmana learned in the Śāstras (shall examine the witnesses)."

The principal points to note in this law are (1) that witnesses are required to *many* and (2) it is only specially qualified persons who may be presumed to speak the truth, who are competent witnesses; (3) they are to be examined by the king or judge and they must answer questions only when asked, (4) the practice of naming witnesses by a party in his pleading is in vogue; (5) no question of qualification of witnesses can be raised in cases of hurt; (6) swearing of witnesses is required by some authorities.

Vasistha

Vasiṣṭha in his 16th Chapter refers to documents, witnesses and possession as three kinds of proof and apparently lays down that in case of gifts of fields or pathways and disputes about dwellings or fields and boundary disputes, documents are the primary modes of proof.

With regard to witnesses Vasiṣṭha too requires specially qualified persons as stated before.

Visnu

With Viṣṇu in its present form the law of Evidence grows more elaborate. He gives a list of persons who cannot be examined as witnesses (VIII 2—4) and this *index expurgatorius* includes the king, an ascetic, a gamester, a thief and an adhyadhīna or dependent person, a friend of a party or one interested in the dispute and also a person who volunteers as a witness without being cited (VIII 3-4). An exception is however made in cases of steya, sāhasa and pāruṣya (VIII, 6). Exceptional qualities are also required to qualify a man as a witness (8 and 9).

In the next sutras Viṣṇu lays down the order of examination of witnesses (10 and 11). Evidence at second hand is admitted on two heads: (a) where a witness is dead or gone abroad evidence may be given by a person who heard his statement (VIII, 15) and (b) hearsay is apparently made admissible by the distinction between witnesses who saw and those who heard (VIII 13).

Testing the testimony by the witness's demeanour is also laid down in VIII 18.

A new and artificial rule of weighing conflicting testimony is laid down in VIII 39. The testimony of majority is to be accepted. Most of these rules are followed in Manu and later-Smṛitis.

Viṣṇu's chapter on witnesses is as follows :—

"2. The king cannot be (made a witness), nor a learned Brāhmaṇa, nor an ascetic, nor a gamester, nor a thief, nor a person not his own master, nor a woman, nor a child, nor a perpetrator of the acts called sāhasa (violence), nor one overaged (or more than eighty years old), nor one intoxicated or insane, nor a man of bad fame, nor an outcast, nor one tormented by hunger or thirst ; nor one oppressed by a (sudden) calamity (such as the death of his father or the like), or wholly absorbed in evil passions ;

3. Nor an enemy or a friend, nor one interested in the subject matter, nor one who does forbidden acts ; nor one formerly perjured, nor an attendant ;

4. Nor one who, without having been appointed, comes and offers his evidence ;

5. Nor can one man alone be made a witness.

6. In cases of theft, of violence, of abuse and assault, and of adultery the competence of witnesses must not be examined too strictly.

7. Now (those who are fit to be) witnesses (shall be enumerated) :

8. Descendants of a noble race, who are virtuous and wealthy, sacrificers, zealous in the practice of religious austerities, having male issue, well versed in the holy law, studious, veracious, acquainted with the three Vedas, and aged (shall be witnesses).

9. If he is endowed with the qualities just mentioned, one man alone can also be made a witness.

Burden of Proof

10. In a dispute between two litigants, the witnesses of that party have to be examined from which the plaint has proceeded.

11. Where the claim has been refuted as not agreeing with the facts (as e.g. the sum claimed having been repaid by the debtor), there the witnesses of the defendant have to be examined as well.

Hearsay

12. An appointed witness having died or gone abroad, those who have heard his deposition may give evidence.

13. (The evidence of) witnesses is (of two kinds): either of what was seen, or of what was heard.

14. Witnesses are free from blame if they give true evidence.

False Evidence

15. Whenever the death of a member of any of the four castes (would be occasioned by true evidence, they are free from blame) if they give false evidence.

16. In order to expiate the sin thus committed (such a witness), if he belongs to a twice-born castle, must pour an oblation in the fire, consecrating it with the texts called Kusmāndi.

17. If he is a Sudra, he must feed ten cows for one day.

Demeanour

18. A false witness may be known by his altered looks, by his countenance changing colour, and by his talk wandering from the subject.

Mode of examination

19. Let the judge summon the witnesses, at the time of sunrise, and examine them after having bound them by an oath.

20. A Brāhmaṇa he must address thus 'Declare'.

21. A Kṣatriya he must address thus "Declare the truth".

22. A Vaiśya he must address thus, 'Thy kine, grain, and gold (shall yield thee no fruit, if thou wert to give false evidence).'

23. A Śūdra he must address thus, 'Thou shalt have to atone for all (possible) heavy crimes (if thou wert to give false evidence'.)

38. That plaintiff whose statement the witnesses declare to be true, shall win his suit, but he whose statement they declare to be wrong, shall certainly lose it.

39. If there is contradictory evidence, let the king decide by the plurality of witnesses, if equality in number, by superiority in virtue, if parity in virtue, by the evidence of the best among the twice-born.

40. Whenever a perjured witness has given false evidence in a suit (the king) must reverse the judgment, and whatever has been done, must be considered as undone."

Narada, Brihaspati and Katyayana

In the works of Nārada, Bṛihaspati and Kātyāyana the law regarding witnesses while substantially the same as in Manu and Yājñavalkya, goes into further details and is elaborated and explained. Thus Nārada classified witnesses into eleven kinds by subtle distinctions (See SBE Vol. XXXIII page 80 seq.). In I, 172—176 Nārada lays down rules based on a principle of *res ipsa loquitur* where no evidence is necessary, but concludes with a verse which says "Some one might make a mark upon his person through hatred or to injure an enemy. In such cases it is neressary to resort to inductive reasoning to ascertain the fact of the matter and stratagems". In I 177 et. seq. Nārada gives a list of bad witnesses who should be excluded. It is noticeable however that in Nārada and Brihaspati, the *index expurgatorius* does not include a king and Bṛihaspati expressly refers to the king as a possible witness.

The Law in Manu

Similarly in Manu, not any and every person can be a witness. Elaborate rules are laid down about the sorts of person who can be witnesses. Manu, for instance gives in VIII 60—71 the following rules :[69]

1. There must be *at least* three witnesses.
2. They must be householders (not ascetics).
3. They must be cited by the parties (arthyukta).

[69] पृष्टोऽपव्ययमानस्तु कृतावस्थो धनैषिणा
अवरः साक्षिभिर्भाव्यो नृपब्राह्मणसन्निधौ ॥
यादृशा धनिभिः कार्य्या व्यवहारेषु साक्षिणः ।
तादृशान् संप्रवक्ष्यामि यथा वाच्यमृतं च तैः ॥
गृहिणः पुत्रिणो मौला क्षत्रविट् शूद्रयोनयः ।
अर्थ्युक्ता साक्ष्यमर्हन्ति न ये-केचिदनापदि ॥
आप्ताः सर्वेषु वर्णेषु कार्याः कार्येषु साक्षिणः ।
सर्वधर्मविदोऽलुब्धा विपरीतांस्तु वर्जयेत् ॥
नार्थसम्बन्धिनो नाप्ताः न सहायाः न वरिणः ।
न दृष्टदोषाः कर्त्तव्या न व्याध्यार्ता न दूषिताः ॥
न साक्षी नृपतिः कार्यो न कारुक कुशीलवौ ।
न श्रोत्रियो न लिङ्गस्थो न सङ्गेभ्यो विनिर्गतः ॥
नाध्यधीनो न वक्तव्यो न दस्युर्न विकर्मकृत् ।
न वृद्धो न शिशुर्यौको नान्त्यो न विकलेन्द्रियः ॥
नार्तो न मत्तो नोन्मत्तो न क्षुत्तृष्णोपपीडितः
न श्रमार्तो न कामार्तो न क्रुद्धो नापि तस्करः ॥
स्त्रीणां साक्ष्यं स्त्रियः कुर्युर्द्विजानां सदृशा द्विजाः ।
शूद्राश्च सन्तः शूद्रानामन्त्यानामन्त्ययोनयः ॥
अनुभावी तु यः कश्चित्कुर्यात् साक्ष्यं विवादिनाम् ।
अन्तर्वेश्मन्यरण्ये वा शरीरस्यापि चात्यये ॥
स्त्रियाप्यसम्भवे कार्यं बालेन स्थविरेण वा ।
शिष्येण बन्धुना वापि दासेन भृतकेन वा ॥
बालवृद्धातुराणान्तु साक्ष्येषु वदतां मृषा ।
जानीयादस्थिरं वाचमुत्सिक्तमनसां तथा ॥
साहसेषु तु सर्वेषु स्तेय संग्रहणेषु च ।
वाग्दण्डयोश्च पारुष्ये न परीक्षेत साक्षिणः ॥

4. They should be free from greed, must know all laws and be competent persons.

5. Parties connected by monetary interests or friends or foes or persons who faults are known, such persons or faulty persons should not be witnesses.

6. The king, artisans, moneylenders, srotriyas, ascetics or persons from a saṃgha, a dependent person, one with defective senses, a person in distress, a lunatic, an inebriate, a hungry or thirsty man, one exhausted with labour, one filled with lust, an angry man, a thief etc. etc.

7. A dependant person, a robber, a man who does forbidden acts (Vikarma), an old man, a child, an antyaja and a man with a defective sense organ (vikalendriya),

8. Women should be witnesses for women, Brāhmaṇa for a Brāhmana, a good Sūdra for Sūdras, and an Antyaja for an antyaja.

9. In sāhasa, strīsaṃgrahana and pāruṣyas witnesses should not be so tested.

10. Where testimony is conflicting the evidence of the majority should be accepted, where the number of witnesses on either side is equal the testimony of those better qualified (gunotkriṣtān) is to be accepted. If both sides are equally qualified the testimony of a good Brāhmaṇa should be accepted.

11. Evidence is competent as to what the witness has seen himself or has heard.

It will be noted that the requirements about the quality of witnesses are not stated in the earlier texts as merely affecting their credibility but as excluding their evidence altogether. But as stated in Manu, these rules appear to be rather directory rules not to accept the testimony of witnesses who are so disqualified, not a law of exclusion of their evidence altogether.

Yajnavalkya on Demeanour

With regard to rules for testing witnesses Yājñavalkya in II 13—15 lays down the following rules.

"He who shifts from place to place, licks his lips, whose forehead perpires, whose countenance changes colour,

Who with a dry tongue and stumbling speech talks much and incoherently, who does not heed the speech or sight (of another), who bites his lips.

Who by mental, vocal and bodily acts falls into a sickly state, is considered a tainted person whether (he be) a complainant or a witness".

As the Mitākṣarā shrewdly points out however this is laid down to show the possibility of falsehood but not its certainty.

These artificial rules of evidence however are substantially modified by Yājñavalkya's general rule (II 19).

"Having discarded that which has (only) an appearance of reality, a king should decide suits in conformity to the nature of things, for even an honest claim, if not properly pleaded, is (liable to be defeated by the adverse party merely satisfying) the legal formalities."

Documents

We have seen before that documentary evidence was not mentioned by Gautama though even Gautama refers to the art of writing. But as early as Vaśiṣṭha, documentary evidence has come into vogue, though apparently it is considered of less importance than the testimony of witnesses. But in all later smritis documents have acquired great importance. Viṣṇu (VII, 1 et seq.) speaks of three kinds of documents, Rajasākṣika, sasākṣika and Asākṣika.

Rājasākṣika documents are documents which are executed in the King's court by the king's clerk (Kāyastha) and attested by the hand of the presiding officer.

The second class of documents are purely private ones, they may be written by anyone, but must be attested in their own hands by witnesses.

Asākṣika documents which are admissible, are documents written entirely in the hand of the party himself. Unless a document falls under one of these three categories, it is not admissible at all.

By the time of Viṣṇu we find already that the necessity of testing documents has been felt. The mere presence of a document is no longer sufficient proof. It is of no effect if it has been obtained by force or fraud (Upadhi). A document which is attested is bad if the attestation is by a witness who is guilty of having done evil things or it is written by a scribe of a similar character. So too are documents made by women, children, dependant persons, lunatics, inebriates or persons under fear, as well as documents which are against the usage of the country. A document is said to be admissible only if it is clear and in accord with law and contains no erasures of letters. Provision is made by Viṣṇu also for testing the genuineness of document by comparison of the handwritings in question, particularly in the case of writers who are dead.

Brihaspati speaks of various kinds of documents which are classified by him into three classes. 1. Rājalekhya, 2. Svayaṃkrita, 3. Svahastalikhita. He mentions documents relating to several kinds of transactions. (1) Partition deeds, (2) gifts of land, (3) sale deeds, (4) mortgage of land or movebles, as well as deposit, distinguishing between deposits for custody and deposit for use,

(5) resolutions of village or local communities in respect of transactions unopposed to the King, (6) Dāsapatra (a document signing oneself as a slave) and (7) Ṛinalekhya of two kinds namely (a) bonds on taking loans with interest and (b) documents of release or satisfaction of debts.

Yājñavalkya is less elaborate but sufficiently comprehensive in his treatment of documents generally (II 84 seq.). He speaks of the necessity of attestation by witnesses, of the nature and contents of documents, and refers to the necessity of endorsement by a debtor of the payment of his debt and of the signature by the witnesses and the scribe.

Kātyāyana adds to the list of documents those regarding purification of a sinner, sandhipatras, sīmāpatras determining boundaries and anvādhipatra or deed of second mortgage.

Special provisions are made for documents made by Kings. Vaśiṣṭha mentions four kinds of such documents, śāsanas or grants, jayapatra or decree, ajnāpatra and prajnāpanapatra. The last two are equally communications of directions by kings, the former being orders to his subordinates and the latter being in the nature of humble submissions to persons to whom honour is due, like the Ṛitvik and Purohita.

Thus we find that while in the early stages of the vogue of documentary evidence the texts tend to take a document as proof without question, in the later texts we find elaborate provisions made for testing of documents, indicating that the forger was already frequently at work. This led to the necessity of proof of documents by oral testimony or divya. Comparison of handwriting is also indicated as a mode of deciding between true and false documents.

Documents obtained by fraud or force or executed by incompetent persons are to be discarded, as also a document which was executed without the executant seeing its contents or having it read over to him.

Possession

Possession as evidence, apparently of right and title is already mentioned by Vaśiṣtha along with documents and witnesses (Likhitam sākṣino bhuktih pramānam trividham smṛitam. Ch. XVI) Later, in the code of Yājñavalkya while the same enumeration is given of kinds of proof it is added that, in the absence of any of these, divya is another mode of proof. While Gautama does not refer to possession as evidence, he recognises title by prescription.

Property possessed by a stranger in the presence of the owner belongs to the possessor according to him, if it is not property of an idiot, minor or of śrotriyas, ascetics or royal officials. A further exception is made however in respect of animals, land and female slaves (Gaut. Dh. S. XII, 37-39). Another old text of Śankha cited in the commentaries is apparently to the same effect though limited to "grāmạ nagaravṛiddhaśrenivirodhe." In such cases, he says "dasavarṣabhuktamanyatra Rājaviprasvāt" (cit Vivāda Ratnākara).

The law regarding possession in both these aspects viz. evidentiary and prescriptive continues, and comes down to Yājñavalkya who says

> Paśyato'vruvato bhumer hānir viṃśati vārṣikī
> Pareṇa bhujyamānasya dhanasya daśavārṣikī,
> Ādhisīmopanikṣepa jaḍavāla dhanair vinā,
> Tathopanidhirājastriśrotriyānām dhanairapi.
>
> (Yājñ. II 24-25)

There can be no mistaking the true meaning of this text of Yājñavalkya. It lays down not only a rule of limitation but also of loss of title by prescription with a few exceptions which are sensible. He differs from the older texts in requiring a longer period of enjoyment in the case of land which in Gautama's text appears to have been excluded from prescription.

It is worthy of notice that Gautama who takes the trouble to enumerate the modes of acquisition of title to property by inheritance, purchase, partition etc. (X, 39-43) does not mention possession there as a source of title. Nevertheless he has this rule of title being transferred by adverse possession. Mitākṣarā commenting on this latter text of Gautama whittles away its meaning on the ground amongst others that possession cannot be a source of ownership as it is not mentioned as such in the former text, delightfully oblivious of the fact that in its argument on the sons' right to ancestral property by birth it explains away Gautama's enumeration of the various titles as not exhaustive (parisankhyā).

When we come to later texts we find that this idea of title being extinguished or created by adverse possession is looked at with disfavour, and various attempts are made by different smṛiti texts to lay down that āgama or title prevails over mere possession and, where āgama can be shown, mere possession even without permission (kṣamālinga) for any length of time would not suffice to dislodge it. This view would reduce the rule of Yājñavalkya to a title by possession only where possession is shown to have had a lawful origin. Others again proceed to require a very long period of possession, e.g. for three generations or for sixty or more years. Commentators almost unanimously accept this position. All these texts are referred to in Kane's History of Dharmaśāstras (Vol. III Chap. XII). Without going into a detailed reference to those texts it may be said that in the later works e.g. of Nāradā, Bṛihaspati and others, the doctrine of prescriptive title is whittled down and possession is made ineffective against an established title.

The reference to the rule in Gautama however puts it beyond reasonable doubt that title by possession was recognised at an earlier stage of the law than that which made it yield to other lawful title (āgama). The competition between Āgama and Bhukti to the disadvantage of the latter was a later development. It is possible that even Gautama's rule with its exceptions and limitations was probably based on an earlier formulation of the law when no such limitations were visualised.

This seems to be similar to the course of evolution of property rights in other systems. We may recall that in early Roman law Quiritarian right to Res Mancipi could be acquired by Usucapio by only one year's possession. A study of Anglo-Saxon and Germanic laws has satisfied scholars that they did not, at one stage, recognise any other right except that of possession and the remedies like the right of pursuit and right to recover possession belonged to the mere possessor and the possessor alone.[70] It is a permissible inference that in primitive law before the abstract concept of ownership was distinguished, possession alone constituted the right to a property. When other lawful modes of acquiring title were recognised, possession was not straightway dislodged from its position as a title, but was required to be of some duration, at first of what would seem now to be an absurdly short time like that in Usucapio in Roman law, but gradually, longer periods like the longi temporis prescriptio of Roman law.

If this can be accepted as a general theory of the evolution of title to property from bare possession, it would seem to be a fair inference to hold that in ancient India at an age beyond the Dharmasūtras, just possession constituted the sole title and that the rule of prescription in Gautama was a development out of and survival of the primitive rule. The reactions of later concept of ownership by āgama on this rule operated in India as in Imperial Rome to lengthen the period of possession required or to a resistance to the idea on the basis of considerations which long operated in England

70 Pollock & Maitland: *History of English Law* Vol. II, Ch. IV.

to prevent the growth of a real law of prescription as distinguished from a mere rule of limitation, barring the remedy but not the right.

The Influence of the Professional Lawyer

The above brief treatment of the development of the law of Procedure and Evidence indicates, as I have observed before, that in the King's Courts law was handled by specialists who had made the study of law their special profession. The law of procedure is found to grow not only fuller in detail as time goes on but become more and more systematic and formal. Distinctions and differences are grafted on older and less precise and definite propositions which are inspired by practical exigencies and by increasing tendency to precision and method.

So too the law of Evidence, starting from vague rules for determining the truth by seeking advice from competent men, grows gradually into a somewhat elaborate code going into minute details such as would naturally suggest themselves to a practical lawyer.

Divine testimony which in earlier days was a matter to be resorted to in every case, becomes gradually restricted to cases where human testimony is not available, and the divyas themselves are humanised. Witnesses originally were only persons of known integrity, held high in public estimation who were summoned by the King at the start. Gradually it became usual for the parties to cite witnesses. Artificial rules about the number and qualification of witnesses tend to be whittled down and a rational mode of judging the testimony of witnesses by weighing it against other testimony as well as by watching their demeanour is gradually evolved.

When documentary evidence came into existence, it appears that the first attitude of law was to regard a document as conclusive. But while the forger was at work at one end, the lawyer at the other was formulating rules for testing the genuineness of the writing and rejecting forged documents. Particular rules were laid down as to the manner of executing the documents, of endorsing payments on bonds for money and attestation by witnesses was made compulsory except on holographs.

There can be no doubt when we look at the picture of the growth of these laws that their development was very largely due to the work of men who had specialised in law.

It does not follow that in those ancient times there were professional lawyers who took up cases on behalf of clients in the manner of the professional lawyers in India today or even in classical Rome.

Parisads

But men who had made the study of law, meaning, not only vyavahāra but the whole sacred law including Āchāra as well, had existed in India from the earliest times. As already mentioned, there appears to have been, in the earliest Vedic times, pariṣads or colleges of learned men. From the reference to the Pariṣad of the Pānchālās in the Bṛihadāraṇyaka Upanisad (VI, 1) it appears that each clan or settlement had its own pariṣad which made it its vocation to specialise in all kinds of learning. Our earliest law books refer to the pariṣads as bodies competent to lay down the law from prejural times. So far as law proper (including āchāra) was concerned the function of the ancient pariṣads seems to have been like that of the Pontiffs of ancient Rome, from whom lay men could seek advice on points of law, auspices and forms.

It seems probable that the learning in law and tradition was handed down from generation to generation in these schools of sages and finally came to be embodied in works like Prātiśālkhyas, Dharmasūtras etc.

In later times these clan or charana pariṣads seem to have gone out of vogue and, while most of the Dharmasūtras lay down that the opinion of pariṣads is good law, they also proceed to define the constitution of these pariṣads. The early tradition was that of the Daśāvara Pariṣad consisting of not less than ten persons is found gradually replaced by that of a smaller number of learned men and according to Yājñavalkya even of a single specially learned Brāhmaṇ—"Eko'pi Brahmavittamah".

In course of time, therefore, there were no special organised colleges or Pariṣads but learned men who had specialised in the study of law were appealed to by the people for advice on questions of law and they generally gave their advice to such clients on receiving what could not be called fees, but honoraria, under different names.

King's Sabha

When King's justice was well established and a sabhā came to be associated with the king, the Prāḍvivāka or Judge, these learned men would be the persons whom the King would appoint as sabhāsadas, and as we have seen, it was their duty to give their opinion on any question arising in the case. We have seen also that besides these appointed sabhāsadas any learned person might attend the sabhā and was entitled to give his opinion whether appointed or not ("niyukto 'niyuktovā").

These sabhāsadas were not expected to be partisans and were by no means retained by either party. On the contrary, they were enjoined to be absolutely impartial, ("Ripau mitre cha ye samāh"). Though, thus, no lawyer in the sabhā was a patron of or in the pay of any client, he might, and possibly could be induced to, espouse the cause of one rather than the other.

As to what actually happened in a Court at a trial we have only one detailed description in an old drama, the Mrichchhakatika where the trial of the hero Chārudatta is given in great detail. In that story however we find no sabhā or sabhāsada. The Court consisted of only one judge assisted by ministerial officers, śreṣthi and kāyastha. Every point of law is taken by the parties and decided by the judge. This gives us no indication about what took place in the case of a regular trial by the King or Judge with sabhāsadas.

Mahabharata Story

We may get, however, some idea of what happened in a King's sabhā when a question of rights was actually debated, in a thrilling scene in the sabhāparva of the Mahābhārata. King Yudhiṣṭhira having been summoned to play a game of dice with Śakuni, who played on behalf Duryodhana, was defeated on every throw by the crooked Śakuni who played with charmed dice.—As a result Yudhiṣṭhira who had pledged all he had, as also the liberty of himself his brothers and his wife Draupadi was not only made destitute but he and his brothers as well as Draupadi whom he had specifically pledged became slaves of Duryodhana.

Duryodhana thereupon sent a messenger (Prātikamī) to summon Draupadi to the Sabhā. Draupadi fenced as long as she could by raising legal obstacles until she was dragged by the hair to the Sabhā by Duhśāsana, brother of Duryodhana.

Draupadi had posed a subtle question of law for the King Dhritarāstra and his sabhā to decide. She asked the King and the sabhā to say whether she had lawfully been made a slave. She did not dispute her husband's right to dispose of her as a pawn in the game, but urged that Yudhiṣṭhira was no longer competent to pledge away her liberty after he had himself become a slave at an earlier throw. She asked for an answer from the King and his eminent sabhāsadas.

She got no ready response from the members of the Sabhā. The first to speak was the Grand Old Man of the Kurus, Bhīṣma who, though very sad at her plight, gave an opinion with characteristic hesitancy trying evenly to balance the rights and wrongs of the act.

"I cannot give a correct answer to thy question," said he "owing to the subtlety of the Law. On the one hand, no one can pledge a thing not his own, on the other hand, a wife is subject to the dominion of her husband. And Yudhiṣṭhira, who would renounce the whole world rather than forsake truth has said that he has lost the throw. In these circumstances I cannot answer your question." (Mah. II 64, 46-47).

Vidura more than once asserted that, after giving himself away, Yudhṣṭhira had no longer any dominion over his wife and he repeatedly invoked the members of the sabhā to give their true opinion. For some time, no one responded till, exasperated by the insults to which Draupadi was repeatedly subjected, Duryodhana's brother Vikarṇa, in a spirited speech espoused her cause and called upon others to give their true opinion. When no one responded, stamping his fist on his other hand, Vikarṇa spoke for himself with fine forensic eloquence.

He raised three points against the servitude of Draupadi. In the first place, he said, Yudhiṣṭhira had pledged Draupadi in a frenzy of gambling. A pledge made in this condition could not be valid. Secondly, Draupadi was the common wife of all the Pāṇḍavas and so Yudhiṣṭhira alone had no right to pledge her. Thirdly, as Yudhiṣṭhira had already been enslaved before, he could no longer exercise any dominion over his wife (Mah. II, 65, 19—24).

The speech of Vikarṇa enraged Karṇa who had so long been gloating over Draupadi's discomfiture and he made a violent speech abusing Vikarṇa. He insisted that even before she had been pledged specifically Yudhiṣṭhira had staked 'all that was his own', and that included Draupadi, so that the last throw was hardly necessary. Even after that he had specifically offered her as a pawn and the other Pāṇḍavas had obviously endorsed his action. He even insisted that Draupadi was not a respectable woman but a prostitute as she was under the sway of several men. (Mah. 65, 27—38).

The sabhā before which this scene was enacted did not precisely answer to the description of the sabhā in the Smṛitis. Yet it was the king's sabhā and it was called upon to decide a question of law posed by Draupadi and, to my mind, this gives us some insight into the sort of debate which might and would arise in a litigation before the King and his sābhā where a disputed question of law or title arose. Each sabhāsada was free to give his own opinion and it is quite on the cards that there would be differences of opinion and different lawyers might espouse the cause of different parties. In any event with a number of members of sabhā each of whom was chosen with regard to his learning in law and each free to give his independent opinion on the case before them as well as to interrogate witnesses, the case of any party who had a case to support or defend was not likely to go by default. Thus though partisan counsel were unknown in ancient India there was at all times a growing body of men who had made the study of law their special vocation and they had a hand in moulding the administration of law in the King's Courts. Outside the Courts too they were apparently persons to whom the lay man would apply for advice on any point of law. Thus their functions nearly corresponded to that of the Pontiffs during the early days of Roman law and of the early jurisconsults whose Responses went to build up and develop the law of Rome.

The development of the law in the King's Court as evidenced by the texts of the Dharmasūtras seems clearly to indicate their handling by such an expert body.

One other result of the law being handled by specialists was their attempt to classify the heads of litigation. Of any pretence to classification we have little evidence in the earliest codes of Gautama, Āpastamba or even Vaśiṣṭha and Baudhāyana. Viṣṇu's code too has no express texts for such classification but his treatment of the laws after introducing the topic of King's Vyavahāra shows that these topics had already fallen into some sort of arrangement.

It is Manu who first formulates the law about classes of topics of litigation which he divides under eighteen heads. Nārada and Bṛihaṣpati have also classified the topics of law under eighteen heads, but these are not exactly identical with those of Manu. A study of these various topics of litigation in the several works give us some idea of the evolution of law in the King's Courts. In later lectures I shall attempt to reconstruct history so far as possible from the topics dealt with by the various sages in their works.

In Manu, Nārada and Bṛihaṣpati topics of Marital relations, Sonship, Inheritance etc. which may be treated together under the name of Family Law, form some of the eighteen topics of litigation. But, reading the older Dharmasūtras, it is clear that Family Law as a whole was, at the start, altogether outside the scope of King's justice or Vyvahāra. This I shall elaborate later on. For the present I shall content myself with saying that, on the whole, it would be convenient to deal with the entire Family Law before dealing with the other topics of litigation in the various lists of Manu, Nārada and Bṛihaṣpati.

CHAPTER IV

MARRIAGE

In the Ṛigveda and the Atharva Veda we have a detailed story of a marriage which is the basis of the ritual of marriage in the Gṛihya sūtras. There are other slightly varied texts which cannot be traced to any Saṃhitā but are to be foand in the Mantra Brāhmaṇa of the Sāma Veda Śākhās and the Mantrapātha of the Yajurveda and which are used in the Gṛihya Sūtras of those śākhās.

Vedic Marriage.

The scheme of marriage envisaged in all these mantras and the rituals of the Gṛihya Sūtras which embody them is as follows :

An adult bridegroom goes to the house of the bride's father. There certain offerings are made before the fire and the girl's family is changed by an appropriate mantra. Thereafter the bride is carried to a chariot which also carries the fire to which the oblations have been made. Mantras which are charms are uttered mainly to keep away evil and ward off accidents on the way. This journey is called *vahatu* which is also the name of the entire marriage ceremony in the Veda.

When the journey is done, the bride is led into the house which the bridegroom has, before this, built[71] and there the fire brought with them is installed as the House Fire (Gṛihyāgni) of the couple before which the couple make joint offerings. The Gṛihyas show that after this the couple sleep together, but with a wand between them. This wand is thrown into water with proper rituals after three nights and then the marriage is consummated with appropriate mantras.

The whole basis of this is the magic of mantras. It makes the wife gṛihapatnī, a term which, in dignity and significance is the same as the materfamilias in Roman law.

The Vedas speak of or contemplate no other form of marriage, nothing else that can give the wife the status of Patnī or legitimate wife.

[71] This house seems to have been built by the bridegroom in contemplation of the marriage as a house where to build his House Fire after leading the bride into it. This seems to be indicated by the fact that Āśvalāyanna Gṛihya puts the ritual of house building (II, 7—9), after the marriage rituals at the bridge's house and before the rituals of a gṛihastha in Adh. III.

It is true that the capture of girls is not altogether unknown to the Vedas. For the Ṛigveda speaks of the carrying away of the daughter (yoṣā) of Purumitra by Vimada.[72] Nor is love-making by youth unknown, as is significantly indicated by a text which is a charm for putting the house to sleep to enable the lovers to meet safely. But these are not marriages. They do not lead to wifehood (patnitva) which is a status in which the girl passes into the gotra of her husband by magic rites.

As already indicated, men being men, the tabus of ritual magic could not put an absolute bar to the physical union of man and woman by the attractions of mutual affection or forcible capture and instances would occur of such unions. But the Vedas or even the Gṛihya Sūtras do not give to girls so united the right of a patni or gṛihapatnī to offer oblations to the House Fire or the right to address the family council (vidatha) as she is obviously entitled to according to the Ṛik mantra in which the bridegroom says to her among other things "Vidathamāvadātha." (RV. X, 85, 27).

In Āsvalāyana Gṛihya Sutras (I, 6)—a chapter which is wholly out of tune with the rest of the Gṛihya Sūtras,—as well as in the Dharma Sūtras we find however various different forms of marriage referred to. The enumerations are not identical in the several Dharma Sūtras and the kinds of marriage approved by each are not also the same.

Kinds of Marriage in Smritis

The kinds of marriage ultimately evolved were eight, though unanimity about the admissibility of most of them was far from being attained even by the time of the present Samihita of Manu.

Brāhma is described as the form in which the bridegroom is invited and given the bride. The essential thing about this form is gift by the father and gift implies gift with water to a bridegroom invited for the purpose.

Daiva marriage also involves a gift of the girl, not to a bridegroom invited for the purpose, but so to say, as a present to the Ṛitvik who performs a sacrifice for her father.

Ārṣa marriage is the form in which the girl is given after receiving a gift from the bridegroom of a couple or two of cattle. We see in later works that there was some controversy over the question whether this receipt of a pair of cattle constituted a sale of the bride.

[72] Rig Veda I, 116, 1.

Prājāpatya also is a gift of the bride only with an invocation to the couple to perform the Dharma together.

All these are forms in which the gift by the parent is an essential part of the marriage.

Now looking at the marriage ritual as embodied in the various Gṛihya Sutras what strikes one at once is the absence of any ceremony of gift of the girl. The ceremonies (which are preceded by a formal betrothal) commence with the ceremonial paṇigrahaṇa or hand-taking.[73] This ceremony, called in Rome *dextrarum junctio*, is universal in the marriage rites to all Indo-Germanic races but neither in the Vedic and Gṛihya Sūtras nor in other Indo-Germanic races is this preceded by any ceremonial gift of the girl.[74] This ceremonial gift, Kanyāpradāna, appears for the first time only in the Āśwalāyana Pariśistha an obviously later composition.

In constrast with these forms of marriage the remaining four are independent of any gift. In these, control over the girl is obtained by methods by which property is acquired whether violently or otherwise.

Rākṣasa, called by Vaśiṣṭha Kṣāttra, marriage is based on the right of conquest and consists solely of the carrying away by force of the bride against her will from her parent's house.

Āsura is simply marriage by purchase, where the girl is acquired by paying a suitable price to the parent.

Gāndharva is love marriage and is completed by a consummation[75] with the consent of the bride.

Paiśācha consists in the ravishment of the girl without her consent while she is drunk or asleep or out of her senses or, according to one authority, in stealing away the girl when her relations are asleep.

Looking at the various provisions of the Dharmaśāstras relating to these forms, one finds almost wild diversity.

73 Apastamba Gr. IV. 11-15.
Atharva Veda XIV 1, 48, 51.
Baudh Gr. I. 6, Sankh I 13, 2.
Manava Gr. I. 10. Pāraskara. I. 6. 3.
Gobhila II, 2, 16, Kaus 76. 5.

74 See Winternitz in Denkschrift der Kaiserlicher Akademie der Wissenschaft. Vol. XL, p. 49.
Paṇigrahaṇa is probably merely a form of the hand-grasp which also seals other solemn covenants among the ancient Germanic races. It was also the ceremony by which the Teacher made a solemn acceptance of his pupil (Asv. Gṛihya XVII, 15, Trav. Ed. p. 77).

75 This seems to be indicated by its description मैथुन्यः कामसम्भवः ।

Gautama recognises the four forms of marriage by gift only, and gives, as the "opinion of some," also Gāndharva and Āsura. This implies that in the society for which Gautama wrote these two latter forms were yet struggling for recognition. He does not mention Rakṣasa and Paiśācha at all.

Āpastamba recognises six kinds of marriage excluding Prājāpatya and Paisācha altogether. This indicates that Rākṣāsa and Āsura forms had vogue in his society while Paiśācha and Prājāpatya had not.

Vasiṣtha mentions the same six forms with the difference that he calls Rākṣāsa and Āsura, Kṣāttra and Mānuṣa respectively. This, to my mind, indicates that in his society, marriage by capture had already become an usual form of marriage among Kṣatriyas and that by purchase an usual form among the common people (Mānuṣa) comprising Vaiśyas and Śūdras. As we shall presently see, the existence of such a stage of society seems to be confirmed by the tevts of Manu.[76]

In an interesting passage Vaśiṣtha quotes, in connection with Āsura marriage, a text to be found in Śānkhāyana Gṛihya (I, 8, 18) and in Maitrāyayania Saṃhitā (1, 10, 11) is quoted :

"Anṛitam vā eṣā karoti yā patyuh kiītā sati athānyai'ścharati"

indicating that there is some evidence in the later Vedic texts of purchase of women. But that text does not go so far as to imply recognition of such women as patñi. This as well as the similar text of Katyāyana

"Krayakrītā tu yā nārī na sā patnī vīdhīyate.
Na sā daive na sā pitrye dāsim tām kavayo viduh"

certainly records an historic truth.[77]

Baudhāyana gives all the eight forms of marriage and he adds that some (eke) praise the gāndharva form on account of its following affection (snehānugatatvāt).

Vishnu gives all the eight forms of marriage in the following order.

(1) Brāhma,
(2) Daiva,
(3) Ārṣa,
(4) Prājāpatya,
(5) Gāndharva,
(6) Āsura,

76 Manu III, 24; contrast V. 6—15, Apast. II, 5, 11. 17—20 II, 5, 12, 1, 2. Vas. p. 6—7. Bandh. 1, II, 20, 2—9.

77 Baudhāyana quotes a variant in the form क्रीता द्रव्येण या नारी etc.

(7) Rākṣasa and
(8) Paiśācha.

Of these the first six are legitimate (Dharmya) and Gāndharva too is approved for Rājanyas *i.e.* Kṣattriyas. Rākṣasa according to him is thus a disapproved or illegitimate marriage for all.

These texts indicate some uncertainties and differences of opinion among the various authors and the schools of law they represent regarding the validity of these new forms of marriage which were intruding into the sacred society of Ārya culture. What a confusion in usages with regard to these forms of marriage was caused is indicated by the several texts of Manu juxtaposed with one another.

Forms of Marriage in Manu.

After reciting the forms in the following order (1) Brāhma (2) Daiva (3) Ārṣa (4) Prājāpatya (5) Āsura (6) Gāndharva (7) Rākṣasa and (8) Paiśācha, Manu goes on—

Saḍānupurvā Viprasya Kṣatrasya chaturo'varān
Viṭśūdrayostu tāneva vidyaddharmyān na Rākṣasam.
III 23

"The first six for Brāhmaṇas, the last four for Kṣhatriyas, the same for Vaiśya and Sūdra except Rākṣasa are known as legitimate."

But, immediately, he goes on to say that the first *four* are praśasta for Brāhmanas, while for the Kṣatriya the *only praśasta form* is Rākṣasa and for Vaiśyas and Sūdras the Āsura form (III. 24).

The very next sloka however indicates that only the first *five* (and not six) are prescribed for Brāhmanas and of these again only three are dharmya and two adharmya. And Paiśācha and Āsura are never to be adopted. Then again he goes on to prescribe Gāndharva and Rākṣasa for Kṣatriyas. (III. 25).

This confusing list is concluded by a text which says that, for Brāhmaṇas, the forms of gift with water, *i.e.* the first four forms, alone are praśasta while for the other varṇas it is *itaretera kāmyayā*, which I understand to indicate that, for all other castes, gāndharva founded on mutual affection is the praśasta form.[78] This gives effect

[78] Manu III. 35, Medhatithi however interprets it as indicating that among other castes brides are not to be *given* unless the bridegroom and bride desire one another.

"Yadi Kanyā varayoh parasparā bhilaso bhavati," he says, "tadā dānam kartavyam netarthā Brāhma vivāhat."

As no text of law speaks of gift as an element of Gāndhárva marriage, the addition of the necessity of gift, according to the wishes of the parties is an obvous

to the opinion of 'some' (eke), referred to by Baudhāyana, who put a premium on mutual affection.

This juxtaposition of such conflicting texts one after another in Manusaṃhitā is quite in keeping with the character and history of Manusaṃhitā as indicated in a previous lecture. Similar instances are to be found elsewhere in Manu *e.g.*, in the texts relating to Niyoga (IX, 51, 57, 64-70) and to the right of the daughters to inheritance (IX, 127-139). These were texts which were current under the name of Manu when the present code was compiled, and they were all placed together by the compiler. There can be no reasonable doubt however that all these texts could not have been in force in the same society and at the same time. They give the different laws that came into vogue in societies separated by time and space.

Evolution of Forms of Marriage.

In recent times in India too we find a multitude of different forms of marriage amongst the different races inhabiting this country. Marriage by capture is still the form in some of the tribes. Actual purchase was widely practised at one time and is still the fact in many societies. On the other hand, marriage by consent of the bride and bridegroom is by no means rare. In the ancient tradition in the Māhābhārata and other works also we find evidence of a number of divergent forms of marriage. Marriage by capture is found to be widely practised among the Kṣatriyas. Instances may be cited as in the case of Bhīṣma carrying away three sisters Ambā, Ambikā, and Ambālikā for marriage with his step brothers.[79] A much earlier tradition is that of Vimada, who carried away Puru's daughter as referred to in the Ṛigveda.[80] Marriage by purchase also is evidenced by the negotiation by Bhiṣma for the marriage of Mādri with Pandu.[81] When the flattering proposal was made to Śalya he humbly pointed out that it was the custom of his tribe that the bridegroom had to give a price which Bhiṣma readily gave and carried away Mādri. Even polyandrous marriages[82] are referred to, which correspond to

gloss prompted by the provisions of later law. Other commentators, *e.g.*, Madhavachārya and Devāṇṇa Bhatta hold however that in Gāndharva marriage there is no gift. See *infra*.

[79] Maha : Adiparva, Chap. 96.

[80] Ṛigyeda, I, 116, I.

[81] Maha : Adi Chap. 107.

[82] Maha : Adi Chap. 116 and other places.

usages amongst some communities in much later times. These instances indicate that in and around societies amongst whom the marriage system of ancient India was evolved, there were various forms prevailing in various communities and in course of time all these various forms have made their way into the sacred law.

In order to find out what was the basic form of marriage we have perhaps to rely more on a study of the ritual than on these recorded facts about marriage. A ritual is a more important institution than mere stray events, for it grows up by a long course of practice and, when established, it is not easily changed.

The Grihya Ritual

Looking at the ritual of marriage in the various Gṛihya sūtras, we find that while they differ in different times in the details, they are all founded upon the ceremony embodied in the Vedic tradition of marriage of Sūryyā with Soma. In this form of marriage the essential features are (1) that marriage is preceded by negotiation and betrothal between the friend of the bridegroom and apparently the father of the bride ; (2) the bridegroom comes and is received as an honoured guest and propitiated with various gifts ; (3) after that follows the hand grasp or pāṇigrahaṇa, a ceremony which symbolises many forms of solemn contract ; (4) a number of ceremonies of magic import for the purpose of driving away evil influence and invoking benevolent gods are performed ; (5) the bride and the bridegroom solemnise their union by uttering sacred texts ; (6) the bride is led thereafter to the husband's home ; (7) in the husband's home she lights the fire and makes sacrifices before it.

Now, these were also the essential features which are further elaborated in each Gṛihya Sūtra and these are the ceremonies which are associated with the particular form of marriage ritual called the Brāhma form in the latest times. We shall not be far wrong in saying that the original form of marriage is to be traced to this particular ritual and everything else that may be found in other places was an accretion from different sources.

Inferior forms of Marriage

Coming now to the several inferior forms of marriage *viz.* Rākṣasa, Āsura, Gāndharva and Paiśācha. The first thing that we notice is that these forms of marriage do not involve a transfer of the Gotra of the bride which was an essential part of the ritual of the Gṛihya Sūtra. They were mere forms of acquisition of ownership over the bride similar to acquisition of ownership over cattle or other property.

Comparing these facts with the history of marriage in Rome we find that the original Roman marriage was a religious marriage, confarreatio, which was practically identical in essential features with the Vedic marriage starting with *dextrarum junctio* and ending with *deductio domum*. The details of the ritual also agree a great deal and the result of such marriage is like that of the Vedic Marriage, consortium ommium vitæ. We find however that in Rome in later days brides were obtained by sham purchase (cœmptio) or by possession (Usus) which are similar to different ways of acquiring property. Even Patricians gradually began to adopt those forms of civil marriage originally prevalent among Plebians and Peregrins and ultimately there was nobody except the Flamen Dialis who were required to marry according to the rite of confarreatio. Similar causes may have similarly led the Aryans of India to adopt forms of marriage founded upon the establishment of ownership over things by robbery, by purchase or by mere consent or ravishment. In Rome the inferior forms of marriage which had not the sanctity of a *justum matrimonum* were in vogue amongst the Plebians and Peregrins who were incapable of marrying according to the religious rites open only to Patres. They were adopted by the Patricians gradually.

In India too it seems probable that these inferior forms of marriage entered into the Vedic Society by a similar adoption or adaptation of rites which prevailed amongst persons who did not belong to the Aryan culture. They may have been the forms practised by people who were not within the Aryan society consisting of three upper classes. They may have been immigrants to Ārya settlement who had come from abroad or they may have been the Anāryas who had adopted Ārya culture and religion. It seems extremely probable that in one or other way these civil forms of marriage came to be adopted gradually in the sacred literature of the Hindus.

That they were gralually adopted is shown by the diversity of treatment of these different forms of marriage by the different Dharma Śāstras, as indicated before. That these forms of marriage may have come from Añarya societies is indicated, but only indicated for one thing by coincidence in the name of Āsura form of marriage which is marriage by purchase. Among the Assurs as well as amongst the

Semitic races generally the form of marriage, even in very much later times, was a formal purchase which may have been originally derived from the real purchase in the past. There is no reason why this form of marriage as first introduced in Ārya society should be called Āsura unless it was obtained from people who were known to the Āryas as Asuras.

It is not necessary to suppose for this hypothesis that the Assyrians extended their empire to the homeland of the Ārya nor that this institution was borrowed directly from real Assyrians. It may have been that the immigrants from the Assur country came and established settlements within the Ārya settlement or it may be that some other races who had this particular institution and whom the Vedic Ārya also called Asuras had brought the institution with them. The point seems to be reasonably clear that this institution could never have been admitted to the name of Āsura unless it was an institution which was known as prevailing among Āsuras. (On Āsuras and Āssyrians, see H. K. Dev in *Vedic India and the Middle East* XIV JRASB p. 129 seq.).

Similarly the Rākṣasa form of marriage which is later called Kṣātra form may have been originally obtained from a race, it may be of cannibals, whom the Ārya called the Rākṣasas.[83] There is no reason why Gāndharva should be the name given to love marriage unless it was the form in vogue amongst people whom they knew as Gandharva (probably from Gāndhara).[84] I think it is a fair inference that these inferior forms of marriage came into the Āryan Society from non-Aryan sources.

Effect of lower forms of marriage

There was a fundamental difference between the ancient Vedic form of marriage and the Āsura or Rakṣasa forms. Vedic marriage was essentially a spiritual union by magic mantras by which the wife became, for all social and religious purposes, one with her husband. She held a dignified position and the courteous and even fulsome terms in which she is addressed by the husband at the marriage ritual in the Vedas, the invocation to her to become the mistress of the household and to address family councils, show the dignity of her position in the family.[85]

[83] See H. K. Dev *op. cit.* p. 140.

[84] In the Rāmāyāna Gāndhāra is expressly spoken of as Gandharvaviṣaya.

[85] RVX, 85, 64.

सम्राज्ञी श्वशुरे भव सम्राज्ञी श्वश्र्वां भव ।
ननान्दरि सम्राज्ञी भव सम्राज्ञी अधिदेवृषु ॥

In marriage by capture or purchase on the other hand the wife is treated as a chattel of which the husband is the owner and master. The wife so procured has none of the honour and dignity of a *patni* or *mater-familias* but is only a *uxor in manu* or little better than a *dasi*. *Baudhāyana* and *Katyāyana* have made the positive assertion that she is a *dāsi*, not competent to participate in the religious rituals of her husband.[86]

After the introduction of these marriages (and possibly also due to the fact that in Aryanised Anārya societies, among whom such marriages had prevailed and survived their Aryanisation, the women never had a better status) there is a definite decline in the status of a wife. She is looked upon more or less as a chattel, a source of offspring, as useful, for instance, as cows with which women are often compared for pointing a legal conclusion.

It was probably when Ārya society began thus to think that wifehood arose not as a result of magic mantras so much as by transfer of ownership by the father, that the idea thus gained ground that as a preliminary to the ritual the father must part with his ownership by some gift even in the ritual marriage. It was thus that the ceremony of Kanyāpradāna may have been added to the ritual of marriage by merely adopting the ritual for the gift of any property, which consists principally of pouring water on the thing given while uttering the formula of gift.

That the original Vedic conception of marriage could not have implied a gift or transfer by the father is indicated by one of the mantras in Rigveda (X, 85, 38–41) in the earliest step of the ritual, which says that the girl first belonged to Soma, who gave her to Gandharva who in his turn gave her to Agni from whom the bridegroom receives her. The idea behind the magic formula therefore is that from birth onwards the girl is possessed not by the father, but by supernatural beings and the husband gets her not by the gift from the father but by the gift of the gods.

Once Kanyā is looked upon as a chattel who can be given by

X. 85, 27.

एना पत्या तान्वं संसृज स्वाधा जिव्री विदथमावदाथ ।

Vidathamāvadātha is interpreted by Sāyana as "go towards home" taking vidatha to mean "home."

86 क्रयक्रीता तु या नारी न सा पत्नी विधीयते ।
न सा दैवे न सा पित्र्ये दासीन्तां कवयो विदुः ॥

A variant of which is quoted in Baudh. Dh. S. II, 1, 20-22.

the father, she is conceived as being capable of being given to a priest or Ṛitvik as a present or a fee. She could be given also for a price which convention fixed at a pair of cattle. It is by no means certain that in the days when this rite first came into vogue a pair or two of heads of cattle was not deemed an ample return for a daughter who, even in the Ṛigveda is not very much prized. In this way gradually, ceremonial marriage came to be diversified into four distinct classes, when, under other influences, as will be presently seen, departures from the original Vedic ritual became acceptable.

Reactions of sacred law

As we have seen, with the possible exception of Gāndharva or love marriage, the inferior types of marriage were probably obtained from Anārya sources. Love marriage may have grown up by itself in the society or obtained from outside possibly from Gāndhāra which was the homeland of Gandharvas.

But none of these forms of marriage were straightway recognised as valid marriages leading to the status of Gṛihapatni for the wife. The sacred law appears to have reacted to the currency of these forms of marriage in society in two different ways. The first attempt apparently was to insist that while he bride could be validly obtained in any of these different ways, as a substitute of gift by the father such acquisitions must be followed by a regular ritual of marriage. This view, is put forward in Vasiṣtha's Dharmasūtra (XVII — 73) but, strangely enough, it seldom finds support in any other text of Smṛiti. On the contrary, there are texts which indicate that in the inferior forms of marriage the gotra of the girl is not changed, because in them there is no gift by the father.[87]

Another form of reaction was to adapt these new and purely civil form of marriage to the religious law. Thus the Āsura form was transformed into the Ārṣa, which was only distinguished from the Āsura by the fixity of the customary price to be paid by the bridegroom before the ceremonial gift of the girl and possibly also by the sacrament to be performed.

The Prājāpatya form of marriage also seems to be a similar

[87] e.g. text of Mārkandeyapūrana cited in Parāśara Mādhrva I, 2, p. 63-64.

ब्राह्मादिषु विवाहेषु यानूढ़ा कन्यका वभेत् ।
भर्तृ गोत्रेण कर्तव्याः तस्याः पिण्डोदक क्रिया ॥
गान्धर्वादि विवाहेषु पितृगोत्रेण धर्मवित् ।

There is complete unanimity among commentators in this respect, seeViramitrodaya on Yajñ. I, 61. Smṛiti Ch.

adaptation. The accounts of Prājāpatya marriage in the Smṛītis are very meagre and little is said about it beyond laying down that the father enjoins the couple to perform the Dharma together. "*Sahobhau charatām dharmam.*" This appears to be an adaptation of the Gandharva form of marriage which was completed by consummation, without reference to the bride's father. This the sacred law disapproves. But it recognises love marriages when the father's blessing was obtained by the couple after their mutual consent when the father may have made a ceremonial invocation to the couple.

Reference has been already made to the various texts in which the Dharmaśāstras recognise the different kinds of marriages. It has been seen that all the forms were not recognised by all the law givers. Gautama refers, in addition to the four approved forms, to the forms of Gāndharva and Āsura as valid marriages "according to some". Rākṣasa and Paiśācha are not recognised by him at all and no distinctions have been made between the quality of validity of different kinds of marriage. Āpastamba does not mention Prājāpatya at all, but recognises Gāndharva, Rākṣasa and Āsura along with the other three forms. He too does not distinguish any form as approved or disapproved. The confusing list given by Manu has been already referred to.

The exclusion of Prājāpatya from the list of Vásiṣṭa and Āpastamba who both recognise Gāndharva seems to lend support to the view advanced above that Prajapátya was merely a Gāndharva marriage sanctified by the addition of father's blessing.

Conclusion

With regard to these facts about the forms of marriage we thus find a mass of conflicting and varied texts. The conclusion which has to be drawn from these facts seems to be that these laws grew up in different societies and different times and were ultimately synthetised into a uniform code, as a sácramental reaction to the vogue of this form of marriage which could not be denied.

Manu's text (III, 25) seems to indicate that at one stage in society Bṝahma, Daivá, Ārsa and Prājāpatya marriage, that is to say, the sacramental marriages had come to be *confined* to the Brāhmaṇas alone, while the other cástes were free to marry as they chose. Quite early in the history of Aryan society it appears that the chief attention of law-givers was to Brahmans who were religious heads and Kṣatriyas from whom came Kings. For others the Smṛities tolerated any form of civil marriage. As Baudhāyana (Gr.

S. I. 2, 14—16) says "Ayantrita-kalatrā hi váiśya-śūdrah bhavanti, karṣaṇa śuśrūṣādi kritvyāt." To Kṣatriyas, who specialised in arms, only marriage by capture or consent was conceded but all civil forms to Vaiśyas and Śudras. This led in time to the stage indicated by Manu (III, 35). This evolution would seem to be similar to the development which took place in Roman law, where, once the civil form of marriage by Coemtio and Usus came to be recognised, they gradually superseded the confarreatic or the religious marriage, with offerings before the fire, altogether for common people, but significantly, the confarreatic was the only form of marriage admissible for the *Flamen Dialis,* the priest of Jupiter in Rome. There, as in India at this stage indicated by Manu, the religious marriage tended to be confined to the class who had special religious functions to perform.

Gradually however, we find a further stage, which may be characterised as the revival of orthodoxy. This is evidenced by the works of the classical jurists, the authors of commentories and Nibandhas. By this time the aberrations from original sacred law seem to have been rigorously suppressed and the sacred law vouched by the authority of sacred texts strictly followed. This probably corresponds to the revival all over India of orthodox Śāstric law in comparatively modern times. At this stage we find all other form of marriage except the Brāhma rigorously excluded from the sacred law although there is evidence that many of these forms survived in custom in different parts of the country.

EXOGAMY.

It appears that, from the earliest times Ārya marriage was strictly exogamous. This is indicated by the ritual of marriage envisaged in the Ṛigveda and worked out in details in Gṛihya Sūtras.

Marriage in the Vedas is called *Vahatu* which means the carrying away of the bride and the ceremony consists of carrying away of the bride in a chariot. There are mantras for greasing the wheel of the chariot and mounting on it and for the safe journey to the husband's home (RV X, 85, 20–30). They all contemplate some long journey and the Gṛihya ritual places some of the mantras as appropriate to a ceremony to be performed in the house of a Brāhman on the way where the couple have to break journey and spend a night. All these indicate that the journey which was taken was not from one house to another in the same village and, considering that the Vedic village was strictly agnetic as indicated before, this shows that the marriage could not take place with an agnate. Besides, the ritual also involves a change of the girl's gotra. Gotra is even now and has always been a strictly agnatic relation and marriage involves change of gotra. It follows that there could not be a marriage with agnates.

No definite information is available from the Vedas as to what other relations were excluded from marriage. In the later Vedic literature, Śatapatha Brāmaṇa I, 8, 3, 6 seems to allow marriage within the third or fourth degree from the common ancestor, though presumably not if the bride and bridegroom are of the same gotra. A text of Paithinasi cited in commentaries (see Mitākṣarā on I, 53) too lays down a similar shorter rule of exclusion when it says "Excluding three from the mother's side and five from the father." A similar text is cited by Nirṇayasindhu as a text of Parāśara who puts the limit at the fourth or fifth generation (Kane, Hist. Dh. Vol. II, Part I, p. 464).

Coming to the Dharmasūtras, Gautama (IV 2 seq.) lays down that the girl to be married must be (1) not of the same pravara (2) beyond seven degrees from pitṛibandhus and (3) beyond five degrees from matribandhus. Vaśiṣtha and Baudhāyana lay down the same rule.

Āpastamba is briefer and excludes only (1) sagotra and (2) Yonisambaddha. II, 11, 15.

These brief rules could not have been the whole law on the subject. They must have conveyed to contemporaries much more than the words conveyed to us.

So, when Manu (III, 5) excludes sapindas of the mother and sagotras of the father and Yājñavalkya (I, 52, 53) excludes (1) Sapindas (2) Sagotras and (3) Samānārṣas, they are probably, not laying down any new law.

If Gautama does not mention sagotras, it is because all sagotras are necessarily samanapravaras. He does not mention sapindas as such, but indicates exclusion of the same relations as are indicated by Manu and Yājñavalkya.

Āpastama's Yonisambaddha — meaning, connected by descent or birth, must have meant the same thing. If it meant literally those born of the same womb the exclusion would be too narrow. On the other hand it might be too wide if it excluded a persons connected by birth. To contemporaries it must have conveyed a more restricted sense.

Pitribandhus and Matribandhus

Who are the Pitribandhus and Matribandhus mentioned by

Gautama? These words have caused much speculation by our judges. Let us however try to find out what the Sūtra authors meant by these words. Bandhu as defined by the Mitākṣarā in one place is a bhinna gotra sapinda that is to say, a sapinda who does not belong to the same gotra. On the other hand in another place, it merely follows an old text quoted, which divides Bandhus into three classes described as Ātmabandhus, Pitṛibandhus and Matṛibandhus. According to that enumeration Bandhu would comprise only nine relations. Father's sister's son, mother's sister's son and maternal uncle's son of (1) a person himself (2) his father and (3) his mother. It is quite clear however that when Gautama speaks of Pitṛibandhus and Mātṛibandhus he does not apply the term in either of the senses of the Mitākṣarā. In point of fact in all the old texts the term 'Bandhu' always means the kindred and kindred, in the old Sutra times, included only agnates. Thus, for instance, when Vaśistha speaks of adoption, and says that it must be done after calling together Bandhus (bandhūnāhūya) and the person adopted to be a Bārdhava, he could not have meant by this term cognates only or at all. He must have understood by the term Bandhu agnates and suggested that the child to be adopted should be a nearest kindred i.e. agnate.

In the Mitākṣarā itself, with regard to distribution of property of merchants who have died abroad, it has been specifically mentioned that their wealth would be taken by the Dāyāda Bāndhavas (Yajñavalkya, II, 264). This same expression has also been used in every Smṛiti in connection with different kinds of secondary sons who are distinguished as Dāyāda Bāndhava and Adāyada Bāndhaves. When Gautama therefore speaks of Pitṛibandhus of seven degrees he could not have meant anything but agnatic relations of the father within seven degrees.

Besides these agnates, the kindred agnates of the mother down to three or five degrees were excluded by several texts. This I am disposed to consider to be an amendment which was introduced in the old law when cognation appears in the scheme of kindred. It does not appear to have been the original prohibition in the Vedic law.

That the scheme of kindred in the Vedas did not include cognates seems to have been indicated the khila text of Ṛigveda which speaks of the maternal uncle's daughter as an eligible bride, so much so that Indra is invoked to take his share as a man takes by preference his maternal uncle's or paternal aunt's daughter. This can only be because when the daughter went out of the kindred by marriage, her father's kindred would not be relations of her son or daughter who have to be excluded from the scheme of marriage.

Marriage with maternal uncle's daughter

This gives rise to a great controversy amongst the authors of legal works. Baudhāyana amongst the Sutras writers recognises marriage of maternal uncle's daughters as well as father's sister's daughter as valid customs in the South and says that this custom can be followed in the southern countries. Authors of commentories are sharply divided into two camps on this question. The northern authors, as also Kumārihaswami who, though a southern Brahmin, wrote in Benares, condemned marriage with maternal uncle's daughter as utterly sinful. On the other hand, leading works in South such as Parāśara Madhaya, Smṛiti Chandrikā and others defend the institution of marriage with maternal uncle's daughter.

It cannot be doubted that the Vedic Khila text (Āyāhīndra etc.) clearly implies that marriage with maternal uncle's daughter was common amongst at least a Śākha of the Vedic Āryas, because mother's kindred were not regarded as kindred. If that is so, mother's brother's or father's sisters' daughter could not be forbidden for marriage. Kinship of maternal relations was later developed (see infra, under Kinship) and, when it was established, and daughter's son began to offer piṇḍas to the maternal grandfather and to participate in piṇḍas offered to him, the maternal uncle's daughter entered into the scheme of kinship as sapinda. It will be seen later that this is so on reference to the law relating to Srāddha, aśaucha and other provisions of the law. This development viz. the inclusion of cognates in the scheme of kinship came into Ārya Society in courses of time. It would be hazardous to say that this development was not the result of mere natural affection or internal evolution as a result of natural changes in social organization. But it seems probable that it was to some extent influenced by customs of Non-Ārya society and came, as will be seen later, through the adoption of the institution of Putrikā.

Remoter relations

In the law as it was developed early in the age of Smṛiti we find it established that marriage is forbidden between Sapiṇḍas both on the father's and mother's side as well as of Sagotras and Samānapravaras.

Pravara is the name given to a number of Ṛishis who are

associated together with the founder of the gotra and all of them are supposed to be ancestors.

The word 'pravara', does not appear in the Vedic literature, in which the word 'ārṣeya' is used (e.g. Ṛigveda IX, 97-51). This word refers to the same thing as pravara, namely; the several Ṛiṣi ancestors of the worshipper.[88] The names of these ancestors had always to be mentioned by way of introduction of the worshipper to Agni who is chosen (pravṛiṇute) for the purpose of the worship. The idea is that by this varaṇa or pravaraṇa, Agni is appointed the priest to offer and carry oblations to the gods who are to be worshipped. Neither the worshipper nor the Ritvikas carry the oblations direct to the gods, Indra, Varuna etc., — except through the intervention of Agni who is thus invoked and chosen as a purohita. We therefore find that in every yāga of the Brāhmaṇas the first step is the pravaraṇa of Agni which is done by reference to the ārṣeya.

The extension of the prohibition in marriage to descendants of all the ṛisis in the pravara seems to have developed later than the days of the Vedas. The basis of this prohibition was a belief in the theory of spirituality of Kinship which seems to have characterised Ārya law from most ancient times.[89]

AGE OF BRIDE.

At what age girls should be married is a question to which law givers have given some attention and, as in other matters, about this also there appears a diversity of texts.

It seems however that in the earliest times as indicated in the Ṛig Veda, adult marriage both for males and females was the rule. It was deemed a misfortune for a girl to remain unmarried for long, but old maids were not considered inconceivable. The story of Ghoṣā[90] who remained unmarried very long until the gods gave her a husband, is indicative of the fact.

The marriage of Suryā and Soma in Ṛig Veda (X. 85) was clearly an adult marriage to which the bridegroom and the bride, and

88 See texts cited by Kane Vol. II, Part 2, p. 487 where he points out also that the names of the Ṛiṣis given in the invocation are the same as those of what are given in later works as the pravara of the worshipper. The fact, that all the pravara Ṛiṣis are not mentioned in the invocation in the Ṛigveda indicates that one or more ancestors were added in later practice until the pravaras became finally fixed.

89 See *infga* under Kinship.

90 Ṛig Veda I, 117, 7; X. 39, 3 and X, 40, 5.

not their parents, were parties. Marriage was preceded by betrothal, a ceremony which was performed by friends of the bridegroom, in this case, the two Aśvins, who came to the bride's house for it.

Marriage followed. Offerings were made to the gods before the fire with various mantras designed to keep away evil genii and to invoke the blessings of benevolent gods. The bridegroom took the hands of the bride and uttered mantras embodying marriage vows by which, among other things they prayed for common life, longevity, progeny, prosperity, for the fidelity and steadfastness of the wife, and so forth. The wife too uttered mantras praying for long life of the husband. (ṚV X, 85, 39)

The final stage of the marriage was the ceremonial consummetion of marriage at the bridegroom's house, after an interval of three or more days. There is one significant mantra which says that the bride first belonged to Soma and then to Gandharva and then to Agni and Agni gives her to her husband. The possession of these gods cover different periods from birth to puberty. (ṚV X 85, 35 — 41)

Another text the meaning of which is obscure is the invocation to Nīlalohita, apparently an evil spirit (R. V. X 85) to leave the bride. What this Nīlalohita is and what he symbolises is not clarified, so far as I am aware, by any commentator. But from the meaning of the word which means "deep red" I am disposed to think that it means a spirit to whom the menstruation of girls was attributed. If this meaning is justified it would seem that the girl is one who has already attained puberty.

All this seems to me to be wholly inconsistent with pre-pubertal marriage of infants.

Already in the Gṛihya Sūtras however we find texts enjoining that a girl should be given in marriage while she is a *nagnikā*. This term itself is variously interpreted. Literally, it would mean a girl who still goes about naked, that is an infant of very tender age. But it has also been interpreted to imply a girl who has not attained puberty.[91]

[91] It may be however that the two senses of nagnikā given in the Gṛihyas were not originally really different. In the first sense nagnikā means a girl who is not yet ashamed to go about naked. But the age at which girls go naked without shame is after all a matter of convention and is very different in different societies and it may well be that at the time when this term was applied to marriageable girls convention did not require a girl who had not attained puberty to cover herself. If that was so the term nagnikā would apply to such girls in either sense. Brihaspati in one of his txets (Text No. 329 in Gackwad's Oriental Series, p. 277) describes a ten year old girl as nagnikā and the texts seems to suggest that the word is used in its literal sense of "a naked girl."

Even those Grihyas however which prescribe that the bride should be a nagnikā, in either sense of the term would seem to be inconsistent in their prescription of rituals. Thus, for instance Gobhila, who, in one text of his Grihya Sutra prescribes that the girl should be a nagnikā, in working out the ritual of marriage prescribes, nevertheless, (1) that the marriage is to be consummated on the fourth night after marriage and (2) that if the girl should be in her monthly course then, consummation is to be deferred for three days thereafter. (II, 5, 7-8) Further, he goes on to lay down "Nājātlomnyām upahāsamichchet" forbidding intercourse with a girl who has not yet grown pubic hair.

These features are substantially repeated in all the Gṛhyas generally and they all contemplate consummation on the fourth day of marriage with mantras by which she is invoked to conceive.

Coming to later times the provision for marriage in childhood grows and parents are required to give girls in marriage before puberty. It is further laid down that if a girl should menstruate in her father's house the father would be burdened with sin. Another provision in the same strain is that if, after puberty a girl is still unmarried, her father or guardians lose their right to give her in marriage, and the girl would be entitled to choose her own husband (svayamvara E.g. Manu IX 90). These subsequent texts, some of them put the age of marriage absurdly low, as low, in fact, as eight years (Manu IX, 94).

Nevertheless Manu, who has texts authorising gift in marriage at those two ages, includes other texts, prescribing that a man should marry at the age of thirty a girl of twelve, an age when most Indian girls attain puberty and further that it is preferable that a girl should remain unmarried in her father's house till her death than be given to an undeserving husband. (IX, 89).

Attempts to reconcile such diversified texts into one single rule embracing all of them are bound to be futile except from an historical point of view. From that standpoint the only explanation that seems to be justified is that these various texts embody rules and usages which grew up in different social environments, at different times and probably in societies far apart from one another. And, at a later age, when the texts all rose to equal authority they were somewhat uncritically mixed up together.

The original rule seems to me to have been, as indicated above, postpubertal marriage. In course of time however customs of marriage at an earlier age grew up in some societies either for natural reasons, or possibly by absorption of non-Ārya usages. There might be natural reasons. Parents may have been prompted to give girls away in marriage at an early age to prevent grown up girls making undesirable marriages, or to prevent girls going astray or being seduced, or even perhaps that the parent might not be cheated of the price of a bride by her running away with a lover, in societies where bride price was or had become customary.[92]

Whatever the reasons, this development occurred quite early in the history of law. Early marriage was however never the universal law. The stories of several swayamvaras and of gāndharva marriages in the Mahābhārata and the Purānas as well as historical instances like that of Rajyasrī, sister of Harṣavardhana, indicate the continued existence of adult marriages.

One thing seems clear. These provisions of the laws apparently grew up in societies where the ownership of children by the father was firmly established and a girl had become more or less of a chattel to be given away or sold. This is not an idea which, in my view was prevalent in the Vedic society, but grew up in time, possibly under alien influence. (*See post*).

[92] Manu IX, 90–93 lays down that if a girl gives herself away in marriage by Svayamvara, as she may after waiting for three years after puberty, the father is not entitled to any Śulka while, on the other hand, the girl is not entitled to get anything from her father as marriage gift nor carry away anything from the father's house. See also Gautama XVIII who says that after three periods have passed the girl can take a proper husband herself after renouncing all ornaments given by the father.

CHAPTER V

MARITAL RELATIONSHIP.

STATUS OF WIVES

The position of the wife in the Vedas is an elevated one and corresponds in some measure to that of the mater-families of early Roman Law. She is mistress of the house. She gives offerings together with her husband before the house-fire and participates in all the affairs. At the same time she owes a duty of obedience to the husband and her husband protects her and maintains her in proper dignity. She is not a slave subject to the absolute dominion of her husband and any maltreatment by her husband seems to have been severely condemned. She is addressed by her husband at the marriage with respect and she is promised a voice in family affairs in the Vidatha or family council, if not the councils of the Kula.

This status of wives in ancient India however underwent a radical change some time after the early Vedic times. This was probably the result of the adoption of the forms of marriage by capture, sale etc. in which wives were treated more or less as chattels. The position in the family of women so acquired would be little better than that of slaves. From being the respected mother of the family, she thus descended to the position of a mere dependant, more or less like a slave. About this time we find the wife very often compared to cows and the children to the increase of cows for the purpose of determining the property in sons and for other similar purposes.

Concomitantly with this change of the status of the wife we find the husband exercising an amount of domination over the wife which is hardly to be distinguished from the domination he exercised over his cattle and there are indirect hints that numerous texts of laws still preserve which show that wives might be treated very much like cattle for producing offspring. One of the methods was for a sonless man to get a son begotten on his wife by another person not only after the death of her husband, but also while the husband was alive. Even in the texts of Āpastamba who forbids niyoga there are passages which indicate that a person might procure offspring on another's wife by agreement. With regard to paternity of the child as late as Nārada we find passages which most strongly indicate that a great deal of laxity in respect of chastity of wives prevailed during some period of the history.

NIYOGA AND KSETRAJA SONS

The institution of Niyoga was one which was foreign to the spirit of Vedic texts. This and the position of wives and widows with regard to their connection with other men may be conveniently discussed by reference to the position of the two out of the twelve kinds of sons referred to in the Smṛitis, — Kṣetraja and the Paunarbhaba.

The Kṣetraja son is described in later books as the son begotten on a widow by a husband's brother or sapiṇḍa, by special appointment, for the sole purpose of raising issue to the deceased husband. The act is accompanied by rigorous forms and all connection with the begetter is forbidden after one or two sons are born. The essence of this institution is that it is a temporary connection for the purpose of raising issue to the deceased.

By the side of this we find also the Paunarbhava son in these enumerations. Paunarbhava is the son of a Punarbhū — a woman who has had a husband before. Her son by a person other than that husband is a Paunarbhava of the begetter.

The distinction between the Kṣetraja and the Paunarbhava lies in this, that the latter is the son of a widow or married woman raised without appointment and that while Kṣetraja is the son of the widow's husband the Paunarbhava is the son of his begetter. This distinction we have to bear in mind in assessing the historical value of the texts.

Two texts of the Rigveda are referred to as evidence of the existence of Niyoga and consequently of Kṣetraja sons. One text which is also cited as authority for the custom of Sati is as follows:

> Imā nārīravidhavā supatni-ranjanena sarpiṣa saṃviśantu
> Anabhravo'namīvā sūratnaṃ ārohantu janayoyonimagre.
> Udīrṣva naṛyabhijīvalokaṃ gatāṣumetamupaśeṣamehi
> Hastagrābhasya didhiṣostavedam patyurjanitvamabhiyaṃ vabhurīyah.

A text which is more pertinent perhaps is the invocation to the Aśvins: (RV 10, 40, 2).

> Kuhasviddosā kuhavastoraśvinā kuhābhipitvaṃ kuru
> Kuhoṣatuh kovā śayutrā vidhaveva devaraṃ
> Maryaṃ na yoṣa krinute sarvastha ā.

The first two couplets of these has been requisitioned by very learned western scholars for the theories that they refer both to the practice of Suttee and to Niyoga upon what I conceive to be a misunderstanding of these texts. They are contained in the 18th Sūkta of the 10th Mandala which consists of verses in connection with the death of a person. It seems to me that the whole Sūkta is inspired by a fear lest death should come to those who are left behind. Death is charmed by this sukta to go by a path away from the worshipper and his offspring and long life is prayed for them and others as a charm for keeping the living out of the way of death. For this purpose everybody alive is asked to attend his duties of life and forsake the dead. Among others, the married women among the relations are asked by the first of these verses forthwith to decorate themselves with collyrium and otherwise go about their duties and to bear children to their husbands. The widow is likewise simply asked to leave her dead husband by whom she had had sons. To impute to this verse an implication that the widow was asked to espouse her devara or that she was preparing to mount the funeral pyre is absurd. It may be that this reading was inspired by the word didhīṣoh which is understood in the sense of the second husband while, as Sāyana correctly interprets it "hastagrābhasya didhisostavedam patyurjanitvam abhiyam vabhūryah" refers to the husband who had taken her hand (hastagrābha) and of whom she had been the jāyā, or bearer of offspring.

There is no reference in this text to the widow being on or near the funeral pyre, nor to the devara whom she is supposed to seek. The context in which these mantras are used in the Gṛihya sutras is that with the second souplet the widow is to be taken by the hand by her son or husband's pupil or devara or a servant of the house. (See Āśvalāyana Gṛhya IV ii, 1, 15). The mention of the son and the servant as uttering these mantras altogether negatives the seggestion that these mantras were understood at the time of the Gṛhya Sūtras to indicate levirate or niyoga, and there is certainly no evidence whatsoever that at any earlier time it was so understood.

The second text asks the Asvins where they had been staying by day and by night and what worshippers were attracting them as *the widow draws the devara to her bed or women attract men.*

None of these texts have reference to the custom of Niyoga as described above. There is no reference in this to the raising of offspring to the deceased, no talk of appointment. On the contrary, the words about widow drawing the devara are justaposed with *women in general* drawing men to their beds, which seem to refer merely to the animal attraction in either case. It is merely a recognition of the fact that in the society which the text depicts it was not a unfamiliar thing for widows to live with their husband's brother, but not necessarily as an approved institution in accordance with Ṛita.

The appearance of this text in the tenth mandals indicates its somewhat late date and its composition at a time when Vedic society had already had many contacts with non-Āryas. The infusion of non-Ārya usages in society was a fact and, it is possible that the association of a widow with her near kinsmen was one of the abuses which had obtained vogue, but was not necessarily recognised as valid marriage or niyoga at this stage of the society.

In the Book of Ruth we find an instance of such a custom among the Hebrews. In the Levirate recognised by the Code of Khammurabi we find yet another such instance. Examples like these in societies surrounding them might have been imitated by some of the Vedic Āryas, or survived among the converted Anāryas after Aryanisation.

A much more significant fact is that, as Manu emphasis in a later text (IX, 65) there is no ritual appropriate to Niyoga or Levirate in the Gṛihya sūtras. The Vedic Ārya had an appropriate ritual for every important act in life and it would be impossible not to have a ritual if this institution was a part of the original Vedic life. As observed before, custom crystallised in a magic ritual may generally be trusted to indicate a more ancient rule than that of any stray texts which have not entered into a ritual. In this case not only is any ritual for niyoga such as is indicated in later Smṛitis entirely absent in the Gṛihya rites, but we find the very text "udīrṣva nārī etc." used in the Gṛihyas for a very different ritual (Aśv. Gr. S). Later on, in Gautama Dharmasūtra and other Smritis when Niyoga is recognised, we find it reduced to a sort of ritual by some strict injunctions about the manner in which alone it could be carried out.

It is only in the Dharmasutras that we first come upon the institution of Niyoga and here we find a great diversity in the provisions of various texts.

Gautama (XXVIII, 21, 22) in dealing with inheritance says "Piṇḍagotrarṣi sambaddhāh Ṛiktham bhajeran strī vā anapatyasya, *vijām vā lipseta.*

The positive provision is that the inheritance to a sonless man goes to his agnates. Then two alternative opinions are indicated by the conjunction Vā. The wife may take the inheritance or she may seek to raise the seed (for her husband).

This clearly refers to the raising of offspring to the deceased by Niyoga. The rules about Niyoga are given in Ch. XVIII in the following terms :

Apatirapatyalipsuh guruprasūtā nartumatīyāt.
Piṇḍagotrarṣisambandhibhyo yonimātrādvā.
Nādeverādityeke nativitīyam.

The points to note in this text are: (1) The intercourse is solely for the purpose of raising issue to the sonless man and not more than two children should be begotten.

(2) The order of relations entitled to raise issue is laid down - sapiṇḍas, sagotras, samanārarṣas, and failing them, any Kinsman, though, "according to some", only the devara is eligible.

But the strange part of it is the provision regarding paternity of the child so begotten. These are:—

(1) the child belongs to the begetter.

(2) In the absence of a previous contract, or where the husband is alive it belongs to him or to both the begetter and the husband.

(3) Where the child is begotten by a stranger it belongs to him or to both but to the husband if he has brought him up.[93]

All this points to a confused state of the law. The *niyoga* of a widow by appointment for raising a kṣetraja son of the deceased is probably there but the paternity depends, not on the husbanding itself, but on agreement with the begetter. In addition a wild variety of cases in which children may be begotten on living peoples' wives is recognised.

Vasīṣtha Dharmasūtra (XVII, 56-57) prescribes similarly, with some rigid limitations, the procedure for raising offspring to the deceased by the widow, adding among others a significant limitation, "Ṛikthalobhānnāstiniyogah", (there can be no niyoga for greed of the heritage), a clause which has important bearing on the law of the widow's heirship.

But earlier in the same chapter he refers to a controversy about the paternity of a child, begotten on another's wife and quotas two texts

(1) Yadanya goṣu vatsān janayate sutān
Gominameva te vatsah mogham syanditamārṣabham
(If a bull labours on others' cows the calves belong to the owner of the cow, the efforts of the bull go in vain). And on the other hand,

(2) Apramattā rakṣantu vainām mā cha kṣetre paravījānivāpsuh
Janayituh putraṃ bhavati samparāye moghaṃ retah
Kuruta tantumetam.

"Protect (the woman) steadfastly and do not sow other's seeds on the field. The son belongs to the begetter in the other world".

93 Janayiturapatyam. Samayādanyatra jivatascha kṣetre parasmat tasya dvayorvā. Rakṣanadbhartureva.

Baudhāyana (Dh. II, 4, 9) gives the formula for niyoga, in significant words. The widow is permitted, after the permission of her Guru, to bear a son *to her devera* in case she has no son.

In II, 3, 17-18 however Baudhāyana prescribes for a Kṣetraja son of the deceased raised by another man and adds that such a son has two fathers and inherits to both. Yet again he quotes the opinion of Aupajanghani, an authority referred to in Brihadāranyaka and Śatapatha Brāhmana who is stated to have said that after death, in the next world, the son belongs to the begetter.

Āpastamba's text (II, 10, 27, 2-3) on the subject is illuminating in its historical implications. He refers to an opinion that a man's wife should not be given to any one except a sagotra, for the interesting reason that is it said that the bride is given to the family and not to the bridegroom alone. On the plea of weakness of the senses of men of his day however he absolutely forbids this practice of giving the wife to the members of the family for procreation of offspring.

Stopping with these authorities, it may be stated at once that these various provisions regarding Niyoga indicate that the institution was just making its way into Arya sacred law and had not yet been quite settled. Taken along with the fact that neither the Ṛigveda nor the Gṛihya sūtras know of any such institution, these texts make it probable that the view about kinsmen begetting offspring on a widow was a new innovation being slowly assimilated to the sacred law.

Some light may also be gathered from the fact that in the Mahābhārata where there are several instances of raising offspring by Niyoga in the Kuru dynasty, the first occasion when it occurs gives rise to a long discussion between Bhīsma and Satyavatī during which Bhīsma finds it necessary to justify by an elaborate argument his recommendation for Niyoga on the widows of Chitrāngada and Vichitravīrya.[94] This fact indicates that the custom was unfamiliar in Ārya society and needed justification by the high authority of Bhīsma just as Draupadī's marriage to five Pāṇdavas required elaborate argument by Vyāsa. Nārada like Pāṇḍu in the

[94] Mahabharata Adi Parva Ch. 103-104 The argument is based merely on precedents in the cases of *Jamadagnya, Utathya, Dīrghatamā* and *King Vali.*

So too Pandu in another passage seeks to justify to his wife the practice of Niyoga by an elaborate argument based on a tradition of utter laxity which was for the first time stopped by Śvetaketu. It is not without significance that the tradition of Śvetaketu referred to locates it in semi-mythical Uttara Kuru and, from Vātsyāyana we learn of the practice of polyandry in several trans-Himalayan countries—a custom which still survives among some of the tribes in the Himalayan region.

Mahābhārata refers to a few precedents e.g. Utathya and Dirghatama, two Rishis named in the Rigveda who are stated in the Mahābhārata and the Purāṇas as having begotten children on other peoples wives. But in the Rigveda (1. 147, 158) no such story about them is recorded.

NIYOGA ANL LEVIRATE

Āpastamba's text gives a pointer to the source of this law. The reason assigned for this institution is stated by him to be the fact that the bride is given to the family and not to the bridegroom alone.[95] This is an idea which is not only natural to a society in which brides are purchased for a price paid out of family property but is actually found among the races who buy their brides. The Hebrews had to pay a price for the bride, or like Jacob, to serve the bride's father in lieu of the price and the Book of Ruth shows that among them Levirate was the law. It is interesting also to note that the Book of Ruth indicates that there was an order of precedence among the kinsmen who are to have the wife of the deceased similar to that indicated by Gautama. In the code of Khammurabi also, Levirate is a recognised institution, and there also bride had to be procured by purchase. All this seems to indicate that Levirate is a natural concomitant of marriage by purchase.

Levirate in these laws means simply that the widow becomes the wife of the Levir. But the code of Khammurabi provides that where the deceased left no son, the first born child begotten by the Levir belongs to the deceased ; subsequent children of course became the children of the Levir.

It is not a conclusion too far fetched, to assume that among the races who lives in the Indus valley and beyond, there were people with cultural affinity to the Semitic races. Pūrānic tradition records an over-running of Ārya territory by foreigners — the Haihāyas who might have had similar customs. On this hypothesis it is reasonable to infer that the institution of Niyoga and the Kṣetraja son were developed as a result of the contact of Ārya civilisation with people of a culture allied to that of the Semitic race. Niyoga or some form of levirate must have been practised in fact in society before it made its way into the sacred law. The Vedic text cited above (Rigveda X, 40, 2) indicates the known existence of some such loose practice.

95 Apastamba was writing at a time and for a society in which Niyoga was condemned. The retention of indirect references to the law of Niyoga in this and one or two other passages only to repel it for his times indicates that before his time the practice had already come into vogue but had gone out of use.

The reaction of the sacred law however to this practice was diversified. In some places and by some authorities, as for instance, in the passages cited by Vaśiṣṭha and Baudhāyana the widow is simply given licence to live with the Devara without reference to any idea of raising offspring to the deceased husband. Other texts e.g. these of Gautama indicate a great deal of laxity in the matter. But the Vedic ideal of constancy and chastity, which we find embodied in the Vedic marriage mantras also, ultimately asserts itself against the growing practice, helped no doubt by changes in social environment about which we can only guess. The divergent views of the paternity of the child also indicates the different reactions of the sacred law upon the invading custom. The text of Aupajanghani, apparently the Vedic Ṛisi of that name, quoted by Baudhāyana and the other texts cited by Vaśiṣṭa and Āpastamba were requisitioned to protest against this practice which Āpastamba definitely forbids.

From the text of Baudhāyana it will seem that the widow was assumed to become a permanent mistress of the devara just as in the Book of Ruth or in the code of Khammurabi. A shade different is the other text in Baudhāyana which describes kṣetraja as a son raised by the widow to the deceased. That this was against tradition is indicated by the reference by Baudhāyana and Vaśiṣṭha and, of course, by Āpastamba to the older Sruti texts to the contrary. Gautama definitely gives paternity to the begetter and yet provides for the husband's paternity by agreement. In fact Gautama's texts go further and indicate a great laxity in the society for which he wrote, in the matter of exploiting the possibilities of women to bear sons to the fullest extent.

All this points to the fact that during the long period covered by these various works the sacred law was gradually digesting a growing custom based on non-Ārya usages, diversified in adaptation, of getting children by others. The ultimate synthesis arrived at is already contained in the Sutra texts like the one of Gautama of the recognition of a Kṣetraja son procreated for the sonless deceased under rigorous limitations against abuse, the adoption in fact of the levirate of the code of Khammurabi to the extent of raising issue to the dead and rejecting the continued cohabitation with the levir. This is the form in which we find the institution of Niyoga continued down to Manu's Code and later.

Later History of Niyoga

The further history of the institution was influenced by several factors. In Gautama's law we find the widow recognised as heir, possibly after the agnates; with a significant addition *vījaṁ vā lipseta*. On the contrary Baudhāyana gives the widow only a right to maintenance. Gautama evidently contemplates that if the widow succeeds in bearing a son by niyoga the inheritance goes to the kṣetraja son. The first step seems to have been to recognise the widow's right to keep the heritage — as a sort of hereditas jacens — so long as she was about raising a son. This evidently led to an abuse of the privilege, so much so, that we find Vaśiṣtha prescribing that there can be no niyoga for securing the heritage, in his anxiety to guard against the property getting into the hands of the widow.

One can imagine that this injunction proved futile and widows went on with niyoga which might conceivably go on for a pretty long time without the lady getting a male child. The society thus got used to the idea of a sonless widow continuing to enjoy the property for life. This may have helped to encourage an opinion expressly voiced by Kātyāyana much later, that the widow was half the body of the man, as she was said to be in the marriage mantras, and as such she was entitled to enjoy his property during her life. Anyhow we find that later law in Viṣṇu and Yājnavalkya recognised the widow's preferential right to inherit to a sonless man without any limitation. Once this was achieved, one of the incentives to the recognition of the practice of Niyoga, which was obnoxious to Vedic notions of chastity was gone and niyoga lost popularity.

Another factor which may have contributed to the gradual disuetude of niyoga was the possibility of getting substitute sons, not only to give solace to the sonless woman but also to fulfil all the religious purposes of the son. The first such substitute was apparently the brother's son about whom Baudhāyana says that where one brother gets a son, all the brothers become blessed with a son thereby. Further development followed as a result of the possibility of adoption which, as we shall see later, was obviously a later development.

As a result of these developments, assisted by the growing popular opinion against the obnoxious practice against which opinions had always been expressed, the practice fell into gradual disuse, until it was possible for the Āditya Púrāṇa to lay down that in the Kali age this practice along with others was no longer allowed. This text or at any rate the universal acceptance which its authority received at the hands of classical authors was the result of a great revival of orthodoxy which occurred sometime after the consolidation of Aryan culture all over India to which reference has already been made.

This tangled history of the institution of Niyoga in the course of its incursion into and the ultimate expulsion from Ārya law is reflected in the multitude of conflicting texts in the present text of Manusaṃhitā.

Manu on Niyoga

In dealing with Stripuṃdharma Manu first refers to the problem, also discussed by some of the Sūtra writers, of the paternity of the offspring of a woman begotten by a person other than the husband. This problem is disposed of by reference to the analogy of seed sown on other peoples' land.[96] The texts which follow immediately lead to no more decisive conclusion than this that wise men should not sow their seed on the wives of other people.[97] Next there follows a more positive statement that if a son is begotten on another's wife the son belongs to the husband of the woman.[98]

Having thus established the question in favour of the owner of the field Manu next proceeds to the question of begetting Kṣetraja offspring to the husband. In verses IX 57-58 it is stated to be a mortal sin for a woman and the man alike where the woman has carnal intercourse with her husband's elder or younger brother. This is immediately followed by texts laying down in some detail the process of Niyoga by intercourse with a devara or a sapiṇḍa solely for the purpose of begetting offspring for a sonless man, as a part of āpaddharma.[99]

96 Manu IX 32-33

भर्तुः पुत्रं विजानन्ति श्रुतिद्वैधं तु कर्तरि ।
आहुरुत्पादकं केचिदपरे क्षेत्रिणं विदुः ॥
क्षेत्रभूता स्मृता नारी बीजभूतः स्मृतः पुमान् ।
क्षेत्रबीजसमायोगात् सम्भवः सर्वदेहिनाम् ॥

97 Manu IX 41

98 Manu IX 48-55. One of the texts in this group is practically identical with a text apparently cited from a Sruti in Vasiṣtha and Baudhāyana.

99 IX 59-63

देवराद्वा सपिण्डाद्वा स्त्रिया सम्यङ्नियुक्तया ।
प्रजेप्सिताधिगन्तव्या सन्तानस्य परिक्षये ॥
विधवायां नियुक्तस्तु घृताक्तो वाग्यतो निशि ।
एकमुत्पादयेत् पुत्रं न द्वितीयं कथञ्चन ॥
द्वितीयमेके प्रजनं मन्यन्ते स्त्रीषु तद्विदः ।
अनिर्वृत्तं नियोगार्थं पश्यन्तो धर्मतस्तयोः ॥
विधवायां नियोगार्थे निर्वृत्ते तु यथाविधि ।
गुरुवच्च स्नुषावच्च वर्तेयातां परस्परम् ॥

This set of texts is however immediately followed by another set severely condemning Niyoga and absolutely forbidding its adoption by the twice born. It is stated that this practice was introduced by the sinful king Vena while he ruled the world.[100]

Then again a reconciliation is sought for texts enjoining Niyoga with these by providing that Niyoga is permissible only when the betrothed husband dies before marriage, when alone the betrothed maiden may have intercourse with her devara, not generally, but with these stringent limitations solely for the procreation of offspring, apparently to the deceased.[1]

In the texts condemning Niyoga above quoted a point is made by Manu which is thoroughly well founded in history. He says,

Nodvāhikeṣu mantreṣu niyogah kīrtyate kvachit
Na vivāhavidhāvuktam vidhavāvedanam punah.

"In the mantras relating to marriage niyoga is nowhere referred to. Nor is there any provision for marriage of a widow in the marriage ritual".[2]

This is quite correct and assuredly a cogent ground for holding that niyoga is altogether foreign to the idea of marital relations in Arya law. His reference to the institution having been promulgated by the bad king Vena when he ruled the world may also be regarded as a pointer to the historical fact pointed out above that the institution came from non-Ārya sources, if particularly, we are right

नियुक्तौ यौ विधिं हित्वा वर्तेयातां तु कामतः ।
ताबुभौ पतितौ स्यातां स्नुषाग गुरुतल्पगः ॥

[100] IX 64-68

नान्यस्मिन् विधवा नारी नियोक्तव्या द्विजातिभिः ।
अन्यस्मिन् हि नियुञ्जाना धर्मं हन्युः सनातनम् ॥
नोद्वाहिकेषु मन्त्रेषु नियोगः कीर्त्यते क्वचित् ।
न विवाहविधावुक्तं विधवा वेदनं पुनः ॥
अयं द्विजैर्हि विद्वद्भिः पशुधर्मो विगर्हित ।
मनुष्याणामपि प्रोक्तो वेने राज्यं प्रशासति ॥
स महीमखिलां भुञ्जन् राजर्षिप्रवरः पुरा ।
वर्णानां संकरं चक्रे कामोपहतचेतनः ॥
तदाप्रभृति यो मोहात् प्रमीतपतिकांस्त्रियम् ।
नियोजयन्त्यपत्यार्थे तं विगर्हन्ति साधवः ॥

[1] IX 69-70.
[2] IX 65

in supposing that King Vena of tradition was the same as the great Vrātya of the Paṇchavimsati Saṃhitā and apparently a powerful non-Ārya conqueror of Ārya land.

Further on, in dealing with the law of inheritance, the present compiler of Manu forgets the strong condemnation of Niyoga in the texts quoted above and quietly assumes that a Kṣetraja son properly procreated by Niyoga succeeds to his father and it is only provided that the son begotten by devara "without appointment" is a bastard. The son begotten by proper niyoga on the other hand inherits just like an aurasa son.[3]

Again, further on, he quietly defines a Kṣetraja son as a son begotten by lawful appointment on the wife not only of a dead man (pramīta) but also of a eunuch or of a person suffering from disease.[4] What is more remarkable is that in the texts which immediately precede this definition, the Kṣetraja son is not only given a position next only to the self-begotten son in inheritance, (IX, 165) but the co-existence of Aurasa and Kṣetraja sons is distinctly contemplated.[5]

Confusing as the juxtaposition of so many conflicting texts relating to Niyoga and Kṣetraja sons in Manu may appear they are illuminating as surviving texts in vogue at different stages of the history of the institution. And they bear out the propositions which I have attempted to establish before, (1) that niyoga was entirely foreign to the original Ārya law, (2) that it entered into Ārya law by adoption by Aryans or by survival among Aryanised non-Aryans of customs prevalent among non-Arya races, (3) that the reactions of the Ārya law to this intrusion were various in various societies and (4) lastly when by a great social revolution society reverted to the ancient Ārya ideals of constancy and chastity the institution went out of use. But it is quite clear that the expulsion of Niyoga was neither consistent nor universal before the classical age of the commentaries. For even in the late works of Nārada, Bṛihaspati and Kātyāyana the institution is described with all the fulness of detail of a living law.

PAUNARBHAVA

It has been pointed out before that the cohabitation of widows with devaras seems to have been established as a fact before it received legal recognition. There was no marriage saṃskara and

[3] IX 143-147
[4] IX, 167
[5] IX 163-164

therefore in early law where saṃskara alone was a justum matrimonium, a widow thus cohabiting could not aspire to the position of a patnī.

Sons of such widows would be Paunarbhavas. Vasiṣṭha's text[6] makes no distinction between the two kinds of Punarbhū and their sons, though one union is adulterous while in the other she has justification, for she is spoken of as marrying (vindate) another husband (Pati). This text indicates that in the second class there is some sort of irregular marriage though not a *justum matrimonium* with a saṃskāra which alone could lead to the status of Patnī.

On the other hand the later text of Yājñavalkya treats the first class of Vaśiṣṭha's punarbhūs as *svairinīs* and limits the term punarbhū to a widow who has gone through a marriage *saṃskāra* with another man.[7] Midway between these two lies the text of Viṣṇu which describes a punarbhū as one who *being akshatā* (i.e. not having attained puberty) has been *saṃskritā* i.e. married with saṃskāra again, and distinguishes those who have not had a second *saṃskāra* as *para-purvā*, while Yājñavalkya's text expressly gives the right to a second saṃskara irrespective of her having attained puberty or not. There are several other texts of Nārada and others which make subtle distinctions between various kinds of *punarbhūs* and *svairinīs* which do not seem to be of any historical importance. (See SBE Vol. XXXIII pages 174 seq.)

What indications about the evolution of the status of the punarbhū do these texts give? To my mind they throw considerable light on the history of the widow's status.

Remarriage of Widows

To start with, we find that in the Vedas there is no remarriage of widows. The Gṛihya sūtras do not give any formula for the

[6] Vasiṣṭha Ch. XVII

पुनर्भूः या कौमारं भर्तारमुत्सृज्यान्यः सह चरित्वा तस्यैव कुटुम्बमाश्रयति सा पुनर्भूर्भवति। या च क्लीबं पतितमुन्मत्तं भर्तारमुत्सृज्यान्यं पतिं विन्दते सा पुनर्भूर्भवति।

"Paunarbhava is the fourth (kind of son). She who renounces the husband of her maidenhood, and associates with another and takes shelter with his kinsmen becomes a Punarbhu. She who, renounces an impotent, fallen or lunatic husband or upon the husband's death weds (vindate) another becomes Punarbhū.

[7] Yajn. I, 67: अक्षता च क्षता चैव पुनर्भूः संस्कृता पुनः।
स्वैरिणी या पतिं हित्वा सवर्णं कामतः श्रयेत्॥

marriage of widows, a point which Manu emphasises in condemnation of niyoga (na vivahavidhāvuktam vidhavā vedanam puṇah). But we find that at one stage the cohabitation of a barren widow wih her devara is tolerated. Baudhāyana (SBE XIV page 227) lays down like Vaśiṣṭha that both the husband and the begetter are the fathers of the child so begotten.[8]

The next stage is marked by Viṣṇu who sanctions a saṃskāra of a widow who is still under puberty. Yājñavalkya also grants a saṃskāra to a remarrying widow expressly without the limitation imposed by Viṣṇu. Nārada's texts are even more explicit and indicate that even widows who were mothers could wed. (Ch XII, 96—100 SBE Vol. XXXIII, p. 184 seq.[9]

It is not without historical significance that no text except the texts of Viṣṇu and Yajñavalkya mention the saṃskāra of marriage in connection with wedding of widows and women of incompetent or deserting husbands. This as has already been mentioned was inconceivable in early law as embodied in the Grihya Sūtra which contemplate a saṃskāra only with a Kanyā (virgin). Later law as it survives in Nārada or Parāśara gives a wide license to wives in particular circumstances, and, in Nārada, makes it her duty to consert with kinsmen. But they say nothing of saṃskāra.

It would seem therefore that the re-saṃskāra of widows and other women never became universal, nor was it an institution which persisted long in such communities as recognised it. And it is clear that in later law a clean sweep was made of all texts that dealt with saṃskāra of widows when very rigid standard of chastity of women was reimposed. It would be quite natural to expect therefore that there should be no extant texts giving special rules with regard to saṃskāra of widows.

It would however be wrong to suppose as Sir Gooroodas Banerjee[10] seems to think, that there were virtually no rules whatsoever, so much so that, for all that the texts lay down, a man might wed his widowed mother-in-law. It is obvious that when saṃskāra was recognised, the whole law relating to the Saṃskāra was attracted to the marriage of widows, including the rules regarding the gift of bride, (except where a maiden too would have the right of svayaṃ vara), the rituals from pāṇigrahana to the saptapadi, as well as rules about prohibited degrees which would apply. Special provi-

[8] Gautama's texts cited before lay down the same rule.

[9] Narāda however does not refer, like Viṣṇu or Yājñavalkya to Saṁskāra of the women.

[10] In his Marriage and Stridhana

sions about widows regarding these things, if any existed, have been obliterated with the disapprobation and disuetude of the institution.

To complete this story it must be added that with the revival of orthodoxy before the classical jurists the Ādityapurāṇa text eliminates the pauṇarbhava with other secondary sons and the texts of Manu in the latest stratum refuses to recognise the possibility of marriage of widows. The commentators are unanimous in proscribing widow remarriage.

Fortunes of Paunarbhava

The fortunes of the Pauṇarbhava son are bound up with these of his mother. When the mother's status was dubious and not that of a wife, he was merely a son born in the family and as such relegated to the position of an Adāyāda. When the mother was deemed to be a weded wife though not a Patnī he rose to higher dignity as a legitimate son, though not so good as one born of a regular wife, but when the validity of widow marriage ceased to be recognised as in the text of Manu, he was relegated again to the low position of other illegitimate sons born in the family.

In broad outline, there can be little doubt that the texts lend countenance to the above story of the evolution ; but it must be confessed that it is not possible to correlate all the evidence so as to prove the theory to the hilt. The place given to the Pauṇarbhava son by Gautama, Baudhāyana and Manu for instance accords completely with their views about the status of punarbhū, as also that given by Viṣṇu, Yajñavalkya and Nārada. But Vaśiṣṭha gives the fourth place to Pauṇarbhava, though his definition of Puṇarbhū does not seem to accord with this view. It must be remembered however that the sutra writers were not thoroughly consistent or logical in working out their opinion. This followed because the entire body of sūtras were not the work of a single author. In the main they embodied the traditional lore in the Vidyāvaṃśa with only occasional amendments by a later compiler to bring the work into line with contemporary usage. It is quite possible that Vaśiṣṭha was recording merely a traditional definition of Puṇarbhū without making a distinction between an adulteress and the other sort while he was also recording an established practice founded on the recognition of a valid widow marriage, though not sanctified by a saṃskāra, of a puṇarbhū of the second class. It will be recalled that by the time of the Dharmasūtras, forms of marriage not accompanied by saṃskāra such as Āsura, Rākṣasa etc. had already acquired legal validity.

The entire development of the law in this as in other matters was not essentially logical. It was conditioned by social usage in the various communities, most probably influenced by practices of non-Āryas as much as by presence of indegenous social and economic necessities requiring plenty of male children. The hankering for sons evidenced by Vedic hymns is evidence of the great social need of sons. The necessity continued and probably increased in later days and in different societies and the law had to adapt itself to the social usages based for the need for man power.

CHAPTER VI.

MARITAL RELATIONS (CONTD).

We have seen that the original form a marriage of Āryas which gave to the wife the status of gṛihapatnī was the one which is founded on the texts of the Ṛigveda, the Atharvaveda and the Mantras derived from them which are enshrined in the various Gṛihyasūtras. There are two most outstanding features of this marriage according to this Vedic ritual which are to be carefully noted. The first feature of this marriage is a spiritual union of the husband and the wife, corresponding to the consortium omnium vitae of Rome a process by which the husband and wife become one, and the second feature which is strongly emphasised is the desire for offspring.

It will be seen later that amongst the ancient Aryans while relationship proceeded along agnatic lines, there was always a tendency to spiritualise that relationship. Father and son were spiritually one as indicated by the Vedic mantra which says, "You are myself bearing the name of son" (ātmāvai putranāmāsi) and the son fulfils important spiritual functions for the father. So too husband and wife are spiritually one and they are unified by the magic of the mantras of marriage. The relationship of sapiṇḍas and sagotras, though founded on a common origin through males, is made a spiritual relationship and, where cognates are introduced into the scheme of kinship, they come by virtue of their giving spiritual benefit.

Fruitfulness

Equally prominent is the anxiety about progeny. The marriage ritual, for instance, Āśvalayana, Gṛihyasutra contains in several stages prayers for offspring by uttering Vedic mantras, taken from the Ṛigveda.

One of the opening mantras by which the unity of the husband and wife is symbolised is

Amo'hamasmi sā tvaṃ sā tvamasya mohaṃ Dyauraham prithivī tvam. Sāmāhaṃ Ṛik tvam. Tāveha vivahāvahai. Prajāṃ prajanayāvahai. Saṃpriyo rochiṣnu sumanasya mānau jīveva śaradah śatam.

(Āśvalāyana Gṛihya V, 5 Travancore Ed. p: 24).

Then again when the wife is brought into the husband's house, the mantra uttered is "Iha priyaṃ prajayā te samṛidhyatam" and the next mantra which is uttered after sitting on red bull's hide is "Ā nah prajaṃ janayatu etc." and so on. (Āsvalāyana Gṛihya VI, 9; Travancore Ed. by Ganapati Sāśtri, p. 31).

Fidelity

The mantras in the Ṛigveda and in the Gṛihyasūtras also emphasise the duty of steadfastness and fidelity of the wife. This is symbolised by the wife being made to tread on a piece of stone with a mantra signifying that she should be fixed as a stone in the house[1], and she is asked while taking the seven steps to follow the *Vrata* of the husband (māmanuvratā bhava.[2] She is taken to see the stars, notably the pole star and Arundhatī as symbols of steadfastness and chastity. (Āśvalāyana Gṛihya Travancore Ed. p. 29).

Correspondingly the wife is invited to take her honoured place in the house as ruling the household and assisting in the council of the family by speaking to them. There is a close analogy in all these, both in the rituals and in the basic concept between the Vedic marriage and the Confarreatio of Rome.

Changed view of relations

As we come to a later age we find that the fundamental concept of the marriage has been considerably changed. The duty of obedience of the wife is changed into a subordination verging on slavery, so much so that the wife could, at the direction of the husband, or her relations after the husband's death be sent to others for procreation. Her status is emphasised as very nearly like that of cattle, the receptacle to hold the progeny of the husband and hardly anything more. While the old idea of chastity and fidelity of the Vedic Mantra waned, the element of authority considerably increased and wives in the late texts were little better than handmaidens or female slaves, as indicated, for instance, in some of the Slokas of Manusaṃhitā.

Now, how did this great change come about and what were the reasons? It is impossible to say with any approach to certainty, because, as we have seen, of the enormous gaps in the historic records and we have only fragments of the long story strewn about in isolated texts.

[1] Asv. Gr. Travancore Ed. p. 25 इम मश्मानमारोहाश्मानमिव त्वं स्थिराभव ।

[2] Asv. Gr. T. VI, 20 Travancore Ed. p. 28

How change developed

It seems reasonable however to infer that the degradation of the wife from the position of the honoured mater-familias dominating the household to that of servitude was the result of the introduction of the inferior forms of marriage founded upon the analogy of acquisition of ownership over the women. The woman who was captured or bought or, perhaps, who chose to elope would not be the woman whom the husband would look upon with the same respect as a woman who was looked upon as a gift of the gods acquired by the magic of marriage rituals. This inference is strengthened when we find it expressly stated as early as in the Baudhāyana's Gṛihya-sūtras that a woman who has been purchased for value is not a patni. She is not eligible for *pitrya* or *daiva* purposes, she is a *dāsī* i.e. a slave. That was the attitude of Ārya society towards the wives who were procured by purchase and it could not have been otherwise in respect of wives who had been acquired by force or even by run-away marriage. It would seem, as indicated before, that the religious form of marriage went, in course of time, at one of the stages indicated by Manu, into considerable disuetude and was practically confined to only Brāhmanas and was not even resorted to by all of them. Naturally, therefore, the society in which, as depicted in the texts of Baudhāyana above referred to, wives were mostly girls who had been procured, not by gift of Agni, but by the forms of capture, purchase[1] etc. which were merely forms of acquisition of property, these wives were looked upon as chattels. That is how the *kanyāpradāna* ceremony which was not a part of the earliest grihyas and for which there is no specially appropriate mantra in the Vedic ritual became a very important part of the ritual of marriage, as we find in Āśvalāyana Gṛihyapariśiṣṭa. The new concept of women as chattels to be given away or sold or carried off and naturally therefore more or less in the nature of a slave in the husband's house was not a concept familiar to the early Ārya. It was one which crept into the sacred law in the ways in which the other non-Ārya concepts crept into it by absorption from non-Aryan practice or by survival amongst Aryanised non-Āryas and this altered status of the wife corresponded to the change in the form of acquisition of women.

Roman parallel

These conclusions are, in my view, strengthened by the parallel in the case of ancient Rome. In the prejural state of Roman

[1] Baudhāyana Dh. S. II, 1, 20-22.

society preserved in her Fas, the only valid form of marriage recognised was Confarreatio, the religious marriage. Even in the later law that was at first the only justum matrimonium which created a *consortium omnium vitae* symbolised by the ceremony of sharing the same piece of bread during the ritual. It gave to the wife the status of a mater-familias who had great dignity and authority though she was *in manu* of her husband. Later on, on the adoption of usages current in Plebian society, other modes of acquiring Manus, in the same manner as any property could be acquired, the wives so acquired only got the status of *uxor in Manu* whose only link with her husband, was subjugation to the authority of the husband until coemtio and usus were later raised to the dignity of a justum matrimonium. Over these women the husband exercised the fullest authority as master and owner. As indicated above, the texts of early law indicate that in ancient India the evolution of this law followed a similar course.

We can trace some intermediate stages in the evolution of the law. In the early Dharmasūtras we have seen that the form of niyoga as ultimately developed was a strictly ritual institution limited exclusively to the procreation of the issue of the deceased. That is a ritual which we find in the later Dharmasūtras and also in Manu, Yajñavalkya and others. But in the earlier Dharmasūtras, as we have seen, the association of wives or widows with kinsmen and others was not limited to the purpose of raising issue to the deceased. In Gautama we find that the paternity of the child depended upon the contract between the husband and the procreator and in the case of *maidens* between father and the procreator. In other words, we find, there was a wide prevalence of extremely lax practices in the relation of men and women, when the institution borrowed from alien races had made their entrance into sacred law. The reaction of sacred law to this was gradually to restrict the operation of these laws within the narrowest limits until ultimately Manu in his latest texts condemned the institution altogether and it had apparently gone out of use.

With regard to the widows, the history of puṇarbhū which has been indicated above also shows that the ancient Vedic concept did not recognise the valid marriage of widows and Manu is perfectly right in the remark, made in the latest stratum of his texts on the subject, that in the ritual of marriage there is no provision for widow re-marriage. But we find that firstly, concubinage with a Punarbhū is recognised as almost a legitimate union. Then again we find such unions are placed under restraint by classifying different classes of

Punarbhūs and Svairinīs until ultimately, in the texts of Viṣṇu, Yājñavalkya and Narada, the use of the term 'Punarbhū' was confined to women who were remarried by *saṃskār*. By the recognition of the saṃskāra marriage with a widow the sacred law put a check upon the lax practices which had prevailed in the society in the earlier Dharmasūtras and the result was that even in the case of widows a marriage Saṃskāra was the only way in which she might have legitimate union with other men.

When we come to still later law we find there is a revulsion of feeling both against the lax practice of niyoga possibly assisted by the abuse of the institution for the purpose of getting the inheritance as indicated by Vasiṣṭha and against the lax relations with widows, until ultimately not only niyoga but also widow remarriage came to be forbidden in the classical period. This was the result of a definite movement towards the restoration of the pristine purity of the ancient Ārya idea and from that time on we find that chastity of women is once again prized as a prime virtue and the union of marriage is looked upon as a union in this life and hereafter. Here again we are faced with a question. What was the reason or the course of development of this new revulsion of feeling against lax practices? This was, to my mind, the result of a great revolution which happened at some time between the earliest Dharmasūtras and the latest Smṛitis and probably coincided with a restoration of society under the authority of orthodoxy after great inroads had been made into the society by alien and heretic sects spreading over the continent. I do not mean the Bauddhas or the Jainas alone, but a number of other communities e.g. non-Āryas, like the Śakas and the Hūnas who spread all over the country and invaded the structure of ancient Vedic society.

Notwithstanding the reversion of society in the classical age to the ancient ideals of society as laid down in the Vedas, however, wives do not seem to have immediately recovered the status which was assigned to them in the Vedic ritual of marriage. They continued to remain in abject subordination.

The abject subjugation of women which was developed in post-Vedic society still continued and was repeatedly emphasised in later Smṛitis and other literature.

Later Developments

In Vedic times, as already pointed out, there are texts which indicate a duty of respect and obedience to the husband as a cardinal obligation. She is to be anuvratā of her husband which literally means that she should follow and maintain the same vrata or duty as her husband. This is emphasised in texts like that of Baudhāyana Gṛihya sūtra which says that she is not independent in the matter of dharma (asvatantrā dharme strī). So too Vaśiṣtha in his Dharma-sūtra says—Asvátantrā dharme strī puruṣa pradhanā nātichraet bhartāram. (The wife is not independent in dharma but is subordinate to man and she must not cross her husband.)

A text of Maitrāyaniya Saṃhitā is often quoted for different purposes. "Atah striyah nirindriyāh adāyadāh", women are without senses and are not heirs. A variant of adāyāda of this text mentioned by Jolly is "amantrakah" signifying that women cannot utter Vedic mantras.[14] Though the quotation as given by Manu confirms this version, ancient scholars were apparently not averse to being somewhat free with Vedic texts to suit their own purposes. In any case, too much importance cannot be given to this stray passage. The whole scheme of the Vedas and the Gṛihya ritual is that the wife was to co-operate with her husband in all religious duties. We find in the Rigvedic text on marriage several mantras uttered by the bride herself. In several Gṛihyasūtras it is the bride herself who utters these mantras, while in others, either the husband or the priest recites them with the prefatory words *Iyam nāri brute,* (This woman says), evidently because the young bride was too modest to speak out. Besides, the daily Gṛihya yajñas had to be performed, with Vedic mantras, by the wife herself when the husband was away. When the husband was present she acted silently while the husband uttered the mantras.

It is clear therefore, even apart from traditional stories in Vedic literature, that women had a right to utter Vedic mantras which was denied to her in later times. Her husband, she only followed out of her duty of respect: She was subordinate to the husband, but not overwhelmed by his domination.

Subjugation of Women

The duty of respect is transformed in later law to abject subjugation. She is regarded as being wholly subject to every whim and caprice of her husband, she could be lent to others for giving birth to offspring. Purānic stories also relate instances in which she is given away or sold by her husband. In the Mahābhārata we find Yudhiṣṭhira pledging away Draupadī as a stake in a game of dice. When a dispute about his right is raised by Draupadī it only

[14] Manu IX, 78 quotes this as निरिन्द्रियाः अमन्त्रकाः

turns upon the question whether, having given himself away in bondage before, Yudhiṣṭhira was still competent to exercise his otherwise unquestioned right to pawn away his wife.

Of a piece with this status of abject subservience to the husband is the text which denies her, along with slaves, any right to property as in the text of Manu which might as well have been taken out of the Twelve Tables which says,

> Bhāryā putraścha dāsaścha traya evādhanāh smṛitāh
> Yat te samadhigachchhanti yasya te tasya taddhanam.
>
> VIII. 416.

That this was not the law of the Vedas is recognised by commentators, and even Manu in common with other Smṛiti writers, elsewhere recognises her rights of property in stṛidhana.

An outstanding example of her better proprietory rights in Vedic literature is the story in Brihadāraṇyaka of Yājñavalkya dividing his wealth between his two wives, as Manu divided his wealth among his sons in the Taittīriya text.

It is possible that during the darkest days of women when they were treated as chattels, they had, as a rule fallen into great depths of degradation themselves. In any case, many a lawgiver has spoken with utmost contempt about women as absolutely unfaithful and always prone to go wrong. Her duty of obedience to her husband is travestied in these texts in provisions about her perpetual tutelage and the imperative need to keep her under watch and protection, not out of respect or tenderness to her, but because she was always likely to go wrong. (See Manu IX, 14-17).

With a reversion of society to Vedic ideals the women got a part of their own back and were not only restored to many of her old rights but in fact gradually given enlarged rights in respect of property as we shall see later. At this period the Smṛiti authors are found speaking with two voices about women, one reflecting the high regard for womanhood based on respect for the mother and the wife in Vedic literature, and the other based on the supreme contempt of womanhood which seems to have flourished in later days.

I have said before how Manusaṃhitā, as we now find it, often records texts in juxtaposition with one another which belong to different ages of society. This is notably illustrated in its texts about women in which the two discordant voices speak at the same time. Thus in III, 55 et seq. we find Manu saying that woman is to be honoured and adorned by her husband, his brothers, her parents and brothers and that the gods live where women are honoured ; that where women weep the house goes to ruin and so on. On the other hand in IX, 14 et seq. the code says that women are by nature corrupt, they do not care for the beauty or age of the man but are attracted by man as such, they are men-hungry, fickle, loveless and even if well protected by husbands, they betray them and so forth. For these reasons, it is laid down, women should be kept under strict control and surveillance. In the same breath however the text goes on to say (IX. 12) that that woman is well protected who protects herself.

Both these sets of texts can be matched by other texts of other authors. The fact seems to be that at the stage marked by these texts the society was affected more or less by two conflicting ideals, one derived from the old Vedic concept of the dignity of womanhood and the other which grew up under the influence of forces which reduced woman to a position of mere slave and child bearer, assisted perhaps by a growing laxity in their morals promoted by that idea. The idea of complete subjugation of women had however come to stay and became a lasting characteristic of the social status of women for a very long time. Yet, as we shall presently see, her proprietory rights were gradually improved.

WOMEN'S RIGHTS TO PROPERTY

Vedic literature has very little to say about the proprietory rights of wives. That she was not incapable of acquiring property is however clear, if from nothing else, from the tradition in the Upaniṣads of Yājñavalkya dividing his wealth between his two wives. Her property however was naturally small. The older texts lay down that her ornaments and the paribhānda or domestic utensils are her own property which must not be divided by her sons after her husband's death (paribhāṇḍam grihe'lamkaro bhāryāyah).

Even before this in the wedding hymn of the Ṛigveda (X, 85, 13 and 38) and in Taittiriya Saṃhitā (VI, 2, 1, 1) we find a reference to pārināhya which are gifts to the bride by the father at her wedding, which according to Taittiriya Saṃhitā is her own property.

There are no texts of the Vedic literature which lay down what properties could belong to women. The tradition of Yājñavalkya however indicates that she could acquire other property on partition by her husband. And the story of Gārgi Vāchaknavi practically competing for the prize of cows given by Janaka indicates that there could be no bar to her acquiring wealth in other ways, at any rate according to the society of White Yajurvedis.

In later Smṛti literature however we find on the one hand, an extension of the kinds of property which she could own, and on the other a stringent rule barring her ownership altogether.

The latter rule is to be found in the text of Manu. "Bhāryā putraścha dāsaścha traya ebādhanāh smṛitah, Yatte samadhigachchhanti yasya te tasya taddhanam." This rule, however, had already become arachaic in Manu's days for, he himself provides for various kinds of stridhana (women's property) which the husband cannot take. Jaimini in VI, 1, 12—14 quotes a variant of this text saying "Bhāryā dāsascha putrascha nirdhanah eva te", but Śabara in his commentary says that incapacity for ownership is not admissible, being opposed to Śruti.

On the other hand we find several enumerations of stṛidhana or women's property in numerous Smṛitis. Thus Viṣṇu in (XVII, 18) enumerates the following as stridhana.

1. Gifts by (*a*) father, (*b*) mother, (*c*) son, (*d*) brother.
2. Adhyagni, *i.e.* gifts before the nuptial fire.
3. Upāgata, *i.e.* what is subsequently acquired.
4. Gift by husband on his second marriage (Ādhivedanika).
5. Gift by bandhus.
6. Śulka or the bride price.
7. Anvādheyaka, *i.e.* gifts after marriage.

In Sutra 22 Viṣṇu makes a special provision for ornaments worn by a woman during her husband's life time which are not to be taken by the heirs of the husband on pain of pātitya.

Manu (IX 194) gives a similar though not identical enumeration but like Viṣṇu he mentions that the kinds of stridhana are *six*, namely,

1. Adhyagni.
2. Adhyāvāhanika.
3. Prītidatta.
4. Gifts by brother.
5. Gifts by mother and
6. Gifts by father.

But in the verses which follow he distinguishes between other kinds of properties of women for the purposes of inheritance.

In these texts are mentioned

(1) Anvādheya or gifts by husband after marriage.
(2) Pitridatta.
(3) Ornaments worn by her during her husband's lifetime.

Thus, though Manu gives six as the number for kinds of stridhana in fact he enumerates a larger number.

Nārada like Manu speaks of only six kinds of Stridhana and enumerates them as follows :—

1. Adhyagni.
2. Adhyāvāhanika.
3. Bhartṛidāya.
4. Bhrātṛidatta.
5. Pitṛidatta.
6. Mātṛidatta.

Bhartṛidāya which would normally mean inheritance from husband is explained by Jimūtavāhana as meaning gift by husband, to make this consistent with his view of stridhana.

Yājñavalkya (II 143) enumerates the following kinds of stridhana.

1. Gifts by (*a*) father, (*b*) mother, (*c*) husband, (*d*) brother.
2. Adyagni—*i.e.* gift before the nuptial fire.
3. Upāgata.
4. Ādhivedanika, gift at the time of the husband taking another wife.

To these he adds an etcetera (*Ādyah*) implying other kinds of stridhanas, and in the next verse he adds

5. Bandhudatta.
6. Śulka and
7. Anvādheyaka.

Kātyāyana in a text enumerates and gives precise definition of different kinds of strīdhana in which he adds the following classes :

1. Adhyāvāhanika, *i.e.* presents to the bride when she is carried to her husband's home.
2. Prītidatta including (*a*) Pādavandanika given to her when she makes her obeisance to the mother-in-law, (*b*) affectionate gift by father-in-law.
3. Saudāyika including whatever is obtained by her before or after marriage, while in her father's house or her husband's, from brother or from parents.
4. Whatever is obtained by a woman by her industry (śilpa).

Two texts of Devals and Vyāsa cited by Jimūtavāhana in his Dāyabhāga are important. Devala's text which seems to be older than the other says

Vṛittirābharanam Śulkam
lābhancha strīdhanam bhavet
Bhoktrī tat svayamevedam
patirnārhatyanāpadi.

Earnings, ornaments, śulka (bride's price) and lābha (profit) are strīdhana which she is to enjoy herself and her husband cannot have it except in distress.

Vyasa's text is significant in specifying as the bride's strīdhana all property which is given to the bridegroom at the wedding:

"Vivāhakāle Yatkimchit varāyoddisya dīyate.
Kanyāyastaddhanam Sarvam Avibhājyancha bandhubhih."

Probable Evolution of Stridhana

On a resume of these texts we find that the meagre references in Vedic literature only indicate a few kinds of properties of women consisting of ornaments paribhānda, and gifts at the time of wedding.

In the dharmaśāstras the number of things which a woman is stated to claim as her property has grown. At one stage they were limited to six classes as indicated by Manu, but the number is soon found to increase and Yājñavalkya refuses to make the list exhaustive by adding an etcetera.

Commenting on the use of this particle (Ādyah) Vijñāneśvara lays down that this indicates all other modes of acquisition of property common to men and women alike such as inheritance purchase, partition etc., and adds that strīdhana has no technical meaning, but means whatever property is owned by a woman.

As a matter of history it seems that Vijñāneśvara was quite right in holding that the word strīdhana when used in the Smritis bears a literal and no technical meaning.

Incidentally, it is worthy of note that while most Smṛiti texts give the wife a right to a share of her husband's property upon partition by sons, such property has not found place in any of the enumerations. Nor, of course have other properties acquired by women by purchase or otherwise been mentioned. But if we take the enumerations against the background of the obviously earlier text that women could hold no property (Manu, VIII 416) it means that these properties were gradually introduced as exceptions to the general incapacity of women for ownership. Viewed in this light, they indicate growing concessions of property rights to women in the same manner as Roman law conceded to women rights to Peculium.

It is not possible to place these various kinds of women's properties in a strict order of evolution, as there is obviously a great gap in the sequence of authoritative texts between the Vedic texts and Manu and others. In these latter we find the penultimate stage of the development of the law including many items while in the former we find only the rudimentary stage of the law of women's property. The texts of Devala and Vyāsa quoted above only show two isolated steps in the development in the interval. There must have been a great many steps by which the early categories of properties grew to their present number to which we get no clue.

Some inferences of a general nature may however be hazarded. Domestic utensils and ornaments were women's properties from the earliest times. Possibly also wedding gifts before the nuptial fire, as indicated by the recognition of Pārināhya, were among the earlier kinds of property recognised. By an extension of this rule property was also recognised in adhyāvāhanika and by gradual further extensions gifts made on other occasions by the various relations were gradually included.

A great extension was given to women's rights of property when Devala included the bride's price (Śulka) and profits (lābha) as women's property. We can guess the reason why in some places śulka which was originally a price paid to the bride's father for procuring the bride became the bride's perquisite. We have seen before that though Āsura marriage was grudgingly recognised, the selling of girls came to be regarded with great aversion and there is a continuous stream of texts condemning the act in unmeasured terms. It is possible that societies in which Āsura marriage prevailed may in some cases have reacted to this approbrium by paying over the śulka to the bride. Thus the śulka may have come to be regarded as the bride's portion in the same way that Mahr became the bride's property in Semitic societies. A further extension is indicated by Vyāsa's text by which gifts to the bridegroom at the marriage likewise became the wife's stridhana. Nārada adds to the list Bhartridāya by which, he undoubtedly indicates the inheritance from the husband, notwithstanding Jimutavāhana's contrary interpretation.

It will appear later, that for most of the time, when these various kinds of women's property were growing the woman did not inherit to her husband at all. Her right to inherit is not recognised by Vaśiṣṭha, Baudhāyana, and even by Manu, Nārada or Bṛhaspati. It was recogised fully only by Viṣṇu, Yājñavalkya and Kātyāyana. It is reasonable to hold therefore that when the earlier texts were enumerating kinds of Strīdhana they contemplated that these alone were properties which a woman could own and no others.

In this connection it is worthy of note that there is a text of Vyāsa (quoted in Dayābhaga page 112) which says -

> Dvisahasraparo dāyah striya deyah dhanasya tu.
> Yachcha bhartrā dānam dattam sa yathākāmam asniyāt.

which indicates a stage at which women's inheritance and possibly also gift by husband to wife were limited only to two thousand niṣkas and no more. Women's property therefore in these texts enumerating stridhanas meant all the properties which a woman could have.

At a later stage when women's rights of property were extended to other properties and when she was recognised as an heir to a sonless husband, Yājñvalkya's text recognised these facts by adding the particle ādyah (etcetera).

Jimutavāhana agrees with Vijñānesvara that strīdhana bears no technical meaning and also that the number six given by the texts of Manu and Yājñavalkya is not restrictive, so that enumerations must be understood to be illustrative only. He would limit the word however only to property over which the woman has absolute powers of disposal, consistently with his view that a wife's right to husband's property obtained by inheritance is limited to enjoyment for life only, without power to alienate or waste. There is no historical justification for this view. When the texts enumerate stridhana they mean that it is hers to deal with as she chooses. Vyāsa's text expressly says so (Sā yathākāmamaśniyat) though he places a pecuniary limit to the woman's property. The other texts can only be properly understood to imply such right. That does not mean that the word stridhana in those texts has the restricted meaning given by Jimūtavāhana. They did not, most of them, contemplate women having any other kinds of property and consequently they could not conceive of adding any qualification as a rider to distinguish these properties enumerated as stridhana from other properties of women.[15]

Constancy and Fidelity

The wife's duty of constancy and fidelity does not end with the death of her spouse according to the spirit of Vedic mantras. Yet, while dharmaśāstras on the one hand lay down rigorous rules of abstinence for a widow, the earlier texts justify a greater or less degree of laxity in respect of sex for widows. This was due to the introduction of the exotic institution of Niyoga.

A significant provision of law is to be found in an oblique reference in the law of debts. Yajñavalkya (II, 46) lays down that a woman is not liable for the debts of her husband or son except in some special circumstances. Sons and grandsons however are liable to pay the debts of a father or grandfather irrespective of any assets obtained from them (II, 50). Any other heir who takes the in-

[15] See also infra on Inheritance, Chapter VIII.

heritance would also be liable to pay the debts of the deceased. Then follows a peculiar provision—debts of a person who leaves no property for his heir are to be paid by his Yosidgrāha i.e. the man who takes his wife. The word used in "Yosid" which would apply to a wife as well perhaps as to a concubine but there can be little doubt that this text envisages a case of the wife of the deceased being taken by another. The liability for his debts in that case goes with the wife. (Yajn. II, 51).

This was apparently a survival from the days when wives had been reduced to the position of chattels who could be taken like other belongings of the deceased, particularly by a devara, and not for the purposes of Niyoga. This was of course inconsistent with latter-day law which even discountenanced remarriage of widows, but the text survived its use as a remnant for commentators like Vijnanesvara to struggle with and get rid of.

One of the effects of the introduction of civil marriages and the consequent degradation of women was a significant relaxation of the rigour of the Vedic law which required an absolute duty of faithfulness to the husband's bed. This is illustrated not only by the texts relating to niyoga and the utilisation of wives to raise offspring by others, already referred to, but also by the attitude of laws, at one stage, towards unchastity of the wife.

In the chapters of the smṛitis dealing with stri-saṃgrahana we find a mixture of texts belonging to several different strata of thought. In many of these, adultery of wives is visited with condign and even terrible punishment. In others the punishment is provided only in cases of adultery with men of lower caste. On the other hand, at one stage, we find that adultery which does not lead to pregnancy is regarded quite lightly. Yajñavalkya, for instance, says: Vyabhichāradṛitau suddhih garbhe tyāgo vidhiyate, Garbhabhartribadhadau cha tathā mahatī pātake. (I, 72).

Manu and other smṛitis have similar texts which say that adultery is washed off with each monthly course.

This attitude of tolerance of unchastity seems to belong to an age when wives were regarded as a sort of slaves or chattels entirely at the disposal of their husbands and mere ministers to their pleasure.

SATI

The revulsion of feeling against the loose practices of latter day society increased the rigours of the life of the widows and not only promoted the prescription of extreme austerity for them but also the encouragement of self-immolation of widows either on the funeral pyre of her husband (sahagamana) or following his death (anugamana).

There is no authority in the Vedas for this practice called Suttee in later days. There is a text of the Ṛigveda (X 18) which, has been relied on by some as evidence of widows burning :

> Udirṣva nāryabhijīvalokam gatāsumetamupaśeṣamehi
> Hastagrābhasya didhīṣostavedam patyurjanitva mabhiyam=
> babhurya
> (Rig Veda X, 18).

This text is addressed to a woman who is probably clinging to the body of her husband and she is asked by it to get up and mind the living and leave the dead. It has been supposed to imply that the widow is preparing to die on her husband's pyre. This I think is a gratuitous assumption. Some indication of its true meaning may be obtained from its application in the Gṛihya sutras e.g. in Āśvalāyana IV, 2, 15 and IV 7, 13 where it has no connection with any such tragic act. The true meaning of this passage has been explained in connection with Niyoga (supra p. 103).

As I have stated before, the ritual literature may usually be relied upon as a truer record of ancient facts than positive enactments of later days. As regards the institution of Sati there is no ritual whatsoever in any of the Gṛihya sūtras, though later ritualists may have pressed into their service Vedic mantras by taking liberties with the text as they have often done.

In the Mahābhārata, however, we find several instances of wives burning themselves on the funeral pyre. In later Smṛitis too we get laws praising the woman who mounts funeral pyre of her husband. The earliest smṛiti authority is that of Viṣṇu (XXV, 14) who prescribes for a widow either brahmacharyya or following the husband (on the funeral pyre).

It is not possible to trace with any precision the source of this practice which was unknown to the early Aryans. But it may have some connection with a practice found in some primitive and ancient societies among whom the dead was disposed of along with his belongings. The dead were buried not only with ample food but also with other things for which he had need while alive, including horses, armour, slaves and sometimes wives or concubines on the basis that these would serve him in the world beyond. We have a passage in the Strīparva of the Mahābhārata reminiscent of such custom, where chariots, clothes and weapons of warriors were burnt in the funeral pyre of deceased warriors.

That this practice of Sati was imported from races among whom the practice of burying the paraphernalia of the dead was in vogue is certain. Such races existed in the neighbourhood of India and in all probability they were to be found in India itself. But the vogue which widow burning obtained was due to other factors.

The strong attachment and devotion to the husband which the Śāstras enjoined was necessarily reflected in the feelings of wives and operated to emphasise and magnify their natural feelings of attachment, so much so that they would fain die rather than live after the dear departed. The rigours and disgrace of widowhood which was looked upon as an accursed state would further emphasise the will to die. But the high merit which attached to sati-hood in public opinion, assisted by the encouragement of persons who would be entitled to inherit to the deceased, apparently added greatly to the impulse to sati-hood even if, as happened in some cases, the women were not egged on and even forced to that destiny. It is not without significance that in more modern times, before the practice was forbidden by legislation, it was more frequent in Bengal where the law gave the inheritance to a widow oftener than elsewhere in India.

Polygyny

Polygyny as an institution has flourished in India from very old times and is evidenced not only by the literature and history of ancient India but also by customary law everywhere. I make bold to say however, that strictly speaking, polygamy as a legal institution did not belong to the earliest stratum of Aryan law. It is no doubt true as pointed out by Kane [in Vol. 2 (1) page 550] that evidence of polygamy is also to be found in Vedic literature. But in judging the evidence of these texts it is necessary to remember that everything that appears in the stories of the Vedas does not necessarily belong to the most ancient stratum of Vedic law. We have to recollect in this connection also that Ṛigveda was probably a collection of the religious institutions of a number of different clans which was consolidated at some remote period of time. The synthetic civilisation that followed does not necessarily embody all the elements to be found in the various examples to be found scattered in the numerous Vedic stories.

Apart from this, it was certainly possible for a man to have several wives in the sense of uxors in Roman law who were not however wedded with a saṃskāra. The mantras in Ṛig Veda X 145 and 159 cited by Kane would be quite relevant even in respect of wives of this character who were not wives by a *justum matrimonium*. The word sapatnī used in these mantras to describe co-wives is not decisive to indicate that they are also patnis in the sense of gṛihapatni. For sapatnī implies only those who have the same pati or master.

Monogamy in Vedic Ritual

To my mind a surer test to judge of the really basic Vedic legal concept would be to consider the ritual of marriage. Now in the ritual of marriage which we find in the Ṛigveda and the Atharvaveda and which is handed down with very little change in fundamentals in the various Gṛihyasūtras, there does not appear to be any rule for a co-wife. The bride and the bridegroom upon their marriage light the Gṛihya fire before which they perform a sacrifice jointly. There is no mention whatsoever of several wives co-operating in the same Gṛihya sacrifice. We find also in the Vedic mantras and gifts of Pārināhya to the bride at the wedding. In later law which permitted polygamy we find that upon a second marriage it was obligatory on the husband to give to his first wife a present called "ādivedanika". This, however, does not find any place in any of the gṛihya rituals nor, naturally, in the Vedic texts. If a second regular marriage during the life-time of one wife was contemplated, we would expect to find the ritual gift of ādivedanika in the ceremonial of Gṛihya ritual somewhere. Altogether it seems to me that the ritual of marriage is altogether inconsistent with the marriage of a man with a patnī alive. Upon the death of the wife even in later law we find that the wife is burnt in the gṛihya fire after which the householder remains without a fire. And the law enjoins that the householder should not remain without a fire longer than necessary and therefore, that he should marry again as soon as possible.[16] There is no provision whatsoever anywhere for the lighting of separate gṛihya fires in the same household by the same husband for separate wives.

At the same time we must remember that the Gṛihya ritual was a religious marriage. Besides the patnī or the gṛihapatnī who was created only by the gṛihya ritual a man might have irregular wives or concubines. That seems to have been freely recognised in practice. But these concubines never had the status of a wife or patnī. Thus it seems that at one stage the widow was recognised more or less as a sort of perquisite of the surviving kinsmen but not as a wife. Such loose connections did not amount to legal or sacri-

[16] Yājñ. I, 89.

ficial marriage. The only legal marriage contemplated was strictly monogamous.

Polygamy in Dharmasutras

As we come to the Dharmasūtras, however, a multitude of wives is clearly recognised—although the gṛihya ritual does not appear to have suffered any change. Here again we find that the right of marriage with a wife alive is sought to be limited by restrictions, some of which are reasonable and some may not appear to be equally reasonable in modern times. One of the reasons was the absence of male children which was in the eye of the Āryas the main purpose of a marriage. Other reasons are given in the following text:—

> Surāpī vyādhitā dhūrtā vandhyārthaghny=apriyamvadā
> Strīprasūśchādhivettavyā puruṣadveṣinī tathā.
>
> Yajn. I, 73.

The effect of this is not a divorce,—The wife would continue to remain the wife. She does not get her freedom by the marriage of her husband and she has got to be maintained properly in the house (Yajn. I, 74) and also to be given a suitable present as a solatium, as already stated, in the shape of ādhivedanika.

While the dharmasastras try to restrict the right to take a second wife by these limitations, in practice however, particularly after the degradation of women about which I have spoken before, free indulgence in polygamy became possible and frequent, specially amongst the kings and chiefs. We must remember also that the institution of polygamy was undoubtedly prevalent amongst the many races of non-Ārya origin who inhabited India round about the Ārya settlements and their influence no doubt greatly helped to extend the scope of polygamy in the Ārya societies.

Polyandry

The institution of polyandry is most certainly non-Vedic. On the other hand in the earliest Vedic times there were many peoples specially in the North, races who were undoubtedly polyandrous and amongst whom polyandry was prevalent even in the days of Vātsyāyana. So too in the South there were numerous polyandrous races of a different type. The Mahābhārata gives the sole instance of polyandrous marriage in the case of marriage of Draupadī to five brothers and in that connection stories are recited indicating that at one time women were absolutely free to have intercourse with whomsoever they chose. It was only śvetaketu who stopped that and introduced the system of marriages. I have referred to this matter before.

This is only a reference to mythical stories of the past brought in to justify that single institution of polyandry in the Mahābhārata, whatever the origin of that particular institution may have been. The reference to the custom of promiscuity as prevalent in Uttarakuru is not without significance, if Uttarakuru is either a mythical or a semi-mythical land lying to the north of the Himalayas where in all probability polyandry or lax systems of marital relations have been prevalent, as indicated by the illustrations given by Vātsyāyana.

Renunciation, Divorce & Remarriage of Wives

There is no text anywhere laying down a law of divorce, a procedure by which the husband or wife could sever the marriage tie. A man could discard a wife and marry another, in later Smritis, under certain limitations as already mentioned under Polygamy, but the wife still remains the legal wife and her marriage tie as a result of her Samskāra is not snapped.

Even an adulterous wife could not be divorced. She might be punished particularly for intercourse with men of inferior castes but she could not be thrown out of the wedlock. We have seen before that the wife is deemed purged of her sin of adultery by a monthly course. The text provides however that if she becomes pregnant in adultery she may be renounced. (Vyabhichārād ṛitau śuddhih, garbhe tyāgo vidhīyate. Garbha bhartrivadhadau cha tathā mahati pātake). The word 'tyāga' in this text clearly seems to imply that she may be turned out of the house, not only for killing the fætus or the husband or for mahāpataka but equally for mere pregnancy in adultery. But the Mitākṣarā and other commentaries would understand the word to imply not turning out of the house but depriving her of privileges and making her atone for her sin by prāyaschitta. The mode of prāyaschitta is of course provided by another text,

Hṛitādhikārām malinām piṇḍamātropajīvinīm
Paribhūta madhaśayyām vāsayed vyabhichārinīm. Yajn, I. 70.

But there is little doubt that the texts gave the option to the husband to turn her out or to keep her in the house for performing her penance. Nevertheless this does not sever the marriage tie. She cannot, after being renounced or turned out, lawfully marry another.

She might live with other men as punarbhū, parapurvā or svairiṇī. We have already seen what her status would be as such. As has been seen before, the Gṛihya ritual of the marriage has no saṃskāra of marriage even for a widow, not to speak of a woman who has discarded her husband.

In dealing with Paunarbhava sons we have seen how widows

and wives of eunuchs and other persons were gradually recognised as capable of remarriage in Viṣnu and Yājñavalkya's texts and how later texts of Nārada, Parāśara and Bṛihaṣpati further relaxed the laws for such wives or widows. This of course implicitly provides that the marriage with the former husband has been dissolved but no text definitely lays down a law of dissolution of marriage either for men or women.

While husbands could thus discard or turn out wives, though apparently not to break the marriage tie, the wife had originally no power whatsoever to discard husbands or leave their husbands on any account, nor even to remarry after their death. Her right to remarry after the husband's death, as also with a husband living, if he was impotent, or had proceeded abroad and stayed away too long without providing for the wife or became a patita was recognised in the late Smṛitis like Nārada, Parāśara and Bṛihaṣpati. Even Manu's text seems to indicate such a right where he provides that a wife should wait for her husband in different circumstances for different periods. These texts are elliptical, as they do not say what she would do after the period is past. This ellipsis is supplied in the text of Nārada which gives her the right to marry thereafter.

Yājñavalkya too makes a similar elliptical statement when he says "Āsuddheh sampratīkṣyo hi mahāpātaka dūṣitam." Where a husband has committed a mahāpātaka, the wife should wait till he purifies himself by a penance. He omits to say what she should do if the husband does not perform the penance. Apparently according to Yājñavalkya also that would justify her in renouncing the husband. Whether in that event she should have the right to remarry Yājñavalkya does not indicate.

It is possible these elliptical texts are so because the texts to supplement them were obliterated with the revival of Vedic orthodoxy.

While thus there is no text or ritual for divorce in Hindu law there is some suggestion of a possible existence of a law of dissolving marriage if we may look upon the ritual of Maruṁakattāyam law as a survival of an ancient Arya ritual.

In the Maruṁakattāyam law there is first a regular and complete ritual Hindu marriage of a Nair girl to a Brāhman, and this is followed immediately by a ceremonial divorce after which alone the girl could enter into a sambandham. It is just possible that something like this ceremonial divorce did exist in Ārya law at a time when the Nairs adopted the Hindu ritual. But it is equally possible that the ritual of divorce was improvised to suit the occasion.

CHAPTER VII

SONSHIP AND KINSHIP

In the later Smṛitis like Manu and Yājñavalkya twelve different kinds of sons are recognised. Six of them are said to be 'heirs and kinsmen' while the other six are mere 'kinsmen and not heirs'. The laws with regard to these secondary sons are not at all uniform in the Smṛitis and I shall endeavour to find out the course of development of the several kinds of sons.

To start with, we find that the Ṛigveda does not recognise any son other than the legitimate or Aurasa son and the Gṛihyasūtras have no ritual whatsoever for the affiliation of the secondary sons. The Ṛik mantras are full of invocations to sons which are only appropriate to the legitimate son begotten on one's own wife, as Zimmer correctly says. (Altindisches Leben, page 318).

The Ṛigveda (VII, 4, 7-8) says "As the wealth (in the shape of sons) of another is to be avoided, so may we be masters of wealth of our own. O, Agni, the child of another cannot be one's offspring. Do not let us be diverted to the paths of fools who think of sons begotten by others as sons. A stranger born of another's loins though very pleasing should not be taken, should not even be thought of in the mind. Then he goes back to the same house. May a vigorous, victorious newly born come to us."[17]

At the same time this text of Ṛigveda discloses an awareness of the existence of the practice of recognising at least one kind of secondary sons, the Kshetraja of later law, sons begotten on one's wife by somebody else, a practice which the Veda strongly condemns as the 'path of fools'.

It seems probable that the 'path of fools' referred to here refers to practices of other communities round about Arya settlements among whom Levirate was a recognised institution. The firmness of the repudiation of it may also indicate that this loose practice may have been creeping into Vedic society to some extent so as to call for this vigorous denunciation.

That this must have been the idea of the entire Vedic society is borne out, not only by other texts, *e.g.*, of Maitrāyaniya Saṃhita and Aupajanghani quoted by Vasiṣṭha and Baudhāyana (q.v. infra)

[17] See also texts of Śruti (traced to Maitrāyaṇiya Saṃhitā cited in Vaśiṣta Baudhāyana and Āpastamba—*supra* p. 106.

but also by the outstanding fact that none of the Gṛihya sūtras which are complete codes of domestic rituals of Vedic society, covering the life of every man, from conception to cremation, has any ritual for making a secondary son. It is hardly conceivable that an important social institution like son-making, if it existed, should not have had an appropriate ritual.

In the Gṛihya sūtras in which rituals, connected with marriage and marital relations, as well as with the conception birth and saṃskāras of sons, apply only to the wedded wife and aurasa son, there is no ritual connected with the making of a son in any way but by begetting him on one's wife.

SECONDARY SONS

By the time of the Dharmasūtras which must have come into existence after a pretty long course of evolution we come upon a very different conception of sonship.

Vaśiṣṭha like the authors of other Dharmasūtras gives a list of twelve kinds of sons six of them being heirs and kinsmen. As will be seen presently, while the number twelve is repeated in every other Dharmaśāstra, their lists as well as the order of precedence vary in the different Dharmaśāstras. A point of importance in Vaśiṣṭha's enumeration however is that he speaks of the twelve kinds of sons as *Purāṇadriṣṭāh*.[18] Purāṇa, in this text did not mean the extant eighteen Purāṇas but tradition. *Purāṇadriṣṭāh* is significant as implying that these secondary sons were the growth out of tradition and custom and could not be traced to Sruti.

In Vaśiṣṭha's Dharmasūtra the six preferred sons are (1) Aurasa, (2) Kṣetraja, (3) Putṛikā (her son is not named as one), (4) Pauṇarbhava, (5) Kānīna and (6) Gūḍhotpanna, while the six who are not heirs but only kinsmen are (1) Sahoḍha, (2) Dattaka, (3) Krīta, (4) Svayamupāgata, (5) Apaviddha and (6) Sudrāputra.

The noticeable thing about this list is that the secondary sons who are preferred as dāyādas were sons born of women of the family while those who are not heirs, were all born or begotten outside the family.

This preference of sons born of women in the family to others affiliated from other families is far from insignificant. It indicates, to my mind, firstly that these preferred sons, whom we should call illegitimate were recognised as sons and heirs earlier than the other

[18] वह्वीनां द्वादश हि पुत्राः पुराणदृष्टाः ।

kinds of sons, and secondly, they were so recognised as being sons of women in the family, while the others were born of strangers.

These conclusions seem to lead to a further conclusion.

In the Ṛigveda and early Vedic society sonship is invariably connected with procreation. In matriarchal societies on the other hand procreation creates almost no relationship ; sons are sons of the mother and her family. The son of a damsel of the family would be a son of the family, no matter how procreated. Thus the sons distinguished as Kanīna or Putrikāputra in later Vedic society would naturally be sons of a matriarchal society. On the other hand, patriarchal societies which permitted the association of widows with the husband's kindred by Levirate would naturally consider the sons of such widows distinguished in later Arya law as Kṣetraja, Pauṇarbhava and Guḍhopanna would be sons of the family.

When such families were gradually absorbed in Arya society, these sons would naturally be recognised as sons by them. The earliest reaction of Arya law to the invasion of these customs would therefore be the recognition of these as secondary sons. When by extension of the proprietory right over sons the other kinds of sons like Dattaka, Kritrima etc. were recognised their position at the outset was inferior to that of other sons.

Later developments however apparently upset this scheme.

Putrikāputra and Kanīna

The picture of the society that we get in the Ṛigveda is that of a strictly agnatic and exogamous society. Daughters on marriage go out of the kinship altogether. The only exception we find is a reference in a solitary text to brotherless daughters sometimes coming back and living with parents like sons.

"Abhrātrikā puṃsah pratīchinameti putratvam."

(RV II, 17, 7 and also IV, 5, 51).

These verses in later times have been referred to by commentators like Yāksa (Nirukta III, 4) as supporting the institution of Putrikā. But a Putrikā as conceived in later Smritis is much more than a daughter living in her father's house ; she as well as her son is deemed to be a son of the father for all purposes spiritual as well as secular. The Vedic text does not go so far and, to my mind, is nothing but a record of an observed social fact.

That the daughter or her son was not conceived as entering the scheme of kinship at all in ancient society is borne out also by the fact that even in the Dharmasutras which recognise the institution of putrikā, she, or any daughter is not regarded as of kindred for other legal purposes of vital importance.

In the law of inheritance (XXVIII, 21) Gautama's Dharmasūtra gives the heritage of a sonless person, to persons connected by piṇḍa, gotra and Ārṣa one after another. Who are conceived of by Gautama as persons connected by piṇḍa we get from his law relating to Śrāddha where they are enumerated as the deceased's own sapiṇḍas, his mother's sapiṇḍas and sagotras. As will be seen later, this scheme, though it gives a status to the mother's paternal relations who are not agnates, does not imply that a daughter or her son is a sapiṇḍa. In Āpastamba's Dharmasūtra the daughter is first recognised as heir only after all sapiṇḍas, sagotras, teachers and fellow-pupils are exhausted, but before the king (II, 14).

Looking further back, the Vedic ritual of Pitripiṇḍayajna, the source from the later law of Srāddha was developed, we find that in that ceremony one offers pindas only to his three paternal ancestors. In fact, as will be seen later, in Vedic Society the daughter or her son was never regarded as kindred, and that society was purely agnatic.

The first step in breaking down the purely agnatic scheme of kinship was the institution of Putrikā and her son as fictitious sons of the Putrikā's father. It will be presently seen that in course of time all the rights of a putrikā were recognised as those of a daughter as such, so that the daughter and her son were recognised as heirs and sapindas, and the door was thus thrown ajar for the admission of cognates into kinship.

It will be useful to consider the provisions of the Dharmasūtras regarding putrikāputra side by side with those regarding Kānīna sons.

Barring the doubtful Vedic text pressed to their use by later law-givers in connection with the Putrikā, we find no trace of her before we come to the Dharmasūtras. But the law in the Dharmasūtras themselves shows that before it was recorded in them, it had already passed through a course of evolution.

Gautama

The original regular procedure by which a daughter's son could be made a son is a definite ritual which is laid down by Gautama in XXVIII, 18 by which the father made a ceremonial declaration with appropriate rites, *viz.*, giving oblations to Agni and Prajāpati, saying that the girl's son was to be his son. This formula we find repeated in other Smṛitis down to Manu.

But already in Gautama's time this formal requirement had been slackened and Gautama cites an opinion held *by some* (eke) that an appointed daughter could be made by mere intention of the father even without this formula (XXVIII, 19, 20).

It may be noted that Gautama (in XXVIII, 18) speaks about *appointing* a daughter and the mode of appointment prescribes a specific ritual but, it may be noted, not the ritual of marriage. In the Sūtras which follow he cites the opinion of some that mere intention without the ritual would be enough.

With this may be compared his description of a Kānīna son as merely born of an unmarried girl. The distinction between Kānīna and Putrikāputra according to him obviously lies in the daughter being *not appointed* in the former case by the father while in the latter case she is specifically appointed with a view to raising a son to him. This distinction was obliterated to this extent only that even without express appointment at the time of her marriage, a married daughter would be a putrikā if there was such intention of the father provided he was sonless. Where such intention too was absent or where the daughter was not married the son might be a Kānīna who is not an heir (adāyāda).

Baudhayana

Baudhāyana in a somewhat cryptic text says that a son begotten on a girl by approaching her is a putrikāputra, otherwise dauhitra.[19] The precise meaning of this passage is by no means quite clear. The word 'abhyupagamya' is explained by Govindasvāmin who, naturally interprets the passage in the light of the later Smṛiti texts, as meaning that the father must have stipulated that the daughter was given with a view to raise offspring for her father.

To my mind this expression bears obvious similarity to the institution amongst the matriarchal races of the South where the husband is a visitor in the wife's house and the children of the wife accordingly become the children of the family of her mother. This expression has got to be taken along with the circumstance presently to be referred to, namely that in the case of a Putrikā properly

[19] Abhyupagamya duhitari jātam putrikāputram anyaṃ dauhitram. II, ii, 15. *Abhyupagamyaa* seems to imply "having approached" which meaning would seem to be more consistent with the history of putrikāputra as I conceive it. But it seems to imply also that the girl should be approached with her father's consent.

so called there is no change of Gotra, as there is no gift of the girl. Taken along with this fact it would seem to suggest that a father of a girl might seek to raise offspring for himself by getting a man to beget a son on his maiden daughter without a ceremonial ritual of marriage. It is such sons begotten on the daughter by a visiting mate who was not, legally speaking, the husband of the girl, which seems to have been the origin of the institution of Putrikā.

"Anyam dauhitram" in the text of Baudhāyana is unintelligible unless the words mean that unless a daughter was so approached, her son would be known as 'dauhitra'. Possibly another passage in Baudhāyana also indicates a similar history.

The precise implication of this text of Baudhāyana would seem to be indicated by his definition of the Kānīna son, (II, ii. 24) which is as follows:

> Asaṃskṛitām-anatisrisṭam yām upayachchhet tasyām yo jātah sa Kānīnah.

"If one approaches a girl, who has not had the saṃskara of marriage and was not given the son born of her is a Kānīna."

As Govindasvāmin quite correctly says, this implies that the girl must be both asaṃskṛitā and *anatisṛiṣṭā,* that is, unmarried and ungiven. If the son is begotten on a married woman, even though she may be given, he would only be a Kṣetraja or guḍhaja according as she was approached with consent of her husband or otherwise. On the other hand if she was unmarried but given (atisṛiṣṭā) for the purpose by her father she would be a putrikā. It is only if a damsel is approached without such gift that her son becomes a Kānīna.

These two texts together indicate that the distinguishing feature of the putrikā is that the maiden is assigned to the begetter for raising offspring to her father, in the same manner as a wife may be given in *niyoga* to raise offspring to her husband. The giving is not a dāna, as in marriage but a mere assignment for the purpose and there was no saṃskāra of marriage.

Baudhāyana cites authority (II, ii 16)[20] which says that the Putrika's son gives the first piṇḍa to his mother, the next to her father and thereafter to the grand-father of the mother. At this stage the Putrikā's son was not at all of the kindred of the begetter. Such kinship was apparently the result of a further development.

[20] Ādiśet prathame piṇḍe mātaram putrikāsutah.
Dvitīya pitaram tasyāstṛitīye cha pitāmaham.

Visnu and Vasistha

Viṣṇu,[21] like Gautama, first lays down that the Putrikāputra is the son of a girl given by a father with an express stipulation that the son born of her was to be his son. But then he goes on to say that even where a daughter is not appointed according to the rule for making a Putrikā she is a Putrikā, if brotherless, going a step further than Gautama in dispensing with an initial intention (abhisandhi) of the father.

Vaśiṣtha[22] seems to differ from these authors in making the Putrikā herself a son. But he indicates by quoting a verse on the process of making a Putrikā, that a Putrikā can be made by a contract *at the time of marriage*, that her son was to belong to the grandfather. As authority he refers to a variant of the Śruti text cited in Nirukta referred to above (Abhrātrikā puṃsah pratīchinam eti putratvam. RV. IV, 5, 51).

Along with this text of Vaśiṣtha should be considered his text about the Kānīna son which is as follows:

Kānīnah panchamo yā pitrigrihe' saṃskṛita kāmādutpādayenmatamahasya putro bhavati ityāhuh. Athāpyudaharanti'.

Aprattā duhitā yasya putram vindati tulyatah,
Putrī mātamahastena dadyāt piṇḍam hared-dhanam.

"Kānīna is the fifth. Where an unmarried (asaṃskritā) damsel, being in her father's house bears through desire (a son) it is said that the son becomes the son of his maternal grand-father. He gives piṇḍas (to him) and takes his wealth."

The only distinction between this and the putrikāputra lies in the absence of the stipulation with the begetter about paternity in the former, but the result is the same, for in either case the son gives piṇḍas to the maternal grandfather and inherits to him.

Viṣṇu in XV, 10-11 gives exactly the same definition of a Kānīna son, but makes a remarkable departure in giving paternity of the son to the man who, later, marries the girl, just like a sahoḍha son and apparently the gūḍhotpanna son. Gautama however considers the Kānīna as a non-inheriting kinsman while he gives to the putrikāputra a high place among secondary sons.

Piecing together these texts one notices at once that, as in the case of secondary sons generally there is a great diversity in the provisions made by the different authorities for Kānīna and putrikāputra, suggesting, to my mind different reactions by different schools

[21] Viṣṇu, XV, 5-6.

[22] XVII, 15-16.

to the absorption of customs foreign to the Ārya law. The custom of having daughters living in the father's house, and without a regular marriage saṃskara bearing sons was making its way in the Arya society and law reacts to this by what I believe to be different ways of recognition of her son.

The first reaction seems to be the one in Gautama. Of the two classes of sons he recognises the putrikāputra who is begotten by the appointment of the father alone as a regular, i.e. dāyāda bāndhava son. The Kānina is an irregular son.

At the next stage, this distinction between the two kinds of daughter's son tends to be obliterated and, Vasiṣṭha, Baudhāyana and Viṣṇu equally consider both to be dāyāda bāndhavas, giving primacy to the putrikāputra,—while Viṣṇu gives the fatherhood of Kānīna to the husband of the girl when married. At this stage it is also to be noticed that the question of the giving of the daughter with a stipulation about the paternity of the son, has lost all significance and Gautama's halting recognition of a son born without express stipulation is extended until in Viṣṇu a brotherless girl is *ipso facto* made a putrikā. A distinction between the putrikā and the mother of a Kānīna still exists, inasmuch as the former must be a brotherless girl while the latter need not be so.

All these texts envisage a condition in which daughters remain in the father's house without a regular marriage saṃskāra with anybody. They would have no status in the husband's family. When a sonless man keeps the daughter with him, her son would become his son. But what if she has no son?

DAUGHTER AS HEIR

Apparently this problem is solved by the text of Vaśiṣṭha making the putrikā herself a son to compensate her for her being deprived of rights in a husband's house.

As we have noticed, none of these texts expressly refer to the putrikā being given with a marriage saṃskāra. The inevitable consequence of such saṃskāra would be that the daughter and the son would pass to her husband's family. But gradually it seems that even a regularly married daughter could be made a putrikā by stipulation and, later, in Viṣṇu by the mere fact of her having no brother. At this stage the distinction between a putrikā and any regularly married daughter would disappear and, we find in Viṣṇu and Manu that daughters, appointed and not appointed, equally take the place of sons and, their son becomes the heir and kinsman of the mother's father.

In later Smṛitis, the Putrikā has lost all her importance. For already the daughter as such is mentioned by them as heir, irrespective of her being a Putrikā,[23] after the sons and the widow. Manu too, while he begins by giving the formula by which a girl could be made a Putrikā,[24] in the immediately following slokas, says that a daughter[25] and a daughter's son[26] as such inherit to a sonless person. In Yājñavalkya the Putrikā is barely mentioned, but the inheritance of the daughter after the widow is well settled.

Obsolescence of Putrika

Now if a daughter and her son inherit as such and if every daughter's son, and not merely the Putrikā's son inherits and, as in Baudhāyana, offers oblations to the maternal grand-father as such, all practical utility of Putrikā disappears, and the institution naturally ceases to exist.

The obsolescence of this custom in the time of Manu and Viṣṇu and others appears from the absence of further details about this institution in any of these Smṛitis.

Manu, indeed, true to its character as an encyclopedæic digest of all texts gives us several texts relating to the Putrikā, which belong to different strata of the history of law. It is singular, however, that in his enumeration of the twelve kinds of secondary sons (IX, 159, 160) he omits any reference to the Putrikā or her son. In another place (IX, 123 et seq.) however he deals with the Putrikā's son, but his treatment of the subject is mixed up with that of the daughter's son generally. As already pointed out, he lays down the law that a Putrikā is made by a contract at the time of marriage (IX, 127), but, immediately after that, he follows with a text laying down that a daughter's son as such inherits to a sonless person and

[23] Viṣṇu, XVII, 4-5.

[24] अपुत्रोऽनेन विधिना सुतां कुर्वीत पुत्रिकाम् ।
यदपत्यं भवेदस्याः स मे पुत्रो भवेदिति ।

Manu, IX, 127

[25] यथैवात्मा तथा पुत्रः पुत्रेण दुहिता समा ।
तस्यामात्मनि तिष्ठन्त्यां कथमन्यो धनम् हरेत् ॥

Manu, IX, 130

[26] दौहित्रोह्यखिलं रिकथमपुत्रस्य पितुर्हरेत् ।
स एव दद्याद्द्वौ पिण्डौ पित्रे मातामहाय च ॥

Manu, IX, 132

offers piṇḍas both to the father and the maternal grand-father (IX, 132). This he emphasizes by saying that the son's son and the daughter's son (not Putrikā's son alone) are equal in all respects (IX, 133, 136, 139). In IX, 140 he lays down the order in which the Putrikā's son offers piṇḍas to his maternal ancestors, while in in IX, 135 he says that on the Putrikā dying sonless, her husband inherits to her, thus indicating that a true husband-wife relation for spiritual and legal purposes now exists between her and her husband. If we remember that the present text of the Manusaṃhitā was essentially a compilation of all the texts of law which were current at the date of compilation in the name of Manu and that accordingly many texts are incorporated in it which had long become obsolete at that date, we shall be able to assess these texts at their proper value. It will then be seen that these texts, so far as the Putrikā's son goes, do not lay down anything which was not already laid down by Gautama, Vaśiṣṭha and Baudhāyana. The other texts, however, which give to the son of the daughter "akritā vā krita va'pi"—"whether appointed or not" the same status as a Putrikā's son, belong to a later stratum already indicated in Viṣṇu. These texts practically nullify the provisions about Putrikāputra who had evidently ceased to be an institution of any practical utility, so much so that he finds no place in Manu's enumeration of the twelve secondary sons. Later Smritis, beyond occasionally mentioning the Putrikāputra among the twelve kinds of sons do not speak of them at all.[27]

The seal upon the obsolescence of the Putrikā along with the various other kinds of secondary sons, except the Dattaka, was set by the text of the Ādityapurāna[28] which gives an index expurgatorius of laws forbidden in the Kali Age and mentions among others the recognition of sons other than Aurasa and Dattaka. This text, as the Smṛitichandrikā, Parāśara Mādhava and others observe, makes the

[27] Narada does not refer to secondary sons. No text of Kātyāyana or Yama is found cited in the commentaries. Two texts of Bṛīhaspati are cited (Col. Dig. V. 4, 304 and V. 4, 225) in which he quotes Gautama, XVIII, 18).

[28] दत्तौरसेतरेषान्तुपुत्रत्वेन परिग्रहः ।

* *

एतानि लोकगुप्त्यर्थं कलेरादौ महात्मभिः ।
निवर्तितानि कर्माणि प्रतिष्ठापूर्वकम् बुधैः ॥

Cited in Smritichandrika (Ed. Gharpure), p. 289 and other commentaries. Mādhavāchārya quoted as from another Smriti a variant of this : Parāśara-Mādhava, Bib. Ind. III, 353.

institution of Putrikā void in the Kali Age.[29] From the historical point of view we can only look upon this as a record of the contemporary fact, that this practice had gone out of vogue.

Unlike the provisions relating to the Dattaka son which acquired the greatest importance in later days when other secondary sons had practically gone out of use, the Smritis contain very little detail with regard to the mode of making a Putrikā, the gotra of the Putrikā's son and the piṇḍas to be given by him. The first reference to the family of the Putrikā is to be found in Vāśiṣṭha's and Baudhāyana's texts already referred to, according to which he offers piṇḍas to his mother next to the father and thereafter to the grand-father of the mother.[30]

In Manu and the later commentaries it is mentioned that the Putrikāputra also offers pindas to his father and is thus a dvyāmusyāyana. On the other hand, in the commentaries like Parāśaramādhava and Smṛitichandrikā it is stated that in the case of Putrikā as well as in marriages like gāndharva marriage, the gotra of the girl is not changed, from which it follows that her son's gotra is also the gotra of her father.

Mādhavāchāryya cites a text of Logakṣī to the effect that "the putrikāputra should give pinda and water to his mother by his maternal grand-father's gotra."[31]

The Smṛitichandrikā holds the same view and with reference to the text of Manu which says that the bride to be married should be not only asagotrā of the father and asapiṇḍa of the mother ; it propounds the riddle, why talk of the sapiṇḍa of the mother at all? By marriage, the mother has become the same with the father and the father's sapiṇḍas are the sapiṇḍas of the mother too. This riddle it answers by saying that this would not always be so. The mother does not become sapiṇḍa of the husband if there is a marriage without gift.[32] This view is consistent with the history of the Putrikāputra. As I have indicated above, the putrikā was not the wife of the husband by a *justum matrimonium*. The husband was only a visitor in his wife's family and could procreate offspring on the wife for the benefit of the father-in-law who would be the father of the son.

[29] Smritic., pp. 288-9, Parāśara-Mādhava, III, 353.

[30] Baudhayana II, 2 to 16.

[31] Parāśaramādhava—I, page 474.

[32] Smritichandrikā, Ahṇika, p. 69. See also Madanapārijāta Bibl. Ind., p. 141.

Suggested evolution of Putrika

These passages seem to me to indicate a course of evolution of Putrikā in Ārya law like this. Sonless persons who had a maiden daughter might keep the daughter in their house ; offspring begotten on her by strangers would be the sons of the girl's father, distinguished later as Kānīna. In course of time this connection with the daughter was regarded as a more or less permanent one and as a sort of marriage,—but not marriage in the full sense, which involves the daughter passing out of the family. The son begotten was the son of the mother's father and gave piṇḍas to him and his ancestors. At this stage the daughter has become a putrikā. She could only be made so by stipulation with the husband who has now married the girl that the sons begotten on her should be the sons of her father. Accordingly the gotra of the son was the gotra of his maternal grandfather.

At a later stage as we have seen from the text of Gautama, Viṣṇu and others, putrikās might be created even without that stipulation or, in other words, whenever a brotherless girl was married. The father might by mere intention make her a putrikā even later.

At this stage of course the marriage having complied with all proper rituals, the daughter must have passed to her husband's gotra. But nevertheless, he was assumed to be offering piṇḍas to his maternal ancestors. The result was that, as a son of his father, the putrika's son offered piṇḍas to his three paternal ancestors, but as a son of his maternal grand-father, he offered piṇḍas to the maternal grand-father and his two paternal ancestors. This development, we find, already taking place in the later Smṛitis, by which the putrika's son and, later, any daughter's son as such began to offer piṇḍas to both sides.

The conclusion to be drawn from an examination of the text, in the light of the historic background therefore, is that the daughter and the daughter's son entered into the legal scheme of kinship in the Ārya law first by the adaptation of some non-Ārya practice in the modified form of Putrikākaraṇa and gradually by the elimination of the formalities until the daughter *per se* became entitled to inherit.[33]

Behind and beyond the earliest stage of the institution in the various texts of Ārya law the law seems to have had a history in matriarchal non-Ārya societies which we may guess.

[33] See article on Putrikāputra by the author in JRASB Vol. IV 1938 No. 1.

I think that we have indications of the kind of non-Ārya societies from whom the custom of putrikākaraṇa might have been developed. In the Marumakattayam and Alya Santana laws we find traces of societies of a matriarchal type in which daughters never leave the house in which they were born. Their mates are visitors to their mother's house and their children are children of the mother's family. We have seen before that the early Ārya settlers had neighbours with whom they had social relations such as the Bāhlikas who apparently were matriarchal and might have had similar customs.

The original customs of such societies when they came into the Ārya fold would be modified by partial adoption of Ārya customs as we can trace in the Marumakattayam and Alya Santana laws. It is possible that in the original non-Arya society of this type the girls were never married at all. They stayed in their mother's home. They formed connection with males, probably subject to tabus, such as we find in Sambandhams of Marumakattyam law, but probably no male could have such connection except with the permission of the male head of the family, and then the children born would be no children of the begetter but those of the mother's family or tarwad. In matriarchal societies where the *Beena* type of marriage prevailed, they would be children of the mother's father.

The effect of such a society coming into the Ārya fold would be of various kinds. One form was what we find in Marumakattyam law. In this, Ārya law was formally adopted in the ceremonial marriage which took place down to the last detail, symbolically, with a Brāhman, followed immediately by a symbolic divorce, so that this so-called husband, was the one person with whom marital intercourse was absolutely tabu. For the rest, once this fictitious compliance with the form of Vedic law had been made the ancient custom of sambandhams with one or more males with the permission of the father would continue and her children would be the children of the girl's father.

A more comprehensive adoption of Ārya marriage by such a community would apparently result in the Ārya marriage being fully implemented, so that the male became the real husband but with the important reservation that the girl would continue to live in her father's house and her children would be her father's children as they did in the pre-Āryan stage of the society. Marriage in Alya Santana law approximates to this form.[34] One step more from this

[34] The husband too might come into his wife's family as illatom son-in-law, if his wife was brotherless.

would be for such society to adopt the Arya law more fully with only a reservation that daughters and their sons could be retained in her father's family. That is the form in which Putrikā was accepted in Ārya law at the earliest stage indicated by Gautama.

Conditions favourable to the adaptation of such customs of matriarchal non-Āryas were also growing in Ārya society. The Vedas already indicate unmarried and even married brotherless daughters living with their fathers. In strict Vedic law they would have no status in the father's family, while they were bereft of any rights in a husband's family. Such a state of things would open the way to adoption or adaptation of these customs of non-Ārya neighbours.

At first the sons of unmarried daughters kept in the father's family might have been recognised as the sons of the maternal grandfather, like the sons by visiting mates in the early matriarchal society. This is a probable explanation of the high position of the Kānīna in some of the earliest texts. Unions with such mates would naturally be subject to the permission of the father. After the custom of procreating offspring by Niyoga on the wife was adopted in Arya society the law might have been extended and fathers of unmarried girls might have got sons begotten for them on thei girls by niyoga.[35] This was perhaps the origin of the putrikāputra. A step further, and this relation of the mate to the daughter might be permanent, subject to the stipulation about paternity. This is the form in which we find the institution in Gautama. We have already seen how the stipulation about paternity gradually vanished and the daughter's son as such stepped into the kinship and heirship to the maternal grandfather even after her marriage saṃskāra.

Some support to this view of the evolution of putrikaputra from non-Aryan sources may be derived from the tradition recorded in the Mahabharata.

There we find two or three remarkable instances of Putrikās. Chitrāngadā and Ulūpi whom Arjun married were not carried by Arjuna to his own kindred but continued to live with their own parents, apparently because that was the custom of the community to which the girls belonged. So too Hiḍimbā the Rākṣasa wife of Bhīma lived on with her family after marriage. It is obvious that

[35] Gautama in XXVIII, seems to contemplate the appointment to raise an offspring to a maiden by providing for the paternity of the son so raised by stipulation and not by a marriage saṃskāra, for the ritual by which the appointment is made contemplates only offerings to Agni and Prajapati and making in their presence the ceremonial stipulation "For me by thy offspring".

these communities were not Āryas, governed, at least originally, by the Ārya sacred law. The presence of Matriarchal societies in many parts of India and beyond its frontiers even today also point to the existence round about the Arya societies, of communities in which mother-kinship was the law. In between purely matriarchal societies and purely patriarchal societies are societies with a somewhat mixed kinship, where the husband comes and lives with the wife and the children of the wife become the kindred of her parents, though the husband also is kindred with them. The system of marriage prevailing in this last class of society is called by Robertson Smith, Beena form of marriage. Evidently Ulūpi and Chitrāngadā belonged to families amongst whom the Beena form of marriage prevailed, in which the daughter remained with the father and her children were the kindred of her father. The Mahābhārata story of Bāhlika a son of a Bāhlika princess married to a Bharata king succeeding his maternal uncle in the Bāhlika kingdom[36] indicates the existence of such societies with which Aryan society had intimate social intercourse. It is likely that the institutions of such societies influenced Vedic societies to adopt the custom with the limitation that sonship of the daughters' son would arise only where a sonless man gave his daughter in marriage with a stipulation that the son of that daughter shall be a son of the maternal grand-father.

Putrika and Epikleros

It is interesting to compare and contrast the institution of Putrikā with the Epikleros in Athenian Law. That law seems to have been derived or borrowed from the law of Moses[37] according to which "if a man dies without male descendants, leaving only a daughter, she is obliged to give her father a posterity to prevent the extinction of his name. The sole daughter of the deceased becomes his heir. But she had to marry a kinsman of the deceased who alone would take the wife with the inheritance.[38] As Professor Balogh points out, this was a device to prevent the inheritance passing out of the family, like Levirate.

The Athenian law seems to have adopted and worked out in detail this law and laid down that where a man dies without sons leaving a daughter she is bound to marry the nearest kinsman, by

[36] See supra, p. 28.

[37] Numbers XXVII & XXXVI.

[38] E. Balogh : *"Some Notes on Adultery and the Epikleros in Ancient Athenian Law" in Studi in Memoria di Emilio Albertario,* Vol. II at p. 701.

being divorced from a previous husband, if she had already been married before to a stranger.[39]

It will be noticed that this institution of Epikleros in Athens is a part of a scheme of disposing of the heritage of which the daughter must be a part. It goes to the kinsman who marries the Epikleros. This is substantially different from the law of Putrikā as developed in the Smritis. In this there is no obligation on the nearest kinsman to marry the daughter for taking the inheritance, nor is the Putrika required to marry the kinsman, as she could hardly do, because perhaps she had already been married to another man and could not renounce him, and, in any case, on account of the law about prohibited degrees.

None the less the Mosaic law or similar institutions among non-Arya races was probably the prototype of the institution which Arya law adapted to make it conformable to their marriage laws. In this form the daughter may be married to any one, who must necessarily be a stranger to the kindred, but her son would be a son of her father. In a completer form this institution may be found in the institution of the Illatom in Alya Santana law.

Viewed in this light the conclusion that the institution of Putrikaputra was adapted from Non-Arya sources seems to be strengthened.

KĀNĪNA, SAHODHA AND GUDHOTPANNA

These three classes of sons along with Kṣetraja, Putrikāputra and Pauṇarbhava sons are classed by Vasiṣṭha as heirs and kinsmen while the others, viz., Sahoḍha, Dattaka, Krīta, Svayamupagata, Apaviddha and Sudraputra are regarded by him as kinsmen but not heirs. As I have suggested before, this classification by Vasiṣṭha was earlier than that by other works.

The reason for the priority of the first group to the others in this list, seems to indicate that they were recognised as sons before the second class of sons were recognised.

If I am right in my view that the Vedic conception of sonship, being confined to Aurasa alone, was gradually modified by the inclusion of Kṣetraja, Putrikāputra and Kānīna under the impact of non-Arya customs, we can imagine the further extension of sonship to other sons born of women of the family, once the idea of procreation in lawful wedlock ceased to be a *sine qua non* of sonship. So other sons born of women of the family were likewise deemed to be sons of whosoever had authority over the mother before any sons of strangers

[39] E. Balogh. op. cit., p. 700 seq.

born out of the family were so recognised. The extension of the concept to the latter class was later and when they were admitted as sons, as kinsmen only, they were not straightway admitted to heirship.

We can clearly distinguish the principle on which Vasiṣṭha's classification is based. The sons who were recognsnied as heirs were all children born of women in the family though not in lawful wedlock. On that principle they were all recognised as belonging to the family. And the only way in which they could be so regarded was by attributing paternity to a member of the family. Thus the Kṣetraja is looked upon as the son of the mother's husband, the Kānīna and putrikāputra as sons of the mother's father, pauṇarbhava as the son of the person to whom the mother belonged and Guḍhotpanna whose begetter was unknown was the son of the mother's husband.

Ownership not the basic principle

It is tempting to infer that the principle underlying the theory of paternity is that the husband or father is the owner of the wife or the maiden daughter. The analogy of women to the field or cattle is often employed in the Smṛitis in this connection. But this is hardly likely for, as will be seen later, the concept of ownership over children was a later development and did not probably belong to the oldest stratum of law and could not account for the inclusion of these children as sons.

It would perhaps be more correct to say that the sonship bestowed on these children was due to the nature of the ancient conception of membership of the society.

To understand this, it is necessary to understand what sonship implied to these law givers. Vedic society like Roman law recognised no one who had not a family or gotra. A man who was without a family or gens could in ancient Roman law acquire a status only by becoming a client of a patrician patron. The position of Vedic society was similar.

The family could have slaves, but sons born of free women of the family could not be deemed to be slaves. For the purpose of status in the family they had to be counted as sons of the Gṛihapatī. To recognise them as sons would not mean giving them the same place as aurasa sons, it would simply mean that they were under the protection of the so-called father, maintained as members of the family and bound to act under the orders of its head. Sonship in their case has a very different implication from the sonship of the aurasa which is so glorified in the Vedas—the son who is the father reborn.

This seems to be the true origin of the recognition of these sons. They must have a gotra of their own and for this purpose alone they are deemed to be sons, gotrabhajāh, but not persons generally entitled to inheritance (dāyādah), this last right having apparently been conferred later.

Dattaka

The Dattaka son has assumed an overshadowing importance among secondary sons in modern law. He alone has survived the orthodox revival which swept away all other sons and added importance to the Dattaka.

Yet in lists of Vaśiṣṭha and Viṣṇu he is only an *adāyada bāndhava* coming not only after Kṣetraja and Putrikā but also after Pauṇarbhava, Kānīna, Guḍhotpanna and Sahoḍha. So too texts of Hārita, Sankha-Likhita, Devala and Yama quoted in the classical works place the Dattaka among Adāyādas.

The Dattaka son did not belong to the early Vedic society. The very idea of a father disposing of a son as property by gift was obnoxious to the Vedic opinion which is re-emphasised by Āpastamba. Furthermore, the ritual law of the Gṛihyas knows nothing of any ritual for giving or taking a son in adoption.[40] A ritual of Datta Homa has since then sprung up, but that is nothing but a ceremonial appropriate to any gift of property coupled with certain adapted rituals appropriate to the natural born son. Vaśiṣṭha's text, which I consider to preserve the earliest authority on the subject, speaks of a person taking a son in adoption making only a Vyāhriti Homa which is merely an auspicious ritual in almost every religious transaction and has nothing specifically appropriate to the taking of a son.

Manu lays down that the adopted son does not carry with him the gotra of his natural father, but takes the gotra of his adopter. When a girl's gotra has to be transferred, the Gṛihya prescribes a mantra and a ritual which is different in different Gṛihyas, but there

[40] The Grihyasutras, including Baudhāyana's have no ritual for adoption any more than for Niyoga, but a supplement fathered or Bodhāyana called Grihyaśeṣa sutra (II, 6, p. 227, Mysore edition) purports to give a ritual for putra-pratigraha. The first part of it is almost a verbatim copy of Vasiṣṭha's short text, followed by a brief improvised ritual and a couple of Vedic mantras appropriate to a saṃskāra of a begotten son. There can be little doubt that this Grihyaśeṣa sutra like Āśvalāyana Pariśiṣṭha is a late work.

is no ritual in Gṛihyas whatsoever for the changing of the gotra of the adopted son.

Vasiṣṭha's text on adoption perhaps enshrines a tradition of the first recognition of the dattaka son. That the law-giver was justifying what was, in his time, an innovation is indicated by his assigning a natural reason for it. He says, "Śukraśonitasanibhavah puruṣah mātāpitrinimittakah tasya dānādhamana vikrayeṣu mātāpitarau prabhavatab."

With this preamble he goes on to prescribe limitations against giving of an only son and against the wife giving without permission of her husband.

Doctrine of father's power of gift

Now, this doctrine of the father's absolute right of ownership over his sons and of the right of both parents not only to give in adoption, but to give, pledge or sell sons is nowhere to be found in the Vedas. The story of Śunahśepha in the later Vedic work Aitareya Brahmana[41] is an apparent exception. But there, Ajigarta gave his son, Śunahśepha, in consideration of getting a hundred cows, to be sacrificed to Varuna in the place of Harischandra's son Rohita. After Rohita had purchased him by giving a hundred cows, he was brought to king Harischandra who was suffering from dropsy on account of his breach of faith with Varuna and he offered Śunahśepha as his substitute to Varuna. The substitute was accepted and the sacrifice was performed with Śunahśepha as a sacrificial animal. When it came to the stage of tying Śunahśepha to the sacrificial yupa, nobody was found who would so tie him. Then Ajigarta came forward and offered to do so for another hundred cows which were given to him. Thereafter when the stage of killing the victim came and nobody came forwadd to undertake the work, Ajigarta offered to behead Śunaśepha for another hundred cows which was given to him. Thereupon Śunahśepha uttered several mantras to appease the gods, one after another, and when he had done, his bonds fell away and Harischandra also was cured.

[41] Aitareya Brahmana Chap. XXXIII. seq.

The full story of Śunahśepha only appears in Aitareya Brahmana which speaks of his father Ajigarta having sold his son to be sacrificed by king Harischandra in fulfilment of a vow to Varuna. In the Rigveda I, 24, 12 there is only a reference to Śunahśepha uttering a hymn to Varuna and being saved. This is followed by several hymns probably meant to have been uttered by Śunahśepha, which however are not the hymns said to have been uttered by him in Aitareya Brāhmana.

Although this story of the sale of a son is there, it was very severely condemned and we find that when Ajigarta came to claim Śunahśepha as his son and asked him to accompany him back home, Śunahśepha called his act towards the son to be more heinous than anything which a Śūdra could do and in this Viśvāmitra supported him.

This does not indicate that the right to sell a son was regarded as endorsed by an Aryan law. After Ajigarta was turned away, Viṣvāmitra asked Śunahśepha to be his son. Then Śunahśepha said, "How could I become your son being of a different (Āngirasa) gotra?" But he added, "if all your sons acknowledge me as your son, then I may become your son." Thereupon Viśvāmitra called his sons, one-half of whom refused to acknowledge Śunahśepha as his son and were for that reason cursed by their father,—while the other half agreed to acknowledge Śunahśepha and accepted his leadership as the eldest.

This is not a story which supports the institution of adoption amongst the Āryas or at any rate in the form which we find in the later Smṛitis. For the Smṛitis recognise the right of a man to take a dattaka son only if he is sonless. But here Viśvāmitra made Śunahśepha his son, although he had a hundred sons alive. And further this was done not by his taking or the father giving as is done in the making of a Dattaka, but by the acknowledgment by the sons of Viśvāmitra. This story, therefore, is assuredly not a precedent for the institution of dattaka or of the father's right of ownership over the son.

Ownership of son not proto-Aryan

It is a somewhat facile assumption that the power of the father in patriarchal society or at any rate in Indo-germanic societies included the power to give, sell or kill a son. The ancient Roman Law which also has the institution of adoption by a formality akin to that of sale of property offers a handy analogy. But while there are sound reasons to hold that the Indo-Germanic races, though probably not racially the same, had a core of common culture developed before they spread out in different directions, it does not follow that property in sons or the institution of adoption was a part of the common culture.[42] On the other hand, the absence of any refer-

[42] Though adoption as an institution is common to many of them there does not appear to be a common name for the adopted son in their various languages as we have in the case of other relations such as father, mother, son etc.

ence to adoption in the Vedas or the Gṛihyas is positive evidence against the view. The struggle for the extension of the notion of sonship to other than aurasa sons, borne out by the examination of the Dharmaśāstras above, also indicates that the notion of sonship by gift and adoption did not arise naturally in Vedic society. The low position given to the Dattaka son in early law is also an indication pointing in the same direction. The first attempts at extension of sonship obviously were to give sonship to boys born in the family. The basis for this extension was not then, as has been pointed out before, the theory of ownership, but physical kinship by birth in the family.

On the other hand the theory of the absolute power of the father over sons is very prominent in Semitic societies. The sacrifice of his son by Abraham is an instance in point. In a somewhat similar predicament, Hariśchandra in the story of Śunahśepha itself could not exercise any paternal authority over his adult son, Rohita, who boldly took his arms and walked out of the house. The idea of unlimited paternal power may be assumed to have permeated the civilisations of the middle East and extended to North West India at least. The sacrifice of Iphegenia in Athens as well as the whole doctrine of Patria Potestas as implying full ownership in Rome may have been adopted from these cultures.[43]

But in Vaśiṣṭha's time the idea was still evidently a new one to sacred law, though it had come into vogue, and Vaśiṣṭha had to explain it by referring to the fact that the father was the author of the son's being. It is noticeable however that Vaśiṣṭha does not speak of the Patria Potestas of the *father* but gives the same right to *both parents* as joint authors of the son's being.

Vinogradoff in his *Historical Jurisprudence* has established that the *jus vitae et nescisque* of the father was not an institution to be found in other Indo-Germanic races. (Historical Jurisprudence I, 232). On the other hand it was a fundamental conception of Semitic races.

[43] Adoption in Roman Law was made by formal sale, with the added contrivance of triple sale by the father which extinguished his authority absolutely and made the son a son under the potestas of the adopter. There was no ritual in the *fas* for adoption. In the law of the *fas* the sale of a son was condemned. This aversion to sale of sons seems to be indicated by the provision of the XII Tables that a father who sells a son thrice loses his Potestas over the son. This law was later used as a device for emancipation of sons. That indicates that in pre-jural Rome neither the *ownership* of the father, nor adoption was known. It must have entered into the jural system, as other institutions did, by adoption of customs of non-Romans and plebians.

This explains the low position of Dattaka in early law. But evidently the doctrine found favour in societies in which the ownership over sons had already become familiar. On the other hand the growing repugnance of society to the illicit origin of the sons begotten on women of the family who had, before this, been recognised led to these sons being pushed down the scale.

Once the theory of ownership over sons against which Āpastamba protested[44] had got a hold, it followed that sons might be made by other modes of acquisition of ownership. The Kṛittrima, Krīta, Apaviddha and Svayaṃdatta are instances of sons of this character.

PĀRAŚAVA

Sūdraputra, who is also called Pāraśrava, by Manu and Yajñavalkya was distinguished by some of the law givers. But he has no logical place in the category of twelve sons. He is, strictly speaking, an aurasa son. His low position is due to the disfavour with which marriage of twice-born classes with Sūdra girls came to be looked upon by later law givers. Even these, *e.g.*, Yājñavalkya, recognise that a twice-born man may marry a Sūdra girl, but they disapprove it (naitaṃ mama matah) because in the wife the father is reborn himself (yadasyām jāyate punah).

Our examination of the law regarding secondary sons thus indicates the profound influence which non-Ārya societies exercised over the development of law in ancient India.

KINSHIP

The family, consisting of a man and woman and their offspring is the germ of every society whether patriarchal, matriarchal or totemic. In course of time families expand into larger groups of society and peoples.

Upto a certain limit, the character of the family determines the character of the wider society of kindred,—though, in the course of later development, the needs of defence and military organisation certainly takes a part in the further development. Where families are originally patriarchal, the first development is one along patriarchal lines. Thus, in Rome, the family expanded into the gens, in Athens into the phratry and genos, while, in matriarchal societies, the family expands into the clan. Each of these early social groups

[44] Apastamba Dh. s. II, 13, 11.

is at the root founded on the fact, which later grew largely into a fiction, of descent from a common ancestor.

Social Groups

From what has been said above about the character of Vedic marriage, it follows that the family grew on patrilinear lines, and consisted of persons descended from a common male ancestor exclusively through males. All indications in the Ṛigveda show that the society which it represents was patrilinear and that cognates or descendants though females had no part in the kindred, though later commentators like Yāska have attempted to read into some texts authority to support the kinship of Putrikāputra.

From the ritual literature of a later age it would seem that, while sons upon marriage set up a separate household, they lived in houses close to one another. In the ceremony of Baliharana in Baudhāyana Gṛihyasūtra we find that after bali offerings were made in every part of the householder's house the worshipper is required "to go out of the house and make the offering in the elder brother's homestead" (Upanişkramya jyeşṭāvakāse). (Baudh. Gr. S II, viii, 30).

Agnatic Groups

The larger groups are mentioned frequently in the Ṛigveda by such names as *jana* and *janma*. The precise implication of these words is a matter of controversy. But whatever they mean, *janma* indicates a group of people connected by birth. *Jana* is evidently a larger group, for each of the peoples among the *panchajanas,* Puru, Yadu, Anu, Druhyu and Turvasu is referred to as a jana which probably nearly corresponds to the Tribe in Roman society and probably to the phratry of Athens which were all units organised for military purposes.[45] Now, we can trace the genealogies of some of these janas in the Ṛigveda. It seems to me not a mere accident that no female or descendant through a female enters into these genealogies and their descent is exclusively through males.

Comparison with early Athenian and Roman social law indicates the same thing. For in Rome the gens consisted exclusively of men descended or, later, supposed to be descended from a common male ancestor. In Athens too the genos and the phratry were similarly groups of agnates. Whatever view we may hold of the theory of the

[45] Ihering in his Geist der Romischen Rechts holds that in Rome the gens and the curiae were expansions of the family, but the tribes were organised on the military principle. (6th ed., vol. I, p. 178).

common Aryan race branching out into these various peoples, there can be no doubt that the linguistic analogies betray a common culture from which the cultures of these several people, including elements of their social organisation started. For among the linguistic affinities we find words indicating several relations. We have common original names for near relations as follows:—

		Sanskrit	*Avestic*	*Greek*	*Latin*	*Germanic*
Father	...	pitā	pitar	pater	pater	fadar
Mother	...	mātā	matar	mater	mater	muotar
Son	...	sunus	hunus	—	—	sunus
Daughter	...	duhitā	dugedar	thugator	—	dauhter
Brother	...	bhrātā	brata	frater	frater	brother
Sister	...	svasā	vahar		saror	swister

There is no such similarity in the names of remoter kinsmen and, Vinogradoff points out, "there is no indication of a nomenclature based on class."[46]

It is noticeable that in Ṛigveda itself though we find references to such near relations as paternal uncle, maternal uncle, husband's brother and such others, there does not appear to be any remoter cognate relations. It is probable that the common stock of these races did not extend beyond the limits of single patriarchal families. Ancestors are often referred to in the Ṛigveda, but they are called by the class name of pitris, indicating, by the way, that the ancestors concerned were all in the paternal line.

In later law we find several important categories of kinsmen referred to, sapiṇḍas, sakulyas, samanodakas, sagotras and samanapravaras. We shall try to consider now what these terms really implied and how they evolved in the religious literature.

SAPIṆḌAS

The term sapiṇḍa is derived from piṇḍa and include all those who are connected through piṇḍa. This expression piṇḍa has been explained by Mitākṣarā as implying the body and, according to it 'sapiṇḍa' includes all persons who are connected with the same body by participating in the particles of the body of the ancestors.[47] In that sense, obviously all descendants of common ancestors however remote would be included. But according to the Mitākṣarā that sense is excluded by the express limitation imposed by texts which

[46] Vinogradoff: Historical Jurisprudence, Vol. I, page 226.

[47] Mitākṣarā on Yājñ. I, 52 (Moghe's Ed. p. 12).

limit the relation to the seventh and fifth generations through the father and the mother respectively.

On the other hand, piṇḍa means the lump or ball of rice which is offered in obsequial ceremonies to ancestors and Jimūtavāhana and many other commentators understand by sapiṇḍa persons who participate in that piṇḍa. According to that view, as piṇḍas are offered to the three ancestors, these with the offeror himself and, on the other hand the three descendants who offer the piṇḍas together constitute the seven members of the sapiṇḍa group.

There can be little doubt that when the Smṛiti texts refer to sapiṇḍa, or connected through piṇḍa, they refer to the offering made at srāddhas.[48]

Looking back at the Vedas we find that the word piṇḍa is not used in the Ṛigveda to signify the funeral repast. It has been used in places to signify the body of the animal sacrificed (I, 162, 19). The word sapiṇḍa seldom appears.

Pitriyajna

Offering of piṇḍas to the three ancestors was however an ancient ritual which, under the name of pitṛiyajña, is described in detail in the Śatapatha Brāhmana, Taittiriya Saṃhitā and in the Gṛihya Sūtras in which it is counted among the Panchayajñas otherwise called Panchamahāyajñas. These include Devayajña, Brahmayajña, Pitṛiyajña and Manuṣyayajña and are among the primary duties of householders (Āśvalāyana, III, 1, 2, see Kane, Hist. Dh. S., Vol. II, Part I, 1085 seq. for details of pitṛipiṇḍayajña). In this yajña balls of rice called piṇḍas are offered to the three paternal ancestors and to them only.

When therefore Dharmasūtra writers like Gautama refer to piṇḍa-sambaddhān as heirs to the sonless they clearly refer to these oblations to the ancestors and mean by this term persons related through these oblations. So too the other Smṛitis, when they refer to sapiṇḍas imply the same persons by this term. The persons related to one another through these piṇḍas are thus apparently the primary group for Vedic Āryas in fact, though they may not have been given that name in the Ṛigveda.

But who were the exact people who, like the Lares of ancient Rome, constituted this group?

[48] Gautama XV, 13, XXVIII, 21; Apastamba Dh. S. II, 6, 14, 2, Vasistha IV, 16-18, Visnu XV, 40 all connect inheritance with *giving* of pindas. See infra, Chap. VIII.

Gautama on Sapinda

In Gautama's Dharmasūtra (Ch. XV, 13) we find that the persons who offer piṇḍas in the absence of sons are stated to be (1) Sapiṇḍas, (2) Sapiṇḍas of the deceased's mother, or (3) his pupil. It seems that the word, 'sapiṇḍa' here includes only agnates, for otherwise the mention of "his mother's sapiṇḍas" separately would be meaningless, as, according to the meaning later assigned to the term, a man's mother's sapiṇḍas would also be his own sapiṇḍas.

In the chapter on Impurities (Ch. XIV, 34) Gautama prescribes a period of impurity of ten days upon the death of an asapiṇḍa-yonisaṃbaddha. The period of impurity prescribed—which is ten days is the same as that for a sapiṇḍa (XIV, 1)—indicates that it refers to very near relatives. Yonisambaddha means relation by birth, *i.e.*, a blood relation. I take this to imply near blood-relation and the whole expression "asapiṇḍda yonisaṃbaddha" to refer to near blood relations who are not sapiṇḍas. Haradatta understands this term to imply samanodakas of later law though that term is nowhere to be found in Gautama, and Bühler translates it as "a relative who is not a sapiṇḍa, a relative by marriage" which is not justified by the original text. To my mind this text here refers to near cognates, for they are connected by birth but are not conceived to be sapiṇḍas. It would follow that Gautama understood by the term sapiṇḍa or piṇḍasaṃbaddha only agnates, while near cognates were regarded by him as asapiṇḍas.

In the ritual of pitṛipiṇḍayajña, we have seen that piṇḍas are offered only to the three immediate male ancestors and to none else. Gautama probably contemplates the same rule and regards other near relations in the same degrees as asapiṇḍas. When therefore he gives the inheritance of a sonless person to piṇḍasaṃbaddhas, he implies agnates only and not cognatic sapiṇḍas of later law who were not kindred in Vedic society.

At the same time we find an innovation, when Gautama introduces the mother's sapiṇḍas of the deceased to offer piṇḍas in the absence of sapiṇḍas. "Mother's sapiṇḍas" in this context would be meaningless unless it implies near relations in her father's family ; and if that is so, the rule indicates that cognatic relationship is coming into some sort of recognition in the law of srāddha though not to sapiṇḍaship. This text would, on this view, indicate a stage in the transition of Vedic society from the purely agnatic to a mixed kinship. As we come to later works, we find cognatic kinship fully established. Piṇḍas are now offered by a man not only to his three paternal ancestors but also to the three paternal ancestors of his mother. He thus becomes a sapiṇḍa of his maternal grandfather as well as of his two male ancestors and his four male descendants who are the maternal grandfather's sapiṇḍas, sapiṇḍa relationship being considered to be reciprocal.

Cognatic Kinship

I have tried to indicate what I conceive to be the agency by which cognates were introduced into the kinship. It was through the introduction of the Putrikāputra. The Putrikā's son is treated as a son and therefore he offers piṇḍas to his mother's father and his two male ancestors, though at the same time he also offers piṇḍas in his father's line.

When in course of time, as pointed out before, the institution of Putrikā was merged in a general law elevating any daughter to her place, the law of piṇḍa applicable to a putrikā's son continued to apply to any daughter's son. One peculiar result when the dauhitra stepped into the position of a putrikāputra was that while on the father's side a daughter's son offers piṇḍas to three generations from the father upwards, on the mother's side the range of piṇḍas goes further up to the fourth ancestor, that is to three ancestors beyond his mother, the mother being ignored for computing these ancestors. The reason for this apparent anomaly is historical and lies in the fact that Putrikāputra was originally a substitute son of his maternal grandfather, and therefore, had, like his aurasa son, to offer piṇḍas to him and his two ancestors. The rule survived the Putrikā and was now applied to dauhitras generally. Kinship with the maternal relations like mother's brother, his sons and so forth necessarily followed. A Putrikāputra being a son of his maternal grandfather would be kindred like a son to all the sapiṇḍas of that grand-father.

The logical working out of this principle gradually led to the inclusion of other cognates like the mother's sister's son etc. into the reciprocal sapiṇḍa relationship for they too now offered piṇḍas to their maternal ancestors, and this in course of time opened the way to complex problems regarding to succession of Bandhus as they were understood by the Mitākṣarā, the last word on which has perhaps not yet been heard in our Courts.

It follows thus that in early Vedic society kinship extended on purely patrilinear lines, just as it did in Athens and Rome, and cognates came into the range of kinship later, as a result of the institution of Putrikā, which itself, as we have seen before, was introduced under non-Ārya influence.

GOTRA

Sakulyas and samānodakas are two classes of agnatic kindred beyond the sapinda group who have been distinguished only in the later Smritis but are not distinguished for purposes of kinship, not only in Vedic literature but also in the early dharmasūtras. The group of kindred next to sapiṇdas which is mentioned in early texts is sagotra or persons belonging to the same gotra.

Kane (op cit Vol. II Part I page 479) points out that there is no positive instance of the word gotra having been used in the Ṛigveda in the sense of the group of descendants of a common Ṛiṣi ancestor. Even in the Atharvaveda (V, 21, 3) where the word 'viśvagotra' is used, 'gotra' obviously means 'a family'. The original meaning of the word was cow-pen and it was apparently extended later to all those who had the same cow-pen, i.e. the kindred living by one another.

On the other hand there is evidence that in Vedic times men used to be called by family names which were the names of the founders of the family. There is reason to suppose that names like Vaśiṣṭha and Viśvāmitra were not merely individual names but names which applied to all persons belonging to families of that name. And in later Vedic literature we find plenty of instances where individuals are indicated by such petronymics. Kane (op cit 479-80) gives a large number of illustrations of such practice. More familiar instances may be found in the Bṛihadāraṇyaka e.g. where Svetaketu is called Āruneya ; and Gārgi is called Vāchaknavi. These ancestral names which were family names ultimately came to be known as 'gotra' names after long generations had passed from the common ancestor. A gotra now came to mean a unit of society consisting of all persons descended in the male line from a Ṛiṣi who was their eponymous ancestor, in fact or by a fiction. This bears an obvious analogy to the gens of Rome which consisted of men who were all supposed to be descended from a common ancestor based upon the evidence of their having the same surname.

Naturally, it is not every man who could be the founder of the family which could go down generations with repute in India or anywhere else. It is only families whose founder was a man of eminence and whose line, for generations, maintained a reputation and could be remembered in the days of his successors by the name he gave them. This seems to be what happened in the case of gotras. Families, expanded into communities, founded by eminent Ṛiṣis whose reputation survived generations later and whose names would be remembered with reverence. These were distinguished as the founders of the respective gotras at a time when it had become the practice to distinguish their descendants by the names of famous ancestors who were deemed to be the founders of gotras and their gotra names survived. Every Brāhmana then went by the name of his illustrious ancestor.

It seems that in this manner some descendants of a Ṛiṣi founder of a gotra became so distinguished on their own account that their descendants would go specifically by their names instead of that of the remoter ancestor. In this manner apparently gotras went on growing in number for some generations in the Vedic age until the further growth was stopped, once the gotras were crystallised in a śāstric formula.

The distinction which gave to these men the eminence deserving perpetuation of their name in their lineage was distinction in spiritual eminence, in religion, science and magic which entitled a person to the rank of a Ṛiṣi or inspired seer. The founders of gotras were therefore only seers, and therefore, Brāhmanas or very learned Kṣatriyas by birth or promotion on account of spiritual eminence. At a time when caste had become hereditary and fixed, therefore, it was only Brāhmanas who could claim a gotra by descent. But the same gotra name was also given to men of other castes who formed members of the same community, of which these Brāhmanas were the spiritual heads. This, which seems to have been a fact, probably became the basis of the theory adumbrated later, that Brāhmanas alone had a prātisvika gotra, i.e. gotra by descent while other people are known by the gotra of their purohit.

This in my opinion was the history of the development of gotra in outline, a concept round which there developed a vast amount of literature, far from consistent throughout, but, like many other branches of ancient knowledge, diversified by interpretations and original contributions of many authors. This mass of materials has been considered and discussed by Kane in his History of Dharmaśāstras (Vol. II Part I page 479 et seq.) He quotes the expression of despair of the author of Pravaramanjari of any attempt to reconcile them. But I venture to think that the history of gotra which I have here attempted to reconstruct would be found to explain satisfactorily from a historical point of view the bulk of what appears in these texts.

If I am right in the view here given it would seem that from the earliest times Vedic societies grew round eminent families or gotras, founded on patrilinear descent alone from a real or supposed common ancestor whose name all members of the gotra bore. But the connection of members of the gotra though founded on a theory of common origin was based essentially on a common spiritual communion between them. As we have seen the founders of gotras were eminent Ṛiṣis who had their specific spiritual creed and cult and members of the gotra were members of a spiritual fraternity founded by them.

Ārṣeya or Pravara.

At the present time at every ritual the person who performs it has to introduce his name in the ritual by referring to his gotra as well as pravara. In the Vedic age however the practice was not to refer to the gotra but to the ārṣeya of the worshippers, called Pravara in later literature.

The practice of invoking Agni at a sacrifice by giving the names of Ṛiṣi ancestors of the worshipper was as old as the Ṛigveda. Thus in Ṛigveda VIII 102, 4, the worshipper says, "I invoke Agni as Aurva, Bhṛigu and Apahnava did". Kane (op cit page 487) who quotes this, points out that the three Ṛiṣis Aurva, Bhṛigu and Apahnava are three out of the five Ṛiṣis mentioned by Baudhāyana as the pravara of the Vatsa-Bhṛigu gotra, which suggests that the two other names were added to the Ārṣeya by later tradition. In Ṛigveda (VII, 18, 21) the worshipper invokes Agni by saying "they who from house to house gladdened thee, being desirous of thee viz. Parāśara, Śatatāyu and Vasiṣṭha, will not forget the friendship of a liberal patron like thee." Kane points out that Satatāyu is the name of Śaktri the son of Vasiṣṭha and that the Pravara of Parāśara gotra is Vasiṣṭha, Parāśara and Śaktri. These and other passages quoted by Kane (op cit 487) amply show that gods were invoked in the earliest days by giving the names of the sacrificer's Ārṣeya. The verb used for invocation in Ṛigveda VIII 102, 4 above in "huve".

In the Śatapatha Brāhmana, wherever the worshipper invokes Agni for choosing him as his agent to carry oblations he is similarly required to introduce himself and invoke the god by his Ārṣeya. The words used are "ārṣeyam pravṛinute". From the practice of this pravarana being made with the names of the ancester Ṛiṣis in the Ārṣeya the new name Pravara for Ārṣeya was apparently derived.

The names of the Ṛiṣis in the several Ārṣeyas or Pravaras indicate that they were the distinguished ancestors of the worshipper in whose name the worshipper introduces himself to the gods. Thus, in the pravara of the Parāśaragotra, Vaśiṣṭha is the father of Śaktri and Śaktri of Parasara. They were all of them very distinguished Ṛiṣis and each of them the founder of a gotra. This shows how, according to tradition a distinguished descendant of a founder of a gotra would himself become the founder of a new gotra, but, none the less, his spiritual connection with his predecessor in the Ārṣeya would continue. Thus the Ārṣeya of men of each of these three gotras would be the same three Ṛiṣis namely Vaśiṣṭha, Śaktri and Parāśara.

In post-Vedic ages gotra names which were handier for the purposes of identification of a man seem to have replaced the Ārṣeya for all purposes except the Vedic sacrifices in which the uttering of the Ārṣeya was imperative to make the mantras effective. and gotra gradually became the more important relationship for practical purposes and we find in the Smṛiti literature that gotra relationship was of great importance for many purposes.

Spiritual Kinship

All these relations of kinship, the sapiṇḍa, sagotra, sakulya samanodaka as well as gotra and pravara were extensions of primary kinship in a family and all arose out of blood relationship, real, assumed or fictitious. Yet blood-relationship was not all of these relations. Their great importance for these ancients lay in the belief in a magic spiritual bond sanctified by appropriate sacrae which was to endure not only here but hereafter. This faith in the spirituality of kinship is the foundation of much that there is in the sacred as well as in the lawyer's law in India.

Thus, the son whose kinship is nearest and most patently physical is conceived, not as the father's flesh and bone but his soul reborn, implying a spiritual bond which is cemented on the occation of each of the eighteen saṃskāras by appropriate mantras. The next group of kindred, the sapiṇḍas are spiritually connected by their common sacrae in honour of their ancestors. Yet larger groups of kindred the sagotra and samanarṣa are likewise connected with one another by participating in the spiritual community of their common ṛiṣi ancestors.

This magico-religious idea of spirituality of kinship made the further extension of kinship beyond blood relations easy and natural for the ancient Indians. The wife is made spiritually kindred by the marriage mantras as a result of which her gotra is changed to that of her husband. So too the adopted son is affiliated to the gotra of his adopter by the magic of mantra.

Besides, we find from the very outset that a spiritual kinship which leads to important results is recognised between the Āchārya and the pupil as also between fellow pupils of the same Āchārya. The relationship was such that on the death of one impurity attached to the others (Gau. XIV, 20). And, in the absence of other kinsmen the right to perform śrādha belongs to the pupil or fellow pupils of the deceased (Gau. XV, 13-14). And the Āchārya or Siṣya and fellow pupil inherit to a dead man after other relations but before the king. (Yājn. II, 135-6).

Philosophers and historians of law have sought for the foundations of kinship in every society in the needs for defence.

Vinogradoff[49] finds the basis of kinship in the necessity for organising for the purposes of defence. That may be a powerful motive for the development of some aspects of kinship, but to my mind it would be going too far to look upon that as the only historical or logical source or basis of organisation of kindred in primitive or ancient society. An equally, if not more powerful motive was spiritual necessity and faith in magic virtues. No family, gens or clan was ever knit together without some sort of magic faith and formula, and, though some scholars like Fustel de Coulanges may have gone too far in exaggerating the role of sacrae and the Hearth Fire, the basis of these rituals in the faith in supernatural bonds was certainly potent in forging the chains of kinship in ancient times. In ancient India the evidence is overwhelming of the importance of this spiritual nexus in the build up of society.

We get evidence in the Vedas and later literature of even wider social units like jana, janma, kula, sreni, gana etc. which were not all of them founded on kinship. Jana and janma were apparently founded on a real or supposed kinship by common descent, but these too, and decidedly the others, were primarily founded on local or occupational community the binding principle in which was very likely the needs of defence of the community and their institutions.

[49] Historical Jurisprudence I, 299 et seq.

CHAPTER VIII

LAW OF INHERITANCE

The law of inheritance in Hindu law has been the part of it which has been most intensively studied in India on account of practical necessities. That law, however, is the law as it was developed almost entirely in the middle ages.

I shall make no attempt in this lecture to go into details of the law of inheritance even in its early stages but only indicate what seem to me to be the salient features in the history of its evolution from its earliest stages down through the ages of the dharma śāstras.

Son

The first point to notice about this is that the rule about the inheritance of the son to the father, which is the primary fact in the books of law proper, was itself a growth out of earlier usage.

The earliest texts that we get in the Dharma-sūtras indicate that sons succeeded to the father upon his death[50]. But it is probable that this rule itself was development out of an earlier practice. It seems to have been usual for a person in old age to retire and, before doing so, to divide his property. We get evidence of this in Vedic texts saying that Manu divided his property (Dāya) between his sons (Taittīriyasaṃhita I, 9, 4 also quoted in a slightly different form in Apastamba II, 6, 14, 10.). In the Ṛigveda III, 32, 2 we find a text "Na jāmaye tānvo rikthamāraika chakāra garbham janitur nidhanam" which has been explained in the Nirukta as follows:

"Not to sisters should the begotten son (Tānva) give the Ṛiktha or inheritance. She is made the receptacle for the child of her husband."

This of course assumes that the son gets the inheritance and only says that the daughter is to get no share of it. The significance of this exclusion of the daughter will be considered later.

The story in the Bṛihadāraṇyaka Upaniṣad about Yājñavalkya and Maitreyī is also an indication of the ancient practice of a person dividing his wealth upon retirement. Yājñavalkya however is said

[50] The word used is 'vibhajeran' shall divide. The primary object of this part of the law is the division of the heritage among sons. The inheritance of others is wholly subsidiary and, in early works very summarily dealt with.

to have divided his wealth between his wives. These texts indicate firstly that the owner of property had a right, at any rate, to dispose of his property, apparently freely and, not only to sons, and, secondly, that good men in old age used to retire into forest settlement after dividing their properties. In making this division the retiring householder was not under any obligation to divide among any particular persons or in any particular manner. It is probable that these texts belong to a time when land or immoveable property had not, at any rate, become an important item of property and the only properties then contemplated were moveables, including livestock.

Disposal of Old Men

It will be remembered that in primitive societies disposal of old men who were of no use to society but were a burden on it was a problem which pressed for solution and the solution was sought in various, sometimes very cruel, ways. Even in ancient Rome according to some, it was at one stage the practice, apparently referred to in XII Tables, of throwing old men from the bridge into the Tiber. This mode of disposing of old men by killing was common usage in primitive societies so long as physical fitness for hunting, fighting etc. was the chief test of social utility of men. In a more settled state of society when wisdom was recognised as of no less value than physical fitness, a wholly contrary attitude towards old age grew up. Old men might be physically unfit but their experience and wisdom were of great value. Where this was recognised, old men were not simply liquidated but treated with honour and often placed in a position e.g. as a Senator in Rome, to guide and regulate people's affairs.

In the ancient Indian conception, the primitive stage had long been passed. Society prized old men for their sagacity but they were to be relieved of the troubles and turmoils of a worldly life, to live in apparent comfort in settlements away from the haunts of the common men and spend their days in the practice of virtue appropriate to that age, and in meditations and religious practices in preparation for the life hereafter, leaving worldly assets to younger people.

This was the humane solution of the problem of old age in ancient India, in keeping with the overwhelming importance of meditation, so characteristic of ancient Indian wisdom, which we find indicated by the texts above referred to.

Succession of sons

The texts of Ṛig Veda (III, 31, 2) and the Taittiriya Saṃhitā above referred to have been followed as precedents in all ages and they show that the practice of division of property among sons by men in old age had been well established, for ancient peoples always have a tendency to follow illustrious precedents. Out of this practice apparently arose the custom of succession of sons to the property of a deceased person even when the father had not made the division in his life time. In this manner the law of inheritance of sons appears to have evolved out of a repetition of this practice of partition by an act inter vivos by what may be called of donatio mortis civilis causa.

But this rule of succession of sons does not seem to have been established altogether without dispute or differences. Faint indications can be traced of the assertion of other ideas in some texts by the very vigour of the repudiation of such contrary views. Thus the Ṛig Veda text cited above, by its vigorous repudiation of daughters participating with sons in the inheritance left by the father, indicates the existence of such a contrary view point which may have been asserted in some societies.

Other views are similarly indicated, for example, by a text quoted in the commentaries, for establishing the right of the sons to inherit, which is rather significant. It says "not brothers, nor parents but sons are the heirs of the father." (na bhrātarah na pitarah, putrāh ṛikthaharāh pituḥ). It may be that this was meant to refute the doctrines or practice which apparently had vogue in some places, it may be among people of alien culture, by which the brother or father if alive, inherited in preference to the son. It is by no means altogether rare to find elsewhere a rule of this kind which has been distinguished by Sir Henry Maine by its Irish name of Tanistry.[51] There might have been instances of peoples amongst whom Tanistry prevailed or it might be that brothers took the property in certain social conditions when the sons of the owner were very young. Instances of brothers of kings succeeding to the throne in preference to young sons are by no means absent in Indian history and legend.

Texts on Inheritance by sons

The earliest law that we get in the texts with regard to inheritance of the sons is indicated in the following texts.

[51] Maine, Early Institutions Lecture VII.

Sānkha cited in Smṛitichandrikā and Mitākṣarā "During the life-time of the father the sons do not enjoy (or divide) the inheritance."

Devala cited in Mitākṣarā "Upon the death of the father, the sons divide the inheritance."

Another text of Śānkha is cited by Mitākṣarā (Ed. Moghe, p. 184), [which is cited by Mayukha (ed. Maudlik, p. 34) as a text of Hārita] "Even when the father does not desire, inheritance may be divided when the father is old and out of his mind or ill."

These texts and similar other texts which can be found in later Smṛitis like Manu, Yājñavalkya, Nārada and others indicate that the father enjoys his property during the life-time and sons only divide between them after his death. Along with these, we have to consider certain other texts which belong to another and perhaps an older stratum of thought which is reproduced in Manu under the law regarding slaves. It says that the wife, the son and slave has no property and whatever they acquire becomes the property of him to whom they belong (VIII, 415). This indicates a condition of society in which the sons not only had no right to the family property but were incapable of acquiring any property at all for their own benefit (See Manu VIII, 415, Sabara on Jaimini VI. 1-12). As pointed out by Sabaraswami in his comment on the text, this is flatly opposed to other texts even in the earliest Dharmasutras which recognise specific property of sons and wives during the life-time of the father. The text of Manu above quoted is perhaps a survival from a condition of society in which the sons were incapable of acquiring any property themselves.

Primogeniture and Uddhara

On the other hand there is a class of texts which definitely lay down that all the property of the father goes to the eldest son alone and it is the duty of the younger sons to live with him just as they lived under their father. Manu for instance in IX 105 seq lays down that "The eldest son takes the entire paternal property and the rest must live under him just as they did under the father. By the birth of the eldest, a man becomes endowed with a son and acquires freedom from the debt to his ancestors. So he is entitled to inheritance. He by whom debts are satisfied and through whom one acquires immortality, he alone is a son born of Dharma, the rest are known as born of lust." On the other hand, Manu continues, "the eldest brother must protect younger brothers like a father and mother." These texts certainly represent a different stratum of legal thought and, as in other provisions in the present Manusaṃhitā different strata are here mixed up together. This again is followed by other provisions about the partition with Uddhāra.

Similarly Āpastamba (II, 6, 14, 10 to 12) refers to this theory of the eldest taking all the property—though he refutes it

"Jyeṣṭho dāyādah ityeke, tachchhāstra vipratisiddham. Manu putrebhyo dāyam vyabhajad ityaviśeṣena śrūyate." Tathāpi 'tasmat jyeṣṭham dhanena niravasāyayantyetachchrūyante.

Another strain of thought is represented by texts which did not give the entire inheritance to the eldest son but gives him a preferential right. These texts lay down that before partition, there is to be a special share of the eldest son set apart after which the rest is to be divided equally. This is called partition with Uddhāra.

With regard to this again the texts are not uniform. Thus Yājñavalkya (II, 114-17) lays down that where the father divides the property between his sons, he can do it as he likes, or he may give a superior share to the eldest or make all of them equal sharers." Manu (IX 112) says "Eldest son takes a 1/20th share as Uddhāra and also the best amongst the things. The second son takes half of that and the younger son takes a ¼th share" that is to say, the second takes ½ of the eldest son's preferential share and the next son takes ¼th of the eldest son's share. Baudhāyana (Dh. S II, 2, 1-6) who absolutely denies the validity of unequal division among sons allows uddhāra of one tenth to the eldest alone.

There is another school of synthetic thought which records "Unequal division or the preference of the son is possible only where the father divides the property. But after the death of the father all the sons should divide equally. These are represented by the text of Hārita cited in the Mayūkha (Ed. Mandlik, page 35) which says "Samāno mṛite pitari ṛiktha vibhāgah."

These various texts have been interpreted variously in the commentaries as laying down one single law Thus, for instance Medhātithi explains the right of the eldest son as given in the text of Manu IX 106 etc. as merely Praśaṃsā or praise of the eldest son. Another synthesis is founded by the text of Manu which says that the sons may live together or separately for the sake of religious merit, for, on partition religious merit increases. So the separation of sons is according to law. Gautama also says that by partition religious merit increases,—the principle being that upon separation each brother has a separate house fire and separate set of sacrifices which brings more spiritual merit.

The suggestion that occurs to one however is that historically these different texts do not fall in one single line of development.

The different texts lay down different laws which prevailed by the custom of different societies. In the age of synthesis which came somewhere about the time of the present Manusaṃhitā these texts were brought together and sought to be explained by so-called reconciliations of conflicting texts. Thus while Āpastamba unhesitatingly rejects the theory of the eldest son taking the property as opposed to Sruti texts, Yājñavalkya in his text (in II, 114 to 117) gives three alternative ways of dividing the wealth :

(1) According to the wishes of the father,
(2) by giving a superior share to the eldest, and
(3) by equal division.

The text of Manu IX, 112 indicates a further original development by which if the eldest is preferred, the second is sought to be preferred also to his younger brother. Medhātithi, as we have found, explains the eldest son's exclusive right to inheritance as mere praśaṃsa, and other commentators follow him in rejecting the exclusive right of the eldest son. But many of them recognise the right of the eldest son to some specific properties as Uddhāra. In the course of time, however, the preference of senior sons apparently went out of use. These diversities in the old texts from the Vedas downwards even with regard to what most people now regard as a primary natural law of the sons inheriting to the father was one of the puzzles which lawgivers had to face as a result of the syncretism in the organisation of ancient Indian society referred to before.

Some of the societies which went to make the synthetic Vedic society had a custom of Tanistry. Others practised primogeniture. Yet others distinguished between sons according to seniority, and so on. When all the sacred texts appertaining to these different societies were lumped together and built into a single revealed code of unquestioned authority the conflict between them had to be faced, and in course of time a fair measure of agreement was arrived at, but not so as to silence all dissent. The agglomeration of all the different views in the series of texts of Manu indicates that each of these texts continued to be followed in diverse societies in his time, until a further synthesis was attempted by the commentaries, though again, not with complete uniformity.

Such diversity would be inevitable even on the assumption of a common single stock from which later Āryas sprang, if we suppose, as seems likely, that the law or practice of inheritance was ultimately founded upon a practice of a man dividing his wealth before death as the Vedic text indicates. In the absence of any curb upon the discretion of the father in making the division, different customs would naturally grow up in different societies, which were later embodied as rules of law in the manuals of those respective societies. It is only when the manuals ceased to be authorities only in their respective schools and each became equal authority for all Āryas that these conflicts would become embarassing and lead to attempts at synthesis in later text books.

In some of the ancient texts we find some reference to the spiritual efficacy of sons as a ground for giving them preference over brothers or others, though their right is not exactly expressed to be founded on such efficacy. But this principle, originally referred to but casually, becomes in course of time a powerful argument for determining the order of succession. In Viṣṇu we find the offering of pindas and taking of inheritance almost invariably coupled together in the formula "pindam dadyāt hared dhanam." Manu not only follows the same formula as a rule but founds upon this superior religious efficacy an argument for preferring the eldest son to others, as stated above.

We shall presently consider the place of spiritual benefit in the theory of succession.

The preference of the eldest son was against the older and more orthodox view represented in Vedic tradition referred to by Āpastamba, by which equal division amongst sons is indicated. [See Apastamba, II, 6, 14 VI, 10, 12 and Taitt., III 194 and II 525 which however speaks of the separating (niravasāyayanti) the eldest son by wealth.] In later days apparently, equal division becomes the rule and is upheld by Mitākṣarā which practically became the universal rule,—though even in later days, the uddhāravibhāga is sometimes advocated.

It seems however that it was not always that all the sons inherited equally. There are indications to show that sons sometimes separated from the fathers' family during the lifetime of the father. Taitt. Samhita, II, 5, II 7 (jyestham putram dhanena niravasāyayanti) speaks of the eldest son being separated by giving wealth. This is probably associated with the idea behind the text of Yājñavalkya viz. Śaktasyāmīhamānasya kiṃchiddattvā prithakkriyā. The eldest son would probably be a person who would, during the lifetime of his father, be earning on his own account and set up on his own. In the very story of Manu having divided his property among his sons we find that one son, not the eldest but the youngest, Navanediṣta, was left out of the division. We find however that that son had an independent life of his own and was probably a sort of an emancipated son. In the later text of Yājñavalkya however it is provided that even in the case of such sons who were śakta (capable) and therefore did not desire to share his father's wealth, the father should separate him by giving him just a trifle (kiṃchit) out of paternal properties and it is only those sons who were dependent on father that would take the inheritance. A trace of this idea is to be found in the emancipation of sons in Rome.

It will be shown later that the theory of the joint family between the father and sons implying jointness in title to the property was not the idea of Vedic society. On the contrary, the idea seems to have been that the sons after their marriage are separated and form separate households. If that is so, one would expect that the inheritance would be divided only amongst the sons who were dependent just as in the law of the Twelve Tables the inheritance went first to the Sui and not to the Emancipati.

Inheritance to the Sonless

In spite of some diversities mentioned only to be repudiated, Vedic society at an early stage settled down evidently to the notion that sons inherited to the father. All the earliest texts of law agree in this though differences exist in respect of the preference of the eldest and of seniors and primogeniture is recognised in some texts.

The law with regard to succession in the absence of sons opens up further room for diversification.

The earliest texts resemble early law elsewhere in not going into details about the persons entitled to inherit. They mention heirs by classes. In early Roman law the inheritance goes first to Sui, that is, to sons under power, and next to Emancipati, sons emancipated, and then to agnates and, failing that, to the gens. In other ancient systems too such as the Athenian, Irish and Anglo Saxon laws heirs after the son are mentioned by classes.[52] So too in the early sutra works in India, the remoter heirs are only mentioned by classes.

Thus Gautama lays down that the men who succeed to the sonless person are persons connected by piṇḍa, gotra and arṣa, the wife being mentioned as a possible alternative.

Āpastamba's rule of inheritance to the sonless is that the heirs are Sapiṇḍas, the Āchārya, the pupils, the daughter and, next, the king. The wife is given only her ornaments, which were recognised as her property from the earliest times (Āpastamba II, 6, 14).

[52] See author's Evolution of Law, pages 126-128.

Vaśiṣṭha gives the inheritance to a sonless man to the (1) Sapiṇḍas, (2) the spiritual preceptor or pupil.

Baudhāyana gives practically the same list and only adds ṣakulyas after sagotras.

It is only in Viṣṇu that we find, for the first time, a rule of succession of various individually named heirs in succession (Viṣṇu XVII) but even in Viṣṇu as well as in Yājñavalkya remoter heirs after the brother's son are named only by classes.

It will be noticed that Gautama and others when they mention the class of Sapiṇḍas and others as heirs do not take the trouble to distinguish between different sapiṇḍas with reference to the nearness of their kinship as does the Twelve Tables with reference to agnati by giving the inheritance to the proximus agnatus. It will not probably be justifiable from this to infer that all sapiṇḍas, whatever their degree of relationship with the deceased would take equally. Here we may remember the warning of Ihering that we must not take early statements of law (Rechtssätze) to contain the whole law. There are generally qualifications to the rule in practical application which were so familiar to contemporaries as not to require express statement or which escaped observation or specification by reason of their very familiarity. It is likely therefore that as between different members of each class some idea of relative propinquity was probably the assumed rule. It is by no means impossible though, that classes may have originally succeeded as a body as seems to have been the rule elsewhere in ancient or primitive laws.

It would be clear however that where sagotras or samānārṣas succeed they must have succeeded as a body, in the same manner as in ancient Rome the gens, which was the successor after the Agnati, took as a body. For there does not seem, at any time, to have been any means to determine the nearness of kinship of these classes.

Later law was developed by working out more detailed orders of succession and also by specifying the individuals who would succeed. This progress was completed only in the works of the middle ages by commentators who went into elaborate discussions on the rival claims of different relations. Already in Viṣṇu however we find a definite order of succession worked out down the brother's son. (Viṣṇu, XVIII—9). Yājñavalkya also follows Viṣṇu in this respect. In some of the later Smṛitis we find rules for determining the degree of propinquity which gives a right to succession (See Bṛihaṣpati S.B.E., XXXIII, page 379).

Theory of spiritual benefit

One of the tests by which preferential right to succession is determined is the right to offer piṇḍas or other funeral offerings to the deceased.

There is a controversy between the Mitākṣarā School of Vijñāneśvara on the one hand and Jimūtavāhana on the other on the question whether the offering of piṇḍas or spiritual benefit is the cause of a person's right to be a sapiṇḍa or to inherit. Jimūtavāhana makes this spiritual benefit the corner stone of his scheme for determining the order of succession, not only to males but also to females. Vijñānesvara on the other hand denies the claim. Succession according to him is determined by propinquity alone. He gives a new meaning to the word sapiṇḍa by taking 'piṇḍa' in sapiṇḍa to mean body, so that sapiṇḍa is a person related by partaking of the particles of the same body. Many other authors like Devaṇṇa Bhatta, who follow the Mitākṣarā generally, are however of a different opinion and consider sapiṇḍa relationship to be founded on community through funeral oblations.

There can be no doubt however that the Smṛitis throughout understand the word sapiṇḍa to mean person connected through funeral oblations. There is no doubt likewise that they generally consider kinship through funeral oblations as a concomitant of right to succeed. Thus Viṣṇu (XV 40) definitely lays down that whoever takes the inheritance is the offeror of piṇḍa.[53] Manu after establishing the right of a daughter's son to inherit goes on to say that he gives two piṇḍas to his two grandfathers (IX, 132) and, further on, says, of a daughter's son, that he offers piṇḍas and takes the inheritance (IX, 136). Jimūtavāhana pertinently points out that the reference to piṇḍa in connection with inheritance clearly implies that Manu considered the offering of piṇḍas as the cause of the right to inherit. Yājñavalkya too after enumedating the twelve kinds of sons goes on that these are piṇḍa givers and heirs one after another (in the order of enumeration).[54]

That the property left by the deceased was charged for performance of his obsequial rites is also stated in a text of Bṛihaṣpati who says that when sapiṇḍas divide the property half the wealth

[53] **यश्चार्थहरः स एव पिराडदायी,** though it is added that a son must offer pinda even if he does not inherit property **पुत्रः पितृवित्तालाभेऽपि पिराडं दद्यात्** (XV. 43).

[54] Yājñ. II, 132. **पिण्डदोऽशहराश्चैव पूर्वाभावे परः परः ।**

must be set apart for the performance of his monthly, six monthly and annual Srāddhas.[55]

On the basis of these and other texts Jimūtavāhana builds up his thesis that preferential right to succession depends upon the amount of spiritual benefit conferred by a person by offering oblations or water to the deceased, a theory which he works out rigorously. Other authors like Devaṇṇa Bhatta also refer to this principle but not with the same consistency.

As against this we have the fact that the earlier sutra works nowhere refer to spiritual benefit in connection with the law of inheritance. It does not necessarily follow that they did not recognise any connection between spiritual benefit and the right to inherit. On the other hand Gautama's scheme of succession is founded on spiritual kinship through piṇḍa, gotra or Ārṣa.

It seems to me that, historically, spiritual benefit and inheritance were correlated with one another from the earliest times though, it may be, not as cause and effect. As I have mentioned before (supra p. 168) kinship in early law was deemed to be essentially not a mere mundane or physical affair but a spiritual relation. One's son and other descendants were kindred physically no doubt, but also through the magic spiritual unity. So were sapiṇḍas, sagotras and samānārsas. Physical propinquity was the fact in the first of these relations but that by itself was neither the whole nor perhaps the vital part of it, the essence was the magic bond which united kindred and which was signalised by appropriate rituals. If that was the fact, it would naturally follow that inheritance and funeral oblations which were equally founded on this kinship would go together. It would follow equally that in case of doubt about the right of succession, the question of spiritual kinship determined by the magic ritual of Śrāddha would be referred to as a criterion. There can be no doubt that Manu was thus applying this test in introducing the daughter and her son into the compact scheme of agnatic kinship. Vijñāneśwara was not departing from the ancient texts in laying down that propinquity was the test for determining the right to inheritance but he did so depart in holding that propinquity was not at all dependent on the piṇḍa theory but merely on physical participation in the particles of a common ancestral body.

We have seen above that the early texts on inheritance are founded essentially on an agnatic scheme of succession and, likewise,

[55] S.B.E. Vol. 33, page 379, verse 61. For analogous history in Roman Law, see Author's Evolution of Law, 2nd Ed., p. 114.

on a total exclusion of females. The only exceptions were the widow in Gautama and the daughter after Bandhus in Āpastamba's text. But from Viṣṇu onwards the widow and the daughter have risen to a definite place in the scheme of inheritance. So too in the case of remoter heirs some principles of preference of individual relations have been evolved.

The order of succession is laid down in Yājñavalkya, practically following Viṣṇu, as follows: (1) The widow, (2) daughters, (3) Parents, (4) Brothers, (5) Brother's sons, (6) Gotrajas, (7) Bandhus, (8) Pupils, (9) Fellow students and failing all the king,[56] except to a Brāhmana's wealth.

This list was further developed in detail by the later commentaries.

I shall now attempt to consider the evolution of heirship of these relations in this order.

WIFE

The wife did not come into the scheme of inheritance without a long struggle and protracted controversy. I shall refer here to the baffling diversity of texts relating to succession to the sonless.

Among Śutra writers Baudhāyana does not give the inheritance to the widow but only a right to maintenance. Vaśiṣṭha and Āpastamba too similarly exclude the widow though the latter includes the daughter.

Manu too (IX, 217) gives the inheritance to (1) mother, (2) father's mother while in IX 185 he gives the inheritance to the father and after him to the brother, and, characteristically provides that when a younger brother takes the inheritance of a sonless elder he should beget a son on the sister-in-law and give the heritage to the son when born (IX, 146). He does not mention the widow as heir at all.

Among other texts cited in the commentaries are those of Devala who gives the heirs in the following order:

(1) Full Brothers or daughters or father, (2) half brothers by a Sabarṇā mother, (3) mother, (4) widow;[57]

[56] Yājñ. II. पत्नी दुहितरश्चैव पितरौ भ्रातरस्तथा । तत्सुता गोत्रजा बन्धुः शिष्य सब्रह्मचारिणः । एषामभावे पूर्वस्य धनभागुत्तरोत्तरः । स्वर्यातस्यह्यपुत्रस्य सर्ववर्णेष्वयं विधिः ।

[57] देवल DB p. 235 ततो दायमपुत्रस्य विभजेयुः सहोदराः
तुल्या दुहितरो वाऽपि ध्रियमाणः पितापि वा ।
सवर्णा भ्रातरो माता भार्य्याचेति यथाक्रमः ।

Śaṅkha whose order is as follows: (1) Brothers, (2) Parents, (3) Eldest wife;[58]

A text of Kātyāyana[59] according to which the order is (1) Father, (2) Brother, (3) Mother and (4) Father's mother.

As against these there are not only the texts of Viṣṇu and Yājña-valkya cited above, but there are (1) a text of Brihat-Manu who particularly specifies that the wife takes the *entire* (kritsnam) inheritance,[60] (2) a text of Bṛihaṣpati[61] and also a text attributed to Kātyāyana[62] (which is in conflict with the other quotation attributed to him above). These texts give the widow the first place among heirs.

It may very well be doubted whether the wife was at all an heir in the earlier strata of law. In the Taitt. Saṃhitā VI, 582 occurs the texts which have been quoted by numerous commentators.

तस्मात् स्त्रियो निरिन्द्रिया अदायादाः
आदायदिरपि पापात् पुंसः उपविस्तरं वदन्ति ।

[58] शङ्ख—स्वर्यातस्य ह्यपुत्रस्य भ्रातृगामी द्रव्यं
तदभावे पितरौ हरेयातां ज्येष्ठा वा पत्नी ।

[59] Kātyāyana—
विभक्ते संस्थिते द्रव्यं पुत्राभावे पिता हरेत्
भ्राता वा जननी वाऽथ माता वा तत्पितुः क्रमात् ।

[60] बृहन्मनु D.B. 230.
अपुत्रा शयणं भर्तूः पालयन्ती व्रते स्थिता ।
पत्न्येव दद्यात्तत्पिण्डं कृतस्नमंशं लभेत च ।

[61] आम्नाये स्मृतितन्त्रे च लोकाचारे च सूरिभिः
शरीरार्धा स्मृता जाया पुण्यापुण्य फलेसमा
यस्य नोपरता भार्य्या देहार्धं तस्य जीवति ।
जीवत्यर्धशरीरे तु कथमन्यो धनं हरेत् ।
सकुल्यै र्विद्यमानैस्तु पितृमातृ सनाभिभिः ।
असूतस्य प्रमीतस्य पत्नी तद्भागहारिनी ।

[62] Kātyāyana 199.
पत्नी पत्युर्धनहरी यास्यादव्यभिचारिणी ।
तदभावे तु दुहिता यद्यनूचाभवेत्तदा ॥
अपुत्रस्यार्थकुलजा पत्नी दुहितरोऽपि वा ।
तदभावे पिता माता भ्राता पुत्राश्च कीर्त्तिताः ।
भ्रातृणामप्रजाः प्रेयात् कश्चित् प्रव्रजेत वा ।
विभजेरन् धनं तस्य शेषास्ते स्त्रीधनं विना ।
भरणं चास्य कुर्वीरण स्त्रीणामाजीवनक्षयात् ॥

Jolly refers to first part of these texts to the Maitrayaniya Saṃhitā where his reading is **निरिन्द्रियाः अमन्त्रकाः** which also seems to have been the original text as reproduced by Manu (IX, 78). Whichever reading of the texts is taken this indicates that wives were not regarded as capable of inheriting the property at the time and in the society in which these texts were written. To the same effect is the text of Manu VIII 416 which says

भार्या पुत्रश्च दासश्च त्रय एवाधनास्स्मृता
यत्ते समधिगच्छन्ति यस्य ते तस्य तद्धनम्

a text which might have been taken equally from the Roman law of the Twelve Tables. Śabara as we have seen in his commentary on Jaimini VI. 112 gives a variant of these texts and says **भार्या दासश्च पुत्रश्च निर्धना सर्व एवते** (vi 114) though Śabara repudiates this view on the ground that it is opposed to Śruti. According to him this text is only meant to indicate the dependence of the wives on the husband.

This text of Manu does not occur in the law of inheritance or other places where the positions of sons and wives are mentioned, but in the section dealing with slaves. It is really a survival of a much more ancient law than is indicated in the other texts of Manu by which wives are said to own separate property (stridhana). It survived in this text only because it was still living law so far as slaves were concerned.

Gautama, the earliest of the Sūtra writers says **"पिण्ड गोत्रर्षि सम्बद्धा ऋकथम् भजेरन्"** and adds as an alternative **"स्त्री बा अनपत्यस्य"** and a further alternative **वीजं बा लिप्सेत.** This brief text to my mind indicates a history by itself and shows how the wives' right to inheritance came gradually to be recognised.

The several stages of the law relating to the inheritance of wives, as I understand them seem to be as follows:

At first, women were incapable of owning property independently of her husband. The only exception recognised was paribhāndam (i.e. domestic utensils) and ornaments (Kane, page 186) unless this itself was an exception grafted on the rule of general incapacity at a later stage.

The next stage was the recognition of the wife's right to some special properties other than utensils and ornaments. These were called strīdhana in its strictly literal sense, i.e., the only properties which could be owned by women. The kinds of such property are seen to grow in course of time.

The recognition of the wife's right to inherit to a sonless man came only when a woman's capacity for independent ownership of property was recognised. When once the latter right was well established, the door was opened for her right to inherit. (*Supra.* p. 125 seq).

But the admission of this right into the orthodox law seems to have been gradual and not free from obstruction either. Such as it was, it seems to me that it was the result of the adoption of the custom of Niyoga in Ārya society from their non-Ārya neighbours.

It will be noticed that the early text dealing with the son's right says, "Not brothers, not parents but sons take the inheritance of the father." This text contemplates and repudiates the rights of brothers and parents alone as possible rivals but not wives, wives being, as another text lays down, nirindriyah adayādāh. The first text recognising a contingent right of the widow is that of Gautama who gives her the right **बीजं बा लिप्सेत.** This text is to be taken side by side with the texts of Vaśiṣṭha which says **"ऋक्थ लोभान् नास्ति नियोगः"** i.e. niyoga is not permitted for greed or desire for the inheritance.

When the institution of Niyoga came to be adopted into the sacred law as I have indicated in a previous chapter, it followed that until a son was begotten on the wife by Niyoga, the inheritance would not pass to the sapindas or sagotras. It would remain, therefore, in the hands of the widow until the son was born, the widow becoming the custodian of the inheritance. The next step would be for her to be the owner, should no son be born by niyoga. The text of Vaśiṣṭha cited above indicates that sometimes widows submitted to niyoga merely from the desire to retain the inheritance in their hands, a practice which he declares invalid.

The Mitākṣarā in dealing with the right of widow to inherit enters into a controversy with those who asserted, apparently even in his own days, that the wife's right to inheritance arose from her right to bear offspring to her husband by niyoga, though he combats this view.

While the history as given above is indicated by what seems to be the logical sequence of the texts referred to above, it would be unhistorical to suppose that this course of evolution was entirely one of natural or logical evolution of the institution in Ārya society or even that the evolution took place smoothly in that order everywhere. It seems more than probable that this last development of the widow's right was largely influenced by non-Ārya law and custom and its adoption did not take place in Ārya society everywhere. In fact, the very controversies in text books on this subject indicate a diversity of opinion which sprang up among different scholars, probably in different Ārya societies.

The foreign origin of the institution of Niyoga has been indicated elsewhere. The reference of this practice to King Vena in Manu may record an historical fact maintained in tradition. King Vena is depicted in the Puranic literature as a tyrant who tried to enforce his divine rights and suffered for his sins, but none the less, a very powerful king who ruled a great empire with an iron hand. He was probably one of the Vrātyas or the Great Vratya, referred to in the Brāhmanas, who ruled Eastern India and probably conquered considerable Arya territory. In his kingdom Levirate may have prevailed and it was therefore supported by the ruler.

Besides, it is also probable that among some non-Ārya races who came into the Ārya fold the wife's right of inheritance was common law and survived their Aryanisation. But, of course, it is a mere conjecture. Evidence of such facts, if true, is completely lost.

When the present Manusamhita was compiled, it is obvious that the institution of Niyoga had gone out of use and was severely condemned as indicated in its texts against Niyoga. Though immediately before these texts, the texts enjoining Niyoga and prescribing its procedure were carefully retained in the present redaction. But the custom of wives holding the property of their husbands had apparently been long in existence and in course of time widows had been recognised as inheriting to a sonless person without any question about Niyoga. This is recognised in the texts of Viṣṇu and Yājñavalkya. The text of Bṛihaṣpati quoted in the Mitākṣarā, Dāyabhāga and other works has merely attempted to establish this doctrine of succession of the women on a new basis. Bṛihaṣpati says that in the Vedas, Smritis and custom, the wife is regarded as half the body of the husband ; so, so long as half the body of the husband survived, no one else would take the inheritance.[63]

Although this seems to be the real history of the widows succeeding to the property in their own right it is clear that in the earliest law, as mother, upon the death of the father, she still had an important place in the family. There are texts which have been

[63] आम्नाये स्मृतितन्त्रे च लोकाचारे च सूरिभिः ।
शरीरार्धा स्मृता जाया पुण्यापुण्य फले समा ॥
यस्य नोपरता भार्या देहार्धं तस्य जीवति ।
जीवत्यर्धशरीरे तु कथमन्यो धनं हरेत् ॥

referred to before which lay down that sons are not to divide the father's property until the death, not only of the father, but also of the mother ; in other words, that the sons should remain joint so long as the mother lives and the mother should be regarded with due respect as the practical head of the family.

We have seen before how the ancient legal idea of the absolute incapacity of women to own any property whatsoever was qualified even in the beginning by her right to paribhānda and ornaments, and how thereafter the list of properties which a woman could possibly hold gradually grew in number. We have seen how these properties were distinguished by the name of strīdhana in a strictly literal sense of being properties of women—for, at that stage, there could be no other properties of women. The list of such properties grew in number and exceeded the traditional number of six. But it was in the late text of Narada, that the heritage from her husband, notwithstanding Jimutavāhana's laboured interpretation to the contrary, was first recognised as strīdhana.

Though the husband's heritage is not enumerated as strīdhana by any author before Nārada, women had already been recognised as heir to her husband who died sonless. Such property would be as much a strīdhana as the enumerated properties in a strictly literal or etymological sense of the term.

We find, however, in a late text of the Mahabhārata a restriction placed on the widow's right to property inherited by the widow. It says :

> Strīnām svapatidāyastu upabhogaphalah smṛitah
> Nāpāharaṃ striyah kuryuh patidāyāt kathaṃchana.

This, which was in the nature more of a moral injunction in keeping with the duty of the widows to live austere lives, is later converted by Kātyāyana into a legal rule in the very texts by which he recognises the widow's right of inheritance. He lays down,

"A sonless widow keeping unsullied the bed of her husband and following her vrata shall enjoy (the inheritance) abstemiously until her death, the heirs of her husband will take after her death."[64]

These texts make the widow more or less a custodian for life of her husband's estate with only a right to abstemious maintenance out of it. She is not expressly declared to be the owner of the heritage.

[64] अपुत्रा शयनं भर्तुः पालयन्ती व्रते स्थिता ।
भुञ्जीतामरणात् क्षान्ता दायादाः ऊर्ध्वमाप्नयुः ॥ Kane's collection, p. 122.

This had the effect of making a difference between the widow's right in her husband's heritage and her property—the strīdhana, in respect of which she did not labour under these limitations, though some authorities sought to place limitations on the extent of the value of her strīdhana, and other texts sought to limit her right of disposing of some kinds of strīdhana by interposing the authority of her husband to prevent it. These strīdhanas were nevertheless, even after these attempted limitations, her own property, which the husband could not take away with impunity and which would not pass to her husband's heirs but to her own heirs. The restrictions were sought to be imposed, as we have seen before, only when strīdhanas ceased to be properties of small value.

For the same reason, it would seem, when women became the sole heirs to their husband's property which might be of considerable value, these restrictions were sought to be imposed on her right of enjoyment and disposal as well as on the order of succession to this kind of property. It is to be noted that in the earliest texts of law which recognise the widow's right of inheritance there is no such limitation nor is there any distinction between the widow and other heirs.

Viṣṇu simply says, "The property of a sonless man goes to his wife, in her absence to his daughter, in her absence to the father" and so on. So that all these heirs are on the same footing.

So too Yājñavalkya in his text already cited says "the wife, the daughters, the parents, brothers, their sons" etc. are heirs one after another. The idea of distinguishing between these heirs in respect of their rights over the property did not arise in the minds of these law givers. It is only when this law became settled that attempts were made to whittle down the rights of the widow by the texts of Kātyāyana and others. But for these texts, it would be obvious that the inheritance would be the widow's property—that is strīdhana and the law regarding strīdhana would apply to this property as well, including the succession of strīdhana heirs. This was not favoured by later law-givers who thus introduced the differences above mentioned between other strīdhana of the wife and the property of the husband "enjoyed by the wife" and followed by the succession of heirs of the husband on her death.

We find however that notwithstanding the inclusion by Nārada of bhartridāya in his enumeration of strīdhanas and notwithstanding Yājñavalkya's expansion of the list of strīdhana by adding an "etcetera", the view could be propounded that the husband's heritage was not the widow's strīdhana, implying that that term had a technical meaning limited to the kinds of strīdhana enumerated in the texts barring Nārada. The foundation for this view was no doubt the text of Kātyāyana (bhunjītāmaranāt).

This view is stoutly combated by Vijñāneśvara who argues with great force that the enumeration of strīdhanas in the texts is not exhaustive but that it also includes all property which a woman acquires by any mode of acquisition open to men, such as inheritance, purchase, partition etc. There can be no doubt that from an historical point of view Vijñāneśvara's contention was right.

But if this view is right, it follows that all the incidents of strīdhana must be equally attracted to property inherited from the husband. She would have absolute powers of disposition over the property, subject, perhaps, to some benevolent superintendence of her kindred and such property would pass to her own strīdhana heirs and not to her husband's heirs. On these points Vijñāneśvara gives no opinion. On both these points the text of Kātyāyana lays down a contrary law and Jimūtavāhana follows the texts of Kātyāyana and the Mahābhārata. While some of the authors, who generally follow the Mitāksara, endorse, in this respect, the view of Jimūtavāhana, Mitra Misra in his Viramitrodaya stoutly controverts him. His argument, buttressed as usual by interpretations of the authoritative texts, is finally wound up by his reference to Jimūtavāhana's own maxim, "a thing cannot be altered by a hundred texts" and he argues that since, according to the authorities, widows have the rights of property, her right of free disposition which is annexed to that "thing" cannot be altered by the texts.

It is not my purpose to discuss further these controversies created by the texts. The only real explanation for these diverse points of view is to be found in the history of the evolution of the woman's right to property inherited from her husband.

The view which history seems to me to indicate is that when the widow's right to inherit came to be recognised it was not contemplated by the law-givers that the widow's right to the heritage would be different from that of any male heirs. They were content to establish her right to the property by inheritance, equally with those of other heirs.

Restrictions on widow's rights.

The problem of restricting her right of disposal or of regulating further succession did not probably arise immediately. The widow in ancient society would be expected to lead an abstemious life in the home of her husband, faithful to her husband's bed and would not be expected to play ducks and drakes with her wealth. On her death her husband's immediate relations with whom she lived would normally step into the ownership of the property which, even during her lifetime would normally have been looked after by them.

When, in course of time, these conditions changed and widows began to leave the protection of their husband's house and to make substantial gifts and sales of property, society would be stirred up by these departures from *boni mores* and seek remedies by imposing restraints which would save what society had looked upon as the normal and proper order of things. The restrictions on her powers of disposition and enjoyment which were originally only moral, now hardened into legal rules. This revulsion of society against practices which stirred their sense of social proprieties would account for new legal restraints like those in the text of Kātyāyana. These new laws were far from revolutionary. They were rather in the nature of conservative reaction against breaches of approved social proprieties When Kātyāyana says that the widow, in order to inherit should be "Gurousthitā *i.e.* living in her father-in-law's house and "dāyadāh ñrdhamāpnuyuh" *i.e.* that her husband's heirs would take after her death, he is really supporting an order of society of the past and merely protesting against departures therefrom.

The effect of these limitations was to raise a new problem about the meaning of the word strīdhana. We have seen before that the word originally meant all the property of a woman. In other words it had a literal and not any technical meaning. We have also seen before that a woman had free power of disposing of her strīdhana, slightly qualified in later law and that her strīdhana passed to her own heirs. But here now was a species of property which women owned but in which her rights were now limited. If strīdhana is given its literal meaning, this too would be strīdhana and there would be a conflict between these limitations and the other provisions of the law relating to strīdhana.

An obvious way of solving this conundrum was to restrict the meaning of strīdhana, or in other words to give it a technical meaning. That this solution was attempted is clear from the vigorous argument put forward by the Mitākṣarā to combat this view. It denies that Strīdhana has any technical meaning and insists that it includes all property that a woman may have in any legal mode of acquisition of ownership, though it omits to work out the full implication of this view in respect of the woman's right of disposal or of the further devolution of the property.

The only other possible view, if one accepts the position which was accepted at this time, that all Smṛiti texts are equally authoritative, was to hold that the word strīdhana had a technical meaning and was limited to those properties which were enumerated as such in the Smṛiti texts. This is the view of the Pūrvapakṣa which the Mitākṣarā puts forward and controverts. There were obvious difficulties in the view, however, as the enumeration of strīdhana by Nārada includes Bhartridāya and Yājñavalkya adds an 'et cetera' to the enumeration. This difficulty was appreciated by Jimūtavāhana who, like Vijñānesvara says that the word strīdhana has no technical meaning, nor is limited to the enumerated varieties, but unlike Vijnaneśvara, he holds that stridhana only includes all properties *ejusdem generis*, namely, all property over which women had power of free disposition which, by the way, begs the question. It is not appreciated apparently that this interpretation too gives to the word a technical (Yogarūḍha) meaning, nor that there are varieties of strīdhana *e.g.* Saudāyika over which the woman's powers are limited by over-riding powers of the husband. Of course there is no express authority anywhere in the Dharmaśāstras for this delimitation of the meaning which is derived by Jimūtavāhana by the fiction of interpretation.

The wife's position, therefore, started from a total absence of her right to inherit. Through the instrumentality of Niyoga she gradually stepped into the inheritance. At first her right was not trammelled by any restrictions, but later, some of the schools succeeded in reducing her right to inherit to a bare right to an abstemious use of the usufruct. Further developments of her position came with the commentaries and Nibandhas in the middle ages. It was however only by judicial decisions by British Indian Courts that the last phases of that history were finally concluded by laying down a law for all India on the basis of the law of the Dāyabhāga and carrying the law further backward than was attempted in any commentary. But with these phases of the history I have no direct concern.

CHAPTER IX

INHERITANCE (contd.)

DAUGHTER

Yajnavalkya

In the text of Yājñavalkya, as already stated, the order of inheritance to a son-less man is as follows:

(1) the wife,
(2) daughters,
(3) parents,
(4) brothers,
(5) brothers' son,
(6) Gotrajas,
(7) Bandhus,
(8) disciples,
(9) fellow pupils of the same teacher.

Other Smritis

Manu also places the daughter practically on a par with sons but next to the sons. But the order of his texts indicates that the daughter and the daughter's son take in preference to the wife who is not specifically mentioned at all by Manu. In Viṣṇu we find a text which places the daughter after the mother. In the older Dharmasūtras, however, the daughter finds no place, except in Āpastamba, after Bandhus. As we have seen before, Gautama gives the inheritance to sons and, in the absence of sons to persons connected by piṇḍa, gotra or arṣa and as an alternative opinion mentions the wife and also indicates an opinion that the wife takes only if she seeks to raise offspring to the deceased. Vasiṣṭha and Baudhāyana do not give the inheritance to the daughter at all. Devala however puts daughter as an alternative to or on a par with brothers.

I have indicated before, (supra p. 139 seq.) in dealing with the putrikāputra how the daughter and her son came into the string of kinship through the medium of the institution of Putrikā. At first a sonless person could, by stipulating at the time of the daughter's assignment, that the son of his daughter shall be his son, make a putrikā. This putrikā is herself a secondary son according to some, while according to others son of the putrikā becomes a secondary son.

Gradually, however, the necessity of that stipulation was eliminated and it has been stated that a putrikā is created by mere intention (abhisandhi mātrāt). A still later stage is indicated that the daughter as such takes the place of the putrikā. The text of Manu, IX 127 and 128, speaks of the putrikā as equivalent to a son. But then in IX 130 he goes on to add "the son is like the self and the daughter is like the son. So how can anybody else take the inheritance while one's self exists (in the shape of the daughter)." And then in verses 132 to 133 he goes on to add that the daughter's son takes the entire inheritance of the son-less man. He gives two pindas to the father and to his maternal grand-father ; and there is no distinction between son's son and daughter's son in the world or in the eye of Dharma, as both proceed from the bodies of the father and the mother. At this stage, therefore, the daughter and the daughter's son by themselves have entered into the scheme of inheritance although they were not heirs under the older law as laid down in the older dharmasūtras.

Kātyāyana and Bṛihaspati lay down very clearly the position of the daughter. Kātyāyana says "The wife is the heir to the husband if she is not guilty of adultery, and in her absence, the daughter *if she is unmarried*."[65] This would indicate that the daughter who takes according to Kātyāyana must be an unmarried daughter,—the married daughters do not come into the scheme of the inheritance according to this text. Bṛihaspati, also, says, echoing Manu "the wife is the heir to the husband and in her absence the daughter. As prescribed, the daughter is born to the man from each limb of the father just like the son. So how can any other take the father's inheritance."[66]

Maiden daughter

The position of the maiden daughter living in the house seems to have been distinguished in Kātyāyana's text from that of daughters who had gone out of the family by marriage. It seems originally to have been obligatory on her brothers to give her in marriage suitably although there is no express text to that effect until we come to the later dharmásāstras. The text of Ṛigveda (III, 31, 2) "Not to daughters should the son give the inheritance, for she is meant to be the receptacle for the sons of her husband," if critically

[65] तदभावे दुहिता च यद्यनूढ़ा भवेत्तदा । Text No. 923 Kane's collection. This text is also attributed to Bṛihaspati Gaekwad Ed., p. 218.

[66] Gaekwad edition, p. 217.

examined, seems to suggest, firstly, that the problem to which this text is an answer could have arisen only with regard to maiden daughters living in the father's family and secondly, that it was assumed that she had to be married by her brothers to bring forth offspring to her husband. Girls who had gone out of the house and gotra could not have been considered in this connection.

We have seen above that Devala's text places the daughter alongside the brother as heir. Āpastamba too in his enumeration mentions the daughter as heir. It would seem that these texts, as well the text of Ṛigveda above cited only contemplated the unmarried daughter living in the father's house, about whom alone the question could arise of her getting the inheritance, married daughters being normally out of the way as belonging to another family.

When therefore later texts like that of Yājñavalkya lay down an obligation on brothers to marry unmarried sisters by giving a quarter from their own share,[67] they were really formulating what was implicit in the social organisation, only defining the precise share which should be given to the sister for her marriage. The share might not have been precisely defined in earlier law or custom, but the right of the unmarried daughter to a charge on the inheritance for her marriage was well understood and this obligation was evidently equally binding on other heirs than the brother. In the earliest law therefore this was all that the unmarried daughter was entitled to in her father's heritage. The married daughter had no rights in it. The maiden also had the exclusive right to inherit to her mother's property or strīdhana in respect of which the earliest texts provide that "strīdhana belongs to daughters, unmarried and unprovided for"—"strīdhanam duhitṛinām, aprattānām apratiṣṭhitānāṃ cha." The natural meaning of this text is that the unmarried daughter who has not been endowed by her father is solely entitled, though it has been interpreted by commentators to give such daughters merely a right of preference over married daughters.

Evolution of daughter's right

The daughter's rights to her father's property was thus originally limited to a marriage portion, the married daughter having no share at all. She first came into the scheme of kinship and inheritance only through the institution of Putrikā and the series of texts of Manu

[67] II, 124. असंस्कृतास्तु संस्कार्याः भ्रातृभिः पूर्वसंस्कृतैः ।
भगिन्यश्च निजादंशाद्दत्त्वांशं तु तुरीयकम् ॥

above referred to seem to represent the evolution of her rights in the father's property in the correct historical order.

As we have seen, the first stage is where a daughter is given away by a sonless father with a special stipulation that a son born of her marriage would be her father's son. This, it may be noted, gives the *son* of the putrikā alone the status of a son to his grandfather, and not to the daughter. At the next stage she is stated to be a putrikā if there was a mere intention to make her one (abhisandhimātrāt). At this stage, it seems the putrikā herself steps into the position of a son, at any rate until she became a mother, though the texts do not definitely say so; but some texts in enumerating secondary sons, mention the son of the putrikā and not the putrikā as such. The next stage is when the daughter as such, putrikā or no putrikā, is deemed to be heir in her independent right, and the son of the daughter is definitely placed after the daughter as heir.

This stage is already reached in the texts of Manu, Viṣṇu and Yājñavalkya of whom the two latter place the daughter as an heir next after the widow. But which daughter? It would seem, as stated above, that in speaking of daughters as heirs these texts might not have originally contemplated married daughters who previously had no rights whatsoever in her father's wealth. And it seems likely that Kātyāyana's text which qualifies the daughter's right by adding "if she is unmarried" was really making explicit what was implicit in the old law as understood by contemporaries. Literally interpreted, this text would suggest a limitation of the right to the unmarried daughter alone, just as, in the case of the mother's strīdhana. In the text of Manu belonging to the latest stage however we probably find a change of social sentiment already made and we may suppose that when he speaks of a *duhitā* being equal to a son on the ground that she saves her father in the next world through her son, he is thinking of the married and unmarried daughter equally. Or, this may have been the germ of a later development which included married daughter also among heirs, postponing her however to the unmarried daughter. When this stage is reached it is obvious that the historic roots of the daughter's right viz., her right to a marriage portion and her right when a putrikā have been completely supplanted by that of her contributing to the spiritual benefit of her father by bringing forth a son.

Character of daughter's estate

The further development and diversification of the law of the daughter's right to inherit has been the work of the commentaries of the middle ages which I do not propose to discuss, except just to indicate one development, viz. with regard to the character of the daughter's right to the heritage and its further devolution.

I have discussed before how the right of the widow was hemmed in by later texts to a limited benefit of the usufruct with a further limitation that on her death the property goes to her husband's heirs. There is no text of the Smṛitis placing any such restriction on the daughter's rights. Early commentaries of the middle ages also do not raise the question at all. Jimūtavāhana in his Dāyabhāga raises the question and insists that the daughter's right to the heritage is limited in the same manner as that of the widow, not because there is any express text which limits such right but on a somewhat curious argument *a fortiori* because, according to him, the daughter being inferior (jaghanya) as heir to the widow, her right cannot be higher than that of the widow. Jimūtavāhana does not advert to the obvious argument to the contrary, that the widow in Kātyāyana's text is to "enjoy the heritage abstemiously (Kṣāntā)" for the obvious reason that a widow's life is supposed to be one of continued austerity, while the daughter as such is under no obligation of abstinence whatsoever.

This view of Jimūtavāhana is not shared by most other commentators, while Viramitrodaya cuts away the root of the argument by saying with reference to the widow that she too has a power of free disposition over the property. Yet, the Judicial Committee has accepted the view of the Dāyabhāga to be the universal law of Hindu India, not only in respect of the widow and the daughter but in respect of every female heir, even where she has inherited to the absolute stridhana property of a female relative. We may say at once that there is no text of the Dharmaśāstras which justifies this view.

THE DAUGHTER'S SON

It is curious that the enumerations of the heirs to the sonless in Viṣṇu and Yājnavalkya do not mention the daughter's son at all but only mention the daughter and then parents and other heirs. Commentators from Vijnanesvara onwards have however included the daughter's son in the list by giving an extended meaning to the word 'daughter' by reference to the particle "cha". To reconcile this text with Manu, they say that this word implies and includes her son. That is a somewhat lame excuse by way of explanation, for, in the same list after the brothers, brother's sons are specifically named and not left to be inferred. On the other hand, as stated above, the daughter's son has been expressly stated to be the heir by Manu.

Looking back at the older texts about the heirship of the daughter's son we find that there has been some amount of confusion between the daughter and her son during the interval during which they were making their way into sacred law as heirs. The earliest stage, as we have seen was when a daughter was made a putrikā by express stipulation at the time of marriage. This stipulation in terms provides that the *son* of such daughter would be a son of her father. On the other hand the old Vedic text abhrātrika puṃsah partīchinaṁ eti etc. (RV. IV, 5, 5) seems to imply the brotherless daughter herself reverting to her father like a son.

In Vasiṣṭha's enumeration of secondary sons Putrikā herself and not her son is named as the son of the grandfather. Yājnavalkya's enumeration of kinds of sons under the law of inheritance however skip over the putrikā and place the son of the Putrikā next after the aurasa. In Manu's text (IX, 127 seq.) he speaks of a putrikā made by stipulation at the time of marriage, but in almost the next verse he says that a daughter is just the same as a son, the self reborn and says "while one's own self (in the shape of a daughter born of his loins) exists how should another take the inheritance?". Then he goes on, "The daughter's son takes the entire inheritance of a sonless grandfather." In IX 135 Manu goes further and lays down that if after a putrikā, a son is born, the inheritance will be equally divided between the Putrikā and the son, the Putrikā, being a woman, not being entitled to preference as elder.

These and other such texts indicate a mixing up of the putrikā and her son and, when *any daughter* replaces the putrikā, between the daughter and her son, until the position was settled by an interpretation of the various texts by giving the daughter and her son places one after another.

In this confusion of texts it is difficult to be definite about the precise evolution of the law as regards the heirship of the daughter and her son. All that we can say is that between the time indicated by the texts of Gautama for instance, when daughters and daughter's son were not heirs at all (though the stipulation in making a putrikā in his work implies sonship of her son) and the time when they were given definite places, a long period intervened during which their claims struggled for recognition in different societies. Different forces operated to bring about their final inclusion. One and perhaps the most important one was the institution of Putrikā by which an appointed daughter's son was made a son by fiction. In some societies, however, the appointed daughter herself became a son. These different forms might have been the results of the adaptation in different places of the respective customs of different non-Arya societies.

Another force of considerable importance was a recognition of the fact that brotherless girls after their marriage sometimes came to live with their fathers as members of their families. In such cases there would be a strong tendency to favour their taking the inheritance.

To justify this, the strength of filial affection might have prompted lawgivers to emphasise the physical fact of the daughter being made out of the particles of the father's body just like a son, as stated by Manu. The influence of this view would make the daughter herself the heir in preference to her son.

Then there was the principle of spiritual benefit which would favour the daughter's son, when he was admitted to a right to give piṇḍas to his maternal grandfather. But Manu uses the same fact of spiritual benefit as a reason for preferring the daughter because, through her bearing the son, the spiritual benefit accrues.

Swayed by these several forces the different law-givers oscillated between these opposite views until the final synthesis postponing the daughter's son to be daughter was reached.

Remoter Heirs

We have seen before that Gautama's formula for inheritance places sapiṇḍas, sogotras and samānārṣas one after another as heirs without any attempt at distinction between different members of the respective classes. Does it suggest the law to be, as we find in some laws of very ancient societies, that each of these classes inherit as a class? It may have been so. But if it was, it is clear that, in due course, distinctions were made between different sapiṇḍas with reference to their propinquity.

However, we find, by the time of Viṣṇu and Yājnavalkya, a definite order of succession among sapiṇḍas after interposing the widow, daughter and daughter's son. We do not know the intermediate stages of this evolution, for, as already mentioned, we have only a handful of source books to fill the gap of the ages between the earlier sutras and these later texts. A hypothesis that the principle of propinquity worked out through ages has led to this resulting determination of the order of sapiṇḍas would hardly be of much help. For propinquity could be determined on different principles. The principle which ultimately prevailed, not in the

Smṛitis themselves, but in the commentaries, was the determination of propinquity on a parentelic basis, that is to say, by exhausting the descendants of the father and then going to the descendants of the grandfather, and then to those of the great grandfather instead of the canonical principle of simply counting the number of males intervening between the propositus and the heir in question. But we do not find any definite authority in the Smṛitis themselves for a rigorous application of this principle beyond a text, applied to sons of sons, applying the rule of succession per stripes to the grandsons, (Anekapitṛikānam tu pitṛito bhāgakalpanā. Yajn II, 120).

All that we find in the dharmasastras themselves is an enumeration of remoter heirs one after another upto a limit. Viṣṇu and Yājñavalkya give the list, as before stated, as follows :

(1) Parents, (2) Brothers, (3) Brother's sons. After this the heirs are simply mentioned by classes as follows, gotrajas, bandhus, pupils and fellow students. But in earlier texts we find a distinction made even among gotrajas. Thus Gautama distinguishes between sapiṇḍas who come first before other sagotras. And Vasiṣṭha, Baudhāyana and Manu speak of a class of sakulyas and another of samānodakas who take before remoter sagotras on apparently a parentelic basis.

Parents

Among parents Viṣṇu places the father first and, next after him, the mother. Yājñavalkya mentions both together without distinguishing between father and mother. Vijñāneśvara interprets Yājñavalkya's text as implying that the mother takes before the father, for the somewhat curious reason that grammatically the compound 'pitarau' is made of the words 'mātā cha pitā cha'—'the mother and the father', placing mother before the father. In this view which is directly opposed to the text of Viṣṇu he is not followed by all the commentators who generally follow him. The other view places the father before the mother.

It is to be noted that the parents are not specifically mentioned as heirs in most previous texts, probably for the reason that they did not contemplate the somewhat rare case of the parent surviving the son.

Brothers

Brothers would be the nearest kinsmen barring sons on a parentelic scheme. As already pointed out however the earliest texts seem to contemplate a view, which is controverted, that brothers and fathers inherit in preference to the son. The sons' position in preference to brothers had already been established from the earliest Vedic times.

Nevertheless it would seem that brothers were given a definite place in preference to other heirs to a sonless person in some societies and this view is reflected in the texts of Devala, Śankha and a text attributed to Kātyāyana referred to above (supra p.). In Devala's enumeration the full brother (or daughters, or father) is first, followed by half-brother by a step-mother of the same caste. Śankha places brothers unambiguously first before all others, while Kātyāyana's text places them only next after father. So too Manu (IX 184), places the father and the brother alternatively as heirs after the son, though this is contradicted by IX 217 where the mother is stated to be the heir to the sonless and, next after her, the father's mother. This diversity must have arisen out of different customs which grew up in different societies. It may be that these variations may have developed in societies which originally followed a custom of Tanistry (which was expressly repudiated by the Ṛigveda) after their adoption of the Vedic law.

Brother's son

After the brother comes the brother's son. In what seems to an older view a special place is given to a brother's son of a sonless person as, equal to a son, and, in fact, a secondary son who seems according to some texts to take before any other secondary son.[68] Other texts relating to adoption enjoin that while there is a brother's son, no other boy should be adopted. It will be noticed that by merely counting the number of males who intervene, the father's brother would be nearer to the deceasd than the brother's son. The brother's son can only be preferred on an implicit parentelic principle.

It is noticeable that none of these lists mention the sons of brother's son, nor for that matter do they mention grandsons and great grandsons of the propositus himself. This does not mean that these remoter descendants of oneself or one's brothers would not be heirs except in so far as they were sagotras. It only signifies that

[68] Manu IX. 182.

भ्रातृणामेकजातानामेकश्चेत् पुत्रवान भवेत् ।
सर्वांस्तास्तेन पुत्रेण पुत्रिणो मनुरब्रवीत् ॥

and Bṛihaspati Smriti (Gaekwad Ed., p. 209).

यद्येकजाता बहवो भ्रातरस्तु सहोदराः ।
एकस्यापि सुते जाते सर्वे ते पुत्रिणः स्मृताः ॥

like all early expositions of law these early texts were not equal to working out the scheme of succession to any but those heirs who would be normally expected to be in existence. Later expositions of law when they bring in these remoter heirs are in most cases working out the implications.

Other agnates

With regard to still remoter heirs viz. sapiṇḍas, sakulyas, samanodakas, and sagotras, these texts only refer to them by classes without taking the trouble to work out any definite order of succession among them. But the principle of the parentelic scheme which was aldeady implicit in the preference of sons of brothers would naturally be extended to these remoter heirs as it was actually done by the commentators in working out the detailed scheme of inheritance. It would hardly be possible to suppose however that all those further details were present to the minds of these early law-givers.

BANDHUS

Yajñavalkya's text introduces, after this, another class, not mentioned in other texts viz. Bandhus. The term has been explained in the Mitākśarā in two different ways, (1) as bhinnagotra sapiṇḍas and (2) as the nine relations viz. father's sister's son, mother's sister's son and maternal uncle's son, of a person himself, of his father and his mother respectively. Our courts have had considerable trouble in interpreting this term in its application to competing claims of different persons.

In dealing with Marriage (supra. p. 95) I have pointed out that this expression (bandhu) is to be found in many older dharmasāstras in other connections and that it originally implied only agnatic kinsmen. In the classification of secondary sons they are distinguished as dāyāda bāndhavas and adāyada bāndhavas. In these texts as well as in the other texts referred to there, the terms bandhu and bāndhava can have no other meaning than kinsmen and agnatic kinsmen. They can have neither of the two meanings which the Mitākṣarā gives.

Yet in mentioning bandhus as a different class after gotrajas, Yājñavalkya must have used the word in a sense different from that of agnatic kinsmen. And it seems that the Mitākṣarā was quite correct in taking the word to mean the persons referred to in a text of Śātātapa as atmabandhus, pitṛibandhus and matṛibandhus. These nine relations were probably indicated by Yājñavalkya by the term bandhus who inherited after gotrajas.

A long course of judicial decisions and learned authors of text-books have laid down, referring to the authority of the Mitākṣarā, that the term bandhu here means all sapiṇḍas who belong to a different gotra and by sapiṇḍa they understood all persons descended from a common ancestor within seven or five degrees, irrespective of whether they participate in funeral oblations or not. With the utmost deference to these authorities, I venture to think that this interpretation of Yājñavalkya's text is not even justified by the texts of the Mitākṣarā and was certainly not contemplated by Yājñavalkya. The Mitākṣarā, in commenting on this particular expression of Yājña-valkya does not say that the term implies *all* bhinnagotra sapiṇḍas, but explains it as meaning only the nine cognatic relations above mentioned.[69] Earlier in his comments on this verse in referring to the expression gotraja Vijñāneśvara puts them in order up to father's mother and then says, "In the absence of the father's mother the sapiṇḍas of the same gotra such as the father's father and others take, *sapiṇḍas of a different gotra having been included by the term bandhu*" (Moghe's Ed. p. 204). Having regard to the fact that in explaining the term *bandhu* itself the author refers only to the nine enumerated relations and no more, it seems clear that this passage does not mean that *all* bhinnagotra sapiṇḍas inherit as bandhus. It only means that the bhinnagotra sapiṇḍas *who can inherit* are included by the term Bandhu.

The Viramitrodaya, dealing with Yājñavalkya's text on inheritance also understands the Mitākṣarā text to include the nine enumerated Bandhus only. But it gives an extension of meaning to the term to include the maternal uncle also. The text mentions the maternal uncle's son as a Bandhu. This, Vīramitrodaya says, includes by lakṣaṇā—a sort of argument *a fortiori*—the maternal uncle himself who is nearer and from whom his son derives his kinship.[70] Neither

[69] बन्धवश्च त्रिविधाः आत्मबन्धवः पितृबन्धवो स्वमातृबन्धवश्चेति । यथोक्तं आत्मपितृस्वसुः पुत्रा आत्ममातृस्वसुः सुताः आत्ममातुलपुत्राश्च विज्ञेया ह्यात्मबान्धवाः ॥ पितुपितृस्वसुः पुत्रा पितुः मातृस्वसुः सुता । पितुर्मातुलपुत्राश्च विज्ञेयाः पितृबान्धवाः ॥ मातुर्मातृस्वसुः पुत्रा मातुर्मातृस्वसुः सुताः मातुर्मातुल पुत्राश्च विज्ञेया मातृबान्धवाः ॥ तत्र च अन्तरङ्गत्वात् प्रथममात्मबन्धवो धनभाजस्तदभावे पितृबन्धवस्तदभावे मातृ-बन्धव इति क्रमो वेदितव्यः ।

[70] योगीश्वर बचनेऽपि बन्धुपदेन मातुललक्षणमन्यथा मातुलानामग्रहणमेव प्रसज्येतेति तत् पुत्राणां धनाधिकारस्ततः प्रत्यासन्नानाम् तेषां च नेति महदनौचित्यमापद्येत ।

This argument would be superfluous if Viramitrodaya, which follows the Mitākṣharā, understood the latter to include *all* bhinnagotra sapiṇḍas as included under bandhus in this text.

the Vīramitrodaya nor any other commentary that I know of interprets Bandhu as embracing *all* sapiṇḍas who belong to a different gotra, whether they take the term sapiṇḍa to mean either participator in funeral oblations or as persons within seven degrees from the father or five degrees from the mother.

Gotrajas

Yājñavalkya's text therefore cannot be understood to include all cognate sapiṇḍas but only the specified nine relations. That is as far as the Dharmaśāstras seem to have gone to include cognates other than the daughter's son as heirs. For the rest, the scheme of succession was purely agnatic and, in respect of gotrajas, including sakulyas and samānodakas, but not including remoter sagotras who seem to have succeeded as a class, on the principle of parentelic succession.

Acharya, pupil etc.

Failing these heirs, the āchārya, the pupil (śiṣya) and fellow-student (sabrahmachāri) take one after another.

The last of the heirs mentioned in these texts is the king, except to the estate of a Brāhmaṇa, whose wealth goes to other Brāhmaṇas. This has been the law from the oldest times from Gautama downwards. This is not the same as the law of Escheat which proceeds on the principle that all property without an owner necessarily belongs to the king. In the Indian texts the king takes not by escheat but as a specified last heir. The exception relating to the property of a Brāhmaṇa is based on the view that a Brāhmaṇa's property is too sacred to be taken by the king on any pretence—a principle which is also repeated in the provision in these laws forbidding the imposition of a fine on a Brāhmaṇa.

JOINT HINDU FAMILY

The Law of Inheritance is one of the eighteen topics of law mentioned in Manu, Narada and Brihaspati, as we shall see later. The name of this topic is always vibhāga or Dāyavibhāga which literally means 'partition of heritage. In the classical works of law of the Middle ages an important controversy meets us at the very threshold of the topic, viz. whether it implies a pre-existing joint ownership of father and sons in the property or whether the sons get a right to partition only after the death of father. As is well-known, this is a fundamental point of difference between the schools of law following the Miṭākṣarā on the one hand and that of the Dāyabhāga on the other. We have seen and discussed the texts relating to the right of sons to inherit to the deceased father. But, in addition, there are other texts which are relied upon for the view noted by Viśvarūpa and, following him, Aparārka and Vijñāneśvara who hold that in the ancestral property, the owner, his sons, grandsons, and great grandsons become co-owners from their birth and the partition which takes places is the partition of the pre-existing property of the sons and others in that property.

A great deal of the later legal literature as well as the judicial decisions in British Indian Courts have dealt with the law of this property of the joint Hindu family and it has been assumed by the scholars that the joint Hindu family in which the father and his sons, grandsons and great grandsons have got equal right of ownership is the primary fact of Hindu law. We shall briefly examine how far that theory is justified.

Texts on absolute ownership of father

We find that the texts of law dealing with this matter of the right of sons in property may be divided into four classes each representing a separate stage. The first class definitely lays down that the father, so long as he is alive, is the absolute master of all the property with the fullest powers of disposing of the property, and, it is emphatically stated, that the sons have no right so long as the father is alive. In this class are the following texts:

Śankha cited in the Smṛitichandrika: "Sons cannot divide the property so long as the father is alive."

Devala: "Upon the death of the father, the sons should divide the wealth of the father. They have no property so long as the father lives faultless."

Manu IX, 105: "Upon the demise of the father and the mother, the brothers should come together and divide the paternal wealth. They have no property in it while they (the parents) live." (anīśāste hi jīvatoh).

Gautama: "Upon the death of the father, the sons should divide the father's wealth or during his life-time at his desire when the mother is past child-bearing."

Sons' limited right to partition

Side by side with the texts of the first group there are ancient texts which indicate that the father is expected to partition the property between his sons in his old age. This is indicated by the text of Taittirīyasaṃhita (III, 194), referred to in many of the Smṛitis, which says that Manu divided the dāya (inheritance) among his sons. One of these texts says that the sons can divide the property when the father is old, and out of his mind (Vriddhe viparīta chetasi). This is stated in the text of Hārita (quoted by Mitākṣarā, Vyavahāramayukha and others) to the following effect, "Even without the desire of the father, partition takes place if the father is off his mind or very old." But there is another text of Harita which is also quoted by Jīmūtavāhana which says, "while the father lives, the sons have no freedom of accepting, giving or pledging the wealth. If the father is in distress or gone abroad, or is suffering from illness, the eldest son should look after the affairs".[71]

In this class also fall those texts which lay down that when the mother is past child bearing and all the sisters have been married out, there may be partition, as in the text of Narada (cited by Mayukha, page 33). These texts however do not go so far as to say that the sons can compel partition.

Restrictions on power of alienation

The third class of texts are in the nature of restrictions of the father's powers of alienation. The following texts cited in commentaries are of that class: "Immoveable properties and slaves, even if they have been acquired by a person himself, cannot be sold without bringing together all the sons. Those who are born, those who are unborn and those who are in the womb—all look for maintenance. There is no gift or sale permitted (Vyasa cited in Dayabhaga).[72] To a somewhat similar effect is a text which says that by the consent of co-villagers, agnates, boundarymen and heirs (co-sharers), by pouring

[71] D.B. I. 42, जीवति पितरि पुत्राणामर्थादानविसर्गाक्षेपेषु न स्वातन्त्र्यं, कामं दीने प्रोषिते आर्तिं गते वा ज्येष्ठोऽर्थांश्चिन्तयेत् ।

[72] स्थावरं द्विपदञ्चैव यद्यपि स्वयमर्जितम् ।
असम्भूय सुतान् सर्वान् न दानं न च विक्रयः ॥
ये जाता येऽप्यजाता ये च गर्भे व्यवस्थिताः ।
वृत्तिं तेऽभिकाङ्क्षन्ति न दानं न च विक्रयः ॥

The last eight letters are also differently quoted as वृत्तिलोपः विगर्हितः which seems to be a better reading.

water and giving gold—these are the six ways in which land passes.[73] It seems, however, that this text is not evidence of a village community or community of ownership but only an injunction requiring a person disposing of land to take counsel of his near relations and neighbours.

Co-ownership of father and sons

In the next class come the texts which definitely assert, contrary to the texts of Manu, Devala and others that father and sons are co-owners of land. To this class belong the following texts: "Of the gems, pearls and corals, the father is the master, but of all the immoveables neither the father nor the grand-father is the master."[74] Similarly Yājñavalkya lays down "In land descended from the grand-father, in Nibandha (a species of incorporal rights) and dravyas (specified things) there shall be equal ownership of both the father and the son":[75] And the text of Viṣṇu says "In grand-paternal wealth the ownership of father and sons is equal".

Even these texts do not go so far as to lay down that the sons, grandsons, great grandsons etc. have a right of enforcing partition against an unwilling father. As we have seen, Gautama's text like other texts of the first group says that after the mother is past child-bearing, the property may be divided at the father's choice.

Right to partition

On the other hand a text of Bṛihaspati cited by the Mitākṣarā and the Vyavāhara Máyūkha (Mandlik, p. 34) clearly suggests that in ancestral lands and houses in the father's hands sons can claim partition without the father's consent, though in father's self acquired properties they cannot.[76]

In connection with the first group of these texts which gives absolute mastery to the father over all property, we find that while

[73] स्वग्राम ज्ञाति सामन्त दायादानुमतेन च ।
हिरण्योदकदानेन षड्भिर्गच्छति मेदिनी ॥

[74] मणिमुक्ताप्रवालानां सर्वस्यैव पिताप्रभूः ।
स्थावरस्य तु सर्वस्य न पिता न पितामह ॥

[75] भूर्या पितामहोपात्ता निबन्धो द्रव्यमेव च ।
तत्र स्यात् सदृशं स्वाम्यं पिता पुत्रस्य चोभयोः ॥

[76] क्रमागते गृहक्षेत्रे पितापुत्राः समांशिनः ।
पैतृके न विभागार्हाः सुताः पितुरनिच्छया ॥
(Bṛihaspatismṛiti Gaekwad Edition, p. 197, Jolly SBE, Vol. XXXIII, p. 370).

ancient legends indicate that a father may give away his all and deprive his heirs, later texts, which may be found in the chapter on the Rescission of Gift, lay down that a man who has his sons or relations dependant on him should not give his entire property. (See infra under Rescission of Gift).

The struggle between the commentaries has been with regard to the question whether the sons have the power to claim a partition against the father and if so, when and under what circumstances? The law as developed in the commentaries like Vijñāneśvara's Mitākṣarā and others has not given a son, grandson or great grandson an unrestricted right to claim partition by reason of their admitted co-ownership of the property. They discuss the different periods of partition with or without the consent of the father and in the latter case they always restrict the right to a time when the father is old or has ceased to care for worldly things and the mother is past child bearing or when the father is off his mind or seriously ill. British Indian courts, however, have extended the law, and the result of the judicial decisions is that of a son, grandson or great grandson not only becomes a co-owner with the father by birth but can claim partition of ancestral property at any time. Leaving out of consideration this later development by judicial decisions, we shall attempt to consider the places of these different texts in the course of the evolution of law in ancient India.

Theory of joint ownership

On the basis of these texts of law a theory of joint family ownership of property has been developed in classical commentaries of Hindu law and this has been considered to be the original state of the law of property in ancient India.

The foundation of this theory is that the father with his adult sons live together in a joint family which has long neen the fact in mediaeval and modern India. This conception, however, does not seem to have been contemplated at all in the early Vedic times. The scheme of life of an Ārya even in the Dharmaśāstras contemplate a tender youth going out of the house to live with his Āchārya, after his Upanayana, as a member of the latter's family and to serve him faithfully until samāvartana or graduation. On completion of studies he makes a ceremonial bath when he becomes a snātaka and leads a life of austerity only less rigorous than that of a student or Brahmachāri. It is his duty then to marry as soon as he can and light his own House-fire, as prescribed in the ritual of marriage, before which he is to make his oblations every day after marriage.

It will be noted that a separate House-fire, not that of his father or brothers, is inconsistent with a joint family. It is not without significance also that the ceremony of House-building in Āśvalāyana's Grihya in II, 7-9 is interposed between the rituals of marriage in the bride's house and those of the daily and periodical rituals of a Gṛihastha in the third Adhyaya. It suggests that a snātaka builds his separate house at the time of marriage and it is to this house that the bride is led and here his House-fire is established. This is wholly inconsistent with grown up sons living in the father's family.[77]

Further, we may notice at the outset that the whole idea of jointness as developed in what I believe to be the later texts of law is practically based upon ownership in land. There could be no idea of jointness of property of the family when ownership of land was unknown. And we must assume that there was a stage of society in which land was not yet property, when land was in fact plentiful and could be cultivated or occupied by any one who chose. Now, looking at these texts we find that in the early Vedic society as also in most societies of the Indo-Germanic culture group, the owner is found freely disposing of his properties without any restriction in the earliest times by way of gift and particularly by division of the property in old age.. I have also referred to the text of Taittirīyasaṃhita embodying the tradition that Manu divided his property among his sons excluding one, the youngest son,—a tradition which took such a firm root in the Indian mind that we find it referred to in many of the Dharmasutras. Such a thing could not be thought of if the sons were co-owners.

We may, therefore, take this state of society as the starting point of the evolution, when the father was the absolute master of the property unhampered by any rights of the sons who were either unmarried or living separately. The texts of Śankha, Hārita, Gautama, Manu and Devala referred to above may, therefore, be looked upon as laying down the law at the earliest stage. At the same time we find from these texts that, like Manu in his old age, fathers were expected to divide their property between the sons. In making such division the father was apparently not restrained by any limitation.

There are texts which seem to indicate that occasionally sons succeeded in dividing the property even in the father's life-time and probably by coercion, Kane (Vol. III, page 564 et seq.) refers to the passage in Ṛigveda I, 75 "Oh Agni ! Many worship you in many places in various ways, they derive from you wealth as from an

[77] RV. X, 7, 7 has an expression "saṃsṛistam dhanam" but this does not refer to a joint family, but only to the wealth jointly offered by two worshippers.

aged father." So also the story of Navanediṣṭa, the youngest son of Manu in the Aitareya Brāhmaṇa (XXII 9) which indicates that the *sons of Manu* divided all the father's property among themselves excluding the youngest son Navanediṣṭa is relied on as indicating that the sons had the right to claim partition against the father in his old age. A different version of the same story is given in Taittīrīyasaṃhita (III, 1, 9, 4 and 5) which does not indicate that there was any force or coercion and which says that Manu himself divided the property between his other sons leaving out Navanediṣṭa who was absent in his Guru's house. In the Aitareya Brāhmaṇa too the story clearly indicates a view that the sons in dividing the wealth had done a wrong. It does not also clearly indicate that the sons had forced the partition. Kane (loc. cit.) refers to several other passages from texts indicating that fathers in their old age had to divide the property among their sons and live upon the sons.

No right to force partition

I am inclined to hold that these passages do not indicate that the sons could, as of right, claim a partition against the father, but rather say that it was felt as a duty of the father to divide the property among the sons and sometimes, when this was recognised, the sons could or would force such a partition against the will of the father. That this was done sometimes in fact by unduteous sons is indicated also by a text of Gautama in dealing with the sacred law regarding persons with whom eating together was forbidden and who could not be invited to a dinner at a Srāddha, (Gautama XV, 15 and 19) where one of the persons to be excluded from the dinner is a son who has enforced a division when the father was unwilling. This indicates that while sons sometimes forced a partition against the will of the father they had no right to do so and they incurred serious social penalties by doing so.

Land as a fund for maintenance

A later stage of the law seems to be indicated by the second set of texts quoted above. Of these the text which lays down that land can be given only with the consent or approval of co-villagers, agnates etc., does not seem to indicate a right of the co-villagers or agnates or boundarymen any more than of the dāyādas to forbid the same, but is one of the numerous instances in which many acts had to be done with such publicity. Thus the adoption of a son, according to Vasiṣṭha, had to be done with great publicity, by inviting of kindred and after notifying the king. The inclusion of co-villagers, boundarymen and of agnates along with the dāyādas seems to indicate that the purpose is to ensure full publicity to all concerned and does not give any co-ownership to any of them.

The next class of texts however, lays down very clearly that immoveable properties and slaves even if they are self-acquired cannot be given without bringing all the sons together.[78] The reason for such rules is also stated and that is, that those who are born and those who are unborn and those who are in the mother's womb—all look forward to the land for maintenance. Therefore, they should not be deprived of it. This text does not indicate a right of the sons and other dependents to the property but rather presupposes that the father can give away the property or sell the property ; only he is under a moral obligation not to give away the fund for the maintenance of his dependents without bringing them together, presumably in order to give them an opportunity to prevent such a sale. This moral obligation of not making a gift or a sale to the detriment of the fund for the maintenance of the dependents is also indicated by the later texts referred to in the chapter of "Rescission of Gift" (q. v. infra) by which a person having sons or other heirs is enjoined not to give away his entire property. These texts are all of a piece with similar provisions of law elsewhere such as in Roman Law by which a provision is made for the heirs getting a legitim in the case of testamentary disposition by the father. At this stage we only find a protest against improvident alienation by the father and these texts are directed towards restricting his opportunity of disposition in the interest of the sons and no further.

The text, "Of gems, pearls and corals, the father is the master. But of the (entire) immoveable properties, neither the father nor the grand-father (is the master)", seems also to fall under this category. This text does not go so far as to say that the ownership of immoveable property *belongs* to the sons or grand-sons. When it says that

[78] स्थावरं द्विपदञ्चैव यद्यपि स्वयमर्जितम् ।
असम्भूय सुतान् सर्वान् न दानं न च विक्रयः ।
ये जाता येऽप्यजाता ये च गर्भे व्यवस्थिताः ।
वृत्तिं तेऽभिकाङ्क्षन्ति वृत्तिलोपः विगर्हितः ॥

The last words are otherwise quoted as **न दानं न च विक्रयः** But I think the other version was the correct one. That indicates that a sale or gift, to deprive the family of its source of maintenance is wrong—but not invalid. The variant according to the rules of interpretation would make the rule a paryudāsa so that the transaction in violation of it would be void altogether.

27

the father is the master 'prabhū' of the moveables, it seems that he can dispose of it at his absolute discretion. But he is not a master in respect of immoveables for the purpose of free disposition.

Equal ownership of sons

The next group of texts, for example, those of Yājñavalkya and Viṣṇu cited above, clearly lay down the law that sons and grand-sons are the owners of ancestral immoveable property equally with the father and grand-father. This recognition of co-ownership of sons and grand-sons grows out of and marks the culmination of the restriction of the right of the father to dispose of the property. Nevertheless, while co-ownership of the sons is thus recognised, it does not follow that the sons necessarily had the right to claim partition against the will of the father but rather, only that such joint property should be left intact.

Right of sons to partition

The last stage however seems to be indicated by the text of Bṛihaspati where he clearly indicates that sons are entitled to have a partition of ancestral houses and lands even if the father is unwilling which was perhaps a logical extension, as understood by the law giver, of the principle of co-ownership.

This seems to be the general outline of the development of the law of co-ownership of father and sons which was not the law in the most ancient stratum of the Vedic society. I must not be regarded as saying that in any particular society this precise order of evolution was followed in regular succession. We must remember that the texts which may be arranged in this evolutionary order are most of them mere stray texts quoted in several nibandhas, from works, of which the originals are missing. They may have been compiled at very different times and in different places. The restrictions on the ownership of the father which we find in these various texts may have developed independently in different parts of the country and in different societies at different times. Thus the earliest restriction on the right of disposing of property may not have developed everywhere but only in some societies where the interest of the sons was safeguarded by moral, and later, by legal injunctions. In yet other societies, this restriction may have been carried further and legal restrictions were placed by way of recognising the co-ownership of sons. In yet other societies the co-ownership of sons may have been recognised without their right of partition against the father's will. And it may be only in some societies that Bṛihaspati's rule giving the sons a right to such a partition was developed. Ages may have passed since these laws were laid down in different societies until the period of consolidation of all texts came, when all these laws were taken as equally authoritative and that led to the controversy about the ownership of the father and sons and the sons' right to partition.

Origin of the law of joint ownership

It is possible to say that this development followed a natural course dictated by the social and economic conditions of society at different stages. Thus it is possible to say that at a time when land was not very valuable, the father's ownership might have been regarded as absolute. But when economic conditions changed and land was not so plentiful, and therefore came to be looked upon as a fund for the maintenance of all, the restrictions might have been applied and they gradually led to the development of the final stage of equal ownership of father and sons.

While this kind of evolution cannot altogether be ruled out, we must also recognise the likelihood of these variations in the law being effected by the influence of alien societies of a type in which the landed property was, by the circumstances of the society, regarded as impartible and in which all the members of the family had equal rights. A typical instance of such an organisation is to be found in the Malābar tārwād which grew up in a matriarchal society. Unlike patriarchal societies where children live under the absolute authority of the father and the property passes from father to son, in matriarchal societies the son is more or less a stranger to the father, even if there was no more than one, and lives with his mother and his maternal relations in a family of which the owners are the females, but whose properties are managed by a male such as the Karnavan and the only productive members of the family are females who are permanent residents in the house. Nevertheless, the females were not regarded as principals or full owners but as subordinate members of the family. They do not become owners and cannot divide the property. In such a society the only suitable form of organisation that can develop with a permanent female population is to give to them rights to enjoy the property only for their lives as a joint impartible property managed by a male in the interest of the entire family.

We have seen before that even in historical times societies organised on matrilinear lines adopted the Aryan culture and also, necessarily, the patriarchal form of organisation of society. Such societies may have carried with them nevertheless their original ideas of joint ownership of land, in which every member of the family had a right, and implanted it upon the Aryan law which they adopted. It is also possible that people in Aryan societies, who were impelled by the extravagance or improper conduct of fathers in disposing of their landed property, when land became valuable, to seek a solution of the difficulty, may have gradually adopted some parts of the laws which they found in force among the neighbouring non-Arya societies built up on matriarchal lines. It is quite possible that in this way the institution of joint family ownership of land gradually made its way into the sacred law of the Aryans.

The sons' right to partition

The texts of the Dharmasastras however did not carry the law all the way. The utmost that they lay down is that the sons are co-owners with the father and, according to the texts of Bṛihaspati which does not seem to have been universally accepted, were entitled to claim partition of the property against their father. This right to claim partition however was not unrestricted. We have seen above in the oldest texts that fathers in their old age used to divide the property and it is only in the old age of the father that sons could expect to have shares in the father's property. The texts therefore lay down rules as to the circumstances in which and the times at which partition could be enforced. These texts have been developed in the commentaries which lay down different times for partition. First, after the father's death, second, during the father's life-time at his desire and thirdly, against the will of the father when the father is old and the mother past child-bearing and, probably even then, only if the father is incapable or off his mind. And we have seen that it was regarded as heinous sin for a son to compel a father to partition property otherwise than under these circumstances. The Mitākṣarā and the commentaries which follow it did not carry the law any further than this and did not give unrestricted right to the sons to compel partition at their mere choice. The father remains the master of the family and of the family property subject to restrictions on alienation so long as he is capable and in full possession of his powers and so long as the mother is not past child bearing. It is by the introduction of the ideas of English Equity regarding joint ownership and the right of partition that the British Indian courts have extended this law so as to give to the sons right to partition without any restriction.

Right of grand-sons etc

It will be seen that all the texts of the Dharmaśāstras referred to refer to the ownership *only of the sons.* They do not refer to the right of the grand-sons or the great grand-sons. The only text which refers to grand-sons says that in the grand-paternal wealth the rights of the sons, and grandsons are equal. This means really that when the property comes down from the grand-father, his son, and grandson are equally entitled.

The Mitākṣarā however has extended the right of the sons to the descendants of the son, not upon any express text of the Śastras, but by interpretation, applied to the law of inheritance as well as partition. For this purpose, however, the Mitākṣarā has to draw the line as the great grand-sons and makes a distinction between succession which is obstructed and succession which is not obstructed to distinguish the class down to great grandson who have rights by birth from that of other heirs.

According to him, the right of the son, grandson and great grandson to ownership of the property of the father is unobstructed (apratibandha). It arises immediately on birth and the presence of the ancestor does not bar their right to the property. On the other hand, the other relations who succeed upon his death have their right to ownership obstructed by the life of the owner. This distinction was necessitated by the extension of the law laid down in the texts from sons to their sons and grandsons who were regarded as equally entitled to the property by birth, in order to prevent the same rule applying to any collateral or remoter relations. This however is a law which was developed in the mediaeval times with which we are not concerned.

Though, under the influence of the authority of Visvarūpa and Vijñāneṣvara, specially the latter, perhaps assisted by the natural desire of sons to have a share in ancestral property everywhere, the Mitākṣarā doctrine has finally prevailed in most parts of India, there were, in the past, societies which stuck to the older view. Of such schools only the school of Jimūtavāhana has survived to this day in Bengal. But his work on Dāyabhāga itself shows that he had illustrious predecessors before him including probably King Bhoja of Dhāra (referred to as Dhāreśvara)[79] who kept up the old law as against the invading innovation.

[79] Jimūtavāhana in D.B. II. 15 quotes Dhāreśvara's opinion explaining Yājñavalkya's text thus :

SELF ACQUISITION

We have seen that in early Vedic society family apparently consisted of the father, mother and small children. Grown-up sons apparently used to set up for themselves after finishing their education. That would seem to be the natural condition of a society of small wealth, when children, on growing up, had necessarily to shift for themselves without recourse to much family wealth. As wealth increased and, particularly, when landed property grew in importance and families began to own considerable landed property, grown-up sons would naturally tend to stick to their parents and look to the father's wealth to sustain them.

So we see that, sometime before the Dharmasūtras, living together of father and grown-up sons had already become a common and even the normal feature. Consequentially people got used to the idea of wealth of the family as a fund for its maintenance.

In a family of parents and small children the natural idea would be that all the wealth belonged to the father, including whatever was earned by the labour or skill of children and, before the law of inheritance grew up, the father would ordinarily distribute his wealth among his sons just as he chose.

This condition of society seems however not to have been expressed except only in the late texts to be found in the present redaction of Manusamhitá. There it is stated that sons like wives and slaves are incapable of acquiring property for themselves and whatever they might acquire would belong to the father.[80]

It followed, therefore, that upon the death of the father all the property including what might have been earned by the sons would fall to be partitioned.

As has been stated before, at the time of the present redaction of Manu and long before that, this text had become quite archaic in so far as sons and wives were concerned. For, even in the oldest Dharmasutras, we find the sons and wives are deemed to have separate property. The text however survives in the late redaction of Manu in the form in which it existed in the remote past because it was a

इच्छया विभागदानप्रवृत्तस्य पितुः पैतामहे सदृशं स्वाम्यं पुत्रैः सह, न तत्र स्वोपार्जित धन इव न्युनाधिकविभागमिच्छातः कर्तुमर्हति ।

Equal ownership of sons being understood as merely a right to an equal share to ancestral property when the father voluntarily divides.

[80] भार्या पुत्रश्च दासश्च त्रय एवाधनाः स्मृताः ।
यत्तु समधिगच्छन्ति यस्य ते तस्य तद्धनम् ॥ Manu VIII 416.

living law with regard to slaves and it is in connection with the law regarding slaves that this text appears in the present Manusamhita.

In the earliest Dharmasutras however the law of inheritance has already grown up and it has become customary, and even praised as meritorious, for sons to divide the property after their father's death.

When grown up sons come into the family and divide their father's wealth the question of the claims of a son by whose labours a part of the paternal wealth was acquired to that part would become insistent. And we find that the law reacts to this claim by a gradual recognition of the claims of the acquirer to his self-acquisitions in a manner somewhat similar to the law of Peculium in Roman law.

Two points peculiar to the Indian law have to be noted however. Peculium in Rome was originally only a part of the father's property entrusted to a son in which the son had no ownership but only limited right of user during the father's life time. Later a new kind of peculium came to be recognised in the shape of Castrense Peculium, which consisted of the earnings of a soldier. From this, by gradual extension, recognition of ownership was extended to other kinds of acquisitions, named Quasi Castrense peculium.

Stages of the Law

In India the earliest texts, as we shall presently see, do not seem to contemplate the son owning the property during the life time of the father. They speak of the right of the acquirer to such property *only at the time of partition* after the father's death. Out of this probably grew up in later times the idea of sons owning such property during the father's life time independently of the father.

Another characteristic feature is that in the earliest texts on the subject we find that the only property so considered as separate property was the property earned by pursuit of learning—vidyādhanam.

With regard to the first of these features we shall presently find that, with only one or two exceptions, from the first to the last the texts clearly envisage only the subtraction of such properties from the hotchpot at partition between brothers and other heirs and do not speak of the son's right to such properties as against the father.

The last feature is worthy of more than passing notice. It indicates to my mind that laws were primarily concerned with the Brāhmaṇas, whose occupation was learning, which meant knowledge of the Vedas in all its branches, and only secondarily with Kṣatriyas and in a remoter degree with common people, the Vaiśyas. The preponderence of the law relating to Brāhmaṇas in all the sections is an outstanding feature of these laws. So we find that here also, when the idea of recognising self-acquisitions was first conceived, the law was confined to earnings by learned occupations which was the special province of Brāhmaṇas.

Before the work of Viṣṇu no other kind of property was distinguished in the same manner, except property won by military prowess, which was for the benefit of Kṣatriyas. Other kinds of self-acquisitions specified, and finally generalised in a rule covering all acquisitions independently of the paternal wealth, were only given in Viṣṇu and the later Smṛitis.

Gautama

The earliest indication that we get of such self-acquisition is probably the text of Gautama[81] (XXVIII-30) which says "What a learned co-parcenar has acquired by his own efforts, he may at his pleasure withhold from his unlearned (coparcenars). But unlearned co-parcenars shall divide their acquisitions equally." This is the germ apparently of the entire law of self-acquisition as developed in later texts. The importance thus assigned to what was later called 'Vidyādhana' indicates the pre-occupation of the early Smṛiti with the Brāhmaṇas only who are the primary objects of regulation as stated above.

Vyasa

This along with the acquisition by prowess (Śauryadhanam) and gifts by father (Saudāyika) were apparently the first to be recognised as properties which did not belong to the co-parcenars. This seems to be indicated by a text of Vyāsa cited in the Dāyabhāga where he says "acquisition made by learning or by military prowess and gifts (by father) are the property of himself and cannot be sought by his co-heirs *at the time of partition.*[82]

We note here that Vyāsa speaks of these properties as "not to be sought *by co-heirs at a partition,*" not that they were the acquirer's independent properties even during the father's life time or before partition. This feature will be found in almost all the texts on self acquisition. Before partition, which is conceived as taking place only on the father's death, all members of the family partook of the benefits of the property and it is only at the time of partition that

[81] स्वयमर्जितमवैद्येभ्यो वैद्यः कामं न दद्यात् ।

Quoted in the Dāyabhāga, Chandicharan's Ed., p. 163.

[82] विद्याप्राप्तं शौर्यधनं यच्च सौदायिकं भवेत् ।
विभागकाले तत्तस्य नान्वेष्टव्यो स्वरिक्थिभिः ॥

these properties had to be set apart. The reference to "co-heirs" (svarikthibhih) indicates clearly that this text applies only to partition between heirs *on the last owner's death,* for Riktha means heritage.

Katyayana

An earlier stage of the law is indicated in a text though it appears only in the late work of Kātyāyana. This text cited by the Dāyabhāga (which by the way is completely contrary to other texts quoted from the same author) says:

"Grandpaternal property, paternal property as well as whatever else is acquired by oneself, all that is to be divided in a partition between heirs.[83]

This, it is hardly necessary to say, is one of the anachronous survivals of old law which abound in the Smṛitis.

Visnu

The later texts of law from Viṣṇu onwards specifically enumerate several kinds of exclusive property of acquirers which include, in addition to Vidyādhanam and Śauryadhanam, the following:

(1) Presents from friends (Maitryam),
(2) Gifts at marriage (Audvāhikam, bhāryādhanam),
(3) Lost ancestral property recovered by one[84] (Hṛitamuddhṛitam),
(4) Offerings given to an honoured guest (Mādhuparkikam),
(5) Gifts by father (Saudāyika) or mother,
(6) Gifts generally.

These specific enumerations are, in these works supplemented by a general proposition that whatever is acquired by one's self without detriment to the paternal property becomes the property of the acquirer which is not to be given to co-heirs.[84]

Evolution of self-acquisition

It seems to me that the evolution of this general principle of self-acquisition followed the prior recognition of specific kinds of self-acquisitions in time. Starting with Vidyādhanam, the law was extended first to Sauryadhanam and Saudāyikam, which are the three things enumerated in the text of Vyasa.[85] Properties acquired at his wedding by the bridegroom seem to have been the next kind of pro-

[83] पैतामहञ्च पैत्र्यञ्च यच्चान्यत् स्वयमर्जितम् ।
दायादानां विभागे तु सर्वमेतद्विभज्यते ॥ Kane's collection Verse 840, p. 101.

[84] Yajñvalkya II, 118-119.

[85] Cited in D.B. (Chandicharan's Ed., p. 173), supra, p. 216.

perty to be distinguished. Saudāyika, originally confined to affectionate gifts by father was naturally extended to gifts by mother or grand-father[86] and other kinds of gifts such as Mādhuparkika which is a gift offered to an honoured guest, and then to gifts by friends (Maitryam) and then to gifts generally, as receiving gifts was the very special mode of acquisition open to a Brahmana.[87]

The law was apparently next extended to whatever was acquired by one's own labour (Sramena yadupārjayet).

A further extension was given by including among self-acquisitions lost family property which is recovered by one, which Yājñavalkya enumerates as a self-acquisition not to be shared by co-heirs. The earlier law regarding this kind of property was apparently very different, as appears from a text of Śankha cited by the Mitākṣarā[88] which only gives a fourth share of the property to the acquirer, the rest being equally divided among all co-heirs.

I have only indicated here the possible lines of development and it is out of question to be precise about the exact sequence of these items. It seems certain however that the law was extended step by step to specific items before the final generalisation was achieved.

The general rule which could be evolved from the specific instances was that what was acquired by a man's own efforts alone would be exclusively his on partition. This generalisation was already made before Viṣṇu and it appears in most works from that time onwards. This principle however appears from the outset to have been qualified by the rider that the acquisition must not have been made at the expense of paternal wealth. If it was made at the expense of paternal wealth, the implication would be that it was merely an accretion and should be common property.

A text of Vyasa[89] cited by the Dāyabhāga makes this implica-

[86] Vyasa cited in D.B. (Chandicharan, p. 173).

पितामहेन यद्दत्तं पित्रा वा प्रीतिपूर्वकं ।
तस्य तन्नापहर्त्तव्यं मात्रा दत्तञ्च यद्भवेत् ॥
स्वामी रिकथ क्रय संविभाग निक्षेपाधिगमाछ च ।
ब्राह्मणस्याधिकं लब्धं क्षत्त्रस्य निर्जितं निर्विष्टं वैश्यशूद्रयोः ।

[87] Gautama.

[88] Under Yajn. II, 118-119.

[89] Chandicharan's Ed., page 170.

साधारणं समाश्रित्य यत्किञ्चिद्वाहनायुधं ।
शौर्यादिनाप्नोति धनं भ्रातरस्तत्र भागिनः ॥
तस्य भागद्वयं देयं शेषास्तु समभागिनः ।

tion express, but at the same time lays down that, even so, the acquirer would get a double share of it as recompense for his effort.

The penultimate stage of this evolution is marked by Viṣṇu and his successors in the texts which I shall now discuss.

Manu

Maṇu says "Vidyādhanam belongs to him whose (acquisition) it is. So also are presents from friends, wedding gifts and Mādhuparkika. Whatever is acquired by the labour of one without detriment to paternal property, that, if acquired by his own efforts and desired by him, he ought not to give (to his co-heirs) except at his own will. When paternal property which was lost is reacquired by the father he should not share that self-acquisition with sons unless he wishes (as it is) his self-acquisition" (IX 206-209).[90]

The last two texts but not the first above have been quoted verbatim in Viṣṇu (Chap. XVIII, 42-43). The first of these texts simply enumerates specific self-acquisitions which seems to me to belong to an earlier stratum than the next text which gives the generalised rule. It will be noted that this text does not in any manner qualify the enumeration of the first text. The third text lays down the later rule with regard to re-acquired property which modifies the law in earlier texts giving only a special share to the acquirer. Even in their juxtaposition therefore it is clear that Manu's texts do not contemplate the limitation of acquisition without detriment to family property to attach to Vidyādhanam, Maitryam, Audvāhikam or Mādhuparkikam, but these are conceived as self-acquisitions simpliciter.

Yajnavalkya

Yājñavalkya's texts (II 118-119) are as follows: "Whatever is acquired by a person himself without detriment to the father's estate (as well as) presents from friends, and wedding gifts shall not belong

[90] विद्याधनं तु यद्यस्य तत्तस्यैव धनं भवेत् ।
मैत्रयमौद्वाहिकं चैव माधुपर्किकमेव च ॥
अनुपघ्नन पितृद्रव्यं श्रमेण यदुपार्जयेत् ।
स्वयमीहितलब्धं तन्नाकामो दातुमर्हति ॥
पैत्रिकं तु पिता द्रव्यमनवाप्तं यदाप्नुयात् ।
न ततपुत्रैः भजेत् सार्धमकामः स्वयमर्जितम् ॥ IX 206-209.

to co-heirs. Nor shall he who recovers lost ancestral property nor what he acquires by learning give it to his co-heirs".[91]

This text gives some countenance to the interpretation placed on it by the Mitākṣarā followed by practically all commentators, that the opening clause "whatever is acquired without detriment to paternal property" qualifies the specific kinds of property enumerated in the later lines. This view leads to the incongruous conception that even a present from a friend or at the wedding may be acquired with detriment to family property. The incongruity of this interpretation was pointed out apparently by Srīkara whose opinions are referred to and controverted by the Jimūtavāhana (Dāyabhāga Chandicharan's Ed., p. 177).

This is a view however which seems to be historically inaccurate. The collocation of Manu's texts, as already pointed out, seems to indicate that the general rule with this limitation did not apply to the specifically enumerated self-acquisitions. But it would seem that the principle of this view had a limited measure of acceptance in Narada's analogous provision that where one brother maintains another brother's family while the latter is learning, the former shares in the Vidyādhana of the latter[92] and also that the Vidyādhana is partible if acquired with the aid of patrimony.

Narada

Narada's text seems to miss the broad general principle and simply enumerates the several kinds of self-acquisitions as follows:

> "Property gained by valour or belonging to a wife (bhāryā-dhanam) and gains of science are three kinds of wealth not subject to partition and so is a favour conferred by the father. When the mother has bestowed her property on any son from affection the rule is the same in this case also; for the mother is equal to the father." (XIII 5, 6).
>
> "When one brother maintains the family of another brother who is engaged in study he shall receive a share of the wealth gained by the study though he is himself ignorant (XIII, 10). A learned man is not bound to give a share of his own wealth against his will to an unlearned co-heir *unless it have been gained by using the paternal wealth.*" (XIII, 11).

[91] पितृद्रव्याविरोधेन यदन्यत् स्वयमर्जितम् ।
मैत्र्यमौद्वाहिकञ्चैव दायादानां न तद्भवेत् ॥
क्रमादभ्यागतं द्रव्यं हृतमप्युद्धरेत्तु यः ।
दायादेभ्यो न तद्दद्याद्विद्यया लब्धमेव च । Yajn II. 118-119.

[92] Narada XIII, 10, 11.

This last qualification to property in Vidyādhana however indicates that the general rule laid down by Viṣṇu, Manu and Yājñavalkya was implicit in this text of Narada.

Brihaspati

Bṛihaspati's text (SBE Vol. XXXIII, p. 371) also merely enumerates the following kinds of self-acquisition without reference to the general rule (1) re-acquisition of ancestral property, (2) Vidyādhanam, (3) Sauryadhanam etc.[93]

This text and the text of Manu IX, 209 are distinguished from other texts cited so far, in as much as they do not apparently limit the law of self-acquisition to the occasion of partition between brothers like the other texts, but prescribe that these are the specific self-acquisitions of the father which he can dispose of at will, unlike ancestral property in which sons have a right. It will be remembered that Bṛihaspati has already developed a rule of son's share in ancestral property in the father's hands to the length of giving the sons a right to partition against the will of the father. It was when this right was recognised that these two texts which, I conceive, belongs to a late stratum, find the need to specify the self-acquired properties of the father which the sons cannot claim.

Vyasa

Vyāsa's texts cited by the Dāyabhāga are as follows:

"What is acquired by one by learning or prowess and the Saudāyika, these are the acquirer's and are not to be sought by co-heirs at the time of partition." "What wealth is acquired by one's own effort without assistance of paternal property is not to be given to co-heirs, nor what is obtained by learning." "What wealth is acquired, with the assistance of common property such as conveyances and weapons, by one's prowess is shared by (the acquirer's) brothers. To him should be given two shares and the rest is to be equally divided."[94]

[93] पैतामहं हृतं पित्रा स्वशक्त्या यदुपार्जितम् ।
विद्याशौर्य्यादिनावाप्तं तत्र स्वाम्यं पितुः स्मृतम् ॥
Bṛihaspatismṛiti Gaekwad Ed., p. 205

[94] विद्याप्राप्तं शौर्यधनं यच्च सौदायिकं भवेत् ।
विभागकाले तत्तस्य नान्वेष्टव्यः स्वरिक्थिभिः ॥
अनाश्रित्य पितृद्रव्यं स्वशक्त्याप्नोति यद्धनं ।
दायादेभ्यः न तद्दद्याद्विद्यालब्धन्तु यद्भवेत् ॥

Here too Vyāsa is talking of the separate property to be subtracted at the time of partition and between brothers or co-heirs. What is special is the positive rule about what the acquirer get when the self-acquisition is with detriment to the family property: in that case the acquirer gets a double share.

Katyayana

Texts of Kātyāyana cited in different commentaries show the law in its final stage in the Dharmasastras. These texts, some of which, though identical in content, have been quoted in different words by different authors, state the law much more fully with all qualifications clearly and explicitly stated and, besides, show a certain amount of advance in details. The several texts including those of the same import, but in different words in different quotations, are as follows:

> "All that (ancestral) wealth which was taken away by force from the family or was lost (to the family) and which was recovered by the father himself by his own efforts, the father is not liable to share with the sons at the time of partition." "That wealth is said to be gained by learning which is acquired by means of learning received from another while subsisting on food furnished by a stranger." "When a matter (a doubt or difficult point) has been placed (before an assembly of learned men) with a wager, whatever is gained by (showing one's superior) learning is known as Vidyādhana (gains of learning), it is not divided at a partition." "What is acquired from a pupil (*i.e.* by the profession of teaching), by performing the work of a priest at a sacrifice, by propounding a question, by solving a doubtful point, by exhibiting one's knowledge, by disputation with a rival, what is gained by deep learning—all this is declared to be vidyādhana and it is not divided at a partition." "The same is the rule even in the case of artisans and whatever is obtained (as a reward etc.) over and above the proper price of an article (becomes the self-acquisition of that member who sells it)." "After vanquishing an adversary in a wager whatever is obtained by (superior) knowledge should be known as vidyādhana (gains of learning) and is not liable to be partitioned. This is the view of Bṛihaspati." "What is gained by an assertion of one's learning, what is obtained from a pupil (*i.e.* by teaching) and what is acquired on the analogy of priests officiating at a sacrifice—all these are known as vidyādhana; this is the view of Bhṛigu." "What is obtained by the superiority of one's learning, and from a sacrificer (by officiating as a priest for him) and from a pupil (by teaching him)—all this is declared to be

साधारणं समाश्रित्य यत्किञ्चिद्वाहनायुधं ।
शौर्यादिनाप्नोति धनं भ्रातरस्तत्र भागिनः ॥
तस्य भागद्वयं देयं शेषास्तु समभागिनः ।

vidyādhana; acquisitions other than these are common (*i.e.* jointly owned) with others." "Bṛihaspati declares that the wealth acquired by valour (in battle) by brothers who were instructed in the family or by the father is liable to be divided (among all the members of the family)." "A learned man should never give to his unlearned kinsmen (brothers etc.) anything from his gains of learning, but a learned man should give his gains of learning to those (of his kinsmen) who are equally learned or more learned than himself." "Where a reward was given by the king (or master) being pleased by the actions of a person who putting his own life in danger did an act of strength (or valour) whatever is thus obtained is the wealth due to valour. (Śauryadhanam). "What is acquired by valour and by learning and what is known as wealth of the wife—all this is not liable to be partitioned by co-sharers at the time of partition." "What is called 'dhvajāhṛita' is declared to be impartible. That is said to be 'dhvajāhṛita' which is recovered from a battle after putting one's life in danger of death for the king (or master) and after putting to flight the army of the adversary." "What is obtained at the time of marriage with a maiden of the same caste is known as 'kanyāgata' (coming with a maiden) wealth, it is declared to be pure and as promoting prosperity." "That is known as 'vaivāhika' (nuptial) which comes with the wife, all wealth of this sort should be known as the means of (performing) dharma (religious duties)." "Whatever is given at the time of marriage as meant for the bridegroom, all that is the wealth of the maiden and it cannot be partitioned by the co-sharers." (Kane's collection, p. 105; trans. p. 307).

The most interesting point to note here is that of different kinds of Vidyādhana described by Kātyāyana. As stated before, the early texts contemplated by Vidyādhanam properties acquired through Vedic learning including knowledge of rituals. Kātyāyana in the above texts specifies different kinds of such acquisitions with interesting detail.

Property won in a disputation in which a wager is laid apparently suggests that sometimes learned disputations were held in which the parties laid wagers on their succeeding to establish their respective theses. Besides, disputations were held at which prizes were awarded, presumably by a king, to the successful disputant, an illustration of which is probably to be found in the story of the Bṛihadāraṇyaka Upaniṣad of a disputation between Gārgi and Yājñavalkya. What is won by a person at these disputations is the first kind of Vidyādhana.

Presents from pupils, the next kind, refers to the rule that, while the teaching was gratuitous, when a pupil living with his teacher completed his education, he had to give a present (vara) to the teacher. A third variety of vidyādhana was the fee or present received for giving an opinion on any question on which advice is sought by a client.

These are varieties of Vidyādhana which are in accord with its original implication. But in Kātyāyana's time the concept had been extended to other kinds of knowledge. Thus an artisan who, by the use of his skill, converts the material to a thing of superior value, such as a picture or an ornament, acquires his remuneration, according to Kātyāyana, by vidyā. A more striking illustration is the gain made by a gambler by his superior knowledge and skill at gambling.

Similarly, Sauryadhanam is illustrated by different items including what is acquired as a reward for doing some great act of valour and dhvajāhṛita or booty snatched away from the enemy in battle.

Wealth obtained on marriage is distinguished as of two kinds viz. Kanyāgata which is obtained as presents at the time of marriage and vaivāhika including all other properties which come with the wife, which is apparently what was implied by *bhāryādhanam* in Narada's text.

LATER LAWS

The last text above cited is based on the view of law developed before this time in a text of Vyāsa, (supra p. 128) that whatever is given to the bridegroom at marriage (vivāhakāle yatkiṃchit varāyoddiśya dīyate) becomes stridhana of the bride. In that view, this formal acquisition by the bridegroom would not make it his property and hence it cannot in any case be brought into the hotchpot at a partition with him.

It is interesting to note the development of this law of self-acquisition, which is to be the separate property of the acquirer, after the general principle was recognised that whatever is acquired without detriment to the family property is the acquirer's separate property. As we have seen, the law began by specifying particular properties which were regarded as self-acquisitions, such as the gains of science, gains of prowess, presents and so on. The general principle was evolved later that whatever is acquired without detriment to the family property is also a self-acquisition. But this generalisation which was originally sought to widen the field of self-acquisition was construed later as a principle of restriction by later commentators whose commentaries have worked havoc with the law of self-acquisition in British Indian Courts. Thus the text of Yājñavalkya according to its tenor clearly suggests as the general rule that whatever is acquired without detriment to the paternal property becomes the acquirer's property. The varieties which are next enumerated are only illustrative and in fact are formulations of what had been recognised as such properties before. But Vijñāneśwara in interpreting these texts has read the first clause as qualifying all the different specific items enumerated and other commentators have followed suit. The texts of Katyāyana partially supports this view. Jimūtāvahana also holds the same view but makes a departure which will be noted presently.

It is obvious, however, that this is a forced interpretation. Presents from friends or presents at the time of marriage or gifts, apparently, can only be regarded as acquired with detriment to family property by a strange interpretation of the words. Vidyādhana or the gains of learning also does not seem to have been contemplated either by Yājñavalkya or any of the early text writers before, from Gautama downwards as property which could in any circumstances become divisible. The general proposition does not seem to have been intended to restrict the specific enumeration in any manner but only to lay down a general rule in addition to the specific instances which are enumerated and which apparently were already recognised by tradition before his time.

The interpretation of Vijñāneśwara however held the ground and was followed by all. Jimūtavāhana however draws a line at regarding the mere feeding at the family expense during the time when the learning was obtained, as a detriment to the family property which would make Vidyadhana a joint property, though some of the above texts do contemplate that Vidyādhana to be self-acquisition must have been acquired by learning obtained while fed by others *i.e.* outside the family. So too he refuses to recognise the Bratabhikṣa or marriage presents as family properties merely because the father of the son at the time of his upanayana or marriage in which these presents were obtained has spent much money.

Another restriction which we find imposed from a pretty early time upon Vidyādhana is that this property, that is the gains of the learning, are divisible only by learned brothers and not by unlearned brothers. Gautama, in his text already cited, says that learned brothers may share in the gains of learning of another learned brother but, he adds, that it is only at the pleasure of the acquirer (kāmam). Other texts do not seem to make that qualification clear. It would seem however, even in these texts, where Vidyādhana is obtained by learning acquired without the assistance from the paternal property, it is not to be divided.

The subsequent development of this law of self-acquisition in the commentaries which had been briefly hinted at has led to much complication in a number of judicial decisions in the British-Indian Courts. With these, however, I am not concerned.

CHAPTER X

TOPICS OF LITIGATION

The enumeration of the topics of litigation (vyavāhārapadas) as we find in Manu, Nārada, Bṛihaspati etc., have no claim to be regarded as a scientific classification of law such as we find in the classical jurists of ancient Rome. The only first attempt at a logical classification is to be found in the text of Bṛihaspati, who seems to have had a flair for classification, and who brings these topics under two broad classes ; those that spring from property and those that spring from will to hurt (dhana-himsa-samudbhava). Even that formula is of little use for scientific division.

But, the enumeration of the topics in the different codes is of great historical value. As we have seen, the list grows from very small beginnings to more and more elaborate catalogues, till Manu or Nārada's eighteen topics can no longer hold all the matters of law dealt with by them, so much so that Nārada has to say that, by subdivisions of the topics, we get as many as a hundred and thirtytwo heads. This development is an index of the development of the king's justice in ancient Indian Law.

We have seen before that by Vyavahāra the ancient Indian jurists understood neither law in general, nor all disputes, but only litigation in the king's court. The different items of litigation dealt with by any law-giver under the head of king's vyavahāra accordingly show what kinds of disputes were adjudicated in the days in the king's court. The expansion of the list as we come to later works would thus give us an index of the expansion of the king's justice.

If we could have all the works of law that ever existed in the past and could arrange the heads of litigation given in them in the order of growing fulness, we could have a fairly complete history of the growth of the king's justice. Unfortunately, however, we have only a handful out of the multitude of works that can be inferred to have been written through the centuries in different parts of this great sub-continent ; and then again the bulk of them not in complete works themselves, but in quotations scattered all over the commentaries or text tooks. It is impossible for us therefore to construct a history of the evolution of the king's justice in India with the fulness and precision with which we can speak about the history of the expansion of the law in Rome or in England. We can only get a broken picture of stages of development separated by large expanses of space and time.

And, of course, we cannot put our finger on the machinery by means of which the stages of expansion were introduced. In Rome we know how the Pontiffs held charge of the forms of litigation and probably developed them, until the Praeter and jurisconsults took up the work of expansion which they achieved by introducing new forms of action by Utilis actions, actions in factum concepta and by edicts. In England we know how the original writs issued by the Chancery were multiplied by writs in *Consimili Casu* and by unchallengeable fictions until Equity intervened and carved out a great and expanding jurisdiction of its own under the Chancellor. We can say nothing like this about ancient Indian topics of litigation. We can only say that Gautama and Āpastamba provided for only a handful of topics, Viṣṇu gave a much longer list and Yājñavalkya, Nārada, Bṛihaṣpati and others give much fuller lists of topics. We cannot say what happened in the long intervals between these stages, nor indicate the machinery by which any particular development was achieved.

Nevertheless, with the materials available to us, we can definitely say that king's justice grew from very small beginnings to a great body of categories embracing the very complex relations of a growing society ; and by a close interrogation of the topics dealt with by different authors we may be able to trace the outlines of some aspects of that evolution. This I shall now attempt to do.

We have seen before that originally it was the people in their various kula, sreṇi and other groups who did justice among members of that group and the king did not figure as a judge in the earliest times. This fact perhaps accounts for the statement by Megasthenes about the extreme meagreness of civil law in India. Megasthenes lived in the Court of Chandragupta and knew only of the matters which came before his court. His statement therefore merely means that such litigations were few and those chiefly confined to crimes, in the king's court. As we shall presently see this fact is also borne out by our earliest Dharmasutras.[95]

[95] What would strike one as most strange in Megasthenes is not that criminal law predominated, but that there was no law of Debt and Pledge in India, and, if the debtor did not pay, the creditor was without recourse at law. Even this, however, would be intelligible when we remember, what we shall find later, that the creditors had large powers of self-help almost on a par with those of a nexal creditor in early Rome. See infra p. 230.

In the earliest codes the Dharmasūtras of Gautama, Āpastamba and Baudhāyana, the topics dealt with under what may be called a section of Vyavahāra as a part of the king's duties are extremely meagre, and, except for the law of debt and deposit, they are all matters which, according to the ideas then prevailing, were crimes, that is, wrongs for which punishment is inflicted by the king, and very prominent among these are the offences against social dignities contrary to the law of Dharma. (Supra p. 45 seq.)

Topics in Gautama

Thus, the rules laid down by Gautama, with hardly a pretence of classification, in connection with king's justice (Chapter XII) relate to the following :—

1. The offences of a Śūdra
   (*a*) for reviling a twice born
   (*b*) for assaulting him
   (*c*) for intentionally listening to the chanting of Veda
   (*d*) for reciting Veda
   (*e*) for remembering Veda
   (*f*) for assuming a position equal to a dvija *e.g.* by sitting on the same seat with him
   (*g*) for having sexual intercourse with Ārya woman.
2. The offence of a Kṣatriya
   (*a*) abusing a Brāhmaṇa
   (*b*) assaulting a Brāhmaṇa
   (*c*) abusing a Vaiśya.
3. The offence of a Vaisya
   (*a*) abusing a Brāhmaṇa
   (*b*) abusing a Kṣatriya.
4. The offence of a Brahmana abusing
   (*a*) a Kṣatriya and
   (*b*) a Vaiśya.
   No penalty for Brāhmaṇa abusing a Śūdra.
5. Theft
   (*a*) by Śūdra
   (*b*) by other castes
   (*c*) some petty thefts.
5. (*a*) Punishment of receiver of stolen property and of servant of thief. Immunity in some small thefts.
6. Punishment and compensation for damage done to crops (*a*) by cattle and (*b*) by other animals, belonging to a person other than the owner.
7. Law of debts, interest, pledge and bailment.
8. Prescriptive title by open possession.
9. Persistence in violations of rules of Varnadharma.
10. Rules about punishment,
   (*a*) no corporal punishment except branding and banishment to Brāhmaṇas.
   (*b*) Punishment to be regulated according to the status and strength of the offender, nature of the crime etc.
11. Punishment for giving false evidence (Chapter XIII, 23).

Features of early law

It will be noticed at once that punishable offences, which were not yet called sāhasa or by any other name, fill an overwhelmingly large part of these topics, practically the only exception being the law of debt, deposit and pledge. The rule of prescription laid down here is only incidental to the law of pledge, just to bring out the exception to the rule of prescription in the case of possession of pledge or bailment.

Another important thing to notice is the preponderance of offences affecting *caste rules,* notably the violation by a Śūdra of the duty of respect and courtesy to the twice-born or Āryas, emphasised by the highly disproportionate punishment for a Śūdra for offences for which Āryas are more lightly treated. Thus for abusing a Brāhmaṇa, a Śūdra's tongue is to be cut off while for the same offence a Kṣatriya's penalty is a fine of one hundred panas, and of a Vaiśya's one hundred and fifty panas. For assaulting a Brāhmaṇa, a Śūdra suffers amputation of the limb with which he strikes, while a Kṣatriya has only to pay two hundred panas. Adultery by Āryas is not even mentioned, but for adultery with an Ārya woman the Śūdra suffers amputation of genitals and forfeiture of property, followed by death if the woman happens to be a guptā—that is, a protected or family woman.

Even more striking is the punishment of a Śūdra for even listening to Veda, for which his ears are to be sealed with lead, while, for reciting it, his tongue would be cut off and, if he has the misfortune to remember it, he is to be cut into pieces. Nor is there need to assume that these were merely penalties held *in terrorem* when we recollect that one of the highly belauded acts of Rāma in Rāmayana is his killing Śambuka for no other offence than his temerity in trying to make a Vedic sacrifice. There is even less need to shudder with incredulity at this when even today some American laws send a Negro to the electric chair for raping a white woman while a white man is not in jeopardy of life for the same offence.

We shall presently see that Āpastamba, Vasiṣṭha and Baudhāyana share most of these characteristics of Gautama's code, though, in some of them, we find slight enlargements of topics of litigation. But, before I pass on to those authors, I should like to invite attention to the historic implications of the law laid down by Gautama in this Chapter.

One must not run away with the notion that the topics dealt with by Gautama in connection with Rājadharma was all the law that there was in his time. Gautama's own work shows on the contrary that, in other parts of it, he deals at considerable length and detail with many topics of law. In Chapter II he deals with the mutual rights and duties of teacher and pupil. In Chapter IV appear elaborate laws about marriage and mixed castes and in Chapter XXVIII there is a somewhat elaborate treatment of the law of inheritance. In Chapter XXIII dealing with penances one comes upon a passage which prescribes that a woman who commits adultery with a man of lower caste should be caused to be devoured by dogs in a public place. All these are topics of litigation in later works, as we shall see.

The exclusion of these topics of law from what is meant to be a chapter on vyavahāra means only this that these were not matters which came up, in his days, before the king's court for litigation. They were dealt with by the Kulas and guilds themselves. The jurisdiction of the king was limited at the time to topics treated in chapter XII which, as we have seen, was predominantly concerned with crimes and serious social misdemeanours and debts.

That this was the fact is further indicated by a late text attributed to Bṛihaspati in Viramitrodaya and other text books which runs as follows :

Guroḥ śiṣye Pituḥputre, dampatyo svāmibhṛityayoḥ
Virodhe'pi mithasteṣām vyavahāro ṇa siddhati.

"Even where there is dispute between them there can be no valid vyavahāra between preceptor and pupil, father and son, husband and wife or master and servant."

Though this text appears in a late work, in which it was obviously opposed to other provisions about litigation between these persons, it is clear that it was a survival of a more ancient rule which now persisted more to register a moral injunction than a legal disability. But, in earlier law e.g. in the days of Gautama, something like this was obviously a rule of law, forbidding, vyavahāra i.e. litigation *in the king's court* between such persons. For these were disputes which could only be decided in the domestic tribunals of the community. And that seems to be the reason why, though legal rules about these relations existed and were laid down by Gautama as binding rules, they were nevertheless not dealt with in the law of the king's justice.

As I have indicated, king's justice was very limited at the start. It started with the king awarding punishment (daṇḍa) for wrongs seriously against dharma. This the king was bound to do by reason of his duty repeatedly emphasised in the earliest law books (*a*) to keep all varnas in their proper sphere of duties and (*b*) to protect people by punishing thieves and criminals.[96] The topics mentioned by Gautama are limited to exactly those functions except practically in the matter of Debt, Deposit and pledge. The probable reason for the inclusion of these topics in the king's vyavahāra in Gautama's law we shall consider later.

Apastamba

As indicated before, the topics of law dealt with as part of king's justice in Āpastamba bear characteristics similar to those of Gautama.

One new feature of Āpastamba is a provision about gambling under public supervision, which I shall deal with later. Barring this, Āpastamba deals with the following:

1. Punishment for adultery with all qualifications relative to to castes of the parties. Incidentally he includes niyoga under adultery, as he forbids the institution absolutely
2. Punishment of a Śudra—
   (*a*) for speaking evil of a virtuous Ārya
   (*b*) for assuming position equal to Ārya.
3. Punishment for homicide, theft and appropriation of land, with differentiation of penalty in the case of Brāhmaṇa offender.
4. Punishment for persistent violation of rules of dharma.
5. Punishment of servants and herdsmen for abandoning work undertaken by them and for other defaults of herdsmen in dealing with cattle placed in their charge.
6. Misappropriation of small properties.

A somewhat interesting provision in Āpastamba (II, 11, 28, 5) is that for punishing cattle for eating crops. The offending cattle has to be kept confined and starved as a punishment.

Baudhayana

Baudhāyana in the chapter on Rājadharma deals with the following topics:

1. The law of self-defence which excuses killing of Ātatāyis.
2. Punishment of Brāhmaṇa by branding instead of death.
3. Punishment for inferior castes killing a Brāhmaṇa for which the sentence is death and confiscation of property.
4. Punishment for murder, differentiated according to status of the murdered.
5. Punishment for killing other people's cattle and other animals.

[96] See supra p. 38. देशधर्मान कुलधर्मान् जातिधर्मान सर्वान् वै ताननुप्रविश्य राजा चतुरो बर्णान स्वधर्मे स्थापयेत् । Vasiṣṭha, IX, 3.

Like Gautama and Āpastamba, Baudhāyana also deals with other topics of law, *e.g.* kinds of secondary sons, marriage and marital relations etc. but in separate chapters. Baudhāyana's treatment of these topics is, however, somewhat ambiguous, inasmuch as Chapter XII where he deals with these topics immediately follows the Chapter on Rājadharma and in dealing with marital relations, he also deals with the punishment of adulterous wives and male adulterers. I am inclined to think however that, none the less, he does not conceive this Chapter as appertaining to king's justice, for such punishments might as well have been imposed by domestic tribunals.

Vasistha

The position of Vasiṣṭha's Dharmasutra seems to be midway between the authors above-named and Viṣṇu. It is difficult to place this work, however, for this particular Smriti is more scrappy, cryptic and unmethodical even than any other Sutra work. Reading it through, one feels somehow that it is not the whole original work but a reconstruction, in which texts are thrown in pell-mell without any connection with the context ; and, on the other hand different texts appertaining to the same topic are placed wide apart. Thus, while the fifteenth chapter deals with a fragment of the law of adoption of sons, followed by other texts wholly unconnected with it, the author returns to the topic of sonship and secondary-sons in the seventeenth chapter, where the texts are followed by fragments of the law of marriage. It is thus difficult to say from the collocation of texts, which of them are topics of vyavahāra. It would seem, however, that the sixteenth to the nineteenth chapters all relate to vyavahāra.

Many of the topics of vyavahāra not specifically dealt with by Vasiṣṭha are obliquely referred to in Chapter XVI in dealing with kinds of evidence. From these references it appears that disputes about pathways, fields and homesteads as well as boundary disputes (sāmanta virodha) were already topics of vyavahāra in Vasiṣṭha. The law of prescription is briefly indicated. The law of Debts and pledges is already there. Questions of sonship and rights of inheritance now appear to be topics of vyavahāra. The topics dealt with by Gautama, such as vākpāruṣya and dandapāruṣya are conspicuous by their absence, though vākparuṣya is mentioned in connection with Niyoga. This seems to indicate, as stated before, that the present text is a fragment of the original Vasiṣṭha and, as such, it is not very helpful in finding from it the precise topics of litigation in Vasiṣṭha's time. Nevertheless, it would seem clear that in Vasiṣṭha's time the king's jurisdiction had already been expanded so as to cover many civil disputes which grow further in the works of Viṣṇu.

Later Smritis

Between the older Dharmasutras and the Smṛitis of Viṣṇu, Manu, Yājṇavalkya, Nārada, Bṛihaṣpati and the Arthaśāstra of Kautilya there is a great gap which may be measured by the difference in the topics of litigation in these works, as compared with those of the Dharmasutras. Manu, Kautilya, Nārada and the texts of Bṛihaṣpati cited in the commentaries give lists of what are stated to be eighteen topics of litigation. But, in point of fact the number is really exceeded. Nārada, Bṛihaṣpati, as well as Kautilya, has a chapter which they call, 'Prakīrṇaka' or 'miscellaneous', which includes many topics which could not be squeezed into the eighteen categories specified by Manu. And furthermore, Nārada says that, by subdivision of these eighteen topics, there may be 132 topics and a hundred different branches. This shows that the topics of litigation which were originally very few, as given in the Dharmasūtras go on multiplying as the King's justice develops and topics tend to be sub-divided by differentiation.

Manu gives the following eighteen topics of vyavahāra :

ṛinadana
nikṣepa
aśvāmīvikraya
sambhūya-samutthāna
dattasyānapākarma
vetanādana
saṃvidvyatikrama
krayavikrayānuśaya
svāmipālavivāda
sīmāvivāda
vākpāruṣya
daṇḍapāruṣya
steya
sāhasa
strisaṃgrahana
stripuṃdharma
vibhāga
dyūtasamāhvaya

Nārada's eighteen topics are differently enumerated and they are as follows :—

ṛiṇadāna
nikṣepa
aṣvāmīvikraya
saṃbhūyasamutthāna
dattāpradānika
vetanasyānapākarma
samayasyānapākarma
kritānuśaya
vikrīyāsampradāna
kṣetrajavivāda
vākpāruṣya
daṇḍapāruṣya
sāhasa
stripuṃsaṃyoga
dāyabhāga
dyūtasamāhvaya
abhyupetyāśuśruṣa
prakīrṇaka

It will be noticed at once that marital relations which was outside vyavahāra in the early Sutras becomes a topic of vyavahāra under the name of stripuṃdharma, and inheritance likewise is included as vibhāga or dāyabhāga in these lists.

We may see at once that, using the nomenclature of this classification, Gautama deals very scantily only with the following topics :

Vākpāruṣya
Daṇḍapāruṣya
Steya
Svāmipālavivāda
Ṛiṇadana
Strīsaṃgrahana

Āpastamba's topics are even briefer. They include only

Strisaṃgrahana
Vākpāruṣya
Steya
Murder (and possibly)
Aśuśrūṣa and Svāmīpālavivāda.

The development from these small beginnings to the eighteen topics of Manu, Nārada, Bṛihaṣpati and others must have taken a considerable length of time and history of which no evidence survives.

It is not only in the matter of the chief heads of topics but also in the matter of contents of each of these that there has been a very great development. We shall indicate the developments by reference to the law of Gautama taken by the side of the laws of Yājñavalkya, Nārada, Bṛihaṣpati or Katyayana.

I shall make an attempt in a later lecture to suggest the course of development of the topics after I have given details of the law under each topic.

LAW OF DEBT

The Law of Debt appears in the earliest law books as a part of the King's Vyavahāra. And yet Megasthenes with direct experience of the Court of Chandragupta goes so far as to say that there was no law of Debt or Pledge in India and that, if a debtor did not pay, the creditor had no recourse at law. Though this may sound extraordinary, the probable explanation is to be found in the fact that the Indian creditor of those days had almost as drastic powers of self-help as the nexal creditor in ancient Rome.

Although this right of the creditor is not mentioned in the Sutras, the texts of Manu and Yājñavalkya may be taken to be expressions of the law as it was always understood. Manu (VIII, 49) says

Dharmeṇa vyavahāreṇa chhalenācharitena cha,
Prayuktaṃ sādhayedartham panchamena valena cha.

"The creditor may realise his debt by moral persuasion, by litigation, by fraudulent means, by fasting at the debtor's door or, fifthly, by force."

In verses VIII 47 and 48 he lays down that the king should compel the debtor to pay, by using the same methods as a creditor might and in verse 50 he says that if the creditor pursues his claim in any one of these ways, he does not become liable to be proceeded against by the king.

To the same effect is the text of Yājñavalkya II 40 which adds that if the debtor complains to the king against the creditor in such circumstances, the complainant should be fined in addition to being compelled to pay the debt.

What the law in the Sutras attempts is practically only to lay down the limits of the claim for interest and that is practically all that Gautama does.

Gautama

The Law of Debts in Gautama is very brief. In Chapter XII, 29 et seq. he provides for a legal interest for money lent at five māṣās a month for twenty paṇas which is to be paid for no longer than a year "according to some". He also lays down the rule which is now known as Damdupat, that interest ceases to run when it has reached an amount equal to the principal. Next follows a provision that where a debt is secured by a pledge which is to be used by the creditor, the usufruct is the interest and no more is payable. He also says that where money is tendered by the debtor but not accepted, interest stops.

Gautama distinguishes between the following kinds of interest.

Compound interest (chakravṛiddih)
Periodical interest (Kālavṛiddhih)
Stipulated interest (Kāritā)
Corporal interest (Kayikā, *i.e.* personal service)
Daily interest and the usufruct of a pledge.

This classification is substantially repeated in the texts down to Manu and Nārada.

There is also a special rule for a special rates of interest in respect of loans of products of animals, of wool and products of field and beasts of burden, in respect of which interest is allowed upto five times the value of the loan.

In Chapter XII, 40 he provides that the debts of a person must be paid by his heirs, but adds that debts due by a surety, a commercial debt and a śulka (customs duties) and debts contracted for spirituous liquor or in gambling or a fine should not be payable by the sons of a debtor.

Narada

Comparing this with the law as laid down by Nārada, we find at once the enormous development that has taken place. In Chapter I where he deals with the liability of father and sons and other co-parcenars for the debts incurred, Nārada says that a father is not liable to pay the debt of the son, but the son must pay the debts contracted by the father—except those which had been contracted from anger, for spirituous liquors, commercial debts and for gambling. But such debts of a son as have been contracted by him by his father's orders, or for the maintenance of the family, or in a precarious situation must be paid by the father. So also what has been spent for the household by a slave, a woman, or an agent must be paid by the head of the household and, when the debtor has incurred debt for the benefit of the family, the debt must be paid by his relations. Coparcenars are liable for debts contracted by another coparcenar during jointness. But, after his death the son of one is not bound to pay the debt of another. The wife is not bound to pay the debt contracted by her husband nor one contracted by her son except where she was a party to the loan. A son-less widow and a person who inherits the estate are liable to pay the debts. The non-liability of husband for the debt of the wife does not apply to wives of washermen, huntsmen and cowherds for, it is stated, that the income of these men depends on their wives.

The rule about a man being liable to pay the debts of the husband of the woman whom he has taken is also to be found in Nārada following others in some detail.

Interest

In Chapter I, 98 et seq. he deals with lending money on interest. The rules about interest are far more complicated than in Gautama. The general rule is an eightieth part of a hundred in every month. The rates vary according to the caste of the debtor. Distinctions are made, as in Gautama, between periodical interest, stipulated interest, Kāyika interest, compound interest and they are described as follows :

"The interest which is payable by the month is termed 'Periodical'. Interest which has been promised by the debtor is 'Stipulated' (Karitā) interest. 'Kāyikā' interest is one pana for a quarter paid regularly without diminishing the principal."

The rule of Damdupat is also mentioned as prevailing in *some countries* but not in others and it is further provided that interest on gold, grain and clothes may be more. It may extend to more than two, three or four times the principal, while on liquids the interests may be eight-fold. In cases of pledges of women (*i.e.* female slaves) and cattle, their offspring is deemed to be the interest on the loan secured thereby.

Provision is made for the creditor giving a receipt for the money received from the debtor. We find in other Smṛitis that the debt is embodied in a document and the debtor when he pays must endorse the payment on the back of the document.

Sureties

In verse 117 *et seq.* Narada gives the elaborate rules for sureties and in the place of the rule of Gautama that a debt incurred by a surety is not to be paid by the sons he introduces a distinction between different kinds of sureties:—

1. Surety for producing the debtor (darśanapratibhuū)
2. Surety for payment (dānapratibhū)
3. Surety for honesty (pratyayapratibhū).

Of these, it is provided, as also by Manu and other Smṛitis, that the surety for payment as well as his sons has to pay his debt. But the sons are not liable in the cases of other classes of sureties. (See Manu, VIII, 159-160).

Pledge

With regard to the law of pledges (Ādhi) a distinction is made in the first place between the pledge which is to be redeemed within a certain time and a pledge which must be retained till the debt is repaid. Another two-fold division is made between a pledge which is not for enjoyment and a pledge for enjoyment. (bhogyādhi). Where a bhogyādhi is given, the use of it is deemed to be the only interest. According to Manu VIII, 144 where the same distinction is made, a creditor who uses a pledge without consent of the debtor is punishable as a thief.

The pledge must be kept in the same condition in which it was given. Otherwise, the pledgee loses interest. So also the pledgee is liable where a pledge has been injured or lost due to the negligence of the pledgee, but not if the pledge is stolen or loses its value without any fault of the pledgee. There is provision also for payment of debts by instalments and also for payment, in cases of the lower classes, by service.

Yajnavalkya

Yājñavalkya also gives a rule with regard to the rate of interest similar to that of Nārada, but he makes an important distinction (II, 38) with reference to the loans given to persons who are engaged in a risky trade by going abroad (kāntāraga) who are entitled to ten per cent and also a special rate of interest for traders by sea who get 20 per cent.[97] This indicates that by this time trade has developed considerably and traders are going abroad not only by land but also by sea. This we see also in other parts of Yājñavalkya, such as the section on "*Sambhūyasamutthāna*".

[97] Manu VIII 159 says in the case of loans to traders by sea the interest settled by people who know the country and the time (देशकालार्थदर्शिनः) is payable.

Instalments

With regard to payment of debts by instalments Kātyāyana limits it only to Brāhmanas who are unable to pay. On the other hand lower castes, if they are unable to pay, should be made to work for the creditor.

Liability for others' debts

With regard to the liability of the husband for the debts of the wife or father for the debts of his son, Yājñavalkya says practically the same thing as Nārada, making an exception in the case of wives of milkmen, vintners and hunters whose debts must be paid by their husbands. (II, 48). The sons and grandsons are liable to pay the debts of the father. But exception is made by Yājñavalkya in cases of debts incurred by wives, or by a person for wine or for lust or in gambling, or debts for fines and for śulka as well as vṛithādana, that is to say, an idle promise of gift.

With regard to grandsons a distinction is made, so that the grandsons are not liable to pay interest though they must repay the principal of the debt. Yājñvalkya lays down that a man who takes the inheritance, as well as a man who takes the wife of the deceased (yoṣidgrāha) has to pay the debts of the deceased and like Nārada, Yājñavalkya distinguishes between sureties for production, for honesty and for payment and says that the sons are liable only for the debt of the surety for payment and not for that of the other two classes.

Pledge

Similarly, the law of pledge is also elaborated. Yājñavalkya lays down that a pledge becomes a property of the creditor if, when the debt has been doubled, it is still not redeemed, and also, in the case of a debt for a limited time, if it is not redeemed within that time. But, a pledge which is used by the creditor cannot cease to be the property of the debtor at any time. Some special rules have also been laid down with regard to gopyādhi bhogyādhi and charitra-bandhaka, the last of which is not lost to the creditor by lapse of time. It is further laid down that if a pledge is not returned after the debt is repaid the creditor becomes a thief of the pledge (ādhistena), that is, is punishable as a thief.

These rules illustrate the development which the law of debt and pledge had in the hands of the subsequent Smṛitikāras by amplification of the law and by differentiation of the concepts of legitimate interest and the liability of sons and coparcenars as well as of the character of surety and the difftrent kinds of pledges.

DEPOSIT (NIKṢEPA)

With regard to 'deposit' (Nikṣepa) the only brief rule which is laid down by Gautama is as follows:

"An (open) deposit, a sealed deposit, an object lent for use, an object bought (but not paid for) and a pledge, being lost without the fault of the holder, (shall not involve) any blameless person".

No doubt this classification of deposits implies that there were some implied differences in the rights and obligations regarding them, but we are only left to guess what they were in Gautama's laws. When we come to later Smṛitis we find a growing elaboration of the law.

Yajnavalkya and Narada

Nārada has elaborate rules for deposit of different kinds and Yājñavalkya distinguishes Upanidhi or a deposit in a container without describing the contents, from bare deposit. Yājñavalkya says that if a deposit is made in a sealed container, without disclosing its contents, the depositee is relieved if only he returns the container as it was, and if the depositee has not returned it when asked for, he is liable to a fine equal to the value of the deposit. But he is not liable to return the deposit if it is lost by act of God, the king or of thieves. In one of the texts he distinguishes between Yāchita, Ayāchita, Anvāhita, Nyāsa and Nikṣepa. This distinction is also to be found in Nārada (see infra). Nārada's text lays down the general rule that the deposit is to be returned to the depositor in the same form in which it was at the time of deposit, and he provides for the punishment for the non-return as Yājñavalkya does. He distinguishes a deposit which is made without disclosing the contents of the container and an Aupanidhika deposit and further classifies deposits into two specific classes,—attested and unattested, that is to say, a deposit made in the presence of witnesses and one without witnesses. In the first case, deposit is to be returned in the presence of the witnesses, while, in the latter, it can be returned without any witness.

If the depositee derives profit through a deposit by using it without the consent of the depositor, he is liable to punishment. Like Yājñavalkya, Nārada provides that the depositee is not liable to pay for loss due to an act of God, or of the king unless he should have acted from enmity. The law laid down applies to all different kinds of deposits, viz. Yāchita, Ayāchita, Nyāsa and Pratinyāsa and an article made over to artisans, as for instance, gold to a goldsmith for making ornaments. Yāchita is what has been loaned for use on special occasions such as ornaments or clothes borrowed to wear at a marriage or other festivals. Ayāchita is a deposit to a third person on behalf of the depositee. Nyāsa is a secret deposit made to a member of the household without the knowledge of the master of the house. Pratinyāsa is a mutual deposit in which the two parties accept deposits from each other.

A peculiar case of deposit is introduced by Nārada viz. where a person takes charge of a wealthy boy. Such a man is treated as a depositee like others, apparently in respect of the wealth of the minor of whom he has taken charge. Asahāya correctly understands this to refer to the case where a man takes custody of a boy who has no guardian. (Nārada II, 15 ; XXXIII SBE, P. 123).

SALE WITHOUT OWNERSHIP

'Asvāmīvikraya' has no place in Gautama's law.

Its germ is to be found in a brief reference to a receiver of stolen property (XII 50) who is to be punished as a thief. A great deal of development and refinement of law was necessary before a person who is not proved to be, knowingly, a receiver of stolen property but has bought it, could be got at. The first reference to this topic is to be found in Viṣṇu. Chapter V. 164-166. Even then, the purchase from a person who is not an owner is not covered.

Yajnavalkya

Yājñavalkya's law with regard to the person who buys or sells property to which the seller has no title is as follows : (II 168-174).

The buyer is guilty if he buys in secret, or from a suspicious character, or at an inadequate price or at an unusual hour.

The owner of the property can get the person apprehended and if necessary he can apprehend him himself.

The buyer can clear himself by pointing out the seller. When the seller is reached the property would go to the owner, the buyer will get back the price he paid, from the seller and the seller would be bound to pay a fine to the king.

Before the owner succeeds, he will have to prove his title or prior possession in respect of the things alleged to have been stolen. If he fails to prove it, he will be fined a fifth part of the value of the thing.

Provision is also made for watchmen or customs officers taking possession of stolen articles when found. Such thing must be kept for a year, pending discovery of the owner. If no owner comes forward to claim it by then, it will be retained by the king.

The law as laid down by Manu and Nārada is practically identical with the law of Yājñavalkya. But an important advance in the law is made in the texts of Bṛihaspati and Kātyāyana, quoted in text books, which recognises purchases in market overt and some other cases. Viṣṇu too among Sutra writers provides for the same immunity for purchase in market overt (Ch. V. 164).

Brihaspati

Bṛihaṣpati says (SBE XXXIII page 335) "when a purchase has been made before an assembly of merchants, the king's officers being aware of it, but from a vendor whose habitation is unknown or when the purchaser is dead, the owner may recover his own property by paying half the price." The principle of this law is further explained to be that both the purchaser and the owner being equally negligent the loss should be shared by them. The owner's fault is want of care in keeping the thing and the buyer's fault is buying from an unknown man.

Complete immunity and apparently also good title is granted to a buyer who buys at a fair price and has notified to the king.

PARTNERSHIP (Sambhūyasamutthāna)

Visnu

The law of Sambhūyasamutthāna is historically very interesting. There is no trace of it in any of the Dharmasutras including Viṣṇu who is so full of details on many other topics of law. Viṣṇu's code knows about criminal combinations of traders and provides for punishment of members of such a combination who corner goods and manipulate prices of commodities (V. 125-26) and the same punishment as for uttamasāhasa is prescribed by him for a partner of a trading partnership selling its goods on his own account (VI. 126). This is practically all that he lays down with regard to trade laws besides prescribing penalties for giving false weights or selling adulterated goods or goods of which sale is forbidden.

Manu

The treatment of the subject in the Manusaṃhitā is interesting. In VIII 203-210 Manu deals with partnership, but only with reference to the rights as between the several Ṛitviks or priests who jointly officiate at a sacrifice. These texts provide as follows:

> VIII 206: Every Ṛitvik must be paid on quantum meruit if he has renounced his work after doing a part of it.
>
> VIII 207: Provides for a case in which such a Ṛitvik may be entitled to the whole fee paid on getting the rest of the work done by a substitute.
>
> VIII 208: Where the fee is paid for a specified part of the ritual (pratyaṇgadakṣinā) it will go to him who did that part of the work.
>
> VIII 209: Details some specific articles which are the perquisites of the Hotā, Adhyaryu, Brahmā and the Udgātā—the four priests who are associated in the sacrifice—respectively.
>
> VIII 210: Lays down the rule about the shares of the respective priests in the rest.

These provisions are followed by the following text:

Sambhūya svaṣu karmāni kurvadbhiriha mānavaih,
Anena vidhiyogena kartavyāṃsa prakalpanā.

"For men who do their work jointly, the respective shares should be calculated according to this rule."

This exposition of the law is intertesting as showing that the origin of the entire law regarding joint enterprise was the customary rule of division of the profits of a sacrifice by the several officiating priests, at a time when joint enterprise in trade or other matters was probably unknown to law. Questions of the rights to shares as between Ṛitviks did not and could not have come originally before the king's courts, but they did come in time and laid the foundation of the law of joint enterprise. This happened at some time between the days of the Dharmasūtras and Manu. In Manu's time other kinds of joint enterprise were known, but were of no such importance as to deserve specific provisions of law, though it is obvious that the rules laid down by Manu for Ṛitviks would be wholly inadequate for a business partnership.

Yajnavalkya

In Yājñavalkya's code, the law of "Sambhūyasamutthāna" enters a completely new phase. It is wholly concerned with partnership in trade including some incidental provisions about customs duties. Yājñavalkya provides as follows: (Yajn. II, 259-265)

> "Among traders who work for profit in partnership, the profit and the loss (are adjusted) according to their share in the entire capital; or according to the agreement.
>
> "If a partner does what the others forbid or disapprove, or if he injures common property by his negligence, he should make good the damage; but he who preserves it from (robbers

or from other) misfortune, should receive a tenth part of it (as his reward).

* * * * *

"The wealth of a (trader) dying abroad shall be taken by his heirs, (Bāndhavas, kinsmen) who may have come, and failing these by the king.

"A man of crooked ways should be expelled (by the other partner) without profits; a partner unable to act, may appoint another man to act for him. In this manner is laid down the law of sacrificers, agriculturists, and artisans."

These rules obviously are much fuller and more relevant to joint enterprise and trade and not only provide for division of profits between living partners, but also for the right of heirs in the profits after the death of the partner. They indicate also considerable development of the system of public regulation and control of trade, and of imposition and realisation of tolls and customs duties by the king's officials. Further particulars of the regulation of trade will be found under Trade Laws (infra). A full picture of the organisation indicated by these rules is to be found in Kautilya's Arthaśāstra.

Narada

Similarly, Nārada (in page 124, Vol. XXX S.B.E.) deals with the rights as between partners and the rights of heirs of partners who, according to him are substituted as partners, and also provides like Yājñavalkya for certain trade laws e.g. payment of duties at toll-houses, the care of the goods of a foreign merchant who dies and such other rules. Nārada provides for officiating priests also as an incidental provision in the law of partnership.

Brihaspati

Bṛihaṣpati's rules (XXX S.B.E., page 336) are much more elaborate, showing the development that has taken place since the law laid down by Yājñavalkya and Nārada. He deals with the authority of one partner to bind others and his liability for unauthorized acts. He refers in particular to trade in gold and silver, joint tillage of soil, trade in thread, wood, stone or leather and the joint work of workmen in building a house or temple, digging a pool, making articles of leather, of musicians who form a company and also to the distribution of booty, obtained from hostile countries, showing how joint enterprise had spread in his time to many forms of trades and joint occupations.

GIFT AND REVOCATION OF GIFT

The next topic to be dealt with is the one called Dattāpradānika or Dattasyānapākarma or Rescission or Revocation of Gifts. It is characteristic of this topic that it appears comparatively late in the history of law and, as I view it, it is indicative of a general feature of the evoluton of ancient Indian law in as much as it shows how a law originally a part exclusively of religion gradually becomes a topic of litigation and positive law.

Gifts in religious law

Making of gifts was an essential and a highly praised duty of the people from the earliest days in religious laws. It is an indispensable part of almost every religious ritual in Vedic times. It seems that the earliest form of it was dakṣinā or a gift made to priests and Brāhmaṇas for officiating at a sacrifice, the giving of which was deemed to be an indispensable part of the sacrifice itself. In big sacrifices made by kings elaborate gifts had to be made as parts of the ritual to learned men. Numerous examples of it are to be found all over the Ṛigveda and other Vedic sacrifices. The biggest gift is enjoined for the Viśvajit sacrifice performed after a comprehensive campaign of conquest at which the sacrificer king had to give all he had.[98]

The story of Nāchiketā in the Kaṭhopaniṣad is an instructive landmark. There the king was making gifts at a Viśvajit sacrifice, but only of moribund cattle "who had had the last drink and the last feed of grass of their life," (pītodakāh jagdhatṛināh). His son Nāchiketā was pained to see this stinginess of his father and felt that he was incurring grave sin. He therefore approached the father who was sitting at the ceremony and asked, "To whom are you giving me, father?" The father was annoyed at the importunity of the son in repeating this question several times and at last burst out in anger and said "I give you to the god of Death". The dutiful son took him at his word and forthwith proceeded to the abode of Death.

The underlying feature of this story is the presupposition that in a Viśvajit sacrifice properly performed the son was a proper or perhaps a necessary gift, indicating that the injunction to give everything at a Viśvajit admitted of no exceptions whatsoever and extended to gifts of sons, wives and all dependants.

Exceptions however were soon ingrafted on this drastic view of the rule in the religious law itself and we find the Sruti text now

[98] See Jaimini, VI, 7, 1-2.

laying down Viśvajiti sarvasvam dadyāt, bhāryā putraścha na dadyāt. (Everything belonging to one should be given at Viśvajit but the wife and the son should not be given). Similarly another exception is seen to develop in another Vedic story which indicates that the Earth, (prithvī), that is, the kingdom is not to be given. The story is that a king had purported to give prithvī, at which the Earth herself appeared in person and protested, with the result that it became incapable of being given. It seems likely however that these exceptions are merely express enunciation of rules which were probably understood before and that their formulation was only made when departures in practice came to be noticed.

At these stages gifts were solely matters of religious law. By making gifts men attained untold religious merit and washed away sins, and the more one gave the greater the merit. Apparently however, some aspects of the law of gift and of what constituted a gift were already developed in the purely religious law. Gift was a ritual, usually accompanied by appropriate mantras and sanctified by pouring water on the thing given. But this only completed the renunciation (tyāga) by the giver which had to be completed by acceptance or (svīkarana) by an appropriate formula by the receiver. Ceremonial gifts thus made had again to be accompanied by dakṣinā.

Gift to Gods

An interesting question arose out of this analysis of a religious gift apparently at a later stage, namely, could there be a valid gift to a deity or devatā?

This problem could not arise in the Vedic times when what was given to gods was only given by oblations to the Fire who was the carrier to the gods and all other gifts were contemplated as given to human beings of spiritual eminence. In later times a practice of giving or dedicating property to deities themselves otherwise than by oblations became common, when apparently Puranic worship of gods in temples came into vogue. The strict Vedic view however was maintained by the Purvamimāṃsā according to which Devatā was not a corporeal being capable of taking and enjoying gifts and therefore incapable of accepting a gift. Śabara in his commentary[99] main-

[99] Mimaṃsa Darsanam, Śabara Bhaṣya IX, i, 6-9, where Śabara vigorously combats the view, based on certain Śruti texts that deities are corporeal and eat or otherwise enjoy things given to them and concludes, यदुक्तं स्मृत्युपचारान्यार्थदर्शनैरीशाना देवतेत्यवगम्यते इति । तन्न । स्मृतेर्मन्त्रार्थत्वादमूलत्वादित्युक्त

tains this and explains expressions like devagrāma and devakṣetra as upachāramātram, a mere figure of speech. What is renounced in the name of a god enriches his worshipper. I venture to hazard a guess that this was the reaction of strict Vedic doctrine to the intrusion of corporeal Puranic deities installed in temples and worshipped by gift of fruits, flowers, food and valuable articles. This intrusion however continued in spite of the protest of Mimāṃsā and ultimately led, in the hands of British Indian judges to the consept of a deity as a juridicial person capable of owning property.

The synthesis between the Vedic concept of impossibility of gifts to deities and what I consider to be the later practice due to inroads of different ideas of worship, so far as it was achieved in Sanskrit works appears to have been this. Gifts could be made to gods but the gifts must be coupled with a formula of remoter vesting (uttarā pratipatti) in a Brāhmaṇa. Without such a remoter gift to a Brahmana the gift becomes infructuous.

Deve dattvā tu dānāni, deve dattvātu dakṣinā.
Tatsarvam Brāhmaṇe dadyāt anyathā nisphalam bhavet.

When a gift is so given, it is kept for the enjoyment of the god for a longer or shorter period according to the nature of the thing given, after which it becomes what is called nirmālya which is to be enjoyed, as a thing sanctified, by the Brāhmāṇa in whose favour uttarā pratipatti is made.

REVOCATION OF GIFT

The religious law naturally did not and could not contemplate a revocation of a gift. It would be a great sin to take back a gift for which the sinner would suffer as a dattāpahāraka unless he restored the thing and performed the appropriate prāyaśchitta, though the religious law, as stated above, did come to recognise some things as incapable of being given. And the law was the same for promises of gift. A gift promised is expressed by the same term as a completed gift viz. *datta* (given).

Manu

The rules regarding gift, having regard to their religious and ritualistic character, were naturally not included originally in the

उपचारोऽपि देवग्राम देवक्षेत्रमिति । उपचार मात्रं । यो तदभिप्रेतं विनियोक्तुमर्हति तत्तस्य स्वं । न ग्रामं क्षेत्रं वा यथाभिप्रायं विनियुंक्ते देवता तस्मान्न सम्प्रयच्छतीति । परिदेवचारकाणान्तु ततो भुक्तिर्भवति देवतामुद्दिश्य यतुत्यक्तं ।

older work under vyavahāra. Litigations regarding gifts apparently came later and perhaps the earliest trace of it under the title dattāpradānika, (literally, non-giving of gift) or dattasyānapākarma (non-implementation of gift) appears in Manu who deals with the topic in two short verses (VIII, 212 and 213) where he briefly lays down the law, following the religious rule, saying that where a gift is made for dharma, it shall not be taken back on the pain of punishment as for theft. Elsewhere, of course, he has a general rule that all transactions by lunatics, inebriates, women or minors including gifts are void. He mentions no other limitation.

Yajnavalkya

Yājñavalkya (II, 135, 175) is more precise and lays down limitations already laid down in sacred law that wives and sons are not to be given and adds further limitations, that the gift should not be to the detriment of kutumbas, (which implies persons who are entitled to be maintained out of the thing) and also that one cannot give what has been already promised to another.

The next verse provides that acceptance of gift *must be open* and not secret, particularly in respect of immovable property and further that what has been promised should be given and what has been given must not be taken back.

Narada

Nārada's treatment of this topic is more elaborate and goes into further details under the following heads:[100]

(1) What may be given
(2) What may not be given
(3) Valid gifts
(4) Invalid gifts.

What may be given is, of course, one's own property only ; but the following things may not be given :

(1) A Anvāhita deposit *i.e.* a deposit made through an intermediary.
(2) Ayāchita deposit that is what has been borrowed for use, such as clothes and ornaments.
(3) A pledge
(4) Joint property
(5) A deposit.
(6) A son

[100] Nārada IV, 1-12.

(7) A wife

(8) The whole property of one who has offspring.

(9) What has been promised to another man.

The possible subject matter of valid gift is all the property which remains *after the expenses of maintaining the family* has been defrayed.

Valid gifts include price paid for merchandise, wages, a present offered for amusement, a gift made from affection or from gratitude, *strībhukti*, otherwise strīśulka and a respectful gift. Invalid gifts are sixteen and include gifts made for fear, anger, hatred, sorrow or pain, or as a bribe, or in jest, or through false pretences or by "a child or by a fool or by a Adhyadhīna, or by one distressed, or by an inebriate, or a lunatic, or in the false hope of getting a reward, as also a gift given to an unworthy man under the impression that he is worthy, or for a purpose wrongly believed to be virtuous.

Texts of Bṛihaspati and Kātyāyana are slightly more detailed, but on these lines.

SERVICE LAWS

There is no general theory of contract in Hindu Law. Several contractual relations have been dealt with under different heads, but not on the basis of contract. The topics of Vetanādāna and Svamipālavivāda are two such heads involving rights and liabilities as between master and free servants.

As will be presently seen, these two topics are separately treated in Manu and Yājñavalkya, but Nārada and Bṛihaspati, for the first time bring them together under a common head of relations of Master and servant of which Vetanādāna and Svamipālavivāda are treated as sub-divisions.[1]

The topic introduced in the enumerations of Nārada and Bṛihaspati (Abhyupetyāsuśruṣa) deals more elaborately with all relations involving obligations to serve, such as studentship, apprenticeship, contracts of service and slavery.

Visnu

As might be expected, the early sutras have no provision whatsoever for any law as between master and servant though some laws about herdsmen are dealt with. The topic is however, dealt with for the first time in Viṣṇu in Chapter V, 153-59 where he says that

[1] Nārada VI SBE XXXIII 128 seq. Bṛihaspati's texts SBE Vol. XXXIII, p. 343 seq embrace Vetanādāna, Svamīpālavivada under one topic of Abhyupetyāśuśrūṣā.

a hired workman who abandons his work has to return all the wages received by him and pay a fine of hundred panas, besides compensating the employer for damage done to the employer's goods. On the other hand, the employer who dismisses a worker has to pay the entire stipulated wages to him and a fine of a hundred panas to the king.

Yajnavalkya

Yājñavalkya's treatment of the law is slightly more advanced and, characteristically, contemplates employment of servants in business and agriculture. In II 193 he lays down that a servant who, having received his wages abandons the work has to pay twice the amount of the wages. If no wages have been received by him, he would nevertheless be liable to pay as penalty a sum equal to the stipulated wages.

In the next verse he lays down a rule for wages where a servant has been employed without any stipulation about wages. In such a case the master has to pay a tenth part of the profit made by him from the business. This rule contemplates employment of workers in trade, in rearing of animals and in cultivation. This as well as the provisions of the laws of Nārada and Bṛihaspati seem to indicate that the normal rule was payment of wages in kind rather than in cash.

On the other hand, if such servant causes loss or diminution of profits by disregarding directions of the master about the time, place or other matter for sale, the servant has to compensate the master at the pleasure of the master. The servant, however, is entitled, under a corresponding rule to an amount above the proper wages if he has secured extra profit by his deal.

Where two (or more) workers are employed, the stipulated wages should be divided in proportion to the work done by each.

A special rule is also laid down for servants employed for carrying goods, in verses II, 197-198. If anything carried is destroyed, otherwise than by an act of God or of the king, the carrier has to compensate the master.

The next rule is interesting, showing that auspicious moments for transportation were observed in the trade, for the law provides that if a carrier raises obstacles at the auspicious moment for starting and delays beyond the hour, he has to pay twice the amount of his wages to the master with proportionate reductions for raising such obstacles after a part of the way is covered.

Manu

Compared with Yājñavalkya, Manu's treatment of the subject in VIII 274-277 is very brief. He simply provides for payment of a fine of eight Kṛiṣṇalas by a servant who does not do a work he has undertaken. But Manu's text makes a concession, not expressed, though probably contemplated, in Viṣṇu and Yājñavalkya in the case of a workman who is ill.

Narada

Nārada's texts mark the fullest measure of development of the law on this subject. Kātyāyana's texts hardly carry the law further than those of Yājñavalkya. Bṛihaspati introduces under this topic some matters which are very remotely connected with it, as will be seen presently, but on the law strictly appertaining to this topic Bṛihaspati's texts are less elaborate than those of Nārada.

I shall, therefore, set out here the texts of Nārada, which, as will be seen, include some provisions elsewhere treated under the separate title of Svāmipālavivāda which disappears as a separate title in Nārada's enumeration of the eighteen topics. It also includes rules regarding payment for connection with prostitutes which Yājñavalkya treats under a different head. Nārada further deals in verses 20 to 22 with other relations not at all connected with the law of master and servant.

Nārada's texts[2] are as follows:

"A master shall regularly pay wages to the servant hired by him, whether it be at the commencement, at the middle, or at the end of his work, just as he had agreed to do.

"Where the amount of the wages has not been fixed, (the servant of) a trader, a herdsman, and an agricultural servant shall respectively take a tenth part of the profit (derived from the sale of merchandise), of the seed, of cows, and of the grain.

"Their implements of work, and whatever else may have been entrusted to them for their business, they shall employ with due care and not neglect them wantonly.

"If one fails to perform such work as he had promised to do, he shall be compelled to perform it, first paying him his wages. If he does not perform it after having taken wages, he must pay back twice the amount of his wages.

"One who abandons merchandise which he had agreed to convey to its destination, shall give a sixth part of the wages. (An employer) who does not pay the wages which he had agreed to give, shall forfeit those wages together with interest.

"A merchant who does not take a conveyance or beasts for draught or burden, after having hired them, shall be made to

[2] S.B.E., Vol. XXXIII, p. 128 *seq.*

pay a fourth part of the hire, and the whole, if he leaves them half-way.

"And so shall a carrier who fails to transport (the goods entrusted to him) forfeit his wages. He shall be compelled to pay twice the amount of his wages, if he raises difficulties at the time of starting.

"When the merchandise has been damaged by the carrier's fault, he shall have to make good every loss, not including such losses as may have been caused by Daiva or by the king.

"For (tending) a hundred cows, (a heifer shall be given to the herdsman) as wages every year, for (tending) two hundred (cows), a milch cow (shall be given to him annually), and he shall be allowed to milk (as his wages all the cows) every eighth day.

"Those (cows) which a cowherd takes to pasture every day, when the night is over, he shall take back again in the evening, after they have eaten (grass) and drunk (water).

"If such a cow meets with an accident, he shall struggle to protect her as best he may. If he is unable (to rescue her) he shall go in haste to announce it to his master.

"Should he neither struggle to protect (the cow), nor raise a cry, nor announce it to his master, the herdsman must make good the value of the cow (to the owner), and (must pay) a fine to the king.

"But the herdsman alone shall make good (the loss of an animal) which has strayed or been destroyed by worms, or slain by dogs or met its death (by tumbling) into a pit, if he did not duly exert himself (to prevent such accidents).

"But, if goats or sheep are surrounded by wolves and the herdsman does not come (to their assistance), he shall be responsible for any (animal) which a wolf may attack and kill.

"But, for (an animal) seized by robbers, though he raised a cry, the herdsman shall not be bound to pay, provided he gives notice to his master at the proper place and time."

Then follow some rules which are somewhat incongruous under this topic, but interesting.

"If a public woman declines to receive a man after having received her fee, she shall pay twice the amount (of the fee). The same (fine shall be imposed) on a man who does not pay the (stipulated) fee, after having had connection with a woman (of this description).

"Should a man unnaturally abuse the person (of a public woman) or cause her to be approached by many, he must pay eight times the amount (of the stipulated fee) and a fine to the same amount.

"If a man has built a house on the ground of a stranger and lives in it, paying rent for it, he may take with him, when he leaves the house, the thatch, the timber, the bricks, and other (building materials).

"But if he has been residing on the ground of a stranger, without paying rent and against that man's wish he shall by no means take with him, on leaving it, the thatch and the timber.

"Hired commodities shall be restored (by the hirer) when the fixed period has expired. The hirer must make good whatever may have been spoiled or destroyed except in the case of (inevitable) accident)."

Many of these rules are also laid down by Manu and Yājñavalkya, but not under this topic.

The topic of Abhyūpetyāsusrusa (non-service where there is obligation to serve) which we find in Nārada and Bṛihaspati is not to be found as a separate topic in Manu. It deals with different kinds of service, that of pupil to his teacher, of apprentice to his master, of a free servant and of a slave. Of these, the relations of teacher and pupil are dealt with in the early dharmasūtras, but they did not and could not form parts of Vyavahāra. Slavery is similarly treated otherwise than as part of vyavahāra in these works. The part of the law which deals with apprentice and his master is altogether new. Viṣṇu and Yājñavalkya briefly deal with non-performance of service by free servants. I shall give here only the law on the topic in its most developed form in Bṛihaspati.

Brihaspati

"The titles of non-payment of wages, and then (of disputes) between the owner (of cattle) and his servants are to follow in due order. Such are the three divisions of (the law of) servants.

"They are pronounced to be of many sorts, according to their particular caste and occupation, and fourfold, according as they serve for science, human knowledge (or skill), love of gain.

"Such of these is again divided (into several species) according to the difference of occupation.

"Science is declared to be a knowledge of (one of) the three Vedas, called Ṛig-veda, Sāma-veda, and Yajur-veda ; for the purpose of acquiring such knowledge, he should pay obedience to a spiritual teacher, as ordained in law.

"Arts (consisting of) work of gold, base metals, and the like, and the art of dancing and the rest are termed human knowledge, he who studies them should do work at his teacher's house.

"He who has intercourse with another man's female slave, should be considered as a slave for the sake of his paramour ; he must do work for her master, like another hired servant.

"The servant for gain (or pay) is declared to be of many sorts, another is the servant for a share (of the gain). Of all, a low, middle, and high sort is distinguished.

"A servant engaged for a day, a month, half a month, six months, two months, or a year, must do the work which he promised to do, and receive the stipulated fee.

"The warrior is the highest of these, the cultivator of the soil is the middlemost, the porter is declared to be the lowest, and so is (a servant) employed in household work.

"A servant for a share of the gain is declared to be two-fold, either serving a husbandman or an owner of cattle, he shall receive, no doubt, a share of the grain produced, or of the milk.

"A third or a fifth (of the produce) shall be awarded to the cultivator of the soil as his share.

"Let that cultivator to whom food and clothing is given take a fifth of the crop, and let him who serves in consideration of the profit (alone) take a third part of the grain produced.

"Should a hired servant fail in the performance of ever so small a part of his master's work, he forefeits his wages, and may be sued in court for his offence.

"When a servant does not perform his work after having received his wages, though able (to do work) he shall be compelled to pay twice as much (as his wages) as a fine (to the king) and (shall restore) the wages (to his master).

"He who has promised (to do work) and does not perform it, shall be compelled to do so by forcible means even, and if, through obstinacy, such a servant should still not do it, as engaged for, he shall be fined eight Krishnalas and his wages shall not be paid to him.

"When a servant, commissioned by his master, does any improper act (such as theft) for the benefit of his master, the latter shall be held responsible for it.

"When a master does not pay wages for the labour stipulated after the work has been performed, he shall be compelled by the king to pay it, and a proportionate fine besides.

"(A man) hired for attendance on milch cows of another shall receive the whole milk every eighth day.

"(A cowherd) shall save cattle from danger of reptiles, robbers, and tigers and from caverns or pits, let him try his best to protect them, call out for help, or give notice to his master.

Some of these rules are of considerable interest as throwing light on the socio-economic organisation of the times. Thus we know the different ways in which servants and labourers of different classes were employed, and how they were remunerated. We have seen before how the previous law provided for remuneration of different kinds of workers. Here we find more detailed rules including an interesting rule of employment of labour for cultivation for a share of the profits which varies from one-fifth of the produce to one-third according as the employer finds food and clothing for the employer or not. The system of share cropping here indicated survives, with variations, to the present day.

CHAPTER XI

TOPICS OF LITIGATION—SVĀMIPĀLAVIVĀḌA

The rules treated under this topic by Manu can be traced to the earliest laws in Gautama and Āpastamba who deal with them in some detail, indicating that both the tending of cattle and protection against depredations on fields by cattle were of great importance to the societies for whom those authors provided.

In later Smritis, these subjects lose a great deal of importance and in Nārada and Bṛihaspati, as we have seen, only a fragment of it is dealt with under the law of master and servant. While this indicates a certain amount of general shifting of the economic centre of gravity of society in their respective times, one special change seems to be indicated. It seems that the herdsmen in Gautama's time were not servants or hired labourers but independent contractors, while in the days of Manu and, more prominently in those of Nārada and Bṛihaspati, they were hired labourers.

It further seems that herdsmen (paśupālas) were a distinct community like cultivators, milkmen, traders, washermen, etc., for Gautama elsewhere says that their guild had full authority, like guilds of cultivators, traders, artisans, etc., in their own respective communities. (Kriṣi-vaṇik-pāśupālyah kuśīda-kāravah sve sve varge).

The different phases of the law on this topic correspond to differences in social and economic conditions of the society at each period and region.

Gautama

In Gautama's law, the only rules which correspond to this topic (XII, 19-26. SBE II, p. 241) are as follows:—

"If damage is done by cattle, the responsibility falls on the owner.

"But, if (the cattle) were attended by a herdsman, (it falls) on the latter.

"(If the damage was done) in an unenclosed field near the road, (the responsibility falls) on the herdsman and on the owner of the field.

"Five Mashas (are the fine to be paid) for (damage done by) a cow,

"Six for a camel or a donkey,

"Ten for a horse or a buffalo,

"Two for each goat or sheep.

"If all is destroyed, (the value of) the whole crop (must be paid and a fine in addition.)"

The concern of the law at this stage was only the compensation for damage done by cattle and other animals belonging to another, and only incidentally to lay down when the compensation would be payable by the herdsman or the owner respectively.

Apastamba

In Āpastamba's Dharmasutras too, the scope of the law is similar, but to the rules regarding the herdsman are added, in the same section, rules regarding a person who having taken land for cultivation neglects to cultivate it. Āpastamba's rules which include a rule about lessees and servants in tillage are as follows[3] :—

> "If a person who has taken (a lease of) land (for cultivation) does not exert himself, and hence (the land) bears no crop, he shall, if he is rich, be made to pay (to the owner of the land the value of the crop) that ought to have grown.
>
> "A servant in tillage who abandons his work shall be flogged.
>
> "The same (punishment shall be awarded) to herdsman (who leaves his work).
>
> "And the flock (entrusted) to him shall be taken away (and be given to some other herdsman).
>
> "If cattle, leaving their stable, eat (the crops of other persons, then the owner of the crops, or the king's servants), may make them lean (by impounding them), (but) he shall not exceed (in such punishment).
>
> "If a (herdsman) who has taken cattle under his care, allows them to perish, or loses them (by theft, through his negligence), he shall replace them (or pay their value) to the owners.
>
> "If (the king's forester) sees cattle that have been sent into the forest through negligence (without a herdsman), he shall lead them back to the village and make them over to the owners.
>
> "If the same negligence (occur) again, he shall once impound them (and afterwards give them back).
>
> "(If the same fault be committed again) after that (second time), he shall not take care (of them)."

Visnu

Viṣṇu's texts (V, 137-150, SBE, Vol. VII, p. 36-37) are of similar import. He lays down that if animals are killed by tigers etc. the fault is that of the herdsman who would have to pay the price of the lost animal to the owner. He also makes the herdsman pay for milking for his own benefit the cattle in his charge. Then he goes on to lay down the measure of damage to crops done by animals. Such compensation is payable by the herdsman and, if the cattle is not in charge of a herdsman, by the owner of the cattle.

[3] Āpastamba II, 28, S.B.E. II, p. 168.

These laws all indicate that the herdsmen were an *independent community* who undertook to graze the cattle of owners as free contractors.

Manu

Manu's rules are more elaborate and not only provide for the matters dealt with above, but also gives detailed rules for keeping cattle, providing grazing grounds etc.

> In VIII 231 he lays down a general rule that during day-time the herdsman is responsible for the animals while by night when the cattle are in the pen the responsibility lies with the owner.
>
> In the next verse he provides for the rate of remuneration of milkmen for milking cows for the owner.
>
> In VIII 233 and 234 he lays down when the herdsman is responsible for loss or destruction of cattle. It is said that he is not responsible for theft if he has promptly informed the owner. If cattle is killed, the herdsman is required to satisfy the owner of the loss by producing identifying parts of the carcass. Where animals are killed by wild animals for want of care of the herdsman, he is liable.
>
> In VIII 238 Manu lays down a rule for keeping a specified quantity of grazing ground outside the village, and, in the following verse he requires persons owning cultivated land in the vicinity of the pasturage to fence their fields with care. If they do not, nobody will be punished if cattle destroy their crops.
>
> In VIII 243 Manu makes an exception by providing immunity for loss caused by cows recently calved, bulls and other animals dedicated to Gods, and he ends the topic with a rule by which the owner of a field is made responsible for loss caused by his own animals and for his faulty agricultural operations, if it causes a loss of the king's share of the crops by diminishing the proper output. For such fault he has to pay a fine equal to ten times the value of the king's share.

Narada

When we come to the Code of Nārada we find a total change in the outlook on this topic of law. Svamipālavivāda no longer forms a separate topic, but is treated wholly under the topic of Vetanādana and herdsmen are dealt with on the same footing as servants. The only rules he lays down with regard to herdsmen exclusively relate to the rate of wages of herdsmen and his liability for loss of cattle in his charge. With respect to the latter item, his rules are almost identical with those of Manu.

SAMVIDVYATIKRAMA

or

SAMAYASYĀNAPAKARMA.

This is a topic of laws of which we find no trace in the earlier codes. It deals with the enforcement by the king of the resolutions and decisions of quasi-corporate groups, of village (grāma), Desa (country) or saṃghas or guilds.

Viṣṇu gives only two brief rules which may come under this topic. In V. 111, he provides for a penalty of hundred paṇas for the man who destroys or misappropriates common property.[4] Lower down he prescribes punishment for the man who steals common property as well as for him who disobeys the decisions of the community.[5]

Manu deals somewhat more fully with this topic in four verses by which he provides for banishment of the man who having joined in an agreement of a village country or guild, disobeys it and also makes him liable to a heavy fine.[6]

Yajnavalkya

The laws regarding these groups, which can hardly be called corporations, grow as we come to Yājñavalkya and to the later texts of Kātyāyana and Bṛihaspati who give detailed rules of conduct of various guilds and associations and as to how their functions are to be performed, as well as about the obligation of obedience to the dictates of these groups and guilds which may be enforced by the king. Kātyāyana makes a significant addition indicating an extension of the king's authority by placing the commands issued by the king on the same footing as decisions of these guilds.[7]

[4] Sādhāranasyāpalapīcha (panaśatam).

[5] Gaṇadravyāpahartā vivāsyāh. Tatsaṃvidam yascha langhayet. V. 167—168.

[6] Yo grāmadeśasaṃghānām kritvā satyena saṃvidam
Visamvadennaro lobhāt-tam rāstrādvipravāsayet.
Nigṛihya dāpayechchainām samaya-vyabhichārinām
Chatuhsuvarnān niṣkan śatamānascha rājatam
Evam daṇḍavidhim kuryyād-dhārmikah pṛithivīpatih
Grāma-jāti-samūheṣu samayavyabhichārinām.

—Manu VIII, 219—221.

[7] Manu in VII, 13 also lays down generally:

तस्माद्धर्मं यमिष्टेषु संव्यवस्येन्नराधिपः ।
अनिष्टं चाप्यनिष्टेषु तं धर्मं न विचालयेत् ॥

An interesting development of the law is to be found in the texts of Kātyāyana and Bṛihaspati which show that the decisions of these groups came by their time to be embodied in documents.[8]

Katyayana

The details into which the law went in the texts of Kātyāyana and Bṛihaspati will be found in the following:

> "Members of groups while strictly adhering to their individual duties (as laid down in the śāstras) should perform all their actions according to the conventional rules of their various groups. If royal edicts (or commands) that are issued are not in conflict with one's duty (as laid down in sruti and Smṛiti), one should, by the king's order, first perform those acts only.
>
> "That wicked man who would not observe the rules put in vogue by the king should be censured and fined as he sets at naught the king's order.
>
> "He (that member of group) who opposes what is reasonable, who gives no scope to the speaker (when the group meets) or who speaks what is absurd, should be made to pay the first amercement. (A significant evidence that decisions of communities were made after free discussion).
>
> "He who is guilty of sāhasa (a heinous crime), who causes a split (in the group) or who destroys the wealth belonging to the group—all these should be proclaimed to the king and destroyed (by the group), this is the view of Bhṛigu.

This is the first and perhaps the only Smṛiti which places the king's order on the same footing as other sources of dharma. The verses immediately preceding it show that this is based on a theory of the divine personality of the king (VII 4-12) a conception foreign to the original Ārya. This view of the king as a law maker does not seem to have made much headway, and his commentator Medhatithi limits this authority of the king by providing that the commands are to be Śāstrāchārāviruddhah and he illustrates such orders as follows :

अद्यपुरे सर्वैरुत्सवः कर्त्तव्यः । मन्त्रीगेहे विवाहो वर्तते तत्र सर्वै संनिधातव्यम् । तथा पशवो नाद्य सैनिकै र्हतथाः न शकुनयो वन्धयितव्या । नर्तिका धनिकैराराधनीया एतावन्याहनि । etc.

These are all particular orders on purely secular matters.

A recent epigraph published by Dr. D. C. Sarkar, however, shows that kings also exercised some power in laying down the law authoritatively when appealed to by a community. See infra.

[8] Kātyāyana in Kane's collection Sl. 254 which defines sthitipatra as follows :

Chāturvidyapuraśreni gaṇapaurādikasthitih.
Tatsiddhyārthe tu yallekhyam tadbhavet sthitipatrakam.

See also Bṛihaspati S.B.E., Vol. XXXIII, page 305.

"He who can eat in the same line with another should be fined if he refuses to do so without pointing out the fault (in him that prevents such commensality of food).

"Whatever debt was incurred for the (purpose of) the group but was misappropriated (lit. eaten up) by them or was applied to their individual purposes must be paid by themselves only.

"Those who (subsequently) enter into groups, corporations and classes become equally entitled to the property and liable to the debts (of the groups) previously (acquired or incurred). One who is inside a group is entitled to a share in the food, the partible things (like grain), in the charities and religious duties (of the group) but one who has gone out (of a group) is not entitled to a share.

"Whatever is obtained by them (*i.e.* by the leaders of groups) or is saved by them or whatever they obtained through the favour of the king should be equally shared by all (members of the group).

"A group of several inhabitants of the same city is called 'Naigama', a troops of persons bearing various kinds of weapons are declared to be 'vrāta'.

"A group of merchants and the like is declared to be 'pūga' and those are said to be pāṣaṇḍis (heretics) who have forsaken the (rules of the) order of ascetics.

"The corporation of Brāhmaṇas is called gaṇa and those who subsist by following some craft are called craftsmen.

"The groups of the followers of Arhat (i.e. the Jainas) and of the followers of Buddha are styled saṃgha and the companies of chaṇḍālas and svapāchas (those who eat dog-flesh) are called gulma.

"Gaṇas, heretics, pugas, vrātas and śreṇis (guilds) and all others who constitute groups are styled vargas (groups). This is what Bṛihaspati says," (Kane's collection of Kātyāyana, P. 255-258).

Brihaspati

Bṛihaspati's texts are even fuller. They provide, in addition to group laws, that the king should settle learned Brahmanas, among these groups and duly endow them to do religious duties for them and also settle their disputes. They are as follows: (See SBE Vol. XXXIII, 346--350).

"Brāhmaṇas imbued with a knowledge of the Veda and sacred lore, learned divines, and persons keeping a sacrificial fire (the king) should worship, establish them there (in his kingdom) and provide a maintenance for them.

"Let him bestow on them houses and landed property, exempt from taxation, declaring in a written grant that the revenue is remitted.

"They shall perform for the citizens constant, special, and voluntary rites, as well as expiatory and auspicious ones, and pass a decision in doubtful cases.

"A compact formed among villagers, companies (of artisans), and association is (called) an agreement (samaya) such (an agreement) must be observed both in times of distress and for acts of piety.

"When a danger is apprehended from robbers or thieves, it is (considered as) distress common to all. In such a case, (the danger) must be repelled by all, not by one man alone whoever he may be.

"Mutual confidence having first been established by means of (a vow with) sacred libation, by a stipulation in writing, or by umpires, they shall then set about their work.

"Enemies, dissolute, bashful, indolent, timid, avaricious, overaged or very young persons must not be chosen as intendants of affairs.

"Honest persons, acquainted with the Vedas and with duty, able, self-controlled, sprung from noble families and skilled in every business, shall be appointed as heads (of an association).

"Two, three, or five persons shall be appointed as advisers of the association, their advice shall be taken by the villagers, companies (of artisans), corporations (or cohabitants), and other (fellowships).

"When a stipulation has been entered in a document as follows, 'The construction of a house of assembly, of a shed for (accommodating travellers with) water, a temple, a pool, or a garden,

'Relief to helpless or poor people, the performance of sacrificial acts, a common path, or defence, shall be undertaken by us in proportionate shares,' that is a lawful agreement.

"(Such an agreement) must be kept by all. He who fails (in his agreement), though able (to perform it) shall be punished by confiscation of his entire property, and by banishment from the town.

"And for that man, whoever he may be, who falls out (with his associates) or neglects (his work), a fine is ordained amounting to six Niṣkas of four Suvarnas each.

"He who injures the joint stock or insults a Brāhmaṇa acquainted with the three Vedas, or breaks the mutual agreement, shall be banished from the town.

"An acrimonious or malicious man, and one who causes dissension or does violent acts, or who is inimically disposed towards that company, association or the king, shall be banished instantly from the town.

"The heads of families, companies (or artisans) and associations, whether inhabiting a town or a stronghold, shall censure and reprimand offenders and forsake them.

"Whatever is done by those (heads of an association), whether harsh or kind towards other people, must be approved of by the king as well, for they are declared to be appointed managers (of affairs).

"Should they agree, actuated by hatred, on injuring a single member of the fellowship, the king must restrain them, and they shall be punished, if they persist in their conduct.

"When a dispute arises between the chiefs and the societies, the king shall decide it, and shall bring them back to their duty.

"Those (companions in trade) who conspire to cheat the king of the share due to him (of their profits), shall be compelled to pay eight times as much, and shall be punished if they take to flight.

"Whatever is obtained then by a man, shall belong to all in common, whether it have been obtained a six month or a month ago, it shall be divided in due proportion.

"(Or) it shall be bestowed on the idiotic, the aged, the blind, to women or children, to afflicted or diseased persons, to persons having issue or the like (worthy persons). This is an eternal law.

"Whatever is obtained or preserved by the members of a fellowship or spent on behalf of the society or acquired through the king's favour, is common to all (members of the society)."

Development of group law

These texts indicate important developments in the law of guilds and other group organisations. We have seen before that in the earliest days of Vedic literature, societies distinguished as Kula, śreṇi, vrāta, puga, and gaṇa in later literature were fully autonomous in all matters relating to them. The exact meaning of the words sabhā, samiti and gaṇa frequently used in the Ṛigveda may be open to dispute, but the references to these and, in particular, the verse in the last hymn of the Ṛigveda[9] clearly indicate the spirit of the Ṛigvedic society where the usual way of doing things in a community was expected to be by agreement in a meeting or association. That is further confirmed by the provision in later Smṛitis giving authority to such group organisations to decide matters relating to themselves.

Later on, apparently the king's authority had to be invoked for maintaining the authority and protecting the properties of the group. For this purpose Viṣṇu provides for the punishment for certain offences against these groups.

As to how the affairs of these groups were administered the early laws say nothing. But the first text of Manu on this topic (IX, 220)

> Yo grāmadeśasaṃghānām kritvā satyena saṃvidam
> Visamvadennaro lobhāt tam rastrād vipravāsayet.

indicates that the affairs were regulated by resolutions or agreements of the group which everybody probably swore to obey (satyena saṃvidam).

[9] समानो मन्त्रं समितिः समानी समानः मनः सहचित्तमेषाम् ।
समानं मन्त्रमभिमन्त्रये वः समानेन वो हविषा जुहोमि ।
[Ṛig Veda X, 191, 3].

Yājñavalkya too (II 18B) speaks of their law as sāmayika or "based on agreement," though he makes an important addition indicating that the king might by his commands impose binding duties on them. A more significant addition is made by Yājñavalkya who lays down apparently that the affairs of the group are not to be be administered by agreement of the group, but by men whom he calls *samūha hitavādi* and their *kāryachintakāh* i.e. the executive of the group, who are required to be specially qualified persons ;

> Dharmajnāh suchayo'lubdhāh bhaveyuh kāryachintakāh
> Kartavyam vachanam teṣām samūhahitavādinām.
>
> II, 191

Thus, in his law the affairs are assigned to be administered, not by the agreement of all members of the group, but to a specially chosen executive of the group.

As yet, however, the groups apparently retain their autonomy, for Yājñavalkya does not yet lay down that the executive head or heads are to be appointed by the king, but only says that specially qualified men shall be deemed to be the executive, apparently by the tacit consent of the group.

Bṛihaspati's text however seems to indicate that the appointment was made by the king in the verse quoted above where he says,

"Whatever is done by these (heads of associations) whether harsh or kind to other people must be approved by the king as well, *for they are declared to be appointed manager.*"

The control of the king by merely issuing commands or rescripts contemplated by Yājñavalkya was thus extended further in Bṛihaspati's text where the appointment is made by the king and he exercises a supervisory power over their decisions.

Bṛihaspati in the above texts also makes an interesting statement about making agreements embodied in a document. Documents embodying agreements or resolutions of such groups are also referred to by Vasiṣṭha. (See supra).

What autonomy existed after this was apparently obliterated in later times in the centralised governments of the Mauryan Empire when according to Greek accounts the administrative machinery of the king extended to the affairs of everybody and were investigated and supervised by the king's officers.

But, in respect of village government as distinguished from other autonomous groups like guilds even texts of Viṣṇu seem to indicate that they were under the administration of Adhyakṣas appointed by the king. The king is enjoined by Viṣṇu to appoint grāmādhyakṣas, daśagrāmādhyakṣas, satagrāmādhyakṣas and deśādhyakṣas. These officials are fixed with duties among others of preventing offences.[10]

LAND DISPUTES.

On land disputes we find pratically no mention in the old Sūtra works. For the first time it appears practically in Manu. In Nārada and Bṛihaspati, it receives its fullest developments.

Visnu and Manu

Manu refers to Sīmāvivāda or boundary disputes as one of the topics of litigation. The only thing relating to boundary disputes in Viṣṇu-sutra is to be found in Chapter V, 172 as a part of what may be called "Criminal Law". There he prescribes that the destroyers of boundaries are to be punished with the highest amercement and the boundaries should again be demarcated by signs. This brief and cryptic reference, however, indicates that there was such a thing as Sīmālinga or signs of boundaries actually maintained in his days. What these sīmālingas are and how they are to be maintained and by what evidence they can be determined, we can only find in the later texts, apparently after boundary disputes, originally the province of village tribunals came to the king.

Manu, however, goes into some details on this topic of litigation in VIII, 245 to 265. He details the manner in which the boundaries are to be demarcated. The demarcation should be by bridges, boundary trees of specified kinds, creepers and reeds of several kinds which were generally indestructible, by tanks, wells and springs and by erecting temples on the boundaries etc. Besides these, there is provision made for creating secret marks underground by burying, under the boundary, stones, bricks, charcoal, sugar and sand, so that they cannot be seen from the surface. The king's judge in a case of boundary dispute is required to determine a boundary by reference to these lingas or signs, and if there is doubt, the matter would have to be decided by evidence.

With regard to evidence, there are certain classes of witnesses who are to be specially regarded as entitled to give such evidence,

[10] Viṣṇu, III, 7-15.

स्वस्व ग्रामाधिपान् कुर्यात् । दशाध्यक्षान् शताध्यक्षान देशाध्यक्षान् च । ग्रामदोषाणां ग्रामाध्यक्षः परीहारं कुर्यात् । अशक्तौ दशग्रामाध्यक्षाय निवेदयेत् । सोऽप्यशक्तः शताध्यक्षाय । सोऽप्यशक्तः देशाध्यक्षाय । देशाध्यक्षोऽपि सर्वात्मना दोषमुच्छिन्द्यात् ।

For translation see S.B.E. Vol. VII, p. 15.

such as villagers living on the boundary (called Sāmantas) huntsmen, milkmen and several similar classes of people and punishment is provided for their giving false evidence.

Under this topic Manu also provides for the punishment of persons who destroy or carry away the boundary marks. By the time of Manu, apparently importance of land as property had increased materially and land disputes had begun to come before the king's court. Yet, Manu is concerned only with the determination of boundary disputes and incidentally thereto, fixing boundary marks.

When we come to Nārada and, still more, to Bṛihaspati we find that land has assumed greater importance and numerous provisions are made in the law for the purpose not only of determining the boundaries, but also for loss, for instance, of protective works, cultivation on boundary lines and things of that sort; and under this topic are again repeated some of the rules already dealt with under Svāmīpalavivāda regarding injury caused to crops by animals.

Bṛihaspati goes into still further details and elaborates laws regarding certain easement rights, as well as some elementary rules with regard to loss by diluvion and gain by alluvion. I shall, therefore, extract here the provisions of the law regarding the boundary disputes in Nārada as well as in the texts of Bṛihaspati.

Narada

Nārada's rules are as follows:—

"Whenever (a decision has to be given) in regard to landed property, whether it be a dike (or bridge), a field, a boundary, a tilled piece of ground, or a waste, it is termed a Boundary Dispute.

Boundary Disputes

"In all quarrels regarding landed property or boundaries, the decision rests with the neighbours, the inhabitants of the same town or village, the (other) members of the same community, and the senior (inhabitants of the district),

"(As also) with those living outside on the outskirts of the village and who live by the tillage of fields situated in those parts, and with herdsmen, bird-catchers, hunters, and other inhabitants of the woods.

"These men shall determine the boundary, in accordance with the (old) landmarks, (such as) chaff of grain, coal, potsherds, wells, sanctuaries, trees,

"Objects of general notoriety, such as ant-hills, artificial mounds, slopes, hills and the like, and fields, gardens, roads, and old dikes.

"When a piece of ground has been carried off by a stream, or abandoned (by the owner) or when the boundary marks have been destroyed, (they shall fix the boundary) according to the inference to be drawn from (an inspection of) of the spot, and according to the traces of possession (held by the former owner).

"Should the neighbours speak falsely, when called upon to decide a question of this sort, they shall all be punished one by one by the king, each having to pay the fine of the (second or) middlemost degree.

"The corporation, the senior (inhabitants of the district) and the rest shall also receive punishment one by one; they shall have to pay the fine of the first degree, if they make false statements.

Judges

"The boundary should not be fixed by one man single-handed, though he be a reliable person. This business should be entrusted to a plurality of persons, because it is an affair of importance.

"Should a single man undertake to fix the boundary (he must do so) after having kept a fast, in a collected frame of mind, wearing a garland of red flowers and a (red) cloak, having strewed earth on his head.

"Should there be no persons conversant (with the true state of the question) and no boundary marks, then the king himself shall fix the boundary between the two estates, as he thinks best.

"According to this rule, let all contests be decided in regard to houses, gardens, reservoirs of water, sanctuaries and the rest, as well as the space intermediate between two villages.

Boundary Plants

"When trees have grown on the boundary (or ridge) separating two contiguous fields, the fruits and blossoms shall be assigned to the owners of the two fields in common.

"When the boughs (or offshoots) of trees grown on the field of one man should take root in the field of another man, they must be known to belong by right to the owner (of that field), because they have sprung forth in another field (than the stem of the tree).

"A cross-road, the sanctuary of a deity, a street and a public road must not be obstructed; (a place for) orders, a terrace, a pit, an aqueduct, the edge of a thatch (syandanikā) or the like (obstructions).

"Should any one cause such obstruction through inadvertency or by force, the king shall impose on him a fine of the highest degree.

Dikes

"The (erection of a) dike in the middle of another man's field is not a prohibited act, as it may be productive of considerable advantage, whereas the loss is trifling. That is to be desired as (comparative) gain where there is (a slight) loss (only).

"There are two sorts of dikes (of water courses), one (called kheya) which is dug into the ground and (another called bandhya) which prevents the access of water. A kheya dike serves the purpose of irrigation, a bandhya dike serves to keep the water off.

"No grain is (ever produced) without water, but too much water tends to spoil the grain. An inundation is as injurious (to growth) as a dearth of water.

"If a man were to put in repair a dike erected long ago, but decayed, without taking the permission of the owner, he shall not have (the use and) profit of it.

"However, after the death of the owner or of another man sprung from the same race (who has succeeded to his property), he may repair the dike, after having been authorized to do so by the king.

"By acting otherwise he will get into trouble, in the same way as the hunter (of the tale). The shafts of him are spent in vain who hits again and again one who has been hit already.

Abandoned Land

"When the owner of the field is unable (to cultivate it), or dead, or gone no one knows whither, any stranger who undertakes its cultivation unchecked (by the owner or others) shall be allowed to keep the produce.

"When the owner returns while the stranger is engaged in cultivating the field (the owner) shall recover his field after having paid (to the cultivator) the whole expense incurred in tilling the waste.

"A deduction of an eighth part (shall be made) till seven years have elapsed. But, when the eighth year arrives, (the owner) shall recover the field cultivated (by the other, as his independent property.)

"A tract of land (which has not been under cultivation) for a year is called Ardhakhila (half-waste). That which has not been (under cultivation) for three years is called Khila (waste). That which has not been under cultivation for five years is no better than a forest.

"A field which has been held by three generations in succession, and a house which has been inherited from ancestor, cannot be estranged (from its legitimate owner) by force of possession, except when the king wills it so.

Mischief by Animals

"When grain has been destroyed by cows or other cattle crossing a fence, the herdsman deserves punishment in that case, unless he should have done his best to keep the cattle off.

"When grain has been destroyed (altogether) with the root, the owner of it may claim a corresponding quantity of grain (as damages), the herdsman shall be corporally punished, and on his master he shall impose a fine.

"A cow within ten days after her calving, a full grown bull, a horse, and an elephant shall be kept off carefully. The owner of any one out of these animals is not liable to punishment (should they do mischief).

"For (mischief done by) a cow he shall inflict a fine of one Māṣā ; for (mischief done by) a female buffalo two Māṣas, in the case of a goat or sheep (trespassing) with its young, the fine shall amount to half a Māṣā.

"The (owners of) elephants and horses shall not have to pay any fine, for they are looked upon as protectors of (the king's) subjects. Impunity is (likewise) granted to (the owner of) a strayed cow, of one that has recently calved, and of one unmanageable

"(As also to the owner of) one that has lost her way, or broken down, or stuck (in marshy ground) or (of) a bull marked with the sign of consecration. Four times (the amount of the damage done) is declared (to be the fine) in the case of (a cow) whose nostrils have been pierced and who abides in the field.

"When the cattle lie down in the field (after grazing), the fine to be inflicted shall be double ; when they remain (in the field for the night), it shall be four times (the ordinary amount) ; when they graze in the sight (of the keeper), that man shall be punished even as a thief.

"When cows, straying through the fault of their keeper, have entered a field, no punishment shall be inflicted on the owner of the cows, the herdsman (alone) is punishable (for the damage done by them.)

"When (a herdsman) has been seized by the king or (devoured) by an alligator, or struck by Indra's thunderbolt, or bitten by a serpent, or fallen from a tree

"Or killed by a tiger or other (ferocious animal), or smitten by a disease of any sort, no offence can be imputed either to the herdsman or to the owner of the cattle.

"When a man claims damages for grain consumed by cattle (grazing in his field), that quantity of grain must be restored to him (by the owner of the cattle), which has been consumed in the field in the estimation of the neighbours.

"The cows shall be given up to their owner, and the grain to the husbandman. In the same way a fine shall be imposed on the herdsman when grain has been trodden down (by cows).

Fencing of Fields

"When a field is situate on the borders of a village or contiguous to a pasture ground, or adjacent to a high road, the herdsman is not responsible for the destruction of grain (in that field), if the field is not protected by a fence.

"On (that side of) the field which faces the road, a fence shall be made over which a camel cannot look, nor cattle or horses jump, and which a boar cannot break through.

"A householder's home and his field are considered as the two fundaments of his existence. Therefore, let not the king upset either of them for that is the root of householders.

"When his people are flourishing, the religious merit and the treasure of a king are sure to be in a flourishing state as well. When (the people) cease to prosper, (his merit and his treasure) are sure to abate as well. Therefore, he must never lose sight of (that cause of prosperity)." (Nārada, Ch. XI, SBE XXXIII, p. 155, *seq.*)

Brihaspati

Bṛihaspati deals with the matter in a series of texts collected from commentaries by Jolly in SBE Volume XXXIII. (Page 351 *seq.*)

Boundary Marks

"The determination of boundaries should be settled at the time of foundation, and it should be marked by visible and invisible signs, so as to dispel doubt.

"Wells, tanks, pools, large trees, gardens, temples, mounds, channels, the course of a river, reeds, shrubs, or piles of stones.

"By such visible signs as these a boundary line should always be caused to be marked ; also by other (marks) deposited underground which the earth is not likely to destroy.

"Dry cowdung, bones, chaff, charcoal, stones, potsherds, sand, bricks, cow's tails, cotton seeds, and ashes.

"After having placed these substances in vessels, one should deposit them underground at the extremities of the boundary. After that, one should take care to point them out to youths and infants.

"These (youths and infants) should again show them to their own children, after having grown old ; by knowledge thus passing from one generation to the other, doubts regarding boundaries may be obviated.

Decision of Disputes

"In disputes regarding a house or field, the decision belongs to the neighbours, as well as to the inhabitants of that town or village or to members of the same society, and to the elders (of that district)

"(Likewise to) husbandsmen, artisans, servants, cowherds, hunters, gleaners, diggers of roots, fishermen, kinsmen, mischief-makers, and robbers.

"After having been adjured by imprecations befitting their station, they shall determine the boundary, and shall indicate the marks deposited underground, as evidence. Such is the law.

"In default of witnesses and signs, even a single man, agreeable to both parties, may fix the boundary wearing a red garland of flowers and a red cloak, putting earth on his head, adhering to truth and having kept a fast.

"Neighbours born in that district, though they be living abroad, are termed natives of the place, they should be consulted in the decision of the suit.

"What they should declare in a doubtful case, as honest men and impartial to both parties, shall be held decisive, thus justice will not be violated.

"These are witnesses in a suit of this kind who know the title of acquisition, the size, the duration of the enjoyment, the name and the characteristics of the land in question.

"The same rule holds good in all suits concerning immovable property. If their statements do not agree, they shall be made to pay the highest fine.

Alluvion, Diluvion and Avulsion

"Supposing a piece of land to have been taken from a village belonging to one man and given to another man, either by a larger river or by the king, what should be decided in that case?

"The land abandoned by a river or granted by the king belongs to him who receives it. Otherwise, there would be no acquisition through fate or the king among men.

"Loss and gain and life among men depend on the act of fate and of the king; therefore, in all affairs, what is effected by them must not be rescinded.

"When a river has been fixed as a boundary line between two villages, it shall never be removed, on account of loss or gain arising (from that river to either village). He who removes it, is liable to punishment.

"The encroachment (of a river) on one side produces an increase of land elsewhere in banks of rivers; that (increase) must not be taken from him (who gets it).

"When land is carried away by a swift course of a river overflowing a tilled piece of ground, the previous owner shall recover it.

Other Rules

"When (however) land is taken from a person enjoying it without a legitimate title of ownership, and given to a worthier person (the latter) must not be deprived of it.

"A house, pool, shop or the like having been used by a man since the time of its foundation, must not be taken from him, nor diminished or altered.

"A window, a watercourse, a peg projecting from a well (used to hang things upon), a shed (erected in a courtyard), a square of four buildings, and a channel for the exit of water (after a rainfall), must not be blocked up, when previously constructed.

"A privy, a fireplace, a pit, or a receptacle for leavings of food and other (rubbish) must never be made very close to the house of another man.

"A passage by which men and animals go to and fro unprevented is called Saṃsarana, and must not be obstructed by any one.

"He who purposely crowds such a place (by carts and the like) or makes a pit, or plants trees, or voids excrements, shall pay a Māshaka as a fine.

"When a man has leased ground, he shall sow and watch it, and reap the harvest in due season. If he fails to do so, he shall be compelled to make good the average value of the crop to the owner."

TRADE LAWS.

Laws regarding trade are conspicuous by a total absence in the Dharmasutras before Viṣṇu. They make their first appearance in short sutras in Viṣṇu. They are parts of the law of crimes.

Visnu and Yajnavalkya

Thus, Viṣṇu refers to the offence of using false balance or weights as also to the corresponding offence of the man who falsely alleges true measures to be false (V, 122-23). Selling imitations as real (124) and illegal combination by traders to cut prices to the detriment of a competitor are likewise offences punishable by the highest amercement (V. 125). The same punishment is to be awarded to each individual seller (V. 126). The sale of goods of which sale is forbidden by the king is punishable with a fine of 10 panas.

If a seller fails to deliver goods to the buyer who has paid the price, the seller is liable to repay the price with interest and to pay a fine of 100 panas (V. 127-8). On the other hand if the buyer fails to buy and the goods sold undergoes a diminution of value the loss (periculium rei) falls on the buyer (V. 129).

There are also provisions about offences relating to the payment or realisation of customs duties on river-borne and land trade, distinguished by the names of tārika or nāvika and sthalaja respectively, which appear to have been realisable by different officers in respect of land trade and river-borne trade.

These provisions are much elaborated by Yājñavalkya under separate heads though not expressly given distinct names as in Manu, Nārada and Bṛihaspati. Some of these *e.g.* falsification of balance or measures are treated along with Sāhasas, while others are treated along with laws later distinguished by the name of vikriyāsampradāna. His treatment of partnership and joint enterprise in trade has been dealt with before under Sambhūyasamutthāna. Some other offences relating to trade namely trading in counterfeit gold and sale of bad meat (vimāṃsa) are dealt with at the end with other miscellaneous offences which the Mitākṣarā has correctly classified by Nārada's nomenclature of Prakīrṇaka.

Now, I shall deal with the development of the part which deals with sales. Viṣṇu, as we have seen, simply lays down that sales are completed by the payment of the price. Thereafter, in his law, the seller is compellable to deliver the goods and the perculium rei in respect thereof falls on the purchaser. Manu and Yājñavalkya for the first time lay down a law for rescission of sales as a distinct topic which has been called Kraya-vikrayānuśayah, or Krītānuśayah. These rules together with the topic of Vikriyāsaṃpradāna contain the laws relating to sale.

Anusaya (lit Repentance) of sales.

Manu

Manu deals with this topic in VIII 222-228 and a noticeable feature of his law is that he deals with the giving of a girl in marriage under this topic somewhat incongruously, though this would be quite pertinent in the case of marriages by purchase.

The general rule regarding rescission is that if a person after sale or purchase of an article wants to rescind it, he can do so by retaking or returning it respectively *within ten days*, but after ten days there can be no rescission, and, if anybody does rescind by retaking or returning the article, apparently without the consent of the other party, he is liable to a fine of six hundred panas (VIII 222-223).

After this follow texts which lay down that one who gives a girl who is not a virgin in marriage by representing her to be a virgin as well as one who falsely calls a girl so given not a virgin is punishable. Then come texts saying that no part of the marriage ritual can be performed in respect of a girl who is not virgin. And the whole topic is then wound up by a text laying down a wide general rule to the effect that these rules will apply to all transactions where a party to it wants to rescind it (VIII, 228).

From the collocation of these texts one would suppose that a marriage of a non-virgin could be avoided and nullified by the husband within ten days, or even that such marriage is void *ab initio*. But that does not seem to have been intended, though the context suggests it.

Yajnavalkya

Yājñavalkya deals with the topic of Krītānuśaya with greater elaboration, which, like his treatment of other trade laws, indicates a greater development of trade and commerce in the society for which he wrote.[11] His texts are as follows:

> "The time allowed (to the vendee) for the examination of seeds, iron, beasts of burden, jewels, females, and milch beasts, is ten days, one day, five days, seven days, one month, three days, and a fortnight respectively.
>
> "Gold is not reduced by fire ; silver loses two palas in the hundred, tin and lead eight ; copper, five ; iron ten.
>
> "In the case of woollen and cotton yarns, the increase is ten *palas* in the hundred ; (so) in (cloth of) middling quality five, and in (cloth of) fine quality three (*palas*).

[11] Yajñavalkya II, 177 seq. Trans. by Mandlik.

35

"A reduction of a thirtieth part is allowed in embroidered cloths and cloths made of hair (wool?). There is neither an increase nor a decrease in the case of silken cloths or barks.

"Where (a thing has) deteriorated, (the artisan) should certainly be compelled to give (compensation), which (men), versed (in the nature) of those objects, may declare (proper) upon ascertaining the (nature of) the place and the time, the use (of the disputed object) and (its) durability or non-durability."

He thus lays down a locus poenitentiae for rescission of sales which is not uniformly ten days as in Manu, but periods varying with the nature of the goods and he makes it clear that this time is allowed *for the inspection* and *testing* of the thing, and the rates of reduction referred to are based on diminution which occurs in testing the article by use. Though Yājñavalkya's text thus clears up and supplements the briefer text of Manu, his law is still wanting in further particulars which were supplied by Nārada in whose texts we find the law on this topic laid down with clarity and fulness.

Narada

Nārada's texts on this topic are as follows:—

"When a purchaser, after having purchased an article for a (certain) price, thinks he has made a foolish bargain, he may return it to the vendor on the same day, in an undamaged condition.

"When the purchaser returns it on the second day (after the purchase has been made), he shall lose a thirtieth part of the price. (He shall lose) twice as much on the third day. After that time, the purchaser is bound to keep it.

"The (intending) purchaser shall first examine an article (before purchasing it), in order to find out its good and bad qualities. That which has been approved by the purchaser after close examination, cannot be returned to the vendor.

"Milch cattle may be examined for three days; animals of burden, for five days, and in the case of precious stones, pearls, and coral, the period of examination may extend over seven days.

"Bipeds shall be examined within half a month, a female (slave) within twice the same (space of time), all sorts of grain, within ten days, iron and clothes, within a single day.

"A worn gown, which is in a ragged condition and soiled with dirt, cannot be returned to the vendor (even) if it was in that blemished state at the time when the purchase was effected.

"Wearing apparel loses the eighth part of its value on being washed for the first time, the fourth part (on being washed) for the second time; the third part (on being washed) for the third time, and one half (on being washed) for the fourth time.

"One half of the original value having been lost, a quarter (of the reduced value) shall be deducted henceforth, till the fringe is tattered and (the cloth) in rags. In the case of battered cloth, there is no rule regarding the reduction of its value (through being washed).

"There is no other way for preparing metallic goods of any sort than by forging it in fire according to the rules (of art). While they are being forged, (the weight of) the metals is diminished by exposure to fire.

"Gold is not injured at all (by such treatment). On silver, the loss amounts to two Palas in the hundred. On tin and lead, the loss is eight Palas in the hundred.

"On copper, as well as on utensils made of it, the loss should be known to be five Palas (in the hundred). As for iron, there is no fixed rule regarding the loss arising on it, because it is different in nature from the other metals.

"The loss and gain arising from the preparation of cloth shall be stated (next). On yarns made of cotton or wool, the increase of value amounts to ten in the hundred.

"(This rule has reference) to large tissue (only). In the case of (tissue of) middle size, five in the hundred (is gained). In the case of very fine tissue, the gain is said to amount to three Palas in the hundred.

"In the case of cloth made of the hair of an animal, and of embroidered cloth, the loss amounts to one-thirtieth. In the case of silk stuff and of cloth prepared from the inner bark of trees, the gain is the same (as the loss in the preceding case). Nor is there any loss (in these cases).

"A merchant who is acquainted with the qualities of the merchandise (he deals in) must not annul a purchase, after having once made it. He ought to know all about the profit and loss on merchandise, and its origin.[12]

The exact import of the deductions prescribed in case of rescission after various intervals is not clearly stated. They indicate either that when a sale is rescinded the sale price to be refunded should be reduced by these amounts. On the other-hand, some of these texts seem to suggest that the reduction in value to the extent specified of the goods returned is not to be taken into account, for instance, the reduction in weight of metals in the process of testing. The latter view is indicated in the comment of the Mitākṣarā on Verse 178.

Under another topic Vikrīyāsampradāna Nārada deals with the corresponding obligations of the seller for non-delivery of goods sold. (Nārada IX ; SBE Vol. XXXIII, p. 146 seq.). For non-delivery the seller is liable to pay the mesne profit he has made if it is immoveable property. Where the market value of the thing falls in the mean time, the purchaser is entitled to get back the difference in price along with the thing itself. Penalties are provided for delivering a thing different from the thing sold and for re-sale of a thing sold to another, except where the purchaser has refused to accept delivery. The purchaser must have tendered the price to make the vendor liable ; otherwise the vendor is free to sell to another.

[12] S.B.E. Vol. XXXIII, p. 149 seq.

Brihaspati

The further development of this law after Nārada hardly shows any improvement. The fragments of Bṛihaspati on this topic collected by Jolly from several nibandhas are obviously incomplete. While some of his texts seem to deny any right of rescission after a sale is completed except where an article (panya, which includes land) has faults which were known to the seller or where the sale was made under the influence of drink or for fear, or where the seller is an adhyadhīna or an idiot. But in the last of the collected texts he evidently contemplates a rescission of sale after inspection within a specified time to the same extent as Manu or Nārada. Bṛihaspati's texts are as follows:—

> "Two sorts of property are distinguished, immovable and movable; when a purchase is concluded, the term 'Vendible property' (panys) is applied to both.
>
> "The purchaser shall examine a chattel himself and show it to others; when, after examining and approving it, he has accepted it, he is not at liberty to return it again.
>
> "The foolish man who sells an article, though acquainted with its blemish, shall have to pay twice its value (to the vendee) and (a fine of) the same amount (to the king).
>
> "What has been sold by one intoxicated or insane, or at a very low price, or under the impulse of fear, or by one not his own master, or by an idiot, shall be relinquished (by the purchaser, or it) may be recovered (from the purchaser) by forcible means.
>
> "Within that period, if a blemish should be discovered anywhere in the commodity purchased, it shall be returned to the vendor, and the purchaser shall recover the price."
>
> [SBE Vol. XXXIII, p. 350].

Katyayana

Kātyāyana's texts (collected by Kane at pages 84-87) do not carry the law as laid down by Nārada and Bṛihaspati with regard to this topic much further except in the following particulars:

(1) He lays down a rule as to what part of the price is properly deemed to be profit,

(2) He provides for the avoidance of sale if the price is inadequate;

(3) In respect of sale of land he dictates that a sale is not complete without the assent of kinsmen for whose assent a definite time is fixed.

(4) He lays down how a sale can be annulled for inadequacy of price.

The texts of Kātyāyana relating to these points are as follows :—

"After dividing the value of a thing into five parts, three parts are declared to be the price of it, the fourth part is the profit and the fifth is meant for truth.

"A compromise and an exchange, if they are unequal, can be annulled for three generations and a sale by order can be annulled up till the 10th year.

"The conclusion is that there can be no lawful sale or purchase of land without securing the approval of the kinsmen (of the seller and buyer) who are neighbours (*i.e.* owners of neighbouring lands) and who are respectable men.

"In the same village a period of ten nights (for vetoing by kinsmen of the sale made by one of the kinsmen) is prescribed ; when (land sold is) in another village, the period is three fortnights, when in another country six months, when the language (of the kinsmen vetoing) is different, a year.

"If the men liable to pay the (land) tax absconds along with surety for the tax the members of the (royal) audience hall should sell the land of the tax-payer for recovering the tax.

"What is decided upon by the neighbours gathering together who know (the land etc. and its value) and who are afraid of sin, as the price of fields, gardens, houses, and the like and of bipeds and quadrupeds, that is said to be their proper price. Dividing that price into eight parts, any price (offered by a buyer) which exceeds by ⅛th or is less by ⅙th (of the price so decided) is to be known as improper.

"All that (*i.e.* a sale for inadequate price) can be annulled even when a hundred years have elapsed. In purchases and sales (a thing) should be sold for that price which the article deserves according to the rules (of śāstra).

"If when a purchase or sale is effected and when the price is less by a fourth, fifth, sixth, seventh or even eighth part (of the proper price arrived at as laid down above), all that becomes (a transaction) for an inadequate price and though carried out must be (regarded) as not done (*i.e.* as invalid). But a purchase is not at all defective when it is (for a price) a little less than (the price arrived at as above).

"But when a purchase or sale falls short as to price by that part, then the transaction, though carried out, is declared by those who know dharma to be invalid.

"A sale of 'uktalābha' kind will be valid if it is for more than half (the price of the thing as settled by the rule above) provided more than ten (years) have elapsed (after the period fixed in it). An avakraya (transfer for hire by a bailee) becomes valid after enjoyment for three generations and a purchase by mutual agreement (between the seller and buyer) becomes valid at once.

"The purchase of an article may be rendered valid even when much less than the proper price has been paid ; but (the balance of the price) would have to be paid with compound interest if there is no agreement (as to the time when the balance of the price is to be paid).

OTHER TRADE LAWS.

As stated before, other laws relating to trade and commerce are scattered over different topics in the books. Of these, the law of Partnership has been dealt with before. (Supra p. 243) Reference has also been made to special laws relating to interest in Yājñavalkya in respect of commercial loans, particularly on trade by sea. (Supra p. 239)

Yajnavalkya

In dealing with the topics of Sāhasa and Prakīrṇaka Yājña-valkya elaborates some of the laws which have been briefly indicated by Viṣṇu.

Thus, in II 238, Yājñavalkya lays down the penalties for a washerman wearing clothes given to him for washing as also for his selling, hiring out (avakraya), pledging or for not returning the clothes when asked for. Manu deals with the same matter in VIII, 396 where he also prescribes that the washerman must wash the clothes not violently but gently on a plank of *simul* wood.

In II 240, Yājñavalkya provides for the punishment of makers or users of false balances, measures and coins as also of forgers of grants (śāsana) and in the next verse he prescribes corresponding penalties for a person who falsely alleges true balances etc., to be false. In II, 244 he prescribes, graduated scales of compensation and punishments for the trader who gives less by using false measures.

Quacks posing as physicians or vets are penalised by the first, middle and highest amercement respectively according as they treat animals, men, or king's officials (II. 242).

Trade offences like adulteration of drugs, oils and fats, salt, scents, paddy or sugar (guḍa) by mixing inferior things are made punishable by fine (II. 245). Faking of merchandise which is made punishable in the following text (II. 246) is interesting as giving instances of the sorts of faking that used to be done. Mud was sold by perfuming it like a scent, skins of common animals dyed to look like richer skins, jewels were faked, cotton yarn made to look like richer stuff, common wood faked as richer wood like sandal, iron faked as silver. These are the illustrations given in the text for which a fine of eight times the price charged is prescribed. Another kind of fraud referred to (II. 243) is changing of containers of goods sold in containers.

In II. 149, Yājñavalkya prescribed punishment for combinations to raise prices by cornering to the detriment of artists and artisans.

In the next verse a similar combination to injure competitors by price cutting is made punishable with the highest amercement. Verses II 251-253 lay down that goods are to be sold at prices fixed by the king. Rates of profit to be allowed to traders in country grown goods and in foreign goods are laid down ; to these are to be added the customs duties charged on goods in fixing the price by the king.

In the Miscellaneous section Yājñavalkya includes two special provisions relating to trade.

Goldsmiths who use false i.e., debased gold and sellers of bad meat such as dog's meat are made punishable with cutting off (according to the Mitākṣarā of nose, ears and hands II, 297). Manu's law in IX, 292 is even more drastic.

For selling articles taken from a dead body the highest amercement is prescribed by Yājñavalkya (II, 303).

The laws relating to trade and commerce and economic relations, while they bring out the progressive effort of the lawyer to meet problems to ensure that justice may be more fully and adequately done, disclose on the other hand, great developments in the economic life of the people.

Economic development

The early dharmasūtras only touch the fringe of economic relations. They are chiefly concerned with little more than money lending, cattle husbandry and the protection of crops against ravages done by cattle. Trade and commerce might not exist at all, for all that these law givers say about them. That was apparently due to two causes. In the first place, trade and commerce was not so considerable or so important for the economic life of the people as to call for their regulation by the law of dharma and secondly such as they were, their regulation was left entirely in the hands of trade guilds themselves.

The text of Gautama "Kṛiṣi-vanik pāśupālyah Kuśīda karavah sve sve varge" shows, on the one hand, that the regulation of economic affairs was entirely left to their own guilds and, on the other hand, indicates the chief economic enterprises of the people in Gautama's time. These were agriculture, small trade, animal husbandry, money lending and handicrafts. These were considered to be matters of too little significance to deserve regulation under the king's superintendence. There was apparently one other occupation of economic value which grew with time, the occupation of priests who officiated at sacrifices, who, as we have seen, were the occasion for the eventual growth of the first law of partnership. (Supra p. 244)

With the progress of society, trade and commerce generally grew in such importance as to form the subject of litigation before the king's courts. And then the lawyer is found to get busy laying down laws growing in elaboration and precision for regulating these relations. The growing importance of trade and commerce is further evidenced, as stated before, by the admission of vaniks or traders, to the King's sabhā to help in the administration of justice.

The law on the topic of Rescission of sale is a prominent illustration of the manner and extent of the growth. The early lawyers contemplated a sale only as a complete transfer of ownership and no question of rescission of sale arose for them. Gradually, however, it was realised that a very disadvantageous purchase is sometimes made by a buyer on the spur of the moment and it would be unjust to maintain the sale without an opportunity to rescind it.

The first reaction of the lawyer to this problem was to lay down a short and simple formula as Manu did. When experience showed that that simple formula was not enough to do justice in all cases and that the same limitation of time for rescission would not be just for all cases the law goes into further particulars as in Yājñavalkya. As more cases come to notice, further particulars are called for and provided by Nārada to meet all such cases to prevent the wrong-doer taking advantage of the limitations of the law. So we find Nārada going into greater particulars. And for the first time he brings out the true principle underlying this law of rescission, which is to provide a reasonable *locus poenitentiae* for the purpose of inspection and trial of the goods by the buyer, varied according to the character of the thing sold. Once this principle is brought out, further developments and limitations necessarily follow with experience and we find Nārada and Bṛihaspati laying down, that there is no such *locus poenitentiae* where goods are taken after due examination and inspection, nor is it permitted in transactions between traders, who ought to know what they are buying and are expected not to buy without due inspection, so that in their case the principle of law is *caveat emptor*. This is now mere common sense.

A consideration of the development of trade laws in the Smṛitis as also the evidence of Vedic literature clearly indicate that trade was not at any rate an important part of the social organisation in Vedic India. As has been pointed out, Gautama classes traders along with cultivators, usurers and artisans as classes who were a law unto themselves, apparently not governed by the Sacred Law. It is only when we come to the Smṛiti of Yājñavalkya that we find trade assuming an importance in law as an item of vyavahāra. In later law, laws regarding trade grow in volume. On the other hand, there is evidence that the Harappan kingdom had a considerable amount of trade with the rest of India and also some trade with foreign countries like Sumer and Accad and in later times trade between India and the Middle East, if not further, was carried on by the Babylonians and Phœnicians.[13] It is possible that the laws regarding trade were developed in the course of development of trade and commerce in Arya kingdoms, possibly on the basis of customs of the pre-Aryan Indians like the Harappan people and also like the Sumerians, Babylonians and Phœnicians of later days. But it is difficult to put one's finger on exactly how those non-Aryan sources, indigenous or foreign, influenced the development of the laws.

GAMBLING

Gambling with dice appears to have been a proto-Aryan institution. It had assumed considerable vogue in the earliest times in India and as far away as in ancient Germany. Tacitus speaks of its vogue among the Germanic tribes among whom pawning away one's liberty was not uncommon. Tacitus speaks of strong and powerful young men meekly following as slaves the winners at a game of dice at which the players' personal liberty was the stake. A parallel at once strikes one in Yudhiṣṭhira pawning his kingdom, his brothers, his wife and himself at a game of dice and numerous other stories of a like character. In the Ṛigveda X, 34, we find a hymn which is really the lament of a gambler who has lost his all by gaming and who warns everybody against indulging in games.

Gambling in Early Texts

Although the institution of gambling is thus as old as the Ṛigveda and even older, it does not find a place in the topics of Vyavahāra in the oldest Dharmasutras. It would seem that in the most ancient stage of our law, it was deemed to be a king's game, and the earliest reference in the laws, barring the texts of Kautilya, is to be found in Āpastamba's Dharmasutra where among the king's duties he is directed to make a house for playing the game. This house was to be open to all the twice born men. Here people played with wooden dice.

We find no reference to gambling under Vyavahāra in Gautama,

[13] Stuart Piggot—Prehistoric India, pages 207 seq: Antiquity, Vol. VII, pp. 169-182.

Wheeler—Ancient India, No. III, pp. 78-80.

Baudhāyana or Vasiṣṭha. Viṣṇu, however, provides for the punishment of persons who play with loaded dice as also those who indulge in other fraudulent practices in gaming (V. 138). On the other hand, he forbids the king to indulge in dice as also other indulgences like wine and women and even hunting (III, 50).

In the metrical smritis with exception of Manu we find that gambling has become a public institution regulated by a sabhika who seems to be an officer appointed by the king to superintend the game, prevent foul play, decide disputes between gamesters and compel payment of stakes. In these works, playing with dice (Dyūta) is coupled with another form of gaming, with animals which is called samāhvaya. Details of the different species of the latter game are only first mentioned by Nārada (XVII, 1). Manu, as will be presently seen, forbids all sorts of gaming altogether. This was a measure of reform however which, if it succeeded at any time, does not seem to have lasted, for in Nārada, Bṛihaspati and Kātyāyana laws of gambling reappear in all their glory, though Kātyāyana prefaces his treatment of the subject with condemnation of gaming on the lines of Manu.

Yajnavalkya

In Yājñavalkya we first find a detailed treatment of gaming. His texts (II, 199-203) are as follows:—

> "The keeper of a gambling-house (sabhika) shall take from a gambler five per cent, when the wager is a hundred (panas or upwards), and ten per cent, in other cases.
>
> "Being well protected (by the king), he shall give the promised share (of his gains to the king, he shall recover the wager, and pay it to the winner (and) being ever patient, (shall speak) the truth.
>
> "(Payment of) that which has been won publicly in an assembly of gamesters in the presence of the master of a gaming house, and when the king's share has been paid, shall be enforced, but not otherwise.
>
> "The superintendents and witnesses in (gaming) transactions (should be) gamblers themselves. A man who plays with false dice, or by deceit, shall be branded and banished by the king.
>
> "Gaming should be allowed under due supervision, as being a means of detecting thieves."

Manu

Quite contrary are the pithy and drastic dictates of Manu who says (IX, 221-228),

> "Dyūta and samāhvaya should be driven out of the state by the king. These two faults of kings are the means for destruction of kingdoms.

> "Dyūta and samāhvaya are open thefts, so the king should always take care to destroy them.
>
> "Games with inanimate things are called Dyūta and what is played with animals is called samāhvaya.
>
> "All who play or arrange for play of Dyūta or Samāhvaya, should be corporally punished by the king whether they are Sudras or bear the signs of the twice born."

And he goes on to say that gamesters, like dancers and other named criminals are secret thieves who should be banished, and ends with a significant text:

> "In ancient times this gambling has been seen to be the cause of great enmity. So no wise men should play games even in joke" IX, 227.

Narada

Nārada, who ignores Manu's condemnation, (XVII, 1-8) gives further details. The instruments of gambling are stated by him to be dice made of slices of leather or ivory, and he speaks of Samāhvaya with birds. The functions of the Sabhika are practically the same as in Yājñavalkya. In XVII, 3 he gives a little detail about when the win is declared at a game of dice. The punishment for gambling offences are, however, far lighter than in Yājñavalkya. He says:

> "Wicked men who play with false dice shall be driven out of the gaming house after a wreath of dice has been hung round his neck, for that is the punishment ordained for them."
>
> "If a man gambles with dice without authorisation from the king, he shall not get his stake and shall have to pay a fine."

To this is added an exception however in the following text:

> "Or let the gamblers pay to the king the share due to him and play in public, thus no wrong will be committed."

These rules indicate a larger vogue of gambling leading to relaxation of restrictions. At the outset the rules contemplated control of the game, professedly to prevent offences by catching thieves, now the control is virtually reduced to one for revenue purposes.

Brihaspati

Bṛihaspati expressly refers to the condemnation of gambling by Manu, but says that other law-givers have permitted it, when conducted so as to give a share to the king. He then goes on to lay down the law substantially on the same lines as Nārada. He however gives further details about kinds of samāhvaya. While in Nārada's text betting at games by *birds only* is mentioned, Bṛihaspati speaks of fight between birds, rams, deer or other animals upon which wagers have been laid.

He adds to the protection given to a player defeated by fraud, a similar protection to one defeated in a secret game and to one who is ignorant of rules. A further relaxation of the rigour of the law in Bṛihaspati is that when the wager laid is one's entire fortune, one cannot be compelled to pay it all, a rule which, if it had existed in his time would have softened the rigour of Yudhiṣṭhira's defeat. Bṛihaspati's justification of gambling under public control like the similar text to Yājñavalkya is ingenuous, for he says that it serves the purpose of discovering thieves (SBE, XXXIII, pages 385-386).

Katyayana

Kātyāyana's text (Kane's collection, pages 113-114) opens with condemnation of gaming as promoting anger and cupidity, creating wicked men, evil and destructive of wealth. But "If it has to remain", he goes on to provide for public gambling under official superintendence in much the same way as others. He says:

> "One should not resort to gambling which inflames the passions and greed (of men), which engenders bad characters, which is cruel, and causes loss of wealth to men.
>
> "Since strife is certain (to follow) from gambling just as poison (is sure to issue forth) from the mouth of a serpent, therefore, the king should stop this vice in his country.
>
> "If it (gambling) has to remain (has to be allowed) he (the king) should allow it to be done openly with an (ornamental) arch erected near the door (of the gambling hall) in order that respectable people may not be mistaken (about its real nature) and he should make it yield revenue.
>
> "The keeper of the gaming house should make the gambling go on and should himself pay to the king (the latter's) dues. He (the keeper) should take from the defeated party ten per cent as his profit.
>
> "The keeper should give to the winner his money (out of his own pocket) and he should recover from the defeated gambler within three fortnights or at once, there is no doubt (about this rule).
>
> "Where (the throw) of a man playing with dice in gambling is the same as or double (of the previous throw) there the (former) gambler is the winner and his protection (from the other gambler) is to be arranged for.
>
> "Or the gambler (himself), after giving to the king his share (of revenue) as declared, should carry on gambling openly. In this way he will be guilty of no fault.
>
> "The keeper of the gaming house should forcibly make the defeated gambler pay what (the defeated) has to pay in the same place (*i.e.*, in the gambling hall) and not elsewhere; since the procedure (in gambling matters) entirely rests with the keeper of the gaming house.

"A person ignorant (of gambling) if defeated should be released (from his liability), but one who knows gambling should not be released if he is defeated in secret (gambling): when one not knowing gambling has lost his all (in a wager), he should not be made to pay his all.

"In disputes (among gamblers), in deciding on victory, in the matter of gain (to the winner), and as regards the means (*i.e.* dice) of those who are (alleged to be) playing with false dice, the keeper of the gaming house, if he is honest, is the final authority.

"In the case of mlechchas, chandalas, rogues, gamblers, ascetics, the decision as to those who (are alleged to) have violated their conventions does not rest with the king."

So, the attempted reform in Manu's text was short lived. His strict prohibition was reduced to a rule of regulated gaming and gaming flourished as before in the times of his successors. The strict supervision at public gaming place for public benefit too was in time relaxed, so that, by paying a fee to the king, everybody was enabled publicly to play any game for an wager. The public benefit professed to be sought from controlled gaming ultimately yielded to a scheme for getting revenue out of this vice.

CHAPTER XII

TOPICS OF LITIGATION—CRIMES.

In dealing with other topics of law we have seen that punishment for certain specific offences in connection with civil disputes and legal procedure is provided in various places, but the topics in Manu, Nārada and Bṛihaspati which deal specifically with crime are :

1. Vākpāruṣya
2. Daṇḍapāruṣya
3. Steya
4. Sāhasa
5. Strīsaṃgrahana and
6. Certain miscellaneous offences in Prakīrṇaka.

The evolution of these topics of law have therefore been reserved for separate treatment under the law of Crime.

We have seen generally how these offences have been treated in the earliest Dharmasutras. Extremely meagre as the laws in those works are, they bring out one characteristic which indicates that the chief concern of the lawgivers was the maintenance of the social order, designated dharma, and very particularly, the social dignities and proprieties. This characteristic appears in a greater or less degree in all the stages of development of the Law but is almost the exclusive motive for the king's interference behind the law laid down in the earliest works. Thus Gautama in treating the offence by word (vākpāruṣya in later nomenclature) is only concerned with objectionable words used by men of lower castes towards Brāhmaṇas and higher castes, and characteristically emphasised the grave social offence of a Śūdra uttering, listening to or remembering texts of the Vedas. Even in respect of adultery or rape the sole offence that Gautama is concerned with is that of Śūdra having criminal intercourse with an Arya woman. We shall see how starting from these laws prompted by a sense of grievous injury to social dignities which alone apparently gives jurisdiction to the king's court the law grows into an extensive and complicated code of crimes in which, caste distinctions certainly persist, but in a far less pronounced measure.

Classification of Crimes

Another distinguishing feature of early law is the practical absence of all attempt at generalisation or classification. Even in

Viṣṇu where the law is seen developed in considerable detail, we have little better than a catalogue of specific unclassified offences.

At some period between the earliest Dharmasutras and Viṣṇu, however, all the punishable offences seem to have acquired the generic names of sāhasas, and they were classified with reference to their seriousness into three classes, first (prathama), medium (madhyama) and highest (uttama) sāhasa with a graduated scale of fines for each class. The use of the expressions prathama, madhyama and uttama sāhasa daṇḍas first appears in Viṣṇu.

Manu's text gives us the first classification of these offences by topics forming parts of the eighteen topics. Apparently however this classification had already grown up in practice before it was definitely set down by name. Looking at Viṣṇu's catalogue of specific offences and in a greater measure in Yājñavalkya who also does not give definite class names, one notices that they are on the whole arranged in an order corresponding to Manu's list.

The first attempt to distinguish laws involving punishment from purely civil disputes was to call them sāhasas. But gradually these sāhasas themselves were distinguished from one another, not merely by the measure of punishment inflicted, but by the nature of the acts penalised. This led to the separation, probably gradual, of theft, violence by words or by hurt and adultery from the generic concept of sāhasa, so that in Manu's classification we arrive at the five heads of crimes separately named and distinguished.

OFFENCE BY WORDS—VĀKPĀRUSYA

The name of this offence in later nomenclature is Vākpāruṣya which, literally means violence by words. But in Gautama or Āpastamba the law of vyavahāra seems to be concerned more with the offence against social dignities and privileges than with violence in words. A Śūdra uttering the Veda, listening to it or remembering it is no violence to anybody, but it is deemed a grave offence against social and religious proprieties. Nor is the act of Śūdra speaking or acting in a manner which assumes an equal position with an Ārya any violence except to social proprieties. Yet these are grave offences for which condign punishment is provided. Of course, using abusive words is referred to as an offence but, it is only a serious offence in a Śūdra against a Brāhmaṇa, and just less serious against a Kṣatriya or a Vaisya. The offence is graduated in respect of other castes, but it is no offence for an Ārya to abuse a Śūdra in any case, least of all in a Brāhmaṇa. (Supra pp. 229-232).

An explanation of this emphasis on offences against social dignities in the earliest law books probably lies in the fact that the king's judicial function originally started from his obligation to maintain social order. That source of the king's first exercise of judicial functions is indicated by two texts of Vasiṣṭha to the effect that the king as well as the Brahmana are the twin upholders of vrata or social order (dvan loke dhritavratau, Rājā, Brāhmaṇaścha vahhu-śrutah) and, that it is the duty of the king to see that each man faithfully performs the duties of his special Dharma. (Rājā chaturo-varṇān svadharme sthāpayet).

Visnu

In Viṣṇu we come upon a far more developed system of laws. He details the following offences which, on the whole, may be classed under Vākpāruṣya ; though mixed up with Daṇḍapāruṣya. (V, 19-39).

> "With whatever limb an inferior insults or hurts his superior in caste, of that limb the king shall cause him to be deprived.
>
> "If he places himself on the same seat with his superior, he shall be banished with a mark on his buttocks.
>
> "If he spits on him, he shall lose both lips,
>
> "If he breaks wind against him, his hind parts ;
>
> "If he uses abusive language, his tongue.
>
> "If a (low-born) man through pride gives instruction (to a member of the highest caste) concerning his duty, let the king order hot oil to be dropped into his mouth.
>
> "If a (low-born man) mentions the name or caste of a superior revilingly, an iron pin, ten inches long, shall be thrust into his mouth (red hot).
>
> "He who falsely denies the sacred knowledge, the country, or the caste (of such) or who says that his religious duties have not been fulfilled by (or that the initiatory and other sacramental rites have not been performed for) him, shall be fined two hundred panas.
>
> "If a man is blind with one eye, or lame, or defective in any similar way, and another calls him so, he shall be fined hundred Kārṣāpanas.
>
> "He shall pay the highest amercement for imputing to another (a great crime) entailing loss of caste ;
>
> "The second amercement for (imputing to another) a minor offence (such as the slaughter of a cow) ;
>
> "The same for reviling a Brāhmaṇa versed in the three Vedas, or an old man, or a (whole) caste or corporation (of judges or others).
>
> "For reviling a village or district, the lowest amercement ;
>
> "For using insulting language (such as 'I shall visit your sister' or 'I shall visit your daughter') a hundred Kārṣāpaṇas ;
>
> "For insulting a man by using bad language regarding his mother (such as 'I shall visit your mother ; or the like speeches), the highest amercement.

"For abusing a man of his own caste, he shall be fined twelve panas.

"For abusing a man of a lower caste, he shall be fined six (Panas) .

"For insulting a member of the highest caste or of his own caste (he having been insulted by him) at the same time, the same fine is ordained ;

"Or (if he only returns his insult, a fine amounting to) three Kārṣapanas.

"The same (punishment is ordained) if he calls him bad names."

It will be noticed that in the laws of Viṣṇu, offences like those of Śūdra reciting Veda disappears, though other new social offences are seen to appear further on. On the other hand, true verbal offences consisting of the use of insulting or defamatory words have been dealt with with much specification.

Manu

Manu's treatment of Vākpāruṣya (VIII, 263-277) shows little development beyond the law of Viṣṇu whose rules are often reproduced in Manu in almost the same words.

Yajnavalkya

It is not until we come to Nārada that we find any definition of Vākpāruṣya. But in Yājñavalkya we find some early attempts at generalisation of the specific offences. In II 204-211 he gives the law as follows :

"He, who, by true, untrue, or ironical (statements) ridicules persons wanting a limb, or an organ of sense, and the diseased, shall be fined twelve and a half paṇas.

"Any one abusing another thus—'I shall have criminal connection with thy sister or thy mother,' shall be made by the king to pay a fine of twentyfive (panas).

"(The fine for abuse) of inferior (people) is half (of the next preceding fine viz. 25 panas) and for abuse of others' wives or superiors, two-fold. (In all other cases, the amount of) fine is to be determined according to the superior or inferior varṇa (class) or jāti (caste) (of the abuser and the abused.)

"In case of abuse of one of the superior class, the fine of two-fold and three-fold (respectively) and of one of a lower class it is to be reduced in the ratio of one-half (according to the class of the abused).

"Let a fine to the amount of a hundred panas be inflicted for abusive words, threatening injury to the arm, neck, eyes, or thigh, and the half of it for like abuse threatening foot, nose, ears, the hand, or the like.

"If this (imprecatory threat) were uttered by a feeble person, he should be fined two panas, but if by one able (to carry the threat into execution), he should be also required to give security for the safety of the person (threatened).

"In the case of abuse (involving) degradation from caste, the fine is that for a middle sāhasa (offence); (in the case of abuse involving an accusation of) a secondary sin, (the abuser) shall be made to pay the fine for the lowest sāhasa.

"The highest fine shall be for him who abuses a Brāhmaṇa learned in the three Vedas, the king, or the Gods. (In the case of abuse) of the caste or the Puga (community) (the fine) is (that for) the middle sāhasa; and (in the case of that) of the village or the district, (the fine) is (that for) the lowest sahasa."

Narada

Nārada in his treatment of Vākpāruṣya starts with a definition and a classification of different forms of the offence. His law goes into further details and contains a few novel provisions.[14] His texts are as follows:

"Abusive speeches, couched in offensive and violent terms, regarding the native country, caste, family, and so forth (of a man) are termed Abuse, (a title of law).

"It is divided into three species, called respectively Niṣṭhura, Aślīla, and Tīvra. The punishment for each increases in severity according as the insult is of a more (or less) serious nature.

"Abuse combined with reproaches has to be regarded as Niṣṭura, abuse couched in insulting language is Aślīla, charging one with an offence causing expulsion from caste is called Tīvra by the learned.

"Hurting the limbs of another person with a hand, foot, weapon or otherwise, or defiling him with ashes or other (impure substances) is termed Assault.

"In both kinds (of insult) five cases are distinguished, when the respective innocence or guilt of the two parties has to be established.

"When two parties have been guilty of insult, and both have commenced to quarrel at the same time, they shall suffer the same punishment, in case that no difference (in their respective culpability) becomes apparent.

"He who is the first to offer an insult is decidedly criminal, he who returns the insult is likewise culpable; but the one who began shall suffer the heavier punishment (of the two).

"When both parties are implicated equally, he of the two shall receive punishment who follows up his attack, whether he was (originally) the aggressor or the defendant.

"If a Śvapāka, Meda, Chaṇḍāla, cripple, one who gains his subsistence by killing (animals), an elephant driver, one deprived of his caste for non-performance of the ceremony of initiation, a slave, or one who treats a Guru or spiritual teacher with disregard

[14] Narada XV, S.B.E., Vol. XXXIII, p. 207 seq.

"Should offend a superior, he shall be punished by whipping him on the spot. Nor do the sages regard bodily injury done to a man of this stamp as (an offence equal to) theft.

"Should any such low person, abhorred by men, insult another man (his superior) that man himself shall punish him. The king has nothing to do with the penalty (to be inflicted on him).

"For these people are the refuse of human society, and their property is (likewise) impure. The king also is at liberty to whip them, but he must not amerce them with a fine.

"A Kṣhatriya who reviles a Brahmana must pay one hundred (Panas) as a fine. A Vaiśya (must pay) one and a half hundred, or two hundred. A Śūdra deserves corporal punishment.

"A Brāhmana shall be fined fifty (Panas) for calumniating a Kshatriya, in the case of Vaisya, the fine shall be half of fifty (i.e. twentyfive), in the case of a Śūdra, (it shall amount to) twelve (Panas).

"When a twice-born man offends against a member of his own caste, (he shall pay) twelve (Panas as a fine). When he utters calumnies which ought never to be uttered, the fine shall be twice as high.

"Even he who truthfully calls another man one-eyed, lame or the like (names), shall be fined by the king not less than one Kārṣapana.

"One must not tax with his offence a man who has done penance according to law, or who has received due punishment from the king. By transgressing this rule, one becomes liable to punishment.

"Two persons, a Brāhmaṇa and a king, are declared to be exempt from censure and corporal punishment in this world; for these two sustain the visible world.

"One who calls an outcast an outcast or a thief, a thief, is equally criminal with those whom he taxes (with their offence). (If he reproaches them) without reason, he is twice as guilty as they are.

"A once-born man (or Śūdra) who insults members of a twice-born caste with gross invectives, shall have his tongue cut-out, for he is of low origin.

"If he refers to their name or caste in terms indicating contempt, an iron rod, ten Angulas long, shall be thrust red-hot into his mouth.

"If he is insolent enough to give lessons regarding their duty to Brāhmaṇas, the king shall order hot oil to be poured into his mouth and ears.

"With whatever limb a man of low caste offends against a Brahmana, that very limb of his shall be cut off; such shall be the atonement for his crime."

Brihaspati

Bṛihaspati's texts go into fewer details and are characterised by wider generalisation and classification. After stating the laws mostly in more general terms he concludes

"This gradation of fines has been declared by me subject to modification by sages in conformity with the (particular qualities) of a man so as either to remain as declared or to be reduced or raised." (See texts of Bṣihaspati in S.B.E., Vol. XXXIII, page 355-357).

Katyayana

Kātyāyana's texts are interesting in respect of the definition which he gives as follows:

"That is said to be harshness of words (vākpāruṣya) when he roars (huṃkara) before another, coughs before him or utters what is censured by people or mimics the words or deeds of another (by way of parody)." (Verse 768 in Kane's collection).

Kātyāyana repeats the classification of Nārada and also the main rules laid down by him.

He makes a remarkable addition, however, by giving place to *apology* as minimising to half, but not excusing the offence altogether (Verse 775 in Kane's collection).

Starting with the indignation against social improprieties in the form of words the law has thus developed gradually into a completer and more intelligible law against insult and defamation by words.

Daṇḍaparusya

The offence of daṇḍapāruṣya has had a more interesting development. Like Vākpāruṣya it started as a code of rules against social improprieties not by words but by deeds. Gautama prescribes a scale of punishment for hurting another, graduated accordding to the caste of the person hurt and of the offender. Āpastamba, while he prescribes punishments for abuse adultery homicide etc., omits mere hurt altogether. Nor does Baudhāyana deals with this topic.

Visnu

In Viṣṇu's work we not only find provision for punishment for hurt, but also for *threatening* to hurt. Hurt itself is distinguished into different kinds with different measures of punishment. Some remarkable features of Viṣṇu's law are (1) a provision of retaliatory punishment for the offence of blinding both eyes of another, (2) the distinction of incapaciating injuries (cheṣtābhojanvyāgrodha) along with beating as Madhyama sahasa, (3) the first prescription of punishment for not running to the rescue of a person who is shouting for help, and (4) the first enunciation of the rule that the offender must pay the *medical expenses* (utthānavyayam) of the person hurt. Viṣṇu's texts so far as they relate to these topics are as follows[15] :—

"If any man raises his hand (against his equal in caste, with intent to strike him, he shall pay) ten Kārṣapanas ;

"If he raises his foot, twenty ;

"If he raises a piece of wood, the first amercement,

"If he raises a stone, the second amercement,

"If he raises a weapon, the highest amercement.

"If he seizes him by his feet, by his hair, by his garment, or by his hand, he shall pay ten Panas as a fine.

"If he causes pain to him, without fetching blood from him, (he shall pay) thirty-two Panas :

"For fetching blood from him, sixtyfour.

"For mutilating or injuring a hand, or a foot, or a tooth, and for slitting an ear, or the nose, the second amercement (is ordained).

"For rendering a man unable to move about, or to eat, or to speak, (cheṣṭābhojana-vyāgrodhe) or for striking him (violently, the same punishment is ordained).

"For wounding or breaking an eye, or the neck, or an arm, or a bone, or a shoulder, the highest amercement (is ordained).

"For striking out both eyes of a man, the king shall (fine him and) not dismiss him from jail as long as he lives :

"Or he shall order him to be *mutilated in the same way* (i.e. deprived of his eyes).

"Where one is attacked by many, the punishment for each shall be the double of that which has been ordained for (attacks by) a single person.

"(The double punishment is) likewise (ordained) for those who *do not give assistance to one calling for help*, though they happen to be on the spot or (who run away) after having approached it.[16]

"All those who have hurt a man, shall pay the *expense of his cure* (utthānavyayam).

"Those who have hurt a domestic animal (shall also pay the expense of its cure)."

The last text indicates that hurt or daṇḍaparuṣya was already being extended by Viṣṇu from the person of the injured party to his belongings. This, we shall find further elaborated in later works.

Yajnavalkya

In Yājñavalkya we not only find a greater elaboration and differentiation of different kinds of hurt, but an extension of the offence of daṇḍaparuṣya to acts like throwing at a person ashes dust etc., though it causes no physical injury, and dirty or unclean things,

[15] Viṣṇu V, 60.

[16] This is the rendering by Jolly. The strictly correct translation would be "For those who do not run to the rescue when (the person attacked is) shouting for help as well as to those near him who run away."

to spitting and also to throwing things which may cause hurt into the house of a person. So too, the offence is extended to causing injury not to the person himself but *to his animals and plants* as also for cutting or damaging trees, creepers, etc., in sacred places like chaitya or cremation ground. In this way the protection given to a man's person from hurt by making it punishable gets an extension to his belongings and from that to other things which are for common use of the community.

The texts of Yājñavalkya[17] relating to this topic are as follows :—

Injury to person.

"In the case of a beating to which there are no witnesses, the determination should be made by marks, circumstantial inferences, popular report, and the like ; lest the marks should be (entirely) counterfeited.

"A fine of ten panas is recorded (as) the punishment for throwing ashes, mud, or dust on a person ; double that sum, for throwing at him filth, the heel or the spittle.

"This (holds, if an offence be committed) against one of the same (class). But (if the offence be committed) against the wife of another or against one of a higher class, (the fine shall be) doubled ; if against one of an inferior class, half the fine, if committed through aberration of the intellect, drunkenness, or the like, no fine shall be inflicted.

"The limb with which any one not himself a Brāhmaṇa gives pain to a Brāhmaṇa, shall be cut off. The lowest amercement is laid down (if the limb or weapon is only) raised, and half of it, if the Brāhmaṇa is touched with the weapons.

"For holding up (threateningly) a hand or a foot, the punishment shall be ten and twenty (panas) (respectively). The middle scale of punishment is declared for all classes for mutual pointing of weapons.

"The (fine) of ten panas (shall be inflicted) for violent pulling of the foot, the hair, the clothes, or the hand (of another), a hundred for violently pulling a man caused to be tied in his clothes, and trampling him under foot.

"The man who causes pain (to another) with a stick or the like, without shedding blood, shall be fined thirtytwo panas, double that sum, if blood be shed.

"The middle fine (shall be imposed) for breaking a hand, a foot, or a tooth, for tearing the ears or the nose, for laying open a sore, and likewise for beating one till he is almost dead.

"In the case of restraint in respect of motion, feeding or speaking (cheṣṭābhojanavyāgrodha) and of injury to the eye and the like, and fracture of the neck, the arm, or the thigh (the fine is that for) the middle sāhasa.

"When several assault a single person, their fine (shall be) double (the fines) already mentioned. That which was taken during the scuffle shall be restored, and a fine (of) twice (the amount shall be paid in addition).

[17] Yājñavalkya II, 212-229. Translation by Mandlik.

"He who (in an assault) inflicts a (bodily) injury, shall pay the expenses of cure, as well as the fine that is laid down for the assault (committed).

Damage to property.

"He who strikes, perforates, breaks or demolishes a wall shall be made to pay five, ten twenty panas, and (all these together with) the expenses (of reconstruction respectively).

"One throwing into the house (of another) a thing (likely to produce) bodily injury should be made to pay sixteen panas and one similarly (throwing) a thing dangerous to life is fined (in the middle amercement).

"For giving pain, drawing blood, cutting off the branches (as horns etc.) or a limb, the fine shall be from two paṇas upwards, in the case of a minor quadruped.

"For cutting off their organs of generation, and causing death, the middle amercement shall be paid (in addition to their value). A double punishment shall be imposed in the case of (similar injury to) superior animals.

"In the case of injury to the branches, or the trunk, or the uprooting of trees which throw down branches, or which are the means of livelihood, the fine is twenty, and twofold (of the preceding fine for the offence next in order).

"In the case of (injury) to trees growing in a sacrificial place (chaitya) a cremation ground (śmaśāna), a boundary, a sacred place, or a temple and the trees well known, the fine is twofold.

"In the case of injury in the aforementioned parts to gulma, guchchha, kṣupa latā (a creeper), pratāna (a creeper without offshoots or knots), osadhi (small plants bearing fruit like paddy), and virudh (plants which grow again after being cut), the fine is half of that before mentioned."

Manu

The extension of the offence or hurt to injuries other than those to the person is more developed in Manu who, in addition to prescribing penalties for hurt lays down in VIII 285-288 penalties for injury to men, animals plants as well as to other things belonging to another person and also compensation for the injury to the owner of the thing, on a scale exceeding the value of the thing. Where injury is caused by a vehicle driven by the accused, that is also a species of daṇḍa-pāruṣya, though Manu lays down an exception where the horse has got out of control and the driver is shouting out to the people on the road.

The following is a summary of the text of Manu relating to daṇḍapāruṣya.

VIII. 279-284. If an antyaja offends a man of superior caste, the limb by which he offends should be cut off. Thus, the hands should be cut for a hurt by hand, the leg for hurting in anger by leg ; for presuming to sit on an equal seat with a superior a buttock should be cut off—(alternatively banishment after branding there) for spitting on another, the lips, and for making water on a person the urinary organ should be cut off, and both hands for assaulting by taking hold of the head or legs or beard or neck.

VIII. 285. A hundred panas for breaking the skin and for drawing blood, for a flesh wound five niṣkas, for breaking a bone, banishment.

VIII. 286-287. Injuries to big trees whose benefits are enjoyed by all, should be punished by fines graduated according to the class of tree. So too, for causing great pain to men and animals fines should be regulated by the nature of the injury.

VIII. 288. Where a person is injured, the offender should be made to pay the expenses for treatment of the injured till recovery.

VIII. 289-90. Where injury is done to the goods of another, whether knowingly or unknowingly, value must be paid to the owner's satisfaction and an equal fine to the king. Particularly for injury to leather wooden or earthen vessels or to flowers, roots and fruits the fine would be five times the value thereof.

VIII. 291-299. For injury caused by a vehicle, the penalty falls on the driver and the owner. But, if the injury is caused on account of the animal having got out of hand or for the breaking of parts of the vehicle and other things beyond control, there is no penalty if the driver keeps shouting to the people. Where the injury is by a sudden diversion from the track by the driver, the owner is liable ; if the driver is expert, he too is liable. But there is no liability if the deviation is necessitated by obstructions on the road. Where the injury caused is the death of a man, the penalty is the same as for theft. For killing animals different penalties are prescribed for different kinds of animals.

The Section concludes with a provision for characteristic cases of justified hurt in VIII, 301-2. A wife, a son, a slave, a dependent and an uterine brother who offends may be beaten, but only with a rope or a cane and only on the back but never on the head. For beating otherwise the punishment is the same as for theft.

THEFT (STEYA).

Punishment of theft and protecting people from thieves were among the chief duties of a king from the very outset and theft is naturally one of the topics of law. This duty was regarded as so imperative that failure to give this protection was from the earliest times a defection of duty, so that the king's officers appointed over villages had to make good the loss of the owner of the stolen things if they could not discover them. This law we find as early as in the text of Āpastamba (II. 10, 26, 8) and it is found elaborated in later works.

Another rule which is enunciated in Gautama (XII, 34-45) and repeated by later law-givers requires the thief who has stolen gold; himself to go to the king with his hair flowing and a wand in hand to confess his fault and ask for punishment. Thereupon the king may punish him or not as he pleases ; in either case he goes off free of sin. This was obviously a penance prescribed for the thief and has survived in law from an earlier pre-juridical state of society when penance was the only sanction against crimes and kings had not yet started to adjudicate and sentence criminals. In early days, when fears of punishment after death were more effective than it obviously became in later times, this might have been actually done by men, and in any case the duty to act thus might have been a more or less effective deterrent against thefts.

Gautama

Gautama deals very briefly with the offence of theft in Chapter XII, 15-18 as follows :—

> "15. The property which a Sudra unrighteously acquires by theft must be repaid eightfold.
> 16. For each of the other castes (the fines must be) doubled.
> 17. If a learned man offends, the punishment shall be very much increased."

This is a striking rule which is the reverse of the scale of punishments for other offences particularly when social dignities are involved. This principle that the greater the knowledge and culture of the culprit, the greater the offence, however runs through all the Smṛitis down to the latest.

This is followed by the rule for theft of articles of small value *e.g.* fruits, green corn and vegetables in small quantities for which a very small fine of five krişṇalas is prescribed.

Wholly out of tune with these texts however are some exceptional rules in Chapter XVIII, 24-31.

> "In order to defray the expenses of a wedding, and when engaged in a rite (enjoined by) the sacred law, he may take money from a Śūdra.
> "Or from a man rich in small cattle, who neglects his religious duties, though he does not belong to the Śūdra caste.
> "Or from the owner of a hundred cows, who does not kindle the sacred fire,
> "Or from the owner of a thousand cows, who does not drink Soma.
> "And when he has not eaten (at the time of six meals he may take) at the time of the seventh meal (as much as will sustain life) not (such a quantity as will serve) to make a hoard,
> "Even from men who do not neglect their duties.

> "If he is examined by the king (regarding his deed) he shall confess (it and his condition).
>
> "For if he possesses sacred learning and a good character, he must be maintained by the (King)."

Contradictions and incongruities like these in these early texts only show that the various rules of conduct derived from different principles have not yet been fully co-ordinated, and the rules of law have not yet been formulated with the fulness derived from later experience nor with precise limitations which might be implicit in early law, but not expressed or found to be necessary by further experience.

With regard to this topic of theft in particular, we shall find that later laws are developed more by removal of these deficiencies than by the addition of wholly new matter.

Apastamba

In Āpastamba's work theft which is lumped with homicide and appropriation of land has been made punishable by confiscation of all property and capital sentence (II, 10, 27, 16). For a Brāhmaṇa who commits these offences the sentence is blinding (II, 10, 27, 17). The rigor of these drastic sentences for all these offences without discrimination is not mitigated by making distinctions according to the quality of seriousness of crime, but by providing for a possible protection of mitigation through a Guru, a purohit, a Snataka or a prince. How these persons can protect is not explained. The commentator Haradatta explains it by saying that these persons could do so by interceding to secure a commutation to a less severe penalty. But it is equally possible that this text implies that by resorting to such pious or influential persons they may obtain a sanctuary which may not be violated.

Vasistha

Vasiṣṭha whose work, as I have observed before, bears signs of being a fragment makes no provision for the punishment of a thief; but that a thief had to be punished was assumed by him in several texts *e.g.,* by the following in Chapter XVIII.

> "The king after punishing a thief, an abhisasta . . . . should fast for one day."

Again

> "The foetus-destroyer transmits guilt by giving food, the wife pollutes the husband by adultery . . . . the thief transmits guilt to the king.

"The wicked man who commits these crimes, while the king holds his power to punish, go pure like honest and virtuous men, after transmitting their guilt to the king, if the king does not punish them his duty as king is polluted."

Throughout the early expositions of law, we thus find the punishment of thieves by drastic penalties is more or less taken for granted and these law givers do not therefore take the trouble to define or discriminate between thieves. Definitions and specifications of penalties, doubtless based on growing practices, grow with time. In Viṣṇusmṛiti, which, as I have said before, seems separated from the earlier Dharmasutras by a long period of slow growth we find the first trace of more detailed laws regarding theft.

Visnu

Viṣṇu (V, 77-90) distinguishes between thefts of different articles and between punishments for them with reference to the values of the stolen articles. His texts are as follows:—

"He who has stolen a cow, or a horse, or a camel, or an elephant, shall have one hand, or one foot cut off ;

He who has stolen a goat, or a sheep, (shall have) one hand (cut off).

He who steals grain (of those sorts which grow in the rainy season) shall pay eleven times its value as a fine ;

Likewise, he who steals grain (of those sorts, which grow in winter and spring, (such as rice and barley).

A stealer of gold, silver, or clothes, at a value of more than fifty Maṣas, shall lose both hands.

He who steals a less amount than that, shall pay eleven times its value as a fine.

A stealer of thread, cotton, cow-dung, sugar, sour milk, milk, butter-milk, grass, salt, clay, ashes, birds, fish, clarified butter, oil, meat, honey, basket-work, canes of bamboo, earthenware, or iron pots, shall pay three times their value as a fine.

(The fine is ordained for stealing) dressed food.

For stealing flowers, green (grain), shrubs, creepers, climbing plants or leaves (he shall pay) five Kriṣṇalas.

For stealing pot herbs, roots or fruits (the same punishment is ordained).

He who steals gems, (shall pay) the highest amercement.

He who steals anything not mentioned above, (shall make good) its value (to the owner).

Thieves shall be compelled to restore all stolen goods to the owners.

After that they shall suffer the punishment that has been ordained for them."

Yajnavalkya

In Yājñavalkya's smṛiti we not only find a more developed penal code but, interesting rules of procedure in dealing with thieves actual or suspected. Specific punishments are prescribed for specific acts, not merely distinguished by the value of articles stolen but also by the nature of the act and a general rule is laid down for adjusting punishment by reference to the place and time, the age, and strength of the accused. He further provides punishment for harbouring thieves.

The procedure prescribed when a theft is committed is to round up all persons who may be properly suspected and put them to the proof of their innocence. If they fail, they are to be given corporal punishments. Duties are also cast upon various persons to catch thieves and bring them to justice. The texts of Yājñavalkya dealing with this topic (II, 266-276) are as follows :[18]

Detection

"A thief is apprehended by detectives, (either as one in possession of) of the lost articles, or (as one to whom the theft has been) traced, or (as one) notorious for previous offences, or as one who lives in unknown places.

"Others should (similarly) be apprehended on suspicion, (such as) those who conceal their caste or names, who are addicted to gambling, treachery, or drinking, whose (face) loses colour and voice falters (267).

Who make (idle) enquiries about another's wealth and houses, who live unobserved, who spend much without having (any means of) livelihood, and who sell lost articles.

If (he who has been) apprehended on suspicion do not clear himself (from that suspicion) he shall be made to give the stolen article, and shall be liable to the punishment of a thief.

Punishment and Penalties

Having caused restitution of the stolen property, the king shall cause the thief to be punished by different modes of corporal punishment (Vividhairvadhaih). A Brāhmaṇa (guilty of theft) should be branded and banished from the kingdom.

The blame attaches to the village officer in the case of a murder or theft in his village until some trace (of the offence) is found ; to the owner of the pasture ground, (for offences in his pasturage) ; to the detectives of thieves, (in case of offences) on a highway, or (in places) other than pastures.

A village shall pay when (the theft takes place) within its limits or that village to which the trace is carried. If (the theft be committed) beyond one krosa (two miles) (from any village), (the communities of) five surrounding villages or even of ten villages (shall pay).

[18] Verses II 277-282 which the Mitaksara includes under Steya do not deal with theft at all but with other serious offences most of which would properly come under strisaṃgrahaṇa.

(The king) shall cause to be impaled on a stake Bandigrâha (sacrilegious house-breakers), likewise those who steel horses and elephants and also violent murderers.

The tongs (*i.e.* the forefinger and index) of the hands of pickpockets and cut-purses should be cut off (for the first offence); for the second offence, they should be deprived of a hand or a foot.

In the case of a theft of inferior, middling and superior articles, the fine shall be according to the value (of the article stolen). In passing sentence, the place, the time, and the age and the ability (of the offender) shall be considered.

To him who knowingly supplies food, place, fire, water, counsel, appurtenances, and (loans for) expenditure, to a thief or a murderer, the fine shall be the highest.

Manu

Manu VIII 303-318 emphasises the duty of the king to punish thieves and to protect his subjects from thieves, the merit achieved by the king doing so and the demerit from failure to do so. This is a duty which arises from his taking a sixth part of the produce as vali or tax. Incidentally he repeats the injunction of Gautama requiring the thief to go to the king to seek punishment and the text quoted by Vasistha :

> Råjabhirdhṛitadaṇḍastu kritva pāpāni manavah
> Nirmalah svargamāyanti santah sukritinah yatha.

Penalties

He then goes to prescribe the penalties as follows in verses VIII 319-335.

For stealing pots and rope from a well—a fine of one masha.

For stealing paddy exceeding 10 kumbhas—death (or corporal punishment).

For stealing less—repayment of eleven times the quantity.

For stealing (1) things measured by weight,
(2) gold and silver and
(3) costly clothes

(*a*) exceeding 100 (panas)—death.

(*b*) exceeding 500—amputation of hand.

(*c*) below that—payment of eleven times the value.

For stealing articles belonging to men of rank and particularly of women and for theft of precious jewels—death.

For stealing capital animals (Mahāpaśu *i.e.*, elephants horses etc.) according to the nature and time of the act.

For stealing cows of Brāhmaṇas, for injuring bullocks and stealing animals—Ardhapādika.

For stealing several minor properties *e.g.* yarn, salt, cowdung, products of animals cooked food etc.—twice the value.
For stealing flowers, green paddy plants etc.—five krişņalas.
For ripe paddy, green vegetables, roots etc.—100 panas.

Then follows a general rule that the limb or part of the body with which the offence is committed should be cut off. No exception is to be made even in the case of the father, acharya, friend, mother, son or purohit, no person is immune from punishment by the king (VIII, 335).

Ground for Enhancement

Manu too repeats the law of Gautama that the higher the status of the offender, the severer would be his punishment (VIII, 336-338). Thus for the offence for which a common man is punished with Kārşāpana the punishment of the king himself would be one thousand, where the Śūdra's punishment is eight units, a Vaisya's would be sixteen, Kşatriya's thirty-two and a Brāhmaņa's sixty-four.

Petty thefts

Taking of things of small value specially in circumstances of distress is not theft, *e.g.*, wild fruits and roots and fuel for making fire and grass for feeding cows is not theft. A hungry twice-born traveller taking two sugar canes or two roots from another's field does not commit theft (VIII, 341).

The man who steals straying cattle or sets them free from tether or carries away a slave or a horse or a chariot is also punishable as a thief.

Most of these texts of Manu betray an earlier and less developed stage of the law which has not yet generalised the offences and punishments as Yājñavalkya or later Smŗitis have done and some of them are clear survivals in the present redaction of earlier texts attributed to Manu which have been brought together by the present compiler.

Narada

Nārada's text as it has come down in the commentary of Asahāya does not contain the texts on theft which Jolly has found only in a Nepalese Manuscript (Sacred Books of the East Vol. XXXIII, pages 223-232).

In this part the author elaborates a procedure indicated by Yājñavalkya for arresting and questioning persons of suspicious character, distinguishing between persons on whom stolen articles have been found. He prescribes punishment for harbouring thieves and receiving stolen property and also lays down rules for pursuit of a thief by following footprints and says that where footprints are lost, neighbours of that place, local officials and governors would be responsible, thus setting an ambitious standard of vigilance not only for officials but for common people.

The offences and penalties particularised by Nārada are almost identical with those of Manu. But he lays down a more general rule as follows :—

> "Manu, the son of the Self-Existent, has declared ten places of punishment, which should be (selected) in (punishing members of the) three (lower) castes, a Brāhmaṇ should remain uninjured always.
>
> (Those places are) the privy parts, the belly, the tongue, the two hands, and fifthly the two eyes, the nose, the two ears, the property and the body.
>
> After carefully considering the (nature of the) offence, the place and time, and after examining the ability (of the offender), and the motive (by which he was actuated), he shall inflict these punishments."

Nārada defines the measures of the three degrees of fines as follows :—

Measures of Penalty

> "The first (or lowest) fine to be inflicted on a guilty person shall amount to neither more nor less than twentyfour (Panas). The middlemost fine shall consist of not more than four hundred, and not less than two hundred (Panas).
>
> "The highest fine should be known to consist of not more than a thousand, and not less than five hundred (Panas). This is the three-fold gradation of punishment, which has been proposed by the Self-existent for robberies."

Again he says :—

> "Punishment is pronounced to be twofold, corporal punishment and fines. Corporal punishment is again declared to be of ten sorts, fines are (also) of more than one kind.
>
> Fines begin with a Kakani and the highest amount of a fine is one's entire property. Corporal punishment begins with confinement and ends with capital punishment.
>
> Fines beginning with a Kākani are declared to amount to no less than one Māṣā. These are called "Fines" amounting to no less than a Māṣā which amount to one Kārṣāpaṇa at most.
>
> Fines beginning with no less than a Kārṣāpana are those amounting to no less than four Kārṣāpanas ; or which begin with two, and end with eight (Kārṣāpanas) or which begin with three, and end with twelve (Kārṣāpanas).
>
> A Kārṣāpana is a silver coin in the southern country, in the east, it is an equivâlent for (a certain number of) Panas, and is equal to twenty Panas.

A Māṣā should be known to be the twentieth part of a Kārṣāpana. A Kākani is the fourth part of a Māṣā or Pala.

By that appellation which is in general use in the region of the Punjab, the value of a Kārṣāpana is not circumscribed here.

A Kārṣāpana has to be taken as equal to an Anaika, four of these are a Dhanaka, twelve of the latter are Suvarna, which is called Dinara otherwise.

For the rest Nārada's texts are practically identical with the law of Manu.

Katyayana

The collected texts of Kātyāyana provide more elaborate rules for arresting and questioning persons liable to suspicion and give some special rules not to be found in other works. His texts are as follows :[19]

"Depriving a man of his wealth, either clandestinely or openly and either by night or by day is known to be theft.

(The king) should carefully examine property (alleged to be) stolen (to see) whether the article passed to the hands (of the alleged thief) from another's hand, or whether he took it up without any intention (of stealing) when it lay on the ground (unclaimed) or whether he actually lifted it away as a thief.

(Where a trader) deals (with his customers) by means of balances, measures (of corn) and measures of capacity that are imitations or substitutes for true ones or not so should be fined the first amercement.

Restitution

What is stolen from the houses in a village, (the king) should make the thief-catchers pay it (to the owners). He should make the guarding officers and wardens of the country (pay the price of stolen articles) if the thief be not found. The property stolen in the village should be restored (or its value be paid) by the headman of the village, in case (the theft took place) in a forest the king must restore (stolen property or its price), but if it took place in a place other than a forest, then it must be restored by the officer appointed to catch thieves.

Whatever is stolen from any person in one's kingdom must be restored by the king, the king should search for the thing lost and if found (after he pays the price to the owner) he should retain (the article) himself. (The king) should restore with efforts the thing itself that is stolen by thieves, in the absence of the thing the price (thereof should be paid by the king), otherwise the king incurs sin. Even when the thief be caught, if the articles stolen be not recovered from him, (the king) should restore the thing (himself) or he should make the thief pay according to his (the king's) pleasure.

[19] Texts of Kātyāyana ed. Kane p. 98, Translations p. 267.

When thieves are being made to restore (articles alleged to be stolen) if there be a doubt as to the offence, the person who was robbed should be made to take oaths or he should establish (his allegation of stolen articles) by (the evidence of) his relatives. Where the owner recovers a portion of his stolen property from a certain person, he (the owner) should recover the rest from the same man, if he (the owner) establishes (the loss of all the articles alleged).

Those who are traitors (or cause destruction of) their country and those who are highway robbers should be deprived (by the king) of their all and should be ordered to be impaled on a stake.

If those who are intent on (*i.e.* whose duty it is to) tracing thieves were to make who is not the real thief to restore (or pay the price of) the thing stolen, the persons so compelled would get back what they had to pay when (the real thief) was found and (the king) should make (the officers guilty of harassing the innocent man) pay (to the latter) double (of the price).

Penalties

The king should cut off that limb of a robber with which he causes loss to another, so that he will not do so again.

If a person takes two cucumbers, or two melons, five mangoes or five pomegranate fruits and a handful of oats or jujubes (from another's land or trees) he does not incur blame.

The Mānavas (school of Manu) declare that those (thieves) who are caught (red-handed) with booty should be at once banished (from the kingdom), but this (punishment) is not approved of by Gautama (the school of Gautama) since it is censured owing to the destruction (or reduction) of people (in the country).

The king, after catching (a Brāhmaṇa) thief and proclaiming (publicly) the signs of his guilt, whether he be caught with booty or not, provided his heinous crime is established as a fact, should deprive him of all his wealth. (The Brāhmaṇa thieves) who are very strong, being guarded with iron fetters, fed on meagre food, should do (hard) labour for the king till their death ; this is the view of Kausika.

When a foreigner steals property from another country (and brings it into a country where he is sojourning), the king (of the latter country) should deprive him of that property and should let him off without punishment.

Those who supply food to thieves, those who give them fire and water, those who purchase (stolen) goods from them and receive (stolen) property from them and those who hide them—these are all declared to be liable to the same punishment (as the thieves themselves).

Where one who is not learned officiates as priest at a sacrifice and where one who is not himself firmly grounded (in any sastra) sets up as a propounder of it, the king should punish both with the punishment for a thief and should make them abide by the (proper) path.

These texts, like others which have been quoted before from other authors in dealing with Vākparuṣya and Dandaparuṣya show some amount of mixing up of different offences which hardly fall under the topic under discussion. This may probably have been due to the fact that certain categories of offences like Vakpāruṣya, Steya, etc., had been firmly established in legal practice and standards fixed for them, so that any new offence would normally be classified under one of the categories already known and provided for. Thus, when Steya was a known category and a person who had not actually stolen a thing but had done something which had the attributes of theft as conceived by the lawyer of the day, such as secrecy or false pretence and for which no specific punishment is already provided would be roped in for purposes of punishment for Steya. From thief to the receiver or the person who harbours or has intercourse with thieves is but a short step. And why not a person who acts and procures money from men by pretending to be what they are not?

CHAPTER XIII

TOPICS OF LITIGATION (*Contd.*)
SEXUAL OFFENCES.

In Manu and Nārada's classification topics of sex relations are treated under two heads. Strīpuṃdharma deals primarily with marital relations while Strīsaṃgrahana deals primarily with sexual crimes. The former has been more conveniently treated in dealing with marriage. We shall deal with Strīsaṃgrahana or sexual crimes.

Gautama

Punishment for adultery and rape is dealt with in the earliest law books, but it is remarkable that Gautama's law makes positive provision only for the offence of intercourse by a Śūdra with a twice-born woman for which the offender suffers amputation of his genitals and forfeiture of property. There is no corresponding rule for punishment of a Kṣatriya or a Vaisya even for intercourse with a Brāhmani woman. (See supra p. 229).

As I understand it, this does not mean that Gautama did not consider other cases of criminal intercourse as wrongs. They were wrongs to be expiated by penances or punished by the community. It is only where the injury was considered to be a great outrage on Dharma as in the case of Śūdra having intercourse with a twice-born woman that the king's justice was invoked.

It is, of course, immaterial for this grievous offence whether the intercourse was with or without the consent of the woman.

Apastamba

Āpastamba deals more fully with this topic (in II, 10, 26, 18-24) in the following terms:

> "A young man who, decked with ornaments, enters unintentionally (a place where) a married woman or a (marriageable) damsel (sits), must be reprimanded.
>
> But if he does it intentionally with a bad purpose, he must be fined.
>
> If he has actually committed adultery, his organ shall be cut off together with the testicles.
>
> But (if he has had intercourse) with a (marriageable) girl, his property shall be confiscated and he shall be banished.
>
> Afterwards the king must support (such women and damsels),
>
> And protect them from defilement.

If they agree to undergo the (prescribed) penance, he shall make them over to their (lawful) guardians.

A man of one of the first three castes (who commits adultery) with a woman of the Śūdra caste shall be banished.

A Śūdra (who commits adultery) with a woman of one of the first three castes shall suffer capital punishment.

And he shall emaciate a woman who has committed adultery with a Śūdra, by making her undergo penances and fasts.

They declare, that (a Brahmana) who has once commited adultery with a married woman of equal class, shall perform one-fourth of the penance prescribed for an outcast.

In like manner for every repetition (of the crime), one-fourth of the penance (must be added).

(if the offence be committed) for the fouth time, the whole (penance of twelve years) must be performed."

The man, it will be seen, is here punished but the woman has to submit only to prayaschitta, after which she becomes free from guilt. In this law too distinction is not made on the ground of consent or otherwise of the woman. The emphasis is on the defilement of the woman which has to be cleared by prāyaschitta.

It is worthy of note in this connection that Āpastamba who elsewhere forbids the practice of Niyoga, considers Niyoga itself as a species of adultery. Conceding that intercourse with a sapinda by her kinsman was permitted in the past it was considered in his days to be a sin for which both the man and the woman would go to hell (II, 10, 27, 2-7).

Āpastamba, it will be seen above, not only condemns adultery of a Sudra with a twice-born but even condemns adultery of a Brahmana with a woman of his own caste though that is only a sin to be expiated by penance, while a Sudra violating a twice-born woman is punished with death.

Visnu

Viṣṇu's text on this topic is brief, but it shows important developments. He makes adultery with a woman of one's own caste punishable and only less so if it is with a woman of lower caste, except where the intercourse is with an antyaja woman, where death is ordained. In his text unnatural sexual offence with cattle first appears.

Manu

In Manu's texts the offence is extended from criminal intercourse to other associations with women short of it. In Āpastamba, we have seen a person entering a woman's apartment is punished. Manu goes much further and specifies other kinds of forbidden association with women (VIII 354).

For talking with another man's wife a man is punishable with first amercement if previously warned (VIII 354), where such previous warning is not found he should be slightly punished (VIII 355).

Defining saṃgrahana Manu says, one who talks with another's wife at a pilgrimage, in the woods or forest, or at the confluence of rivers is guilty of saṃgrahana. Joking, playing, touching ornaments, sitting on the same bed or seat, these are all offences of strisaṃgrahana.

So too where one touches a woman in an improper part, or being touched she does not resent, all this done by mutual consent constitutes saṃgrahana (VIII 257-9).

The texts prescribing punishment for saṃgrahana defined like this seem hardly consistent. For, while VIII 359 prescribes death for a non-Brāhmaṇa who commits this offence, in VIII 361 it is said that one should not speak to another's wife if forbidden, if one does so even when forbidden, he pays a fine of one gold niṣka.

Some exceptions are provided for. Thus beggars, singers (vandinah), priests chosen for a sacrifice, and artisans may talk to other people's wives (VIII 360). So on the other hand, wives of chāranas who live on their charms and draw men to themselves, as well as female slaves, mistresses of another and women who have renounced the world may be spoken to, but a slight fine may be imposed for such intercourse.

With regard to virgins the law is varied by circumstances. If a virgin is violated without consent, the punishment is death, but not where she, being of the same caste, consents (VIII 364). The virgin herself if she seeks intercourse with a man of superior caste is not punishable ; if she has intercourse with a man of inferior caste she must be restrained within the house (VIII 365). The man who has intercourse with a maiden of superior caste is punished. If he seeks a girl of the same caste he must pay the śulka, if the father is agreeable (VIII 369), *i.e.*, he will marry her.

For raping a maiden, amputation of two fingers is prescribed, but a fine of two hundred panas if the girl is willing (367-368).

For adultery by a woman, even feeding by dogs is prescribed, while the man is to be laid on a hot iron and burnt (371-2). Variations of punishment are prescribed for different castes including ghastly penalties besides fines (VIII 374-385).

Narada

Nārada deals with Strisaṃgrahana not as a separate title but as part of the chapter on Stripuṃdharma. His attitude towards women is much softer than Manu's. As is well-known, he prescribes remarriages for widows and for women who are abandoned or those whose husbands are impotent. (XII 95-101). In justification of the wife taking another husband it is cynically stated,

> "Women have been created for the sake of propagation, the wife being the field and the husband the sower of the seed. The field must be given to him who has the seed. He who has no seed is unworthy to possess the field." (XII, 19).

In consonance with this is the provision in XII 61 as follows:—

> "A man is not punishable as an adulterer for having intercourse with the wife of one who has left his wife without her fault or of one impotent or consumptive if the wife herself consents."

For other cases of adultery as well as individual relations with another's wife or a maiden and other sexual offences, Nārada's penalties, if less condign are on the whole in conformity with those of Manu and Yājñavalkya. He says,

> "To meet with another man's wife in an unreasonable hour or place, and to sit, converse, or dally with her, these are the three grades of adultery.
>
> When a woman and a man have meetings at a confluence of two rivers, at a Ghat, in a garden, or in a park, it is also termed saṃgrahana.
>
> By the employment of go-betweens, dispatch of letters and other criminal proceedings of various kinds, adultery may be found out by the knowing.
>
> If one touches a woman in a place (where it is) improper (to touch her) or allows himself to be touched (in such a spot) all such acts, done with mutual consent are declared to be saṃgrahana.
>
> Bestowing attentions (on a woman) sporting (with her) touching her ornaments and clothes, sitting with her on a bed, all such acts are (also) declared to be adulterous.
>
> If a man seizes a woman by the hand, by a braid of hair, or by the border of her gown, or if he calls out "Stop, stop", all such acts are (also) declared to be adulterous.
>
> By the sending of clothes, ornaments, garlands of flowers, drinks, food and fragrant substances, adultery may (also) be discovered by the wise.
>
> When a man, actuated by vanity, folly or braggartism, declares himself, that he has enjoyed the love of a certain woman, that is also termed an adulterous proceeding.
>
> When a man has connexion with a woman of his own caste, a fine of the highest degree (shall be inflicted on him);

and the middling fine, when he has connection with a woman of lower caste, and capital punishment, when he has connection with a woman of superior caste.

(When he has connexion) with a maiden against her will, he shall have two fingers cut off. If the maiden belongs to the highest (or Brahman) caste, death and the confiscation of his entire property (shall be his punishment).

When, however, he has connexion with a willing maiden, it is no offence, but he shall bestow ornaments on her, honour her (with other presents), and (lawfully) espouse her.

A mother, mother's sister, mother-in-law, maternal uncle's wife, father's sister, paternal uncle's (wife), friend's (wife), sister, sister's friend, daughter-in-law,

Daughter, spiritual teacher's wife, Sagotra relation, one come to him for protection, a queen, a female ascetic, a nurse, an honest woman, and a female of the highest caste.

When a man carnally knows any one out of these (twenty) women, he is said to commit incest. For that crime no other punishment than excision of the organ is considered (as a sufficient atonement).

When a man has sexual connexion with (small) cattle, he shall pay one hundred (Panas) as a fine, (for sexual connexion) with a cow, he shall pay the middling fine, and the same (for sexual connexion) with a low-caste woman.

Let a punishment be inflicted by the king on him who has intercourse with a woman, with whom it is forbidden to have intercourse, and let such sinners be cleared (of the moral offence committed by them) by performing a penance.

Intercourse is permitted with a wanton woman, who belongs to another than the Brahman caste, or a prostitute, or a female slave or a female not restrained by her master (niṣkāsini), if these women belong to a lower caste than oneself ; but with a woman of superior caste, intercourse is prohibited.

When, however, such a woman is the kept mistress (of another man, intercourse with her) is as criminal as (intercourse) with another man's wife. Such women, though intercourse with them is not (in general) forbidden, must not be approached, because they belong to another man."

"When a married woman commits adultery, her hair shall be shaved, she shall have to lie on a low couch, receive bad food and bad clothing, and the removal of the sweepings shall be assigned to her as her occupation.

A Kṣatriya woman shall wait six years or three years, if she has no issue, a Vaisya woman shall wait four (years), if she has issue, any other Vaisya women (*i.e.* one who has no issue), two years.

No such (definite) period is prescribed for a Sudra woman, whose husband is gone on a journey. Twice the above period is ordained, when the (absent) husband is alive and tidings are received of him.

The above series of rules has been laid down by the Creator of the world for those cases where a man has disappeared. No offence is imputed to a woman if she goes to live with another man after (the fixed period has elapsed)."

Brihaspati

The fragments of Bṛihaspati dealing with the subject collected by Jolly do not give a complete idea of his whole law on the subject. But these texts are distinguished like other passages of Bṛihaspati by his attempt to classify and generalise. His text are as follows :—

"The two kinds of injury (abuse and assaults) and the three kinds of violence have been declared. Learn the threefold (offence of) adultery, which is productive of sin.

The two first kinds of it are connected with violence and deception respectively, the third kind springs from sensual desire ; the last is again of three sourts, being of the first, second, or highest degree.

When a man has intercourse with a woman in secret against her will, when she is asleep, or disordered in her intellect, or does not notice his approach, it is (termed) forcible enjoyment of a woman.

When he conducts her into his house under false pretences, and after giving her intoxicating drugs, has intercourse with her, it is considered fraudulent enjoyment of a woman.

When a man exchanges looks with a woman or sends her messages, and has intercourse with her impelled by sensuality, it has to be considered as (adulterous intercourse) springing from sensual desire.

Winking (at a woman) smiling (at her), sending her messengers, and touching her ornaments or clothes, is termed as adulterous act of the first (or lowest) degree.

Sending perfumes, garlands, fruit, spirituous liquor, food or clothes, and conversing with her in secret, is considered an adulterous act of the second degree.

Sitting on the same bed, dallying, and kissing or embracing each other, is defined as an adulterous act of the highest degree by persons acquainted with law.

For these three gradations of adultery, the first, middling, and highest fines shall be inflicted respectively, the fine shall be even higher than that in the case of a very rich man.

(The king) shall confiscate the whole wealth of him who violates an unwilling woman, and having caused his penis and scrotum to be cut off, shall cause him to be paraded on an ass.

When a man enjoys a woman by fraud, his punishment shall be confiscation of his entire wealth, and he shall afterwards be branded with the mark of a female part and banished from the town.

The highest fine (shall be inflicted for connexion) with a woman of equal caste, half of that (for connexion) with a woman of inferior caste, but a man who has connexion with a woman of higher caste than his own, shall be put to death.

When a woman has been enjoyed against her will, she shall be kept in the house well guarded, smeared (with ashes) lying on a low couch, and receiving a bare maintenance only.

To atone for her sin, she shall be caused to perform the Kṛichchra or Pāraka penance, in case she had intercourse with her equal in caste, but if she has been enjoyed by a man of inferior caste, she shall be abandoned and put to death.

> When a woman comes to a man's house and excites his concupiscence by touching him or the like acts, she shall be punished, half of her punishment shall be inflicted on the man.
>
> Her nose, lips and ears having been cut off, she shall be paraded in the streets and plunged into water, or she shall be torn to pieces by dogs in a public place frequented by many persons."

It is worthy of note in this connection that in dealing with stripuṃdharma, Bṛihaspati prescribes strict chastity and forbids Niyoga and has a specific provision for a strict surveillance of the married woman by her mother-in-law and other wives of the family, reflecting more or less the condition of young wives in Hindu society in later days (XXIV, 2 in S.B.E. Vol. XXXIII).

Katyayana

Kātyāyana too attempts a classification which, if not logical, is illustrative of the sort of things punishable according to him. The only fragments of his texts collected by Kane are as follows :—

> "Adultery is said to be ninefold, *viz.*, when it is accompanied by the employment of a go-between, being together at an improper time and place, falling on a woman's neck or seizing her hair or the border of her sari (or gown) seizing a woman, by the ear, nose or hand, sitting or taking food with her on the same seat.
>
> When a man has forcibly had sexual intercourse with a woman, capital punishment is to be inflicted in that case (by the king) since it is a violation of (good) conduct.
>
> An unchaste woman who, being under the influence of lust, herself amorously approaches a man should be released by the king's order after being proclaimed (as unchaste) in the presence of people."

SĀHASA.

The term 'Sāhasa' has been defined by Manu and others as offences done with violence. In these books the word thus signifies a specific class of offences.

The term does not appear in older law books, but in Viṣṇu, as has been already pointed out, the classification of penalties for offences as those for Sāhasas of the first, middle and highest degree are specified. We have seen that in the earlier Dharma-sutras we have nothing more than specific penalties. These were presumably all the offences which then came within the ambit of the king's justice. Between these and Viṣṇusmriti, the number of such offences are seen to have been multiplied. It seems that with the multiplication of such offences, they were together given the general name of sāhasa, and, before the time of Viṣṇu they were classified into sāhasas of the first, medium and the highest degree, with definite measures of penalty for each.

This classification of penalties for offences continues in all late smṛitis, though the offences for which they are prescribed are no longer called by the generic name of sāhasa but have specific names of their own. In Viṣṇu we find a long catalogue of numerous offences which are none of them specifically called sāhasa, but, in prescribing the penalty for them, the terms, prathama, madhyama, and uttama sāhasa daṇḍa are used. This indicates, to my mind, that with the expansion of the king's jurisdiction and a corresponding development of laws of specific offences, these came to be differentiated gradually from the general concept of Sāhasa, leaving the name sāhasa to apply to a specific class of offence, accompanied by evidence. Probably however, a trace of the old use still survives in the law about abetment and instigation where the instigators of sāhasa alone are referred to, as liable to double the penalty of the criminal himself, though the rule in the way it has been applied appears to apply to all offences.

Manu

Manu who gives the first classification of eighteen topics makes sāhasa one of such topics. In VIII 332 he distinguishes theft from sāhasa by saying that what, when done with violence, is sāhasa becomes steya without such violence. In the verses specifically referred to sāhasa, he does not specify or prescribe punishments for specific kinds of sāhasa, but merely enjoins the king to punish men guilty of sāhasa and on no account to let them off, either for friendship or on receipt of even vast wealth (VIII 347). In this connection he lays down a law of self-defence in a somewhat characteristic fashion in VIII 348-351. He prescribes that the twice born shall take arms in revolutions affecting the twice born. Even killing is justified for self-defence for saving sacrificial fees and for protecting women and Brahmanas. No matter whether he is respected person or a child or an old man or a very learned Brahman, if a man is an ātatāyi, he should be killed without consideration.

Viṣṇu too indicates as if sāhasa was already a distinct kind of offence when in prescribing Divya he speaks of Rajadroha, sāhasa, Nikṣepasteya as distinct offences (Viṣṇu IX 2, 3 and 22). But though defined by Manu as any offence which is accompanied by violence, the exact conception of sāhasa was never precisely delimited.

Yajnavalkya

Yājñavalkya gives a narrower definition of sāhasa as the violent appropriation of common property, (sāmānya dravyam prasabhaharaṇāt sahasaṃ smṛitam II, 230) but in the texts which follow under this topic he includes many offences which are anything but violent. Some of these have been referred to under trade laws. Others are offences against social dignities and privileges and acts which were deemed to be against public policy.

A general rule about punishment of abettors and instigators of sāhasa which is to be found in II 261 is probably of general application to all offences.

The texts of Yājñavalkya under sāhasa are as follows:—

> "When common (as well as another's) property is forcibly carried away, that (act) is called sāhasa (a heinous offence). The fine (in such a case) is (ordinarily) twice the value (of the thing taken away) but fourfold when the offence (is) denied.
>
> He who causes the commission of a sāhasa shall be made to pay a double fine ; and he who does the same by saying—'I will give (such a reward)' shall be made to pay quadruple the amount.
>
> For him who abuses or disobeys the venerable, who beats his brother's wife, who does not give what is promised, who breaks open a house sealed,
>
> Or who does an injury to his neighbour, or his blood relations, or the like, the fine is fifty panas. This is invariable rule.
>
> He who wantonly consorts (*i.e.* without Niyoga) with a widow, who does not run to help when there is a cry for help, who needlessly halloes (for aid), he who being a Chandāla touches men of the higher (classes),
>
> Who feeds a Śūdra ascetic (of the fourth order) on religious or obsequial (occasions), who pronounces an improper oath, who (although) disqualified performs religious rites,
>
> Who destroys the virility of bullocks or inferior quadrupeds, who conceals common (property), who destroys the foetus of a female slave,
>
> (Or) whoever being the father, and the son, the sister and the brother, the husband and the wife, and the preceptor and the pupil abandon each other when (the person abandoned is) not degraded shall be fined a hundred (panas).
>
> A washerman wearing the garments of another shall be fined three panas, and in cases of sale, hiring out, pledge, or a loan on request, ten panas.
>
> For witnesses in a dispute between the father and the son, the fine is three panas (and) for him who engages himself therein, the fine is eight-folds (*i.e.* 24 panas).
>
> He who makes false balances, false royal mandates, false measures, and false coin, as well as he who adopts them (knowing them to be false) shall be (liable) to the highest fine.

That tester of coins (Nāṇakaparīkṣakah) who pronounces a genuine (coin) false, and a false one genuine, shall be made to pay the highest fine.

A quack, falsely (setting himself up as a physician) treats the lower animals (ordinary) people or officers of the king, shall be amerced in the lowest, the middling, and the highest fine (respectively).

He who restrains one not deserving to be restrained, or lets off one (who was specially) called up, before the purpose (for which he was called) is accomplished, shall be made to pay the highest fine.

He who abstracts one-eighth share (of an article sold) by a (false) measure or balance, shall be fined two hundred (panas) where a greater or a lower (share is abstracted), a proportionately (higher or lower fine should be imposed).

He who adulterates with inferior (articles), vendible medicines, oils, salt, perfumes, corn, coarse sugar and the like, shall be made to pay sixteen panas.

When (by some operation) inferior earth, hide, gem, yarn, iron, wood, bark, or cloth is made (to appear to be of) a superior kind, the fine is eight-fold of the (commodity) to be sold.

Palming off

He who pledges or sells a sealed casket (fraudulently) substituted (for a superior casket shewn) or the counterfeit of a natural vessel shall be fined (in the following manner).

(When the value of the thing palmed on the buyer, or a pledge is) less than a pana, the fine is fifty (panas) (when) a pana one hundred (panas), (when) two panas, two hundred (panas) when the value is higher, (the fine is) higher.

Prices

For those knowing whether (the price set by them) is higher or lower (than the maximum rates fixed by the king) unite in fixing a price too heavy for Kārus (workmen) and Silpins (artisans) the fine is the highest.

For those traders who conspire to obstruct (the sale of a commodity by demanding it), or selling it at an improper price, the highest fine is laid down.

The sale or purchase (of articles) should every day be made at the rates fixed by the king, the profit derived in this manner is declared (to be) propitious for traders.

A trader shall make five per cent as profit on commodities of the same country, and ten (per cent) on the foreign, if the purchase and sale take place immediately, (*i.e.* on the same day as that of the purchase).

The rates should be so fixed (by the king) as to be advantageous both to the buyer and the seller after adding to the (cost) value of the commodity, the expenses incurred.

Non-delivery on Sale

He who having received the price of a vendible thing does not deliver it to the buyer, shall be caused to deliver it together with udaya (*i.e.* either profit or interest) and if (the purchaser) be one come from a foreign country, also the profit which would have accrued to him in that foreign country.

A commodity once sold may be sold again, if the purchaser should not desire to take it, when the first purchaser not having received it (when offered) it is (afterwards) destroyed that loss (being) due to a default (on the part) of the purchaser, shall be (borne) by the purchaser.

If a commodity, which (though sold) was not delivered on demand, (and if it) be injured by an act of God or the king, the loss shall fall on the vendor.

Where (one) sells (a thing) previously sold to another, (or sells a thing) with blemishes, as (one) without a blemish, the fine is twice the value (of the article).

No trader shall recede from a sale, unless he has grounds to complain of ignorance (that his bargain has been) too cheap or too dear. He who does (so recede without such ground) shall be liable to a fine of one-sixth of the value of the article)."

Narada

Nārada is more logical and precise in his treatment of sāhasa and represents a more developed stage of law, though he too includes under the topic of sāhasa rules about theft generally, on the excuse perhaps, that theft, if only accompanied by violence becomes sāhasa. I give below texts of Nārada relating to sāhasa: (Tit XIV).

What is Sāhasa.

"Whatever act is performed by force (sahasā) by persons inflamed with (the pride of) strength, is called Sāhasa (a heinous offence); sāhasa (force) means strength in this world.

Manslaughter, robbery, an indecent assault on another man's wife, and the two species of insult such are the four kinds of Heinous Offences.

It is again declared to be threefold in the law-books, viz. (heinous offences) of the first, middle-most and highest degree. The definition of each kind shall be given as follows.

Destroying, reviling, disfiguring or otherwise (injuring) fruits, roots, water and the like, or agricultural utensil, is declared to be Sāhasa of the first degree.

(Injuring) in the same way clothes, cattle, food, drink, or household utensils, is declared to be Sāhasa of the middlemost degree.

Taking human life through poison, weapons or other (means of destruction), indecent assault on another man's wife, and whatever other (offences) encompassing life (may be imagined), is called sāhasa of the highest degree.

Gradation of punishment.

The punishment to be inflicted for it must be proportionate to the heaviness of the crime, (so however as) not to be less than a hundred (Panas) for Sāhasa of the first degree, whereas for

Sāhasa of the middlemost degree the punishment is declared by persons acquainted with the law to be no less than five hundred (panas).

For Sāhasa of the highest degree, a fine amounting to no less than a thousand (Panas) is ordained. (Moreover) corporal punishment, confiscation of the entire property, banishment from the town and branding, as well as amputation of that limb (with which the crime has been committed) is declared to be the punishment for Sāhasa of the highest degree.

This gradation of punishments is ordained for every (caste) indiscriminately, excepting only corporal punishment in the case of a Brāhmaṇ. A Brāhmaṇ must not be subjected to corporal punishment.

Shaving his head, banishing him from the town, branding him on the forehead with a mark of the crime of which he has been convicted, and parading him on an ass, shall be his punishment.

Those who have committed Sāhasa or either of the two first degrees are allowed to mix in society, after having been punished, but if a man has committed Sāhasa of the highest degree, no one is allowed to speak to him, even when he has received punishment.

Theft—a kind of Sāhasa.

Theft is a special kind of it. The difference between (Sāhasa and theft) is as follows. Sāhasa is where the criminal act consists of a forcible attack, theft is where it is done by fraud.

That (theft) is again declared to be threefold by the wise, according to the (value of the) article (purloined) whether articles of small, middling or superior value have been stolen.

Earthenware, a seat, a couch, bone, wood, leather, grass, and the like, legume, grain, and prepared food, these are termed articles of small value.

Clothes made of other material than silk, cattle other than cows, and metals other than gold, are (termed) articles of middling value, and so are rice and barley.

Gold, precious stones, silk, women, men, cows, elephants, horses and what belongs to a god, a Brāhmaṇ, or a king, these are regarded as articles of superior value.

Taking away by any means whatsoever the property of persons asleep or disordered in their intellect or intoxicated is declared to be theft by the wise.

Where stolen goods are found with a man, he may be presumed to be the thief. (The possession of) stolen goods may be inferred from a luxurious mode of life. Suspicion arises where a man is seen in bad company or indulges in extravagance.

Those who give food or shelter to thieves seeking refuge with them, or who offer them (to escape) though able (to present them), partake of their crime themselves.

Withholding help in distress

Those who do not come to offer assistance, when people are crying out (for help) within their hearing, or when property is being taken away, are likewise accomplices in the crime.

That series of punishments, which has been ordained by the wise for the three kinds of Sāhasa, is equally applicable to theft; according as it concerns one of the three species of article in their order.

Tracing of thieves.

When cows or other (animals) have been lost, or when (other) property has been taken away forcibly, experienced men shall trace it from the place where it has been taken.

Wherever the footmarks go to, whether it be a village pasture ground or deserted spot (the inhabitants or owners of) that place must make good the loss, unless they can prove the footmarks to go out of that place again.

When the footmarks are obscured or interrupted because (they lead to) broken ground or to a spot much frequented by other people, the nearest village or pasture ground shall be made responsible.

Where two persons have gone the same road, the offence, as a rule, shall be imputed to him who stood charged with other crimes before, or who associates with suspicious characters.

Chandalas, executioners, and other such persons as well as those who are in the habit of roaming at night, shall institute a search (after the thieves) in the villages ; those living outside (of inhabited places) shall search (for them) outside.

When the thieves are not caught, the king must make good (the loss) from his own treasury. By showing himself remiss (towards criminals), he would incur sin and would offend both against justice and his own interest."

Brihaspati

Bṛihaspati's text, which I have quoted before gives a similar definition of Sāhasa which is as follows :—

Manuṣya māranam steyam paradārābhimarṣanam
Pāruṣyamubhayaṃcheti sāhasam syat chaturvidham

Accordingly he includes under this topic much of the law regarding theft, and also many miscellaneous offences (See Texts of Bṛihaspati in S.B.E. XXXIII, p. 363 seq).

Real offences of violence or sāhasa proper are treated by him as follows :

Violence is declared to be of five sorts, and of these, manslaughter is declared to be the worst, those who have perpetrated. it, shall not be amerced in a fine, they shall be put to death by all means.

Both notorious murderers and secret assassins shall be put to death by the king by various modes of execution, after their property has been duly seized.

When several persons in a passion beat a single individual (and kill him), the responsibility of his death shall be charged to him who strikes the fatal blow.

He who struck the fatal blow shall have to atone for his offence as directed, the first aggressor and the associates shall be punished half as much.

The decision should be given after carefully ascertaining by signs the less or greater severity of a wound, the seat of vital power, the strength (of the murdered individual), and the repetition (of the blows or cuts).

Where the corpse is found, but the murderer cannot be discovered, the king shall trace him by drawing an inference from previous enmities of his.

His immediate neighbours, and their neighbours, as well as his friends, enemies, and relatives, shall be questioned by the king's officers employing towards them the (four) expedients of conciliation and so forth.

The (guilty) person may be found out from his keeping bad company, from signs (of the crime committed), and from the possession of stolen property. Thus has been declared the method of discovering murderers and robbers.

He who has been arrested on suspicion and does not confess his guilt, shall clear himself (from suspicion) by ordeal, this rule holds good for causes of every sort.

He who has been cleared of guilt by ordeal shall be released ; he who has been convicted shall be put to death. By punishment (of the wicked) and release (of the virtuous), the renown and religious merit of a king is increased.

Katyayana

Kātyāyana defines sāhasa as an offence committed with violence. But he too includes under this topic some other offences of a miscellaneous character. His texts are as follows :—

"That is declared to be sāhasa which is an act done with force.

Robbing in the presence of guards, carrying away a thing by force sāhasa is of this kind, while (mere) theft is said to be concealing (*i.e.*, depriving a man stealthily).

Where an offence coming under the name sāhasa has taken place without (leaving) indicatory signs (for fastening the guilt), the person (charged with sāhasa) must establish his innocence by oaths (and ordeals). This is the rule in all disputes.

If several men violently beat one man to death he out of them who gives the fatal blow is declared to be the murderer.

Self-defence—Ātatāyi

One who is the author of the murder by (actually) killing (the deceased) would be liable to be killed in various ways. One should certainly kill without waiting for consideration a man coming with the intention of destroying (a life or a dam).

No blame attaches to him who kills wicked men (Ātatayi) that are ready (to kill another), but when they have desisted from their attempt (to kill), they should be captured and not killed.

If a man superior in austerities, Vedic study and birth becomes an ātatayin (a desperate felon), killing him is not proper, killing is prescribed for a sinner of a lower class. This is the view of Bhṛigu.

He who is about to use his sword, poison or fire, he whose hand wields a drawn bow, who kills by the incantations contained in the Atharvaveda, who is a backbiter conveying to the king (information that would lead the king to harm a man), who assaults another's wife, who is bent upon finding out weak points in another (and striking him there)—all these and the like should be known as ātatayin.

The wicked man who robs a man of his fame and his character, who deprives (one) of dharma and artha (are said to ātatayins), he who not being charged (or accused) before proceeds to take life or rob (a man) of his all or to commit similar offences is to be known as ātatayin.

One who kills animals having (sharp) claws, horned animals, animals with fangs or tusks, and elephants and horses and other animals when all these are ātatayins, does not incur any blame.

Even a Brāhmaṇa deserves to be killed if he be guilty of causing abortion, if he be a thief (of gold) or if he strikes a Brāhmaṇa woman with a sharp weapon or if he kills an innocent woman.

That man who causes (slight) injury, breakage or total destruction of (valuable) articles would be liable to the first amercement and the owner of the article is entitled to get (another similar) article (or its price).

He who steals, breaks or burns the idols of Gods or who causes damage to temples should be punished with the first amercement.

He who causes a breach in a rampart wall or pulls it down or shatters it, or obstructs the flow of water (running in a water channel), should be awarded the first amercement."

The conclusion about the nature and history of Sāhasa that is suggested by this confusing mass of texts is as before mentioned, that Sāhasa was the name originally for all punishable crimes then known. Bṛihaspati's definition comes nearest that sense of the term. When after new kinds of offences came to be known they were placed under one or the other of the categories already known, however, Sāhasa long continued to be the residuary category under which all such offences would usually be placed. At a later stage, when the contents of Sāhasa had become more or less fixed, need was felt for a new category and Prakīrṇaka was devised under which all offences not otherwise classed were placed.

MISCELLANEOUS (PRAKĪRṆAKA)

As has been mentioned before, the eighteen topics of Manu did not include any miscellaneous section. But already in Manu some matters not properly germane to certain heads were squeezed into inappropriate heads. Later development of law made it more difficult to squeeze all topics into Manu's eighteen heads. Nārada therefore reclassified the eighteen topics into seventeen heads and added a fresh topic called Prakīrṇaka or miscellaneous. The name Prakīrṇaka was already known in connection with the law of Penance, for instance in Viṣṇu who describes it thus:

> "Yadanuktam tat prakīrṇakam,"
> "What has not been (already) said is Prakīrṇaka."

And he goes on to add that in respect of Prakīrṇa sins the wise man will perform penances with reference to their gravity or lightness under the advice of Brāhmaṇas.

That apparently gave the lead to Nārada for placing unclassified offences under the topic of Prakīrṇaka. The last set of Yājñavalkya's texts is also included in the Mitakṣarā classification under the head of Prakīrṇaka.

Narada

The description rather than a definition of Prakīrṇaka by Nārada is as follows:

> "Prakīrṇake punarjñeya vyavahāra Nṛipāsrayāh,
> Rajnamājnāpratighātastatkarma karanam tathā
> Purah pradānam saṃbhedah prakṛitīnāṃ tatheiva cha
> Pākhandinaigama-Śreni-ganadharma viparyayah
> Pitāputra vivādascha prāyaschittavyatikramah
> Pratigraha vilopascha kopa āsraminamapi
> Varṇasankaradoṣāscha tadvrittiniyamastathā
> Na driṣṭam yaccha purveṣu sarvam tat syat prakīrṇaka".

> "Under the head of Miscellaneous (Disputes) are comprised lawsuits depending on the king (such as) transgression of the king's commandments and obedience towards his injunctions.
> Grants of town, the division of the constituent elements of a state, the duties and the reverse of heretics, followers of the Veda, corporations (of merchants) and assemblages (of kinsmen).
> Disputes between father and son, neglect of (prescribed) penances, abstraction of gifts (made to worthy persons), the wrath of anchorites,
> Sinful confusion of castes, the rules regarding their means of subsistence, and (in short) whatever has been omitted in the preceding (titles of law), are treated under the head of Miscellaneous."

The texts of Nārada included under this topic however hardly covers a fourth of this ambitious catalogue. They are concerned mostly with the king and his royal dignity and duty and with Brāhmaṇas. (See Nārada, XVIII, SBE, Vol. XXXIII, p. 214 seq).

Yajnavalkya

The texts of Yājñavalkya treated under this topic answer this description a little more adequately. The offences dealt with by him (in II, 295-307) are wrongs affecting public law viz :

(1) Fraudulent misdescription by the writer in a royal grant regarding quantity of the grant.
(2) Letting go a thief caught, without surrendering him to the king.
(3) Polluting a Brāhmaṇa, Kṣatriya or Vaisya with forbidden food.
(4) Dealing in faked or impure gold.
(5) Sale of bad meat *e.g.* dog's meat.
(6) Injuries caused through animals, with exceptions.
(7) Falsely calling a lover a thief by woman caught in adultery, and releasing him on receiving money.
(8) Speaking evil of king.
(9) Injuring the king.
(10) Revealing the king's secrets.
(11) Selling articles taken from the body of a dead person.
(12) Blinding both eyes of a person.
(13) Carrying out orders of a master in foreboding evil of the king.
(14) Assuming the signs of a Brāhmaṇa by Śūdra for a living.
(15) The offence of giving a false decision by a member of the king's sabhā found upon a review of the decision by the king.
(16) Contempt of court by saying that one is not defeated even though defeated in a litigation.
(17) The king's sin in receiving a fine wrongly imposed on a person which has to be expiated.

Brihaspati

Bṛihaspati introduces the topic Prakīrṇaka with a text which suggests that it deals with litigations instituted by the king himself, but he gives under this head some general rules about punishment particularly of a Brāhmaṇa, and also certain rules about the respective validity of two different transactions between the same parties. (SBE, Vol. XXXIII, p. 386 seq).

Certain forbidden practices referred to are curious. Thus Bṛihaspati says:

> "Forbidden practices are found among the Southerners in the present day, (such as) matches with a maternal uncle's daughter, in spite of the prohibited degree of relationship on the mother's side (causing such unions to be illegal).
>
> The highly reprehensible custom of a brother living with his deceased brother's wife, and the delivery of a marriageable damsel to a family is found in other countries.
>
> What is more, matches with a mother occur among the Pārasikas. The inhabitants of some countries do not allow the presentation of fresh gifts (of food) at a Śrāddha offering to those Brāhmaṇas who have been fed at a Śrāddha held on the eleventh day (after the decease of a person) or at some other Śrāddha.
>
> Others, after lending grain, take twice as much back in the autumn season and occupy the embanked land, after having received twice the amount lent.
>
> Though the principal has been repaid. This is reprehensible also. Such forbidden practices (the king) should check (when they are resorted to) through folly.
>
> Such customs as are not opposed to the laws of particular countries and castes or other (corporations), every king should establish in accordance with the sacred law, after consulting the law books)".

The reference to the Persian custom is probably based on a garbled information about Khetukdas marriages between brother and sister in the early Median law.

CHAPTER XIV

RETROSPECT AND CONCLUSION

I have given so far what I conceive to have been the course of evolution of ancient Indian Law generally and with reference to the particular topics of law so far as they were evolved in the period covered by the Dharma Sastras.

We shall now be in a position better to appreciate the entire course of the evolution from a brief retrospect of the history of the topics of law I have so far given.

Positive law, that is, law enforced by sovereign authority emerges when the king begins to administer justice and develops into vyavahāra. It has its roots in usages and institutions of pre-jural society.

PRE-JURAL SOCIETY

So soon as man begins to build a society, that is, so soon as man has ceased to be confined to a family group ruled by the might and authority of its head, the need arises for a certain measure of delimitation of the interests of each member of the society however small it may be. This delimitation is not done by a conscious agreement, as the authors of the theory of a social contract imagine, but simply by men falling into habits which make it possible to avoid violent conflicts. These habits grow in time into customs and usages which people feel constrained to follow, less by external compulsion than by an inner restraint.

What promotes and sustains this inner restraint in primitive society is magic, a belief in supernatural agencies which punish transgressions of usages and can be assuaged by magic charms and rituals. Religion which implies a faith in Gods who punish and also protect comes next, but early religion is also largely affected by faith the magic virtues of Mantras which can force the Gods to help. Magic and religion support the customary law and produce a sense of constraint which was as powerful in the early stages of society as any caused by fear of punishment by Kings and Judges. Society as it existed in the early Vedic age appears clearly to have been in this later stage when magic has been partially superseded by religion. The conception of right and wrong is represented by the concept Ṛita, which like Physis of the early Greeks represented the principle of order in the universe. Right conduct, the right ritual and in fact right everything, including the correct order of the universe is Ṛita, and the great God Varuṇa is the upholder of Ṛita. He punishes the person who does anṛita and to him the wrongdoers pray for forgiveness with appropriate mantra and ritual.

The temporal guardianship of the law of Ṛita vested apparently in the community to which the man belonged. They would punish the wrong doer and require him to perform the ritual penance that would expiate the crime. The prescription of the proper ritual and proper punishment would be made by those who specialised in the knowledge of Ṛita, the Brāhmaṇa who makes a study of the law his occupation and who would advise the community in the matter. The king was there, but he was nothing more than the leader in battle and the protector of the people ; the administration of the laws or justice was none of his business. Later Vedic literature in the Brāhmaṇas no doubt speaks of the king as awarding daṇḍa or punishment. But that does not necessarily involve adjudication. It merely contemplates the might of the king coming down on the manifest wrong doer or one adjudged to be so by his community. So far as it was a matter of sacred law, it was for the Pariṣad to advise on. For the rest, each community small or large was the only administrator of law and justice.

KING AS JUDGE

The emergence of the king as judge was gradual. The first step was when the king was invested, as in the Brāhmanas, with the duty and right to punish—to award daṇḍa. That this did not necessarily imply any sort of adjudication is illustrated by many stories even in later society, for instance, the story of Rāma proceeding to punish Śambuka for attempting to perform a Vedic sacrifice ; or Sita to satisfy his subjects. The manifest wrong doer or a notorious offender was simply punished by the might of the king.

When we come, after a great gap in the history, to the age of the Dharmasūtras the king is already a judge, and decision of disputes, Vyavahāra, is an important function of the king. But the disputes which the king decides are almost exclusively offences which are considered by people of the age to be grave transgressions of socio-religious conventions. Practically the only civil disputes which the king deals with are debt, deposit and pledge, on the principle, no doubt, that non-payment of a debt is as great an offence as theft. For the rest, all disputes are still settled by the various Kulas, Sreṇis and other organisations who do justice among their members.

In the earliest days of the king's assumption of judicial powers, we find the king assisted and advised by the Purohita who is the power behind the throne. And in the Dharmasūtras too we find it a primary duty of the king to appoint a very learned Brāhmaṇa as his Purohit and to act according to Dharma on his advice.

The Purohita is an important institution from the earliest days of the Vedas. In the Ṛigveda we find how kings were guided and led by Purohitas like Vasiṣṭha and Viśvāmitra and, as appears from the story of the fortunes of Triṣṭu, the choice of the Purohita made all the difference in their fortunes in war with rival tribes. In administering daṇḍa, and later, in doing justice the king would naturally be guided by his Purohita.

At a later stage we find the king enjoined to have a sabhā of learned men, who have mastered all the Vedas, with whose advice he is required to administer justice. Then we find another functionary the Pradvivāka, originally, probably, a foreman of the sabhā, but eventually emerging as a Judge. These sabhāsadas, the Pradvivāka and the Purohita were all learned Brāhmiṇs fully conversant with the secrets of Dharma, who, between them, share the bulk of the administration of justice which, it was always presumed, should be according to Dharma. Between them, these classes constituted a body of experts and specialists in law and performed functions nearly analogous to those of the College of Pontiffs in ancient Rome.

SOURCES OF LAW ADMINISTERED

Where was the law to be found which these persons would administer? Theoretically, it was always the Veda which was assumed to be the sum total of all knowledge that there is or could be. But Āpastamba lets out the real source of the law they administered when he says that it was Sāmayāchārika law, that is, the law laid down by agreement of the learned which is presumed to be based on the Veda. That leads us back to an earlier stage, before the king was judge, when learned men of every community made a special study of laws in their Pariṣada and laid down the law for the community. Before the constraint exercised by the king's authority it was these people who specialised in the knowledge of the law which was in fact laid down by custom sanctified by a religious and moral sanction.

At that stage the law in ancient India corresponded to the Fas of ancient Rome which people felt to be binding and which was declared for them by the learned. Step by step after the king began to a administer justice, some of the rules of this Dharma or Fas came to be enforced by the king with the advice of the learned in law.

Much of the development of law as given there was associated with the increase of the authority of the king in the course of this history. We have seen that the king in the Ṛigveda was in fact merely a military head, though in the later Vedic literature he is conceived of as awarding punishment. The king when he emerges as a Judge, as he does at the time of Dharmasutras, decides disputes, but only in accordance with the sacred law or the customary law which he is required to ascertain from competent authorities. It is remarkable that there is no text of law which gives the king any authority to legislate, or to make new laws, except in a belated reference in Manusamhita where Rajakṛitadharma is referred to as being binding upon the people.

But, it appears that this law-making power of the king was never absolute or unrestricted. It was generally confined to making orders in respect of matters which were not covered by the books of law. Medhātithi in his commentary on the text of Manu illustrates this Rājakṛitadharma by reference to orders which are in the nature of commanding particular acts to be done in respect of matters not governed by the law. An inscription which has been published recently by Dr. D. C. Sarkar[20] seems to give some indication of cases in which the king could even in the 6th century A.D. be supposed to have laid down the law. The inscription recites that a community of merchants resident in the State asked the king to state the law by an Āchāra-sthiti-patra and the king by his orders laid down the law in answer. He did not arrogate to himself real legislative functions but purported only to lay down the rules which were to be deemed to have been in force in his time and to make some administrative arrangements. The laws were more or less in the nature of declaratory laws like the Twelve Tables, and not legislation proper. At no time, therefore, covered by the Smṛitis does the king appear to have had any real legislative authority and in the Middle Ages it is perfectly clear that the king never had or purported to exercise any sovereign legislative functions in respect of matters which were already covered by the law,—though in the sphere of matters of conduct of the people which were not covered by such laws he might make the necessary orders not inconsistent with the sacred law or the customary law. And the sources of law up to the latest time continued to be what they always were, viz. in respect of matters

[20] J.R.A.S.B., Vol. XVI, p. 113 seq.

which were dealt with by the sacred law, the law of the Śrūti and the Smṛiti and, in respect of other matters outside the domain of the sacred law, by the customs and usages of the people.

Customs

With regard to customs and usages which were enforced as laws, a close analysis of the laws would show us that there were three distinct attitudes of the Dharmaśāstras with regard to three separate categories of customs. With regard to matters of sacred law or ritual, the only custom which was recognised was custom which bore upon it an impress of sanctity, raising a presumption of origin in some lost text of Śruti. This first class comprised the usages of Ṛiṣis who were reputed seers of the Vedas whose every action might be expected to have been in accordance with some rule of the Vedas which they knew but which is not known now. So too were the customs of countries, differently specified, which had an ancient reputation of being peopled by men who scrupulously followed the sacred law unsullied and, still later, customs very generally in vogue among people generally for which no earthly (driṣṭa) motive would be assigned. From this class of customs there arose a presumption of origin in lost Vedas and which therefore was recognised as presumably founded on Śruti unless opposed to an express text of the Vedas. This is the custom which is referred to by Āpastamba as ānumānika law which may be repelled by an express text of Śruti and with regard to which elaborate rules were gradually formulated in the schools of Mimāṃsā philosophy.

The second class of usages which did not bear any similar insignia of Vedic authority were (*a*) usages on purely secular matters which had or could have no scriptural basis, or (*b*) customs and usages of people who were deemed to be more or less beyond the pale of sacred law, not only antyajas and heretic sects, but also people who followed what was then deemed to be lowly occupations, agriculturists, traders, usurers etc.

A third class of cases where rules and customs followed in a society were, in course of time, recognised and tolerated from considerations of policy without scrutinising their character sacred and profane was constituted by the laws and customs of conquered territories after subjugation.

In course of time these different attitudes to different classes of customs appear to have been mixed up and the attitude towards laws of conquered territories probably tended to be extended, so that more and more customs came to be recognised as law than Gautama or

Āpastamba ever conceived and perhaps a very substantial part of the lives of the population came to be regulated by customary law without a critical study of their claim to authority on these principles.

Evolution conditioned by growth of custom

The evolution of law was at all times conditioned by the growth of these customs. Each new law-giver embodies in his Code every established custom which was recognised in Courts in the society in his day. On the other hand the introduction of new customs and new conditions of society gave rise to new problems which had to be worked into the framework of the sacred law which courts had to administer. What was the religious law to be applied to a new set of circumstances of the society for the time being? The law-giver had to supply it within the frame-work of the sacred law.

This we find done at almost every stage of the evolution of law. A case worthy of note where the method of evolution is almost writ large is the development of a law of partnership. Joint enterprise in trade and commerce was unknown to the early lawgivers who had no rules to regulate it. But usage and custom had a rule about the division of the perquisites of priests who jointly officiated at great sacrifices. This law though first laid down in Manu was clearly an ancient practice recognised in sacred law. Manu formulates this law precisely and then says that that would be the law in cases of all joint enterprises. When new problems arose which could not be solved by the application of these rules, new rules were evolved and led to further developments which we can find in the texts of Yājña-valkya, Nārada, Bṛihaspati, Kātyāyana etc. (Supra, p. 243 seq).

The story of this and similar stages of evolution of laws prominently brings into relief the fact that far from India being the unchanging East as it was conceived by Westerners of the past, society was always undergoing a continuous transformation from age to age. From the age of the Ṛigveda of practically a purely agricultural and pastoral community we pass on, by stages which cannot unfortunately be clearly distinguished, to the age of Yājñavalkya and his successors when trade and commerce, by land and also by sea had grown considerably in importance, with the resultant elevation of the social status of traders, who were in course of time admitted to seats in the king's sabhā. A great economic and social change is indicated by laws like this.

The whole story of this change cannot unfortunately be unfolded. For, far too many links in this chain of progress are missing during the age of Dharmasastras for which we have neither epigraphic evidence nor accounts by foreign observers like the Greeks, the Chinese or the Arabs which can be unmistakably referred to this age. We know from the evidence of later times that at some ancient time Indians of some parts of this great country had become maritime adventurers who braved the seas to carry their commerce to distant countries and also carried on foreign trade by long routes. We also have very dependable evidence from the days of Alexander the Great onwards of a constant intercourse with states as far distant as Rome and China, including diplomatic contacts, exchange of religious, philosophical and scientific knowledge as also a commerce in art and industrial products. I have indicated also from the evidence of archaeological discoveries and of the Ṛigveda that even in the remotest past intercourse of some sort existed with outlying countries, of the Vedic Aryas as also of the other important element of Indian Society, the people of the Harappan Empire.[21]

It is possible that this intercourse with foreign peoples stimulated trade and commerce among the people which is partially reflected in the laws. It is possible also that the usages of trade and commerce which were ultimately enshrined in the laws were borrowed from or influenced by usages of foreign commercial races of ancient times like the Babylonians, Phoenicians and others, but of this we can lay our finger on no evidence in the present stage of our knowledge.

The story of the evolution which I have so far attempted to give shows however that right through the Dharmaśāstras, the ancient laws registered a notable progress from more or less rudimentary laws of a simple society to a very complex structure in continuous response to the changing conditions of a very complex society. We have seen likewise that with regard to some elements of the social structure reflected in the laws, notably in the family law, it can be stated with confidence that some part of the development was due to foreign or non-Ārya sources.

EXTENSION OF VYAVAHĀRA

While the consideration of the topics of law from the earliest to the latest Dharmaśāstras has unmistakeably shown that the form as well as the content of the laws have grown considerably, we are not

[21] In an interesting paper on *Vedic India and the Middle East* in XIV J.R.A.S.B., p. 121 seq. Mr. Harit Krishna Deb has discussed evidence of contacts westward so far East as Egypt. His conclusions however require further examination.

in a position to say how precisely it grew from stage to stage. A few lines may however be indicated as very probable.

Thus at the start, family law which was most intimately connected with religious and ritual law as well as with the authority of domestic tribunals was not included in the laws of the King's court.

The text which is an anachronous survival in Bṛihaspati, to the effect that no dispute between (1) Guru and pupil, (2) Father and son, (3) Husband and wife, (4) Master and servant (or slave) could raise a vyavahāra, indicates the original state when these disputes did not come before the King's court but were disposed of by domestic tribunals.

So too it would seem that disputes about land and its cultivation, trade disputes and disputes between herdsmen usurers or artisans did not come to the Court. This is indicated by the text of Gautama "Krişi vanik pāśupālya kuśīda kāravah sve sve varge." Their guilds and village authorities decided all such disputes between themselves. As between them and others however disputes could and did come before the king, for from the earliest law we find provision for disputes between creditor and debtor, herdsmen and the owners of cattle or persons whose crops were destroyed by cattle.

We can almost trace how these items gradually entered into the sphere of king's justice.

The earliest stage

The earliest topics of the king's justice seem to be fairly represented in the scanty list of disputes dealt with by Gautama, Āpastamba and Baudhāyana. They were chiefly offences which the society of those days deemed so grave as to deserve condign punishment—offences, primarily affecting the social order. Thus theft is punished by the king because, to protect people from thieves and robbers was a primary duty of the king. On the other hand hurt, abuse and adultery are only punished if they are a grave violation of social proprieties and caste privileges and decorum.

There was as yet no attempt to generalise or classify. Specific offences were separately punished and measure was laid down for their punishment.

Apart from these punishable offences the only apparently civil action which came to the king's Court from the earliest time was probably an extension of the law of theft. Withholding payment of money or thing borrowed was only a step removed from theft, in that the possession of money or thing had originally been taken by consent. The rigour of the law of Debt, even down to the days of

Manu and Yājñavalkya shows that a defaulting debtor was looked upon as a sort of criminal against whom creditor might take any means fair and foul in a manner slightly less rigorous than the Nexal creditor in the Twelve Tables.

Manu says,

"A creditor can realise his dues by dharma (*i.e.* by gentle moral appeals), by litigation, by fraud, by fasting at the debtor's door or by force."

Yājñavalkya adds, "The King must not forbid (or stop) a creditor who is attempting to realise his debt, and if the debtor, pursued by a creditor doing so, applies to the King, the debtor will be punished by the king and made to pay the creditor his dues." (II. 40).[22]

When debt became cognisable by the king, its immediate effect was a regulation of interest and payment *e.g.* by service or by instalments and formulation of appropriate rules for rights and duties regarding pledge, (ādhi), suretyship (pratibhū) for liability of heirs and others of the actual debtor and so forth. These are all the things that early law of Debt provides. We have seen how these laws grow and gain not only in volume but in differentiation and detail. (Supra, p. 236 seq).

The development of this early law was by processes which may be brought under three different heads. Firstly, there was the natural development with the increasing complexities of social relations and logical extension of prnciples. Next there was the extension of the King's jurisdiction to matters which were originally matters for domestic or guild tribunals. Lastly, the laws also developed by infiltration of customs and usages of alien society, either due to adoption or adaptation by the Aryas of foreign customs or to the survival of alien customs in such communities after their adoption of Arya culture.

Natural development

The first kind of development which may be called "a natural development" is illustrated by, for instance, the development of the Law of Deposit by an obvious extension of the Law of Debt.

The topic of Deposit (nikṣepa) was an obvious extension of the law of debt. It is slightly treated by Gautama but as time goes on it is seen to branch out into different laws for different kinds of deposits for which provision was made with increasing definiteness.

[22] In the Āchara-Sthitipatra in J.R.A.S.B., Vol. XVI, p. 113 there is reference to a practice of debtors being handcuffed.

Similarly a developments out of the law of Theft was, as we have seen, the law of Asvāmīvikraya. The primary law was the punishment of the thief and of a person presumed to be a thief by having the stolen property on him. Receivers of stolen property, harbourers of thieves, their servants and other accessories were gradually roped in. But soon the Court was confronted with a person who had stolen property on him but proved that he had bought it. He could not be dealt with straight off as a thief and the need for special provision for him led to the topic of asvāmīvikraya. We have seen how the law developed until a purchase in market overt came to be deemed to clear the purchaser even without producing his vendor.

The early topic of the law of herdsmen and their liability to owners of cattle and to persons whose crop was destroyed similarly led, with change of social conditions to the growth of laws regarding free servitors and their wages which were first dealt with as a separate head of Vetanādāna until by the time of Nārada and Bṛihaspati they were more or less amalgamated with the law regarding herdsmen.

Encroachment on domestic tribunals

The second type of development due to the extension of the King's law to matters which were in the exclusive jurisdiction of domestic or communal tribunals is illustrated by the development of the Law of Strisaṃgrahaṇa. Adultery and sexual offences were matters for the sacred Law relating to penance from the earliest times. It entered into Gautama's law in a rudimentary form by extending the king's jurisdiction to sexual offences only where they were of a type which grievously offended the sense of social proprieties of the community.

Marriage and marital rights and transgressions were the subject matter of religious and social regulations from early times. But they were matters exclusively for the domestic tribunals. As we go on however we find all these matters of marital rights and transgressions brought within the sphere of the king's law ; and these laws, we find, grew gradually in elaboration till two full-fledged topics of litigation under the names of "Stripuṃdharma" and "Strisaṃgrahaṇa" appear in a developed form in the latest of the Dharmasastras.

Land laws which were originally a matter for the village tribunal made a modest entry into the list as "Boundary disputes" and in the hands of the jurists of the King's Court it was soon elaborated, apparently by a gradual recognition by the King's court of growing customs, into an elaborate code of land laws such as we find in Nārada and Bṛihaspati.

Disputes regarding guilds and communities which were the original and autonomous social units in very ancient times came gradually under the sphere of Kng's law as disputes relating to these guilds came to be agitated in the court of the King'; and we have seen how these topics gradually developed into a topic of "samvidvyatikrama" (Supra p. 259). Trade and commerce which was previously in the hands of guilds also came in and accounted for the heads of sambhūya-samutthāna, vetanādāna, abhyupetyāśuśrūsa, karya-vikrayānusaya. Inheritance too came in as vibhāga.

Alien influence

Instances of the third influence namely, the absorption of alien laws, customs and usages can be notably dicated in the sphere of family law by the development of the law of marriage, sonship and kinship, as already pointed out.

On these lines it is possible to imagine a course of development of the topics of vyavahāra. And, we have seen that each head of law, since it was first introduced gradually expanded into more elaborate and precise rules according to felt practical necessities. This development was very largely the work of learned men who from the earliest times specialised in the knowledge of law and with the introduction and expansion of king's justice grew into a body of practically professional lawyers who had the duty to advise the king in the administration of justice and also assisted in solving problems of law for the people who appealed to them,—as the Romans appealed to the Pontiffs or to the jurisconsults.

Smriti law was practical law

By closely following the course of evolution of the topics of law we can thus easily dispose of a criticism which was once made, for instance by Nelson,[23] but which is not much heard of now, that the Smṛitis were never practical laws but more or less of an ideal code somewhat like Bentham's Theory of Legislation, spun out by the imagination of priestly scholars, but never really the law actually administered, before the British rule. The course of the history here outlined is enough to demolish this thesis even without reference to the numerous epigraphs of the middle ages which show that the law of the Smṛitis was then more or less scrupulously followed by kings and the people in their transactions. For the law could not have

[23] In his *Prospectus on a Scientific Study of Hindu Law*, p. 44 and p. 161.

developed gradually in details in the way it did unless the developments were called for by the practical needs of its administration.

The character of the so-called Codes and digests is perhaps to some extent responsible for this misapprehension. For no dharmaśāstra (with the exception of Nārada, unless it is only a part of a fuller code) is exclusively concerned with law but deals with all other religious duties and obligations as well, and the purely legal part of it is also deemed to be a part of dharma. In the parts dealing with the vyavahāra portion too, strictly legal rules are very much mixed up with injunctions of purely religious and moral obligation. Administrators of law in those ages however had little difficulty in distinguishing between injunctions relating to matters enforced by courts and purely moral injunctions. They already had rules of interpretation originating in connection with Vedic texts and rituals, gradually developed into the various Mimāṃsā rules. When law givers laid down laws they may be presumed to have been aware of the basic principles of these rules and have written in recognition of them.

Besides, even in laying down rules about legal duties they never forgot that these duties were based on religious notions about right and wrong. This is emphasised in many places by elaborating the law of religious obligation in dealing with purely legal duties on that topic. To Western lawyers and scholars of the nineteenth century familiar with only clear cut rules and principles of law this unfamiliar mixing up of moral and legal rules was confusing and inconsistent with the character of the books as practical laws. But this is a character arising out of the fact of all laws being deemed to be grounded in dharma or moral and religious duty which is a characteristic of law throughout ancient Indian history. The inscriptions of Asoka no doubt proclaimed laws which people were bound to obey but these laws were freely mixed up with moral and religious injunctions. That did not make these inscriptions any less practical laws.

The Austinian conception of positive law, as commands of the sovereign enforced by his might, irrespective of whether they are morally right or wrong was never recognised in ancient or mediaeval India. Every law was dharma and had its root and justification in eternal principles or right conduct according to current ideas of right. The ancient law-giver in laying down the law is therefore found frequently to go off the track of pure positive law and treat the laws as parts of religious and moral duty, and therefore, while giving the dictates of law on any topic, be it the law of debts or the law of evidence or of marital relations, bring in, along with the strict law on it, purely moral laws and duties connected with the topic.

CONCLUSION

In conclusion I wish to make it clear that the last thing I wish is to be dogmatic in any opinion which I have expressed here. The field of investigation necessary for adequate theories on the matter is so vast and the materials are so scanty that no one can feel sure about the conclusions he draws from the evidence. And, personally, I must frankly confess that my knowledge of the entire subject is far from nearly complete.

Nevertheless, I have felt impelled to place before the world such conclusions as I have drawn from my studies on the subject, only because the sands of my days are running out and I am approaching the end of my life's labours. I shall appeal to all those who read my book to take what I have said here in a spirit more of criticism than of faith. And I shall feel myself amply repaid if these studies inspire some people with new lines of thought and impel them to make further researches on the history of laws and social organisation of ancient India, which is of such great importance for a scientific study of Comparative Sociology and Historical Jurisprudence, and facts about which are so little understood as yet, in spite of the work of generations of great scholars. I conclude in the trust that my efforts will help in some small measure in inspiring endeavour to that end.

INDEX

A

B

C

E

F

G

H

I

L

M